AF478126

Exile, Murder and Madness in Siberia, 1823–61

Also by Andrew A. Gentes

EXILE TO SIBERIA, 1590–1822

RUSSIA'S PENAL COLONY IN THE FAR EAST: A translation of Vlas Doroshevich's "Sakhalin"

Exile, Murder and Madness in Siberia, 1823–61

Andrew A. Gentes

First published 2010 by
PALGRAVE MACMILLAN

Palgrave Macmillan in the UK is an imprint of Macmillan Publishers Limited, registered in England, company number 785998, of Houndmills, Basingstoke, Hampshire RG21 6XS.

Palgrave Macmillan in the US is a division of St Martin's Press LLC, 175 Fifth Avenue, New York, NY 10010.

Palgrave Macmillan is the global academic imprint of the above companies and has companies and representatives throughout the world.

Palgrave® and Macmillan® are registered trademarks in the United States, the United Kingdom, Europe and other countries

ISBN 978-0-230-27326-9   hardback

This book is printed on paper suitable for recycling and made from fully managed and sustained forest sources. Logging, pulping and manufacturing processes are expected to conform to the environmental regulations of the country of origin.

A catalogue record for this book is available from the British Library.

A catalogue record for this book is available from the Library of Congress.

10   9   8   7   6   5   4   3   2   1
19   18   17   16   15   14   13   12   11   10

Printed and bound in Great Britain by
CPI Antony Rowe, Chippenham and Eastbourne

*Dedicated to my teachers,
Tom, Pat, Wilfred, and David;
and to the victims of the so-called
War on Drugs*

Contents

List of Tables

Preface

This book continues the history of tsarist Siberian exile I began with *Exile to Siberia, 1590–1822* (2008). Whereas it is desirable that readers be familiar with this previous work, such is not necessary to understand the present work on its own terms. All dates conform to the Julian, or Old Style, calendar, which during the period covered here was 12 days behind the Gregorian calendar. This book uses a number of terms and acronyms with which readers may not be familiar, and so I have provided both a glossary and a list of acronyms' definitions. The transliteration of Russian terms accords with the Library of Congress system, except that in the body of the text I have deleted any diacritical mark that comes at the end of a word so as to facilitate use of the possessive case. Nonetheless, some idiosyncratic transliterations remain because I have quoted other scholars' translations. Finally, I have attempted to convert from Russian to their original Latinate spellings the names of, especially, Polish actors. This has proved rather difficult at times and admittedly involved some guessing, and there are some exceptions to this rule for reasons explained in footnotes. I apologize ahead of time for any errors.

Acknowledgements

Many persons offered guidance, insights, suggestions, criticism, instruction, encouragement, and assistance during the many years I worked on this project. I wish to thank Tom Gleason, Pat Herlihy, Steve Marks, Andrei Znamenski, Adele Lindenmeyr, Bob Elson, Max Okenfuss, Matthew Light, Olaf Mertelsmann, Will Sunderland, Marshall Poe, Sarah Badcock, Benjamin Schenk, Andreas Renner, Daniel Kaiser, Mark Steinberg, John Randolph, Virginia Martin, Norihiro Naganawa, Dave Pretty, Steven Seegel, Eva Maria Stolberg, Tamara Troyakova, Leland Turner, and Michael Finke. I am especially grateful to Bruce Adams, who in a rare act of generosity gifted me his research materials upon retirement, and Anatolii Remnev, who kindly gave me copies of his publications as well as his student Aleksandr Vlasenko's doctoral dissertation, which filled in many blanks regarding developments in Western Siberia. Thanks are due once again to Michael Strang and Ruth Ireland at Palgrave, and to my manuscript's anonymous reader. The views expressed here are my own. I benefited from the comments and interest shown by participants at the Living in Exile Conference at James Madison University (2002), the Tenth British Universities Siberian Studies Seminar at the University of Houston (2004), the XVIth Biennial Conference of the Australasian Association for European History sponsored by the University of Sydney (2007), the 2009 Ralph and Ruth Fisher Forum on Russia's Role in Human Mobility at the University of Illinois at Urbana-Champaign, and the XVIIth Biennial Conference of the Australasian Association for European History sponsored by Flinders University (2009). Support for the research and writing of this book came from the Woodrow Wilson Center's Kennan Institute, the University of Queensland's Centre for Critical and Cultural Studies, the Australian Academy of Humanities, and Hokkaido University's Slavic Research Center. I am grateful to the staffs of these organizations as well as those of the University of Queensland's Social Sciences and Humanities Library, Hokkaido University's Slavic Research Library, the University of Illinois at Urbana-Champaign's Slavic Research Library, the library of the Russian Academy of Sciences' Far Eastern Branch, the Russian State Library, RGIA DV, GAPK (State Archive of the Maritime Region), GARF, GAIO, the Irkutsk Regional Museum's library, the Rare Books and Manuscripts Division of Irkutsk State University's Main Library, the New York Public Library's Manuscripts and Archives Division, and the Library of

Congress. Without librarians' and archivists' dedication to their professions this book would not have been possible. I would also like to thank Maney Publishing for permission to use in Chapters 3 and 4 material from an article that appeared in *Slavonica* in 2007. Finally, I wish to acknowledge the good spirit that helps me in all things.

AAG
Washington, DC

Acronyms

EOGU — Eniseisk General Provincial Administration (*Eniseiskoe obshchee gubernskoe upravlenie*)

GAIO — Irkutsk District State Archive (*Gosudarstvennyi arkhiv Irkutskoi oblasti*)

GARF — Russian Federation State Archive (*Gosudarstvennyi arkhiv Rossiskoi Federatsii*)

GUVS — Main Administration of Eastern Siberia (*Glavnoe upravlenie Vostochnoi Sibiri*)

GUZS — Main Administration of Western Siberia (*Glavnoe upravlenie Zapadnoi Sibiri*)

IGP — Irkutsk Provincial Administration (*Irkutskoe gubernskoe pravlenie*)

MVD — Ministry of Internal Affairs (*Ministerstvo vnutrennykh del*)

OPT — Prison Aid Society (*Obshchestvo popechitel'nago o tiur'makh*)

RGIA — Russian State Historical Archive (*Rossiiskii gosudarstvennyi istoricheskii arkhiv*)

TobPS — Tobol'sk Exile Office (*Tobol'skii Prikaz o ssyl'nykh*)

ZhMVD — Journal of the Ministry of Internal Affairs (*Zhurnal Ministerstva vnutrennykh del*)

Glossary

Arshin	unit of measurement equal to 71 cm or 28 in
Assignats	paper rubles with a value less than for silver rubles
Bezpopovtsy	schismatics who abjured priests
Brodiagi	vagabonds, usually fugitive exiles and penal laborers
Brodiazhestvo	the crime of "vagabondage"
Desiatina	unit of measurement equal to 1.09 hectares or 2.7 acres
Dobrovol'nye	"voluntaries," term for family members who accompanied exiles
Gimnaziia	high school
Guberniia	province
Katorga	penologico-administrative regime; penal labor; collective noun for penal laborers
Krai	unorganized territory
Meshchane	category of petty urban dwellers
Narodnost'	"nationality-ness"
Narod	the (common) people
Obrok	peasant dues
Okrug	"district"
Ostrog	Siberian fort
Plet'	three-tailed whip
Popovtsy	schismatics who used priests
Raznochintsy	persons without clearly defined class status
Shliakhta	Russian term for Polish gentry class
Shliakhtichi	members of the Polish gentry
Sibiriaki	Siberian Russians
Skopchestvo	crime of castration, or belonging to the *Skoptsy* sect
Skoptsy	self-castrating religious sectarians
Soslovie	social estate
Starozhily	"long-term residents," i.e., Siberian Russian peasants
Uezd	"district" (in use before 1822)
Ulozhenie	Law Code
Volost'	canton
Zavod	industrial township

Introduction: Geography, Penality, Power, and Resistance

Siberia dwarfs European Russia. Nearly 5,000 miles east to west, over 2,000 miles north to south, and covering over six million square miles, it is immense. Its western and eastern halves are distinct from one another. The Enisei River marks the division between the Western Siberian Plate, a geologically young platform of sedimentary rock, and the much more ancient Siberian Platform. Stretching from the Krasnoiarsk-Novokuznetsk-Rubtsovsk line east to Irkutsk and south of Lake Baikal, the mountains from which the Enisei springs date back 700 million years and are Siberia's second oldest geological formation. The geology east of Lake Baikal and the Lena River is more recent. The so called Russian Far East is Siberia's youngest and most active region: at 230,000 square miles Kamchatka is one of the world's largest peninsulas and has several volcanic mountains over 10,000 feet; Sakhalin—589 miles long and covering nearly 48,000 square miles—is one of the world's largest islands.

Most of western Siberia is flat and marshy, except for the Altai Mountains. The region's low elevation and the fact that its rivers remain frozen in the north long after they thaw in the south, together transform its southern steppe into possibly the world's largest springtime bog. The waterlogged, spongy soil spawns hordes of insects that plague residents in summer. The landscapes of eastern Siberia and the Russian Far East are more variegated. A combination of mountains and marshy lowlands characterizes the topography north of the 60th parallel between the Lena and Enisei rivers. Rugged mountains dominate the landscape east of the Lena. Along the lower Pacific coast, weather and temperatures resemble those in the coastal regions of Oregon and Washington.

Siberia contains the largest river systems in the world. Moving from west to east, the first is the Ob and its basin, which includes the Irtysh, Tobol, Ishim, Tom, and other rivers. Considered as a single river, the

Ob-Irtysh is 3,361 miles long and drains a territory of nearly two million square miles. The next mighty river is the Enisei, fed, all from the east, by the Upper Tungus, Lower Tungus, Chuna, and the swift-flowing Angara. The Enisei basin is nearly as extensive as the Ob's and the Enisei River, though 1,200 miles shorter than the Ob-Irtysh, still ranks as one of the world's longest. At 2,800 miles, the Lena is regarded by geographers who refuse to consider the Irtysh and Ob as one river to be, in fact, the world's longest river. Draining the heart of eastern Siberia, it culminates on the Arctic coast in an enormous delta of some 19,000 square miles. Its major tributaries are the Kirenga, which originates in the mountains west of Lake Baikal; the Vitim and Olëkma, which drain the huge Vitim Plateau east of the lake; and the Aldan, which meets the Lena just north of Iakutsk and is itself fed by the Amga and Maia, both of which drain the Aldan Plateau south of Iakutsk. The basins of these three major rivers—the Ob, Enisei, and Lena—cover a combined area larger than Western Europe. Siberia's fourth major river is the Amur. It originates southeast of the Vitim Plateau and flows for 1,800 miles before emptying into the narrow Tatar Straits that separate Sakhalin from the mainland. Its basin is smaller than those of the other rivers (1,500,000 square miles) and includes only two main tributaries, the Argun and Shilka, the former originating across the border in China, the latter near Nerchinsk, east of Chita. Since 1860, the Amur-Argun has demarcated nearly the entire length of the Russo-Chinese border.

There is only one lake in Siberia that need be mentioned here, yet what a marvelous lake it is! Containing almost 15,000 cubic miles of water, or 20 percent of the world's surface fresh water, Lake Baikal forms the centerpiece of the surrounding region's unique natural environment. Almost 400 miles long and 30 miles at its widest point, it covers 20,000 square miles. At its deepest are 5,314 feet of water to fathom before reaching a bottom that is itself thousands of feet thick due to the silt collected in what is actually one of the world's oldest canyons. Twenty-seven islands dot its surface, though the largest one by far is Ol'khon—Asia's Avalon where, legend has it, Chinggis Khan lies buried. A total of 336 rivers—the major one being the Selenga, which originates in Mongolia—feed the lake from surrounding mountains and plateaus. The Angara is the only major river that drains Baikal, drawing its waters through Irkutsk, 40 miles west of the lake. Given its central location, length, and the invisibility of the opposite shoreline at most points, it is no wonder that during the nineteenth century locals called Baikal "The Sea." But its water is so pure that three feet of ice can be seen through like glass.

The myth that all Siberia is permafrost and covered year-round in snow is still popular. However, the *tundra*, a permafrost landscape of limited vegetation, exists only north of the 60th parallel. Most of Siberia is instead covered by the *taiga*, a belt of coniferous and deciduous forests ranging between 600 and 1,200 miles wide and stretching from European Russia to the Pacific coast. South of the taiga, in the west, lies the *steppe*—large, flat, treeless; whereas Zabaikal´e and the southern half of the Russian Far East resemble northern North America in terms of climate, vegetation, and soil. Although Siberia's average daily temperature is 32° F, its population is predominantly settled far south of the 60th parallel, so that most Siberians live at nearly the same latitudes as European Russians. This was even more the case during tsarist times, before the Soviet government built several large cities in the north. St Petersburg and Moscow are actually farther north than most of Siberia's largest cities. Summer is balmy: July temperatures average 65° F in Irkutsk and 75° F in Vladivostok. Yet if Siberia is warmer than might be expected, winter spares no part of it. Coastal regions benefit from the Pacific jet-stream, but are nevertheless punished by Arctic gales that push the wind chill factor dangerously low. However, nothing compares to the interior's temperatures, which are life threatening. Irkutsk averages 5° F in January, though the temperature can easily drop to –30° F, at which point atmospheric moisture freezes to form a kind of spectral fog and you must constantly blink your eyes to keep them from congealing. Yet even these temperatures pale beside those of Iakutsk, located at the 63rd parallel on the banks of the Lena, where January temperatures average –45° F (were it not for the river they would be even colder). The enormous Sakha Province, for which Iakutsk today serves as capital, warms up as might be expected in summer, with July temperatures averaging between 35° F and 66° F depending on location. Nonetheless, Sakha's northern city of Verkhoiansk holds the record for the coldest temperature ever in a continuously inhabited city or town: –90° F.[1]

Siberia's size, geography, and weather significantly limited the tsarist government's ability to administer the exile system. The very remoteness of the places to which convicts were sent was part of their appeal to punishers, yet northern flowing rivers, dense taiga, mountains, and featureless steppe hampered efforts to move guards, supplies, and convicts from west to east. Huge ice floes during spring thaws made the crossing of rivers a suicidal enterprise. Few and poor roads, long distances between settlements, and murderous bandit gangs played havoc with communications. The distance from St Petersburg to Tobol´sk,

Omsk, Irkutsk, and Iakutsk extends to 3,500 nautical miles, yet the topographical miles that needed to be traversed were at least three times as long. People and supplies took months, sometimes years, to reach destinations. Orders disappeared along with their couriers; and if finally received by their nominated executors, they were often no longer relevant. Haphazard communications allowed Siberian officials to routinely ignore orders from the capital or regional superiors and to embezzle goods and monies they later claimed never to have received. "There is not a country in the world where words correspond less to the reality," complained Mikhail M. Speranskii, Siberia's governor-general from 1819 to 1822.[2]

In 1839 Siberia's adult male population totaled nearly 600,000.[3] As of 1858 its male/female population totaled nearly three million.[4] Within an empire of nearly 70 million people[5] Siberia was sparsely settled, though like European Russia most inhabitants were peasants. The climate made daily life more difficult for them than for their European counterparts. Shorter growing seasons necessitated that more land be cultivated and that harvesting be done more quickly. The ever-present threat to Siberian peasants' existences rendered them desperate and ruthless yet also hard-working and independent. The absence of a landed gentry who in European Russia sometimes assisted their serfs in times of need, and the sparseness of government officials and institutions that might have provided similar assistance made for a thin line separating *Sibiriaki* (Siberian Russians) from starvation or cannibalism. The state officially owned all land but managed it poorly, and so what fertile land there was acquired a value greater than elsewhere in the empire, a value measured not by its salability but what individuals did with it. As early as the late seventeenth century *starozhily* ("long-term residents," also designating Siberian Russians) complained about a lack of good land and petitioned the tsar to abolish exile. They did not want to give up cleared parcels to convicts who would not cultivate them. As Siberia's exile population grew its countryside became increasingly violent. Exiles shunned by villagers or who chose not to remain in assigned locations fled to join an expanding population of vagabonds known as *brodiagi*. Brutalized by inhumane treatment and the natural environment, *brodiagi* begged from, robbed, and murdered *Sibiriaki*, who responded with lynch mobs and murder. By the early nineteenth century Siberia was a Wild East where the will to survive rendered another's life easily dispensable.

*   *   *

While it is important to bear in mind the conditional factors imposed by nature, nature is no substitute for human volition in explaining the development of the exile system, about which there was nothing inevitable or natural. Certain authorities chose to send certain groups of people along certain routes at certain times to certain destinations: the concatenation of these choices created and conditioned Siberia's exile population. I describe the origins and first 230 years of exile in *Exile to Siberia, 1590–1822,*[6] which readers should turn to for a full explanation of developments preceding those covered here. However, the present book may be approached on the basis of the following brief outline of earlier developments.

Almost immediately after its invasion of Siberia during the 1580s, Muscovy began using exile to settle its newly acquired territories. Exiles then served one of essentially two roles, as either a state servitor (usually, a Cossack) or an agricultural peasant. Both roles supported the highly lucrative fur trade that Muscovy inherited from the Mongol Empire after its collapse, and so exile from its very beginnings served primarily statist rather than judicial or penal goals. Exile nonetheless also served to rid European Russia of criminals and other undesirables, including prisoners of war and those the crown regarded as political threats. Following the 1649 *Ulozhenie* (Law Code) that formally acknowledged Siberian exile as a punitive tool, common criminals came to represent the majority of exiles. Further adding to their numbers was the substitution, in 1753–54, of permanent exile for the death penalty for serious offenders, who were sometimes accompanied by their families to Siberia, which now came to be known as the "land of criminals." In 1696, Peter I's establishment of *katorga* (penal labor)—a penologico-administrative entity that commandeered a large slave labor force for industrial projects then mostly located in European Russia—marked the next major development influencing Siberian exile. At first, *katorga* replaced exile as the regime's preeminent form of penality;[7] but after Peter's death in 1725 penal laborers were increasingly assigned to Siberia's growing metallurgical industry. Besides mines and smelteries, convicts also labored in Siberia's salt works, distilleries, and textile mills.

Despite a lack of concrete data, it is apparent that exiles' numbers grew with each successive reign, especially after empresses Elizabeth Petrovna and Catherine II granted exilic authority to serf owners and self-regulating communal organizations (*obshchestva* and *meshchanstva*). Deportees' overwhelming numbers combined with Siberian officials' corruption and malfeasance to result in dehumanizing conditions. Despite Petersburg's half-hearted efforts to use investigations and trials to force administrators into line, the situation deteriorated further as the nineteenth century began. Scandals and disasters that also victimized exiles led both to Alexander I naming M. M. Speranskii as Siberia's

governor-general and eventually to the Siberian Committee's 1822 Siberian Reforms—a collection of regulations intended to incorporate Siberia
into the empire and systematize its administration yet that also took
note of its regional peculiarities. Two regulations dealt specifically with
exile and produced for the first time what can be called an exile *system*.
Enamored of the emerging notions of rational government, Speranskii
idealistically believed he held the key to unlock a better future for
Siberia.

This book continues the history of Siberian exile by addressing the
period 1823 to 1861, during which 300,000 people were exiled to Siberia.[8]
This time-span embraces the final years of Alexander I's and the early
years of Alexander II's reigns, though my analysis focuses mainly on the
reign of Nicholas I (1825–55). In addition to discussing statecraft, administration, penality, and exilic society, I am concerned with tsarism as a
socio-cultural phenomenon. The book begins with the upsurge in exiles'
numbers immediately following the 1822 Reforms and goes on to explain
why Speranskii's system came to ruin as early as the 1830s. Exile exemplified tsarism's overall disorder and was a harbinger of the greater disorder to come. The 1861 serf emancipation did not fundamentally alter
the exile system, but did precipitate a surge in exiles' numbers much
greater than that immediately following the 1822 Reforms for reasons
I will explain in a later book.

I view the Siberian exile system similarly to the way Émile Durkheim
regarded punishment in general, insofar as its rules and forms related to
larger societal structures. For Durkheim, punishment reflected the morality of the "collective conscience" at work. This is admittedly something
difficult to measure, though the notion carries some resonance, as we
shall see. Durkheim nonetheless conceded that more concrete factors also
condition what he characterized as punishment's essential qualities. One
factor was government, especially absolutist government, which wrests
control over punishment away from society and places it in the hands of
the state in such a way that individuals come to be treated not as citizens
but as property.[9] This commodifying process lay at the heart of the tsarist
government's relationship towards society, though was by no means
unique to Russia. Nonetheless, with particular reference to Russia I believe
that attitudes toward, and uses of, criminalized subjects reflected an epis-
temological conflict between executors of sovereign and those of state
power during the period 1823–61.

In *Discipline and Punish*, Michel Foucault argues that beginning in the
late seventeenth century rehabilitative disciplinary strategies increasingly
replaced retributive punishments in accordance with the needs of the

burgeoning nation-state. Emblematic of this process was the phasing out of corporal punishment, torture, and dungeons and their replacement by both the modern penitentiary and a penology based on normalization and discipline. The simultaneous development of military drills and standardized piece-work provided both models and analogies for this normalizing and disciplining of what would idealistically become docile bodies. For Foucault, Europe's overall disciplinary trend found ultimate expression in Jeremy Bentham's plans for the Panopticon, a prison that suggested "a historical transformation: the gradual extension of the mechanisms of discipline throughout the seventeenth and eighteenth centuries, their spread throughout the whole social body, the formation of what might be called in general the disciplinary society."[10] If *sovereignty* had been the preeminent form of power during the early modern era, then *discipline* was its successor. Admittedly, tsarist Russia lagged behind Western Europe in several important categories; but as a land-based military power following Napoleon's 1815 defeat this Eurasian empire was *non pareil*. During the relatively peaceful period that followed, the autocracy, state censor Aleksandr Nikitenko observed, "set itself the task of disciplining the country."[11] As Frederick Kagan explains in his recent study of Nicholas I's military reforms, the immediate motivation for this disciplinary strategy was to provide manpower and means for Russia's enormous army.[12] So profound was the impact of Napoleon's 1812 invasion upon the psyches of Russia's leaders—an impact that may be likened to that experienced by Soviet leaders during World War II—that they became obsessed with disciplining both the military and civilian sectors, indeed with militarizing all Russia in order to steel it against future invasions and internal disturbances.

During his 1978 lecture series at the Collège de France, Foucault significantly modified his ideas about power, and these modifications offer further ways to conceptualize power in tsarist Russia. Foucault now mused "that the panopticon is the oldest dream of the oldest sovereign: None of my subjects can escape and none of their actions is unknown to me." He therefore proposed "a completely different economy of power... —an absolutely new political personage that I do not think existed previously [to the eighteenth century]... and this new personage... is the population."[13] Foucault was now also reconceptualizing the state: at the end of one lecture he rhetorically asked, "What if the state were nothing more than a way of governing? What if all these relations of power..., what if these practices of government [of which he had just given examples] were precisely the basis on which the state is constituted?" And he stated more emphatically: "the state is only an episode in government, and it is not government that is an instrument of the state."[14] This notion of the state as a set of processes or strategies rather than an institution disrupted the chronological development of power he had previously mapped out in *Discipline and Punish*:

> So we should not see things as the replacement of sovereignty by a society of discipline, and of a society of discipline by a society, say, of government. In fact we have a triangle: sovereignty, discipline, and governmental management, which has population as its main target and apparatuses of security as its essential mechanism.

Foucault nevertheless saw a historical transition, "from the eighteenth century," of "three movements—government, population, political economy," that together rendered "government management" the pre-eminent form of rule.[15]

Foucault tended to use "governmentality" rather than "government management" in subsequent lectures. Governmentality will be addressed in a moment. But first it is necessary to emphasize that his notion of a power triangulation best explains why the forms of Russian penality I rather simplistically identified as "pre-modern" and "modern" in my previous book were, in fact, coeval, as I nevertheless also argued. Foucault's later model is especially useful for understanding developments in Russia between 1823 and 1861, when the autocrat's prominence alternately facilitated and impeded ministerial efforts to construct an effective bureaucratic administration and police apparatus.

Foucault originally defined governmentality as: 1) "the ensemble formed by institutions, procedures, analyses and reflections, calculations, and tactics that allow the exercise of this very specific, albeit very complex, power that has the population as its target, political economy as its major form of knowledge, and apparatuses of security as its essential technical instrument"; 2) the tendency in the West for "government" to eventually outweigh sovereignty and discipline as the preeminent form of power and hence lead to creation of "governmental apparatuses... [and] development of a series of knowledges"; and 3) a process whereby the state of justice that characterized the Middle Ages turned into an administrative state that was itself "governmentalized."[16] Taking each of these points in reverse order, it may be seen that between the time of the 1649 *Ulozhenie*, which replaced most sentences of capital punishment with exile, and 1753–54, when capital punishment was abolished *de jure* for all but a few offenses and a ladder of punishments established, medieval retributive justice was largely replaced by governmentalized processes redounding to the benefit of an administrative state rather than the sovereign's personage. With regard to the second point (and Foucault included Russia as part of the West[17]), Catherine II showed at least an academic interest in Beccaria, Montesquieu, and other Enlightenment thinkers' penological theories insofar as they amounted to newly-minted knowledges useful for statist applications, even though her interest had little bearing on policy.[18] Finally, Foucault's first, wide-ranging, point problematizes the relationship between Siberian exile and tsarist governmentality and highlights our main concern here.

In part because Foucault did not so much elaborate his analytics with concrete historical examples as stake signposts for subsequent investigations, scholars have since refined and reconceptualized governmentality. In their recent *Foucault, Cultural Studies, and Governmentality* Jack Bratich et al. regard governmentality as "an analytic perspective that defines the state's role as one of coordination, one that gathers together disparate technologies of governing inhabiting many sites."[19] Mitchell Dean similarly modifies the term while suggesting that any analysis of government address four issues: 1) ontology, or *what* is being acted upon (e.g., the flesh of the body, the population); 2) ascetics, or *how* this governance is supposed to occur; 3) deontology, or subjectification—*who* individuals or population become when so governed; and 4) teleology, or the *why* of this governance—i.e., its *telos* or goal.[20]

Given these categories, and bearing in mind Durkheim's notions of punishment's structural significance and government's reduction of citizens to state property, the ontology of tsarist governmentality during the period 1823–61 comprised three main targets: the individual imperial subject, the collective imperial population, and the soul (in the Foucauldian sense of a subjectified inner existence disciplined through rewards and punishments). In terms of ascetics, tsarist governmentality maintained aspects of paternal despotism but also increasingly involved an emerging bureaucratic consciousness. The deontology of tsarist governmentality turned on maintaining and disciplining individuals so as to render them docile bodies serviceable to statist goals that were typically—though not always—economic in nature. Toward achieving these goals, this deontology further necessitated invention of a "population" upon which the state could exercise power through various knowledges expressed largely via statistics. Finally, the teleology of tsarist governmentality vacillated between the following: 1) a return to a Christian pastoral form of government wherein the tsar would serve as shepherd for his wayward flock; 2) construction of the New Jerusalem—that is, an end to history and the creation of heaven on earth;

and 3) a void, which in and of itself represented tsarism's end and therefore the conclusion of a self-abnegating and nihilistic journey and was as such the very antithesis of *telos*. With regard to this nihilistic journey it must be acknowledged that the imperial exhaustion that eventuated in World War I was by no means particular to Russia.[21] But it was sooner evident in Russia than in England or France, as the decision by Nicholas I to plunge into the abysmal Crimean War demonstrates. This irrational charge into the telic void also exemplified the absurdity that the teleology of the state is the state itself. In other words, the existence of the state is its own *raison d'état*, and so by definition it has no real goal.[22] Subconsciously acting upon this realization, tsarist Russia was developmentally far ahead of its European neighbors in this sense.

Nicholas, who may have killed himself due to the frustrations he faced as head of state, possibly reached this very same conclusion. "The domestic affairs of the country are all going extremely badly," observed Mikhail Bakunin in 1847. "There is complete anarchy under the label of order." This founder of anarchism was by no means a disinterested observer, but his opinion was shared by many across the political spectrum who perceived as did he the hollowness at the heart of power:

> The facade of bureaucratic formalism conceals terrible wounds; our administrative, judicial, and financial systems are all a lie—a lie to deceive foreign opinion, a lie to lull the conscience of the sovereign, who all the more willingly lends himself to it because the real state of things scares him.[23]

As an historical phenomenon, governmentality was precipitated by the Treaty of Westphalia that in 1648 ended the Thirty Years War—by several measures Europe's most destructive war ever. Westphalia laid the basis for cameralism, which relied upon *Staatswissenschaften* ("sciences of state") to develop practical solutions to prevent a relapse into chaos and barbarity. Walter Pintner has argued that a cameralist tradition began in Russia no later than Peter's reign (1694–1725).[24] However, a reading of the 1649 *Ulozhenie* in light of Westphalia suggests that it did so earlier. *Staatswissenschaften* "tended to view governing as more impersonal, an administration of a population which consisted of an ensemble of people and things," writes David Lindenfeld in his study of German statecraft.[25] Altogether *Staatswissenschaften* made up a *Polizeiwissenschaft* ("political science" or "public administration") that originally endowed "police" (*Polizei*) with the following verbalized meaning: "the set of actions that direct… communities under public authority." Simply put, at the time of its invention "police" meant "good government."[26] Eventually the notion of "the general welfare," which emerged alongside ideas of natural and inalienable rights, assisted cameralism to the extent that *Polizei* increasingly amounted to "the assertion of the will of the ruler over the estates in the name of the common good," explains Lindenfeld, who adds, "Political science thus represented the application of absolutist social discipline in the name of a secularized natural law, which provided the ends to which such discipline was directed."[27] However, these ends embodied in notions of secular law tended to serve mostly the interests of the state rather than society. Blind faith in the state and in administrative procedures may be summed up as governmentality.

Governmentality's development also turned on the discovery of economy as a "key dimension of reality"[28] rather than simply an extension of good household management. Economic historians disagree as to when the modern notion of economy emerged,[29] though it is fair to say it was embodied by fifteenth-century mercantilism. Of course, the emphasis then was on accumulation rather than capitalization; yet by coinciding with the greater killing power that the invention of gunpowder gave to military forces economy facilitated the policing of populations so as to make the state a more efficient financial enterprise. Colin Gordon, discussing Foucault's proposed transition from a pastoral form of power to governmentality, accordingly writes of the emergence of an "economic pastorate"[30]—an idyllic combination of pastoralism and governmentality. During the early modern period the emphasis was on controlling the economy; but in the mid-eighteenth century François Quesnay and other French *philosophes* envisaged economy as guided by natural laws that best operate with minimal government interference. Their Physiocracy ("rule of nature") introduced *laissez-faire* economics. However, Quesnay did not advocate a completely hands-off approach for government; rather, he believed it should use its power and authority to insure that economy's laws follow their natural course. Quesnay began publishing his Physiocratic precepts during the Seven Years War (1756–63) with an eye towards both increasing royal revenues and lessening the burden on the French peasantry. He argued that only agriculture produces wealth and that the only legitimate basis for taxation is land rent, or "the net product." To increase net product agriculturalists need to own the land they work because, as Elizabeth Fox-Genovese tartly puts it, "no one in his right mind willingly undertakes hard labor without being assured of the absolute right to the fruits of that labor...." To reflect the natural order economy's operations should be as unfettered as possible by tariffs, import duties, and other restrictions. Yet whereas government was to be essentially a caretaker and securer of private property, the Physiocrats did not demand that it insure any presupposed *political* rights and instead called for "legal despotism," by which they meant "a sovereign, assisted by administrators, and a group of magistrates to serve as the custodians of the fundamental laws of the realm. No restrictions except the sovereign's own sense of responsibility to observe the laws hampered the free exercise of authority."[31] Physiocracy spread throughout Europe, though sovereigns and administrators simply chose those elements they found most useful and ignored the rest. Early in her reign Catherine II solicited the advice of Physiocrat Pierre le Mercier de la Rivière and approved the founding of the Free Economic Society, yet expanded serfdom in direct contravention of Quesnay's axiom of private ownership. Physiocracy's influence none-theless helps account for her efforts to expand Russian territory and develop agricultural colonies—policies her successors continued.

Nicholas I and his finance minister Egor F. Kankrin strongly favored agricultural over industrial development.[32] True, this reflected their prejudice against urban life and their support of a landed gentry whose heyday had come and gone,[33] but they also hoped to improve conditions for state peasants. This goal reflected the need to augment state rev-enues; yet it was equally redolent of the paternal and rustic connotations Nicholas associated with *narodnost* ("nationality-ness"). Therefore, by embracing agricultural rather than industrial development the autocracy evinced its idyll of an economic pastorate. All the same, the case should not be made too strongly. Nicholas never devoted much attention to economic matters and Kankrin, despite pursuing a fundamentally pes-simistic agenda to control finances by simply limiting expenditures, failed to augment state revenues. Nicholas's predecessor had left him a state debt of nearly 590 million ruble-*assignats*. But he learned nothing from Alexander I's profligacy, and during the period 1823–31 the government accumulated 70 million rubles in debt and by 1832 was 823 million rubles in the red.[34] And this was long before the deficits incurred by the Crimean War. Pavel D. Kiselev, a progressive reformer in comparison to Kankrin, had some voice in economic policy. But his support for the tsar's militaristic predilections in nearly all policy areas superseded any bene-ficial influence he might have brought to this role. His 1836 inspection tour "convinced Kiselev more than ever that the immorality and cor-ruption both of the local administrators and of the unfortunate peasants themselves was the major barrier to economic progress," and so the land reforms he promoted amounted to a call for greater policing rather than fundamental socioeconomic change, writes Pintner.[35] W. Bruce Lincoln similarly found Kiselev's land reforms limited to administrative measures.[36] These reforms made no practical impact in Siberia,[37] but do reveal the regime's attitude toward governing civil society.

Policing, control, and the mentality necessitating them, as opposed to a commitment to genuine political, social, and economic reform, predicated the creation of statistics, police forces, and population. As throughout Europe so in Russia, the increasingly complex relationship between state and society resulted in governmental power challenging that of the sovereign. "[K]eeping [*sderzhivaia*] the Russian chariot on the path of Western European development for thirty years," wrote a commentator from the vantage point of 1870, "Emperor Nicholas gave us the time to prepare ourselves and the possibility of embarking upon that wide path now being revealed to us by his successor [Alexander II]."[38] As this writer probably unintentionally suggested, Nicholas did more to *restrain* (another translation of the verb *sderzhat*) Russia from proceeding down a Westernizing path rather than move it forward. His 30 years on the throne represented time lost rather than time gained in this sense, and when it turned muddy his successors failed to keep the chariot on the path at all. Yet Nicholas is not a one-dimensional figure: by embracing and idealizing autocracy while fetishizing state service he embodied the contradictions and tensions between sovereign and governmental power. This made him the true heir of Peter I, who also failed to reconcile the contradiction between wanting both a well-regulated police state and the despotic joy of having one's every whim fulfilled. By centralizing both His Majesty's General Staff and the Imperial Chancery Nicholas exhibited the disdain military minds often have for bureaucracy and its functionaries; on the other hand, he was willing to undertake reforms, though not toward any goal of "liberalization" or "Westernization" but rather to strengthen his autocratic regime.[39] That his own interests might differ from or even undermine those of the state was something he seems never to have fully acknowledged, except perhaps near the end of his life.

That said, the chariot whose reins Nicholas firmly grasped was burdened by much useless cargo. The emperor "cultivated a great self-sufficiency and decided all questions with brief and irrevocable commands," writes a Soviet biographer,[40] but "[n]owhere else is master more fawned upon and less obeyed," observed a contemporary.[41] Many of Russia's top officials were sycophants as well as being—like their subordinates—indolent, corrupt, and jaded. Others, most notably Aleksei A. Arakcheev, whose "emergence," notes Daniel Orlovsky, "was a symptom of institutional weakness in the central government,"[42] carved personal fiefdoms out of the ruling apparatus. Such destructive tyrants earned and deserved opprobrium from those who, however sometimes misdirected their actions, were motivated by something other than solipsism. As Lincoln so felicitously explains,[43] these old-school bureaucrats were gradually replaced by a qualifiedly different caste that viewed civil service as a profession and sought to fulfil its duties according to a combination of rational principles and high ideals. Moreover, this younger generation found some support among several of Nicholas's top officials, including Kiselev, Aleksandr I. Chernyshev, and Speranskii.

Foucault argued that governmentality finds its foremost expression in the ascetics of biopolitics, whereby officialdom creates and uses statistics—the preeminent science of statecraft—to more efficaciously govern that "massified" subject, the population, which is "not a primary datum [but] …a series of variables."[44] In Russia, biopolitics can be seen to have begun with the revisions, or censuses, Peter I used to improve tax collection and military conscription and which allowed the police to come into its own. John LeDonne has shown that the policing of the population significantly expanded under Catherine II.[45] Following establishment of the Ministry of Internal Affairs (MVD) in 1802, statistical record-keeping expanded as well (hence the only reliable figures on the exile population date from 1807). A report generated in 1830 by the Irkutsk *guberniia* administration typifies this new trend in statistical reporting: it shows the number of prisoners and transferees kept in *guberniia* prisons the previous year, the total number of days spent in these prisons, and the costs associated with their incarceration, maintenance, and transfer.[46] Similarly, the MVD's journal routinely published statistics on various matters. A statistical table from 1840 informs readers that more than 8,000 exiles passed through Kazan's transfer prison the previous year.[47] Such data were often presented with little or no analysis because, like the state, they were their own *raison d'être*, the supposed need for them being a justification of the existence of the agencies that produced them.

Towards the goal of a well-managed economy, mercantilist or Physiocratic, any cognition of population, statistics, and police necessitated administrative systematization, i.e., bureaucracy. Bureaucracy is regarded here as a particular—though excessively prominent—ascetic component of the type of governmentality that finds expression in the state. To better consider the way bureaucratic power functions, it is best to view it as a set of processes and strategies rather than an institution. "Foucault holds that the state has no… inherent propensities; more generally, the state has no essence," notes Gordon. "The nature of the institution of the state is, Foucault thinks, a function of changes in practices of government, rather than the converse. Political theory attends too much to institutions and too little to practices."[48]

Peter Berger et al., in their study *The Homeless Mind*,[49] write that the relationship between bureaucracy and society that so characterizes modernism is, theoretically, arbitrary and unnecessary, in contrast to that other characteristic, technology, which is absolutely necessary to produce, say, an automobile. Defining reality as essentially synonymous with consciousness, they offer the following definition of modern bureaucratic consciousness: 1) it is concerned with orderliness; 2) it believes in the general and autonomous organizability of social life; 3) it promises predictability; 4) it offers a general expectation of justice resulting from moralistic application of technologically-facilitated anonymity; and 5) it fails to separate between means and ends to the extent that procedures become as important as ends, if not more so. As its authors acknowledge, this is a prescriptive model not too dissimilar from Max Weber's model of bureaucracy, though unlike his it defines a consciousness that produces and is reflexively conditioned by the practices noted above. Keeping in mind the deontology of governmentality mentioned above, it is important to note that bureaucratic consciousness subjectifies the client, whose relationship to bureaucracy is in the first place almost entirely passive and whose just treatment necessitates his or her being stripped of personal identity and rendered a nominally integrated representative of a statistically defined population. Indeed, whether the client is treated justly or unjustly, he or she will be subjectified qua *victim*.

Despite its inclusion of reformers, the tsarist bureaucracy during the period 1823–61 generally evinced not rationalization but the "[r]ed tape, routine, and slowness"[50] that is summed up in the word *formal´nost*—that seemingly witless following of rules for rules' sake. "[B]ureaucratic formalism in the provinces was an unacknowledged substitute for the correct hierarchical organization of authority which the Russian administration lacked," writes S. Frederick Starr.[51] This was so. But *formal´nost* existed in large part because it gave a petty civil servant considerable power over a victim of nearly any status or rank. "By virtue of their offices, these despots oppress the country with impunity, and incommode even the Emperor," the Marquis de Custine complained of those he disparaged as "subaltern employés." "This is the bureaucracy, a power terrible every where [*sic*], because its abuses are always in the name of order, but more terrible in Russia than any where [*sic*] else."[52]

Bureaucracy's ascetics involve depersonalization and statistical formulation because they are discursively self-referential and, like the state, their own *raison d'être*. Hence:

> Bureaucracy, especially in the political sphere, *locates* the individual in society more explicitly than work. It "reminds" him of his macro-social connections over and beyond his private life. Thus it is potentially more threatening or more "inspiring," as the case may be, than work. The more frequently the individual comes into contact with bureaucracy, the more frequently he is forced into structures of meaning beyond those of his private life.[53]

By way of summing up the anomic, alienating, uprooting effects of modernization Berger et al. coin the term *homelessness*, for which "exile" may serve as an analog both generally and in the specific case of tsarist Russia.[54] Indeed, the autocracy's lack of a coherent economic policy, its fetishization of service and *narodnost*, and the inanity of the MVD's and other agencies' statistical data rendered an individual exile's *labor* less important than his totemic signification of both the sovereign's and the bureaucracy's subjugation of the tsarist subject, the imperial population, and the soul.

All of which may suggest a rather gloomy picture of the inexorability of homelessness/exile. But Berger et al. further suggest that the defense against such alienation is cultivation of the private sphere. Toward pursuing an analysis of Siberia's exile population, let us relate this notion to a similar one of Foucault's that he terms "counter-conduct" and defines as a form of resistance against the "conduct of conduct" bred within a "state of obedience."[55] Foucault posits five forms of counter-conduct, though for our purposes only two need be mentioned here. The first is asceticism, which in this case refers to a way of governing the self and eventually assumed primary importance in Foucault's later works on sexuality.[56] But for our immediate purposes literary critic Michel de Certeau offers a more concise framework for understanding this activity. In *The Practice of Everyday Life* Certeau uses linguistic theory to analyze such "discursive" activities as walking and cooking by noting that, at the point of enunciation, an actor does not need to know the language produced by hegemonic elites because s/he is "consuming" this language and using it in makeshift (*bricolage*) fashion to "compose the network of an antidiscipline [read: 'counter-conduct' or 'cultivation of the private sphere']...."[57] Certeau further develops this notion by explaining that if a strategy is a "calculus of force-relationships which becomes possible when a subject of will and power... can be isolated from an 'environment,'" then "[t]he place of a *tactic* belongs to the other. A tactic insinuates itself into the other's place, fragmentarily, without taking it over in its entirety, without being able to keep it at a distance." As such, tactics become "victories of the 'weak' over the 'strong' [and include] clever tricks [and] knowing how to get away with things...."[58] In other words, Certeau's analytics acknowledge subjects' agency and autonomy within a generally oppressive system.

The second form of counter-conduct identified by Foucault and considered here is the formation of communities. By way of example he cites the religiously heretical communities formed during the Middle Ages, though there is no reason counter-conduct communities cannot be secular. Such communities cultivate through Certeauean tactics those private spheres that are the defense against homelessness/exile. With regard to Siberian exile, five counter-conduct communities may be said to have existed. First was the community of Siberian officials who habitually produced a network of antidisciplinary acts that constituted an entire sphere of counter-conduct. There is abundant evidence of the disparity between Petersburg's orders and Siberian officials' behavior. For instance, writing years after the event, a former *katorga* official recalled that he did not report two men he knew to have escaped from their places of exile because he believed they were occupied at the time by more rehabilitative activities. "Whether what I did in both instances was bad or good, I don't know," he writes. But nowhere in his published memoir does he reflect that he broke the law.[59] Certainly, not every act by Siberian officials was planned or even intentional; but their sum total was sufficient to cause their collective behavior to be perceived by contemporaries as idiosyncratic or, in other words, antidisciplinary.[60] Siberia's second counter-conduct community was its exile population, made up of administrative exiles, exile-settlers, penal laborers, and others. Contemporaries were at pains to define the exilic community and document its behavior, and so allowance must be made for the way it was discursively constructed when consulting certain sources. But it remains clear that as a group exiles were antidisciplinary if only because they did not behave as authorities intended. Third were the distinct communities of political exiles formed by the Decembrists and Polish revolutionaries (and later by exiled *narodovol´tsy*, Marxists, and Socialist-Revolutionaries), each of whom maintained considerable autonomy and managed to flout the autocracy's attempts at disciplinary control within certain boundaries. Fourth was the equally distinct community formed by penal laborers in the various locations to which they were assigned. Finally, there was the community of vagabonds, or *brodiagi*, who in Siberia were usually fugitive exiles. These groups will be detailed in the following pages, but it is important to add here that each developed behaviors which, when recognized and approved by other members in the community, provided individuals with emotional gratification and were thus reinforced to the extent that they came to be repeated automatically and unconsciously. Work by William Reddy and others on the cultural construction of emotions is important toward better understanding how these counter-conduct communities developed and perpetuated themselves,[61] and the very existence of a hegemonic tsarist political culture served as an antithesis that allowed these counter-conduct communities to strengthen their internal cohesion. As Foucault observed, such communities are intimately bound up in the genesis of the state.[62]

To summarize the discussion so far, a tension was evident in Russia during the period 1823–61 between long-established sovereign power and emerging governmentality. Part and parcel of this governmentality was the development of a bureaucracy, whose procedures and goals often conflicted with those of the sovereign. The state increasingly sought to dominate society through political science, which yielded an understanding of society as "population." However, far from being an inert referent for statistical analysis, society responded with counter-conduct, which was itself empowered by the state's hegemonizing activities.

*   *   *

A major question throughout this book is why, if exile was so evidently unsuccessful, was it not abolished? To answer this in terms of episte-mology—because repudiation of the hallowed tradition of exile threat-ened the monarch himself. Like the spectacle of public execution, exile signified the tsar's godlike authority to banish a subject from the Edenic body-realm and cast him into darkness.[63] "The prince should exercise his authority boldly, lest chaos and criminality thrive," writes Jean Bethke Elshtain in *Sovereignty*. "He is God's rod and vengeance."[64] Banishment to Siberia, or even more so the threat of such, conferred upon the tsar the much desired recognition of his godlike powers. Nicholas I's desire to be recognized, to be *seen*, was extreme, almost infan-tile, and was manifested by the various ways he used to inform subjects that he was always watching them. For example, court medaller Fedor P. Tolstoi minted a medallion that was distributed to notables upon

Nicholas's ascension to the throne depicting the new sovereign's "All-seeing Eye" (*Vsevidiashchoe oko*).[65] "He is a man of talent and of resolution," Custine perceptively observed, "...but he wants magnanimity: the use that he makes of his power only too clearly proves this to me."[66] Ironically, Nicholas lost sight of his goals because he could not distinguish the point at which his desire to supervise state activities became a manic obsession. "This was the unique, personal legislation of the emperor, which inevitably had a fragmentary and haphazard character," A. E. Presniakov writes. "Cropping up on one occasion or another, it transformed the activity of the higher authorities from generally planned efforts to largely uncoordinated decrees."[67]

Nonetheless, the exile system (with the emphasis on "system") also validated bureaucrats, though they needed it in a way different than did the emperor: for them, it offered a proving ground for experiments in social engineering. Just as, writes Elise Kimerling Wirtschafter, "the growing contradiction in the government's policy of promoting bureaucratic rationality while preserving the existing social order"[68] found reflection in the vagaries of military justice, so too was it reflected in the exile system, which, like the Nicolaevan administration generally, was managed almost entirely by men with military backgrounds. Indeed, Russia's militarization of the civilian sector probably reached its apogee under Nicholas;[69] and in any case, militarization encapsulated the dichotomy between the arbitrariness of sovereign power and the iron logic of bureaucratic uniformity, with some officials hoping to perpetuate the good old days and others taking their cue from Western countries' increasingly professionalized institutions. However, the reforms proposed and acted upon between 1823 and 1861 were intended not to *Westernize* Russia but to strengthen the autocratic regime.[70] Siberia became a battlefield in the struggle between sovereignty and governmentality over how the state should be strengthened because exile was a pressing issue that embraced the entire empire. Officials both inside and outside Siberia therefore sought to enhance their careers by improving exile's management and utility. For this and other reasons to be discussed few during this time questioned its probity.

"All independence of thought and action seemed to [Nicholas I] inadmissible 'arrogance and opposition,' and all hope lay in stringent execution of orders and in unquestioning obedience," writes Presniakov. "He regarded his ministers as mere executors of his will, not as plenipotentiary and responsible directors of distant departments."[71] This is something of an exaggeration but it identifies wherein lay the rub, for "[i]f the bureaucrats could not circumvent the tsar, neither could the tsar readily circumvent the bureaucrats."[72] Caught in the middle of this struggle for power Siberia's exiles and non-exiles were its victims, but they fought back on their own terms.

1
The Surge: Exile and Crime in Siberia

During his brief stint as Siberia's governor-general from 1819 to 1822, Mikhail M. Speranskii realized far-reaching reforms were needed to redress problems involving its territorial and administrative organization, indigenous population, and exile system. Discussion of the 1822 Siberian Reforms falls outside the scope of this book. I detailed the "Regulation on Exiles" (*Ustav o ssyl´nykh*) and "Regulation on Exile Transfer within Siberian *Gubernii*" (*Ustav ob etapakh v sibirskikh guberni-iakh*) in my previous book, where I concluded as follows:

> The 1822 reforms are most significant not for having meliorated an inhuman penal system, but rather for attempting to systematically exploit deportees through an administrative infrastructure and set of regulations that, if followed... would ensure clock-like efficiency.

Speranskii, I added, "presaged those twentieth-century technocrats who imagined people as machines serving the high purposes of... the state."[1] Much in these two regulations either never went into effect or failed from the start. Personal rivalries, both among members of the Siberian Committee and more generally, possibly played a role in undermining these regulations. The number of top figures in government remained low throughout this period;[2] petty jealousy and back-stabbing were especially detrimental; court politics predominated over professionalism; personalities rather than offices determined the making and implementation of policy. Speranskii's social awkwardness and inability to ingratiate himself isolated him from other officials, many of whom could not stand him. His associations with many young noblemen who eventually became Decembrists led to his victimization at the hands of Nicholas I.[3]

Speranskii however had his allies, including the courtly and well-mannered chief of the Third Section Aleksandr Kh. Benkendorf. Universally regarded as a scatterbrain, if not something of a simpleton (he reportedly sometimes had to rely upon a calling card to remember his name), Benkendorf nevertheless enjoyed Nicholas I's confidence more than anyone. In his "Report on Public Opinion during the Year 1827" he offered the emperor his evaluation of Speranskii and other major figures. Classifying both Speranskii and his earlier patron Viktor P. Kochubei as among Russia's leading dignitaries (*sanovniki*) and "those contented" with the *status quo*, Benkendorf added that Speranskii

> is seen as tops by all intellectual and gifted people of the middle class, for example, the literati, merchants, and urban bureaucrats. In difficult circumstances a significant number of them turn to him as if to an oracle, confiding to him their fears, hopes, and innermost thoughts. He is accessible and popular, and cordially invites their confidence. They regard his word as prophecy. He is, it seems, completely devoted to H[is] M[ajesty] the sovereign emperor and his prevailing system [*sushchestvuiiushchii stroi*], the maintenance of which he supports with all his might, praising highly the sovereign's person and smoothing over the future with reassuring predictions.[4]

Whether or not personalities and infighting played determining roles, it is certain that the 1822 regulations failed because the regime clung insistently to a traditional view of exile and its functions and began exiling larger numbers than ever before. "Siberia was for Russia a deep sack," said foreign minister Karl Nesselrod, "into which we tossed our social sins and riff-raff in the form of exiles and penal laborers and so on."[5] Nonetheless, there is no substance to historian Abby Schrader's claim that "Speranskii's project... to rehabilitate criminals and turn them into productive colonists... depended upon the massive expansion of the exile system."[6] On the contrary, Speranskii designed his reforms in the expectation that no more than 2,000 exiles per year would enter Siberia.[7] There was no cause-and-effect relationship between the reforms and the burgeoning numbers of exiles. Explanations lie elsewhere.

During the period 1819–23, 4,570 people per annum were exiled to Siberia.[8] In 1823 alone, that is, when the 1822 Reforms took effect, 6,796 people were exiled. This figure nearly doubled to 12,050 in 1824. The year of Alexander I's death (1825) witnessed the highest number (12,508) deported to Siberia prior to serf emancipation, though figures during the first three years of Nicholas I's reign were similar.[9] During the period 1823–60 the average yearly number of exiles was 7,719 (8,335 if accompanying family members, or so called *dobrovol´nye* ["voluntaries"], are included)—a figure significantly higher than when Speranskii was conceiving, drafting, and introducing his exile regulations. Between 1823 and 1845, the year a new *Ulozhenie*, or Law Code, modified the exile system, a total of 202,348 exiles and 22,764 *dobrovol´nye* entered Siberia.[10]

Accounting for the surge in exiles' numbers strikes at the heart of tsarist penality and society. Soviet historiography held that the state's growing reliance upon exile was a response to the heightening "liberation movement in Russia."[11] Indeed, Pavel D. Kiselev's investigations at the time showed both the state's and landowners' peasants' living standards were worse than imagined; and largely as a result of this peasant revolts increased from 148 during the period 1826–34 to 216 during 1835–44 to 348 the following decade.[12] But the Marxist interpretation fails to account for specific policies and puts the cart before the horse insofar as it portrays deportation rates as a *response* to this "liberation movement" (itself a lukewarm qualification of the "revolutionary movement" Lenin insisted could only be led by a professional vanguard). Moreover, it fails to acknowledge that communal assemblies (*obshchestva* and *meshchanstva*) were responsible for over half those deported by administrative procedures during this period.

In fact tsarist Russia's increasing use of exile was more insidious than Soviet historians were willing to acknowledge, because it manifested the ascetics of a governmentality geared toward producing a docile population of serviceable bodies and reflected the growing economic pressures peasants faced. As both the state and the nobility sunk further into debt the peasantry was pushed to increase production. The autocracy's reluctance to tax the nobility to support its enormous military expenditures led it to squeeze as much as it could out of the rest of society. To satisfy these demands authorities increasingly relied upon the use and the threat of exile. Meanwhile, peasants turned on their neighbors and likewise increasingly used and threatened exile through administrative procedures.

In addition to this economic determinant there was a less tangible but no less real factor increasing the use of exile. Under the combined influence of militarism and neo-Classicism government leaders felt a growing compulsion to cleanse society—a clean society being synonymous with a well-ordered one comprised of serried ranks and straight lines.[13] Beginning with Paul's reign (1796–1801) this epistemology found expression on the parade ground and through the construction of monuments and palatial buildings. The well-drilled battalion rendered individual soldiers' movements limited, measured, and predictable; within the cityscape huge monuments and palaces fetishized balance, stability, and time-lessness while diminishing human beings. These spectacles and structures were intended to overwhelm spectators with the power of the state and to naturalize or, in Clifford Geertz's formulation, *essentialize* the state.[14] As something natural, the state became a living being; as something essential, its life and health had to be maintained through high standards of purity and harsh retaliation against threats to that purity. If for no other reason than to protect the state and those who benefited most from its existence "the ongoing emergency of the Napoleonic Wars... demanded a greater militarization and regimentation of society," writes Alexander Bitis.[15] Militarization turned the empire into a police state long before 1881, when historians have traditionally marked its inauguration in reaction to Alexander II's assassination. Not only did the military soak up most of the state's finances, but under Nicholas "the War Ministry was the third largest ministerial employer of *civil* officials...."[16] Given the arbitrary control senior officers exerted over the lower ranks (*nizhnye chiny*), the military's growing dominance over society was fraught with consequences. "Like the biblical God," writes one historian, "commanders were supposed to be both merciful and 'terrible.'"[17] Nicholas, whose imperial suite in 1853 "included 45 generals and 48 colonels,"[18] held this to be axiomatic.

Following Napoleon's 1812 defeat Alexander I had ordered several neo-Classical structures built in Moscow, the most significant being the Cathedral of Christ the Savior, an homage to God for delivering the realm from the Corsican Satan. Yet at the same time this didactic memorial situated the Romanovs within a mytho-history that commenced with Classical Rome and continued through Biblical times. Nicholas maintained this grandiose obsession with purity and order by, *inter alia*, perpetuating his father Paul's "paradomania" with as many as 40,000 soldiers marching around the Alexandrine Column outside the Winter Palace.[19] State increasingly replaced God during the transition from Alexander's to Nicholas's reign, though reverence for either sufficed for reactionaries who wanted to rid society of its riff-raff. Aleksei A. Arakcheev, who served under both tsars and was rumored by peasants to be a cannibal, was a catalyst for this transition. Whereas Alexander saw "order, ... cleanliness, ... symmetry and elegance" in the military colonies Arakcheev began establishing during his reign,[20] Nicholas considered them models for exile settlements he later constructed in Siberia. The transition from a mystical politics dedicated to establishing heaven on earth to a mythopoeic politics glorifying Russia's past found reflection in efforts to endow government with renewed moral authority, and so "Nicholas sustained the symbolic preeminence of the autocrat not by elevating himself to celestial spheres," writes Richard Wortman, "but by abasing his subjects...."[21] "Not by daring and rash dreams, which are always destructive, but gradually, and from above, laws will be issued, defects remedied, and abuses corrected," the young tsar declaimed in his coronation manifesto.[22]

Nicholas backed up these words with brute force. The army ruthlessly crushed peasant rebellions while military courts summarily punished civilians who fit into any of 41 separate categories. Military tribunals operating under field regulations that allowed execution of the condemned within 48 hours were supposed to be disbanded after 1815 but became a permanent fixture in 1831, and field regulations were thereafter routinely used. Between 1827 and 1846, 3,400 people were exiled to Siberia "by simplified military-judicial procedure." It is indicative of Nicholas's view of justice that in 1848, after learning of disorder in the Siberian goldfields, he ordered: "try all the guilty [*sic*] forced labourers by Field Regulations."[23]

This heavy-handed conduct spawned development of counter-conducts among peasants anxious to preserve their private sphere that was the *mir*, in all its connotations of "commune," "world," and "peace." As we shall see, within Siberia as well, everyone from high officials to fugitive penal laborers contributed to strategies of antidisciplinary behavior in the face of St Petersburg's onslaught.

Most significantly for the exile system, this statist puritanism found expression in ukases promulgated in 1821 and 1823 to prohibit the longstanding practice of enlisting petty criminals (*malovazhnye*) and vagabonds (*brodiagi*) in the military. Most such offenders were now to be exiled to Siberia instead. Citing problems with *brodiagi* and criminals already in the military, Emilii-Karl L. Vitgenshtein (Wittgenstein) and Fabian V. Saken fon-der-Osten (Sacken von der Östen) had suggested this ruling to Alexander I, who himself expressed concern in 1817 about convict recruits' influence on fellow servicemen in Orenburg and Siberia. Alexander was also doubtlessly troubled by a series of sixteen "collective protests" by army regiments between 1820 and 1825, the most significant being the Semenovskii Guards' mutiny of October 1820 and the Orlov Affair of 1821–22. The first involved officers marshalling lower ranks to protest against their regimental commander's personal excesses. It bears little resemblance to the Decembrist Uprising of five years later, except that several officers participated in both acts and were both times equally obeyed by their troops. Perhaps sensing an omen, Alexander disbanded the Semenovskii regiment, ordered the ringleaders to run a thousand-man gauntlet as many as six times, and distributed its lower ranks among units in the Caucasus and Finland. An undetermined number were exiled to Siberia. In January 1821 he created a military secret police whose small number of spies operated principally within the officer corps. These spies exposed the Orlov Affair, which in late 1821 led to senior officers M. F. Orlov and V. F. Raevskii being charged with circulating subversive literature connected to disturbances by the 16th Division.[24]

Like its surveillance of officers, the autocracy's exclusion of petty criminals and *brodiagi* from the military was intended to insure troops' integrity and loyalty. A "cleansing" (*ochishchenie*) of petty criminals from fortress garrisons accordingly began in 1823.[25] As for deporting *brodiagi*, this was nothing new. Early in his reign Peter I had "launched a full-scale assault on begging and vagrancy" that included ordering *brodiagi* exiled to Siberia. In Evgenii Anisimov's words *brodiagi* came to be "viewed as an alien body in the social organism... "[26] Nonetheless, concludes Adele Lindenmeyr, "The actual results of all these decrees were extremely meager," and *brodiagi* were probably more often assigned to the military.[27] Government officials and scholars would debate what to do with *brodiagi* and beggars until the end of the imperial era.[28]

Brodiagi were actually being created by the military itself, since nearly all soldiers who survived to complete their 25-year terms were, upon release, incapable of productive labor. Invalided veterans unable to secure a spot in one of the invalid units established during Catherine II's reign were, in the language of the law, released "on their own sustenance." Some of the hundreds of thousands invalided between 1815 and 1825 received pensions, but these totaled less than 750,000 rubles in value. In 1854, in the midst of the Crimean War, "pensions expenditure was less than half a million silver roubles, compared with an overall military budget of 178.6 million," writes John Keep.[29] It is ironic that when, in a fit of magnanimity, Nicholas hastened by three to five years the retirement between 1826 and 1829 of more than 45,000 soldiers,[30] he inadvertently created several thousand new itinerant beggars and dependent villager dwellers. An 1834 law granting indefinite furloughs to certain soldiers who had already served for 20 years[31] had a similar effect. Indeed, given the widespread application of the charge of *brodiazhestvo* (vagabondage), military veterans quite likely accounted for most of the empire's *brodiagi*. Even if only a small portion of the 48,812 soldiers known to have been "lost to various causes in [the war year of] 1827" alone[32] were incapacitated upon retirement, the enormousness of their numbers and impact on society between 1823 and 1861 becomes apparent when considering that Russia had a standing army of 800,000 men.

The struggle against *brodiagi* intensified considerably with issuance on 23 February 1823 of the regulation colloquially known as the *"Brodiagi Regulation"* (*Ustav o brodiagakh*).[33] *Brodiagi* and petty criminals who would earlier have been "exiled to the military" were now put at the disposal of several government bodies, including the MVD, Ministry of Finance, Main Administration of Communications (*Glavnoe Upravlenie Putei Soobshcheniia*), and Ministry of War and assigned to labor in "ports, Ekaterinoslav's factories, the mining and salt-making industries, and to jobs under the direction of Communications." The MVD had authority over several areas related to exile, including the capture of fugitives, providing for sick and crippled exiles, provisioning and settling exiles in Siberia, and the construction of transfer prisons and way-stations (which in 1833 became the new Department of Communications' responsibility). The Ministry of Finance dictated taxes and duties for exile-settlers, the paying and withholding of their salaries, and other financial matters affecting them. The Ministry of War was responsible for convoying exiles along the march-route to Siberia, providing guards along the way and at *katorga* sites, and operating the military courts to which exiles were subject.

Brodiagi and petty criminals unsuitable for labor were now to be administratively deported for settlement in Irkutsk *guberniia*. Those already in the military were to be purged and also exiled. The only ones exempt from these provisions were the elderly or physically disabled, and vagrant orphaned children, who were to be remanded to institutions operated by the Social Welfare Boards (*Prikazy Obshchestvennago Prizreniia*).[34] Created by Catherine II's 1775 Statute on Provincial Administration, these boards were responsible for operating "almshouses, orphanages, special institutions for the incurably ill, insane asylums, workhouses, and houses of correction, along with schools and hospitals," and as of 1862 oversaw "524 hospitals, 39 insane asylums, 111 almshouses, 23 orphanages…, and 30 houses of correction and workhouses." But lack of oversight and funding led to their becoming both harmful to those they were supposed to help and "symbols of the evils of bureaucracy and centralization," writes Lindenmeyr.[35] Eventually, *brodiagi* were mostly sentenced to "exile to resettlement" (*ssylka na vodvorenie*)—a vaguely defined category introduced during the 1850s that eventually referred exclusively to those convicted of *brodiazhestvo*. But even then the term was misleading, since *brodiagi* were forced to serve a one-and-a-half year labor term before being assigned to the countryside. For instance, all 849 *brodiagi* deported to

Tobol´sk *guberniia* during 1861 went directly to the Ekaterinsk or Uspensk distillery.[36] A law of 29 March 1828 made *brodiazhestvo* a criminal offense punishable by the courts,[37] though it is clear that before this date some defendants were convicted by the judiciary.

The *Brodiagi* Regulation and related legislation created a vicious circle that significantly expanded the exile population, most directly by allowing deportation of those who would earlier have become servicemen. Arrested in Vil´no *guberniia* in 1824 for *brodiazhestvo*, Dmitris Zakharevich and Leon Parfenov were spared corporal punishment but nevertheless sentenced to exile to settlement (*ssylka na poselenie*), soon to be followed by Iakub Shileiko.[38] The loss of potential recruits meant the military had to increase its levies, especially during the wars against Persia and Turkey (1826–29). Three levies during 1827–28 drafted a total of 256,817 recruits; seven levies between 1827 and 1831 yielded approximately 500,000 recruits; and throughout Nicholas's reign nearly three million men were drafted.[39] Such high demand for cannon fodder increased the number of draft evaders. "Upon the first rumours of an upcoming levy," states an 1832 military report, "the majority of people with names on recruitment lists hide away from their dwellings."[40] They had good reasons for doing so: a 25-year term, drills in "stick-academies," meager rations, gauntlets of switchwielding soldiers, compulsory settlement in a military colony, exposure to cholera, typhus, and tuberculosis, and so on. "During the first quarter-century of Nicholas's reign," writes Lincoln, "it has been estimated that 1,028,650 men in the army perished from disease alone."[41] Designated recruits, besides hiding from authorities, "cut off an index finger... drank poison or acid hoping to damage their internal organs," or "simply took flight," sometimes "en route to induction centers."[42]

Draft-evaders who were captured but could not be identified were exiled as *brodiagi* under the new law; those who mutilated themselves (*chlenovrediteli*) were sometimes exiled too. Exiled *chlenovrediteli*'s numbers were small (853 between 1827 and 1846[43]), but their cases created legal and administrative problems. For instance, the Senate debated what to do with exiled *chlenovrediteli*'s wives. It was bad enough for a village woman to be a "soldier's widow" (*soldatka*), but she faced much greater scorn if she stayed behind as an exile's wife. Many therefore shared their husbands' fates and marched with them to Siberia. In 1831 the serf Melanii Moiseeva petitioned the Nizhegorod administration for the right not to accompany her husband and to live where she wanted. Reasoning that both *soldatki*'s and exiles' wives were anyway freed from serfdom because of their husbands' status, the Senate granted Moiseeva's petition and ordered that its ruling set a precedent for future cases.[44] It is doubtful, however, that further provisions were made for these women.

Even more sobering to imagine are the effects of another ruling concerning the children of *brodiagi* condemned to exile. This time the State Council played the decisive role, also in 1831, though unlike the Senate it faced an invidious dilemma between sending the children of *brodiagi* and (in most cases) their wives on a march described as "in all respects difficult… [and] exhausting," or seizing and thus depriving these children of "the care that children necessarily need" from their parents. Supported by the emperor, it chose the latter course. Children of exiled *brodiagi* were now to be remanded to the social welfare boards, with boys, "when they reach that age that enables them to enter Military Orphanages, relocated to those Orphanages," and girls institutionalized "until that time when they have the means to provide for themselves." The question of how to dispose of nursing infants was particularly thorny. After some debate, councilors decided that mothers would not commence the march until six months after their infants were weaned, at which point the boards would seize their babies and the mothers would be dispatched to Siberia as usual.[45] This law appears to have been enforced inconsistently. Nonetheless, comparison of several figures suggests that children seized by the state in this way may have numbered in the thousands: Kazan's transfer prison processed 497 children during 1839 alone; during the period 1854–60 over 2,400 children entered the exile system; 1,665 did so in 1861 alone.[46] Of course, these figures concern children who were *not* seized; but they nevertheless hint at the number who would have been seized, moreover because *brodiagi* constituted the largest category of exiles. It should be added that convicted minors (*nesovershennoletnie*) were also subject to exile (though unlike adults, not corporal punishment). Those aged ten to 13 could only be exiled to settlement, while those aged 14 to 17 were eligible for *katorga*. Between 1847 and 1852, 205 boys and 172 girls were exiled to Western Siberia, 161 (including 51 girls) to *katorga*.[47]

The military's growing number of resentful recruits seems to have at first resulted in larger numbers being punished with exile. Soldier Pavel Antipov was convicted for participating in the insurrection among Novgorod's military colonies during the 1831 cholera epidemic. He received a severe punishment of 30 lashes with the knout. After arriving in Irkutsk in 1833, Antipov served his *katorga* sentence, first in Irkutsk's textile mill, then in the Ilginsk distillery.[48] During the peacetime years 1836–38 an average of 5,386 men per annum deserted the military. Keep mentions a Private P. Zhuravlev who deserted three times despite (or perhaps because of) repeated corporal punishments, and another deserter who was exiled to *katorga* after running the gauntlet.[49] "Desertion was not just a means of self-help but also a blow against the absolutist military system," he elsewhere writes, noting that the desertion rate for the Second Army was just below 1.5 percent per annum during the period 1819–21.[50] The 1832 military report quoted above states that recruits who were given leave were kept under constant surveillance, but that nevertheless "desertion occurs very often."[51] In 1829, the second and final year of the Russo-Turkish War, the government offered soldiers and gendarmes a bounty of ten rubles for every "*brodiaga*, fugitive, and other persons without passports" they captured.[52] It circulated a listing of spaces in the empire's various forts that were available "for soldiers convicted of a fourth escape."[53] That same year, officials related the emperor's concern that Catholic monasteries were harboring *brodiagi* and deserters, as they had supposedly done during the late eighteenth century.[54] Petersburg's military reforms eventually helped reduce the desertion rate to just 0.1 percent for the period 1836–50.[55] All the same, an 1877 official review of the history of *brodiazhestvo* opined that fugitive soldiers and serfs together accounted for the majority of pre-emancipation *brodiagi*.[56] According to S. V. Maksimov, "Nearly unwavering consistency distinguished the number of *brodiaga*-deserters who fled the difficulties of military service and all the overwhelming and sometimes compellingly unseasonable circumstances of this type of official obligation."[57] Deserters from the Siberian military sometimes formed bandit gangs with fugitive exiles. One that included five deserters and over 20 *katorga* convicts terrorized Krasnoiarsk *okrug* during autumn 1842.[58]

Like similar laws in Western Europe and the United States at the time, the *Brodiagi* Regulation was sufficiently vague to be applied against a range of undesirables. Officials used the charge of *brodiazhestvo* to deport *meshchane* involved in the 1831 cholera riot in Staraia Rusa. Dissident peasants like those involved 15 years later in Viatka and Kazan *gubernii*'s "potato riots" were often exiled as *brodiagi*.[59]

Most significantly, "*brodiazhestvo*" facilitated deportation of the elderly and the mentally and physically disabled. Malfeasance in this area was so widespread that on 4 August 1827 the Senate "forbade the removal to Siberia for *brodiazhestvo* of the aged, deaf, mute, and blind...." The following year senators ordered elderly *brodiagi* sent to workhouses instead, but allowed healthy female *brodiagi* to continue to be exiled to Siberia so as to increase its Russian population.[60] These laws were rarely enforced. In June 1830 the Tobol´sk Exile Office (TobPS) informed the Senate:

> [V]arious *Guberniia* Administrations are for *brodiazhestvo* exiling to settlement in Siberia elderly men and women between 70 and 90 years old, as well as the blind, deaf, dumb, insane, emaciated, maimed, and such like who are not at all suitable for a Siberian settlement....[61]

Most were being exiled without having committed "any crime at all… and cannot complete the march and find themselves in City Hospitals [along the way]," where they were routinely ignored by staff who resented having these wretches foisted on them. Despite the Senate's 1827 ukase as well as others before and since that ordered such persons placed under the care of their *guberniia*'s charitable institutions (*blago-tvoritel´nye zavedeniia*), officials were clearly using the *Brodiagi* Regulation to shift the burden of supporting them to other regions (i.e., Siberia, if these people got that far). The charitable institutions the Senate so casually invoked hardly existed, however, and so *guberniia* administrators often felt they had no other choice. This situation renders understandable, if no less reprehensible, the decision by Arkhangel *guberniia*'s governor-general to pay a villager ten rubles to keep a madman chained inside his hut—he was doing him a favor by not deporting him to Siberia.[62] Little had changed by the end of Nicholas I's reign, when the Ministry of State Domains reported on the woeful lack of institutions for a total of 73,000 state peasants who needed care because of senility, mental incapacity, illness, and so on. This figure excluded serfs and was probably too low anyway.[63]

Upon joining the convoys bound for Siberia, such vulnerable persons faced a high likelihood of dying before reaching their assigned destinations. Guards regularly rode or put supplies in the carts supposed to carry sick exiles to hospital.[64] Hospitals and infirmaries with uniformly high death rates replicated transfer prisons' and way-stations' terrible conditions. Way-stations sat on stone foundations, were made of wood, and consisted of a single large ward with sleeping platforms (*nary*) running along the walls. They sometimes had two levels of platforms and a row down the middle, but even then the parties were usually too large and so many slept on floors inches thick with filth. With almost no light and atmospheres suffused with carbon dioxide and perspiration from hundreds of unwashed bodies, these were kennels for the damned. After nightfall doors and windows were locked and a *parasha*—a large open vat—placed in the corner: hours before daybreak it would be overflowing with human waste. "The stench from the *parasha* is unendurable," reported one official, but of course exiles had no choice but to endure it. Legislation passed in 1840 resulted in some new way-stations being built, but they were allowed to dilapidate like their predecessors. This legislation was followed two years later by a rule allowing priests into way-stations "for the edification of criminals being exiled to Siberia." Deportees were informed of their "responsibilities to faith and morality."[65] A way-station's infirmary usually consisted of a single room with six beds and no physician, and most of the hospitals that accepted exiles were for some reason so far from the march-route that many patients died before ever reaching them. In November 1839 GUZS allowed exiles to be interned in hospitals previously reserved for the military's lower ranks, but reversed this decision five years later.[66] In 1861, of the 1,844 patients already *in situ* or admitted that year to Tobol´sk *guberniia*'s prison hospitals, 107 never left them alive. In other words, more than one out of every 17 patients died. The death rate was still higher in Tobol´sk's six almshouses, which unlike the hospitals were mostly located along the march-route and housed many exiles.[67]

Creation of special correctional battalions provided another way to persecute a homeless population that increasingly challenged city authorities and reflected peasants' increasing hardship. These battalions were separate from the military, technically under local governors' control, and so did not violate the *Brodiagi* Regulation. The first were established in Novgorod and Pskov around 1828. As of July 1830 eight battalions existed in Odessa and Novorossiia consisting of *brodiagi*, deserters, petty criminals, and others who before 1823 would have been assigned to fortresses or workhouses. Additional battalions later arose in Moscow, Brest-Litovsk, Kronshtadt, Kiev, Ekaterinoslav, and elsewhere. The 1822 Reforms and other legislation had called for exiles to be permanently or temporarily assigned as laborers for use by local civilian administrations, but provided few instructions regarding this. Correctional battalions were designed more precisely to fashion deviants into serviceable bodies according to a military model. These battalions already mostly included *brodiagi* when, in 1838, the State Council ruled they should be reserved only for them. However, at some point a separate category of battalions was established to deal with convicts from the nobility. Even noblemen guilty of murder or robbery were assigned to these, on the supposition that the same law protecting them from corporal punishment also rendered them "petty criminals" (*malovazhnye*) and thus prevented their being exiled to settlement or to *katorga*. Correctional battalions for noblemen existed until 1845, when Nicholas decreed that they be used only for commoners.[68]

Correctional battalions were also established in Siberia, though whether they were reserved for local offenders or were destinations for convicts from elsewhere is not clear. Nonetheless, it is fair to suspect that a large percentage of these battalions' prisoners originated outside Siberia because many exiles escaped only to be rearrested. An 1862 report describes a Tobol´sk *guberniia* institution it likens to a correctional battalion but specifically calls "the Omsk exile-settler labor battalion," which suggests it was the only such battalion in the *guberniia*. During 1861 this battalion inducted 16 new convicts and released five, so that its roster now totaled 74. The report mentions that legislation passed in 1859 ordered laborers who completed a four-year term within the battalion be assigned to resettlement in Eastern Siberia, whereas those who served briefer terms were to be assigned to "*starozhil* villages in Western Siberia." "[L]ike a correctional battalion," Omsk's labor battalion was reported to be "maintained on the land taxes account and is being housed in an unsuitable dilapidated building managed by the Social Welfare Board." The battalion cost the *guberniia* administration 2,365 rubles 44 kopeks to maintain during 1861, and "earned" (i.e., "performed labor valued at") only 914 rubles 70 kopeks. Not only were funding and living arrangements deplorable, but management was "chaotic." The report concludes with an unconvincing expression of hope for future improvement.[69]

Between 1827 and 1831, 16,985 subjects were exiled for *brodiazhestvo* compared to 9,163 between 1842 and 1846. In 1827, 4,739 were exiled; in 1846, just 1,449.[70] For various reasons the number exiled as *brodiagi* would increase considerably after 1861,[71] but this earlier decline after an initial spurt shows that correctional battalions and the Senate's rulings had a dampening effect. Nicholas's government also chipped away at the *Brodiagi* Regulation in order to expand its pool of military recruits, even if this risked lowering the army's morale and dependability. In 1830 the Senate confirmed lower court rulings of 1828 and 1829 that assigned two serfs charged with *brodiazhestvo* to the military, explicitly stating that these cases established a precedent.[72] Another ruling of March 1832 assigned all able-bodied convicts to the military rather than exile. This was followed by an 1836 law that assigned able-bodied convicts under 35 to the military; those between 35 and 39 to correctional battalions; and those 40 and older (or younger but disabled) to settlement in Siberia.[73] Along with the other factors already mentioned, this legislation reduced the number exiled for *brodiazhestvo*. However, on 23 November 1853 a statue, entitled "On Measures to Restrict the Growth of Prisoners in Places of Confinement and to Transfer Criminals to Exile Sites away from Siberian Residents," allowed correctional battalions, workhouses, and prisons to turn over surplus prisoners for resettlement in Siberia and introduced to the exile system the category "resettled laborers" (*vodvoriaemye rabochie*). Initially, this category included convicts skilled in trades who were to be distributed so as to introduce their services to Siberia's remote *okrug* and *volost* centers. But "resettled laborers" soon came to refer only to *brodiagi* exiled to factories and *zavody* ("industrial townships," see Chapter 7) or, if they were women, to hospitals to work as laundresses.[74] From the beginning administrators were confused by this new category, and this probably explains why it did not have an immediate impact. However, after 1861 courts relied upon the statute to exile *brodiagi* in larger numbers than ever before.

All told, the 1823 *Brodiagi* Regulation had a terrible impact on Siberia. The 48,566 *brodiagi* exiled between 1827 and 1846 accounted for 30.4 percent of all exiles (159,755, including those administratively deported).[75] Many so called *brodiagi* were in fact old or physically or mentally afflicted. The Siberian Committee found that as of 1833 "the senile [and] those incapable of any kind of work" comprised 20.5 percent (20,570) of Siberia's exile population of 100,086, with females in this category totaling 2,673.[76] Comparable figures the following year were 23.2 percent (22,508) of a population of 97,121.[77] Not everyone included in these figures were victimized by the *Brodiagi* Regulation: many deportees were crippled by the march to Siberia or their exilic conditions, others became senile long after they arrived. But the Senate's 1827 ukase against deporting such persons was routinely flouted and TobPS, which processed nearly all exiles entering Siberia, received many persons it never should have. Of the 6,807 exiles it processed in 1833 it immediately assigned 14.2 percent (968) to the category officially called "incapables" (*nesposobnye*).[78] In July 1842 Tomsk governor Stepan P. Tatarinov reported to the Ministry of State Domains on those exiles in his jurisdiction who were not, like many, lodging in the homes of state peasants: of the 5,563 who were married, 848 were incapacitated; and of the 16,302 who were single, 2,835 were incapacitated.[79] How these people fared once they arrived in Siberia will be discussed in Chapter 2.

*   *   *

The disorganization and casuistry of Russia's judiciary also contributed to the surge in exiles' numbers. Some sympathy is due judicial officials, for under Nicholas I the Ministry of Justice was sorely under-funded.[80] As early as 1826 a backlog of more than two million cases awaited adjudication; and in a single year the Third Section received nearly 15,000 personal denunciations, petitions, and other administrative cases to address. Benkendorf inveighed upon the emperor to rule on as many cases as possible and to order courts to hasten theirs, but no single person could have dealt with all these matters alone, and when in 1842 Nicholas ruled that those filing false denunciations would receive the punishments otherwise reserved for the accused this only added the need to investigate denouncers to the gendarmerie's numerous responsibilities.[81]

Lincoln suggests that Speranskii's codifying of laws during the 1830s succeeded in creating something very close to rule-by-law under Nicholas.[82] But Samuel Kucherov's observation that "[t]he work of codification entrusted to M. M. Speranskij did not change anything in the field of the court system and its functioning" is much closer to the truth.[83] Juridical historian Nikolai S. Tagantsev remarked on the law code's "special shortcomings"[84] that delayed emergence of genuine legal rights. Beholden to the rich and powerful, tsarist courts remained far too hideous to consort with Themis, the goddess of justice. During the period 1834–45 the acquittal rate among the nobility was 56 percent while among state peasants and serfs it was 42 percent. Similarly, 42 percent of landowners charged with abusing their authority were acquitted in 1834 while just 18 percent of peasants charged with insubordination were.[85] The pressure Benkendorf put on hapless judges only made the situation worse. Sidney Monas writes that when they failed to speedily process their backlog of cases the Third Section would send "assistants" who mocked any pretense of legality:

> N. M. Kolmakov, a notable jurist, related in his memoirs how a gendarme officer, dispatched to a certain appellate court which had lagged behind in its decisions, forced the judge to decide all pending cases while he stood there. The judge attacked a mountain of paper, deciding alternately "upheld, reversed; upheld, reversed." The job was soon done, and the gendarme returned satisfied to St. Petersburg.[86]

Like the abusive use of the *Brodiagi* Regulation the charge of "bad behavior" (*durnoe povedenie*) contributed to exiles' numbers. This vague accusation allowed landowners, communal assemblies, and local officials to have an individual administratively deported without his or her being charged or convicted of a crime. According to regulations passed in 1827 landowners were not to deport the senile, crippled, or those over age 50; single mothers accompanied by boys under the age of five or girls under age ten were not to be deported, unless their husbands were military recruits.[87] Like those judicially-convicted as exile-settlers (*ssyl´no-poselentsy*) administrative exiles were for the most part assigned to peasant villages; unlike them they retained their rights. They could return home after five years but only with their commune's permission, which was often not forthcoming. Between 1827 and 1846, 65,774 men and 14,135 women were administratively deported to Siberia, 63 more than were exiled as a result of criminal convictions.[88]

Following investigations in 1811–12 that exposed administrative exile's abusive use Alexander I abolished landowners' exilic authority. But the Senate reversed this with legislation of 1823 and 1824. The growing concerns about *brodiagi* heightened the state's reliance on civilian authorities and so this return of landowners' exilic authority, coincidental with the *Brodiagi* Regulation, is not surprising. Many in government considered administrative exile indispensable for regulating the countryside in the absence of a strong police presence there. The return of this authority may also have been a sop to serf owners at a time when Alexander was rumored to be contemplating emancipation.[89] With emancipation fever sparking unrest in the countryside Petersburg concluded that landowners' and village communes' ability to employ this essential component of peasant justice (*samosud*[90]) was especially necessary. More generally, the overburdening of the judicial system required that administrative exile be available to dispatch petty thieves and violent drunks who would otherwise further clog up the courts. A tradition dating back to early Muscovy (if not earlier), administrative exile was therefore sanctioned by the government because it had nothing to replace it with.

The charge of "bad behavior" targeted peasants. Of the 9,564 exiled for this reason during the period 1835–46, 5,747 were privately-owned serfs and 2,910 state peasants. Another set of figures shows that during the period 1827–46, 13,015 were exiled by landowners, communes, and local officials for "bad behavior" and that they accounted for 16.7 percent of administrative exiles and 8.1 percent of those in all exile categories combined. The rising numbers of such exiles (1,249 during the period 1827–31; 2,775 during the period 1842–46) partially made up for the decline in the number exiled for *brodiazhestvo*.[91] Communal assemblies appear to have relied upon this punishment more often than did landowners and district officials: in 1833 the former sent 259 men and 24 women to Siberia for "bad behavior," whereas the latter sent 86 men and 81 women.[92]

Petty criminals, *brodiagi*, and those evincing "bad behavior" were just some of the groups the state wanted to quarantine and, if possible, normalize using the exile system. The short-lived Ministry of Police, which after 1819 was absorbed by the interior ministry, had as part of its mandate the assignment of Roma to permanent settlement in cities and villages, despite the government's acknowledged difficulty in persuading them to forsake a nomadic life.[93] Under Nicholas I Roma appear to have been dealt with more harshly than before. In April 1840 the MVD announced "decisive measures for eradicating the *brodiazhestvo* of Gypsies..." and reported a plan to put them in state settlements by early 1841: they were to be deported, provisioned, and settled "per the [1822] 'Regulation on Exiles.'"[94] State settlements for exiles had by then existed for some time in Siberia (see Chapter 6). Policies directed at Roma during this period need more research, but the 1840 plan clearly reflected the general obsession with cleansing and ordering society.

The regime also used exile to rid the Caucasus and Central Asia of Muslims and other inhabitants. In 1827 the Senate ordered *brodiagi* who were either Muslim or from the Caucasus assigned to fortresses in Finland.[95] Given that many would have been elderly, crippled, or mentally afflicted, the Senate was knowingly condemning many to death in an unfamiliar and hostile climate. Likening this particular decision to ethnic cleansing would be going too far, but other evidence shows that in addition to individual political and religious figures[96] ethnic groups were targeted by the Russian military. In 1822 Robert Lyall, an English botanist and member of London's Royal Asiatic Society who had been living in Russia for several years, traveled with a fellow countryman and two Italians to the Caucasus. Unlike many foreign visitors Lyall knew Russian. In Georgia he learned from a Russian officer that the region's commander, General Aleksei P. Ermolov,

> was so incensed against the Tchitchéntsi [Chechens], one of the most ferocious and untamable of the Caucasian tribes, that he was now sending off great caravans of them to Siberia. They are seized and kept prisoners till a sufficient number is collected, and then they are transported to the East for life.... The Kabardians too have lately been expatriated, and their country given to others of the more tranquil tribes. Indeed, I have been informed, that it is intended to establish Russian colonies in these regions, so as more effectually to repress the highlanders of the Caucasus....[97]

Ermolov routinely executed captives in public spectacles designed to instill fear and dread among a population he regarded as "barbarous Asiatics." He even boasted to Nicholas of having tortured a captive before hanging him. The incident displeased the emperor and helped lead to Ermolov's eventual dismissal.[98]

Early nineteenth-century circulars identifying fugitive exiles include disproportionate numbers of Arabic, Turkic, and Persian names among persons accused of trying to escape to Bukhara, which seems to have been a metonym for all regions such persons normally came from.[99] In 1833 Kazan and Orenburg *gubernii*, which despite comparatively small populations each had large Tatar/Kazakh populations, generated more exiles than any other *gubernii*.[100] Orenburg, Kazan, Saratov, and Simbirsk *gubernii*, also with large Tatar/Kazakh populations though small populations overall, were among the top ten exile-generating *gubernii* during the period 1827–46.[101] In 1830 the MVD circulated instructions that Kazan officials had obtained from a local imam named Akhun Siagtiv concerning the proper disposal of "Muslim corpses."[102]

Still other documents show that Muslims and other southern peoples were targeted with exile. In September 1828 Eastern Siberia governor-general Aleksandr S. Lavinskii ordered all those exiled for counterfeiting assigned to Zabaikal´e. His subordinate, Irkutsk governor Ivan B. Tseidler, reported that "among them are a large number of Tatars, and in recent years Tatars, Georgians, Armenians, and Kirgiz have been exiled to this [Irkutsk] *guberniia*, and their numbers are increasing...." Tseidler calculated that 1,653 "Tatars, Armenians, Georgians, Kirgiz, and other Asiatics" had been deported there between 1823 and mid-1828 and blamed them for numerous "murders, robberies, thefts, escapes, and border-crossings." Between 1825 and mid-1828, 234 were reportedly responsible for "192 cases of theft, murder, arson, escape, and robbery." Twenty-three others crossed into China during 1827 alone and, wrote Tseidler, "According to the Chinese they are also causing great difficulties [there]...." Chinese officials were being reasonable, but he feared attitudes might change depending on China's internal affairs. Tseidler opined that because they were being assigned to a region foreign to their lifestyles Caucasians were trying to escape to the mountains while others were seeking freedom on the Kirgiz Steppe, where, however, "Mongols" were forcing them back into Russia. The biggest problem, however, was that "having no women to marry, they are unable to establish [homesteads in] their settlements and [instead] wander among the Russian villages doing virtually nothing...." The peasantry hated them for their "inclination to criminality, their unwillingness to work, and for not establishing homes...." They were being reassigned to Zabaikal´e for these reasons, he explained, where there were currently "absolutely no Tatar villages" and no organized *volosti* and thus "stern measures" would be needed to contain them, though Tseidler did not specify what these might be.[103]

There is some evidence that other ethnic minorities were singled out for exile. George Jewsbury writes that Bessarabia's constable for Ismail threatened locals with exile, and Bitis makes a similar claim regarding Russia's man in charge of the occupied Danubian Principalities.[104] Also targeted were those in what is today Ukraine. Kherson, Kiev, Chernigov, Poltava, and Kursk ranked among the top 11 *gubernii* generating the largest numbers of Siberian exiles during the period 1827–46.[105] This was probably largely a result of the retaliation that followed the November Insurrection (see Chapter 5), though Ukraine had a disproportionately large number of the peasants who accounted for the majority of exiles.

Christian sectarians were also targeted.[106] As of the early nineteenth century, most sectarians in Siberia were descended from either those who migrated soon after Patriarch Nikon's reforms or others who settled during Catherine II's reign. But there were later arrivals. In 1833, 85 men and 11 women entered Siberia as punishment for "crimes against faith,"[107] though it is difficult to tell how many were punished specifically for heresy. In 1844 the Committee of Ministers ordered peasant Sergei Alekseev, discovered conducting Old Believer prayers and rituals in his home, exiled "for resettlement" to a "distant region of Siberia determined by the ranking local commander." Alekseev was subsequently assigned to Iakutsk *oblast*, though relieved of taxes for three years to better allow him to establish himself. Similarly punished were Old Believers Ivan Gordovskii, Timofei Trifonov, and others deemed "especially dangerous" for having beaten up fellow believer Ivan Trifonov after he suggested they accept a priest from the "One True Faith" (*Edinoverie*).[108]

In his "Report on Public Opinion during the Year 1829" Benkendorf included schismatics (*raskol´niki*) in a list of ten "discontented elements." It is indicative of the regime's blinkered attitude that whereas he gave reasons for each of the other elements' discontent ("so called Russian patriots," for example, asserted that the imperial family was of German origins "and were dreaming of idiotic reforms in the Russian spirit [*v russkom dukhe*]"), he offered no opinion as to why schismatics might be discontented.[109] Yet Benkendorf was not mistaken that they were. In 1843, 22,000 schismatics in Eniseisk *guberniia* "rioted" and "thrashed the constable and nearly killed the governor." Fortunately, a courageous and diplomatic lower-ranking officer named Konstantin S. Beznosikov defused a tense standoff that prevented the villagers' annihilation by 10,000

Cossacks.[110] Whether this incident was caused by repression specifically aimed at schismatics or suffering in general is not clear, nor is it clear if it was isolated or part of a larger pattern, but Eniseisk was not the only region with a large Old Believer population. The MVD reported 19,169 "schismatics of various sects" in Zabaikal´e *oblast* as of 1859, evenly divided between males and females and nearly all assigned to Verkhneudinsk *okrug*. The large majority—17,879—were *bezpopovtsy* (that is, they abjured priests, as opposed to *popovtsy*). The category "Molokans, Dukhobors, and *Ikonobortsy* [an ancient Orthodox sect]" included just three males, but there was a much larger number of *Skoptsy* (discussed below).[111] Tobol´sk *guberniia* had a population of 20,642 schismatics in 1855;[112] and a population of 23,758 in 1861—an increase of 766 over the previous year. *Bezpopovtsy* outnumbered *popovtsy* ten to one, and there was a handful of members of lesser sects.[113]

Native-born or recent arrivals, Siberia's schismatics were kept under close surveillance. In October 1843 the MVD reported to GUVS that the Holy Synod had learned of a significant Old Believer presence around Irkutsk. Meetings were taking place "night and day" in the homes of such people as "Zaigraev and Butkovskii, in Tarbagataisk *volost*; Ivan Danilov, in the village of Kunaleisk; Vlasov, in Kuitun; [etc.]." Governor-general Vil´gel´m Ia. Rupert was asked to use all available resources to limit their activities. In particular, the MVD wanted to know if Danilov and Zaigraev,

> who formerly pledged allegiance to the One True Faith but have returned to heresy [*v raskole*], may not have a legal decision brought against them for this; if not, then would it be possible to order them immediately brought before a strict court?[114]

Rupert forwarded the report to Irkutsk's civilian governor, who in April 1844 responded that the local constable had taken "proper measures" to limit Old Believers' activities but not yet acted against Danilov and Zaigarev. The MVD persisted, and the following year the IGP reported that the case against "the Peasant Danilov is proceeding. Also, with regard to the Peasant Zaigarev, he has been removed to Minusinsk *okrug*, Eniseisk *Guberniia*, by decision of the Committee of Ministers."[115] Persecution of Old Believers continued under Alexander II. In 1862 Irkutsk's MVD branch reported to GUVS concerning one Iakov Krashenin, exiled to an unspecified "distant" location by the Tobol´sk judiciary for turning his son into a schismatic. As per his rights under a Senate ruling of 30 June

1860, Krashenin had petitioned to transfer to an Old Believer community in Zabaikal´e.[116]

Despite their small numbers, *Skoptsy* were the most viciously persecuted of schismatic sects—a persecution, moreover, that personally involved the emperor, since the law required him to confirm each sentence against religious sectarians.[117] *Skoptsy* believed their founder Kondratii Selivanov to be "the reembodiment of the original Redeemer."[118] But aside from this heresy, officials were more horrified by their practice of castrating or mutilating their sexual organs and for refusing to reproduce. *Skoptsy* were sometimes sentenced to *katorga*. In 1825, 34-year-old Mar´ia Nikolaevna Lysova, of Taurida *guberniia*, was convicted and sent to Irkutsk's textile mill. After 17 years she was unable to work anymore and put in a settlement.[119] Several years before Lysova's conviction a military court sentenced Aleksandr Semenov, of the same *guberniia* and close in age, to the Aleksandrovsk distillery near Irkutsk.[120] *Skoptsy* received corporal punishment in only a few instances. Trofim Pozdniakov was convicted of castrating himself in 1829, given 30 lashes, and exiled to Eniseisk *guberniia*, to Cheremkhovsk village, which seems to have been reserved for *Skoptsy*. That same year 45-year-old Stepan Iudakov of Tambov *guberniia* received the same sentence.[121] A military commission gave a particularly harsh punishment to Koz´ma Ivanov, a 26-year-old "soldier's son," sentencing him to pass twice through a gauntlet of 500 soldiers followed by eight years *katorga* on the Åland Islands. Ivanov's date with the gauntlet was eventually cancelled in exchange for a longer sentence in Nerchinsk *katorga*.[122] Because Zabaikal´e's exile-settlers tended to be former penal laborers, *Skoptsy*'s declining numbers there (never very large to begin with) suggest few were ever sentenced to *katorga*.[123] In 1846, 16, including all eight members of Prokhor Smol´nikov and his wife Elisaveta's family, were exiled to Iatkusk *oblast* and put at what was termed the "disposal" of the Russian-American Company. The document's description of Prokhor as a "farmer" suggests his family served more or less as company serfs.[124] Others were punished with assignment to the military. In 1819 the Committee of Ministers—which had an inordinate interest in persecuting *Skoptsy*—ordered the Zuev brothers assigned to the military; several years later Matvei Labanov, a peasant from Kaluga *guberniia*, was similarly assigned.[125] In 1841, 25-year-old Matvei Golubstov, a Cossack from the Caucasus's Ekaterinograd *stanitsa*, was assigned to the military, but upon being judged unfit was exiled to settlement in Siberia instead.[126]

Despite inconsistent sentencing procedures *Skoptsy* were usually exiled to settlement in Eastern Siberia. Western Siberia always had a small population of *Skoptsy*. For instance, only 94 were living in Tobol′sk *guberniia* as of 1861.[127] In 1835 Vasilii Smorodin, a peasant from Iaroslavl *guberniia*, was exiled for "being a *Skopets*" (lit., for "*skopchestvo*"[128]) and assigned to the remote village of Isitskiustantsaia in Iakutsk *oblast* where, as of 1846, the 64-year-old was listed by officials as a "farmer, no family."[129] A decade later a Perm court convicted peasant Egor Kir′ianov of castrating himself and sentenced him to Turukhansk *krai*, but he died in nearby Kungur's transit prison before he could be convoyed there.[130]

Eastern Siberia's *Skoptsy* population grew slowly, from 267 males and 48 females in 1831 to 312 and 94 in 1852. During this same period the number assigned to *okrug* cities declined as the number in the countryside grew. For example, in 1841 the city of Krasnoiarsk counted 36 males and five females, yet by 1852 seven males and no females were living there. Similarly, Irkutsk and Nizhneudinsk each had one male as of 1848, after which no more *Skoptsy* were allowed to reside in these cities.[131] Officials feared their influence over city dwellers at the same time they were using them to populate the countryside. "As of 1849," writes Laura Engelstein, "over 900 Skoptsy exiles were distributed across six Siberian regions, almost two-thirds in Enisei Province alone."[132] Nevertheless, the government wanted them kept in discrete communities. By 1857, 643 were in Eastern Siberia, the majority (428) having been assigned to Eniseisk *guberniia*, where they congregated in Minusinsk *okrug* and Turukhansk *krai*. The 92 then assigned to Irkutsk *guberniia* were clustered in either Badaisk *volost* in Irkutsk *okrug* or Chermykovsk *volost* in Balagansk *okrug*. Zabaikal′e *oblast* had a population of only 23 *Skoptsy* as of 1857, half of whom were living in Barguzin *okrug*.[133]

In May 1852 interior minister Lev A. Perovskii asked Eastern Siberia governor-general Nikolai N. Murav′ev for data to produce "a list of all Schismatics and Jews living in the Empire."[134] Murav′ev seems to have suspected Perovskii's motives, for at the same time that he provided some of the figures asked for he penned an internal memorandum in which he complained, "it might happen that with every year [the *Skoptsy*] would decline were it not for the addition of those exiled to settlement from Russia's interior *gubernii*," and added, "The greater part of *Skoptsy* located in Irkutsk *Guberniia* own homes, farms, and distinguish themselves through hard work...." Their numbers had been expanding since 1840 in Minusinsk *okrug*, where most engaged in agriculture and lived in Tesinsk *volost* between the rivers Kuriatyi and Kanga.[135] Eniseisk governor Vasilii K. Padalka shared Murav′ev's view, noting in a July 1853 report that most *Skoptsy* were peacefully engaging in agriculture. All were under local police's "special surveillance," and only a few were spreading their "fanaticism" to others. During the previous five years only 16 had been "incorrigible" and, as a result, were transferred to Turukhansk *krai*, which was also the sole location of the nine instances of castration learned of during that period. Padalka optimistically concluded that *skopchestvo* was on the decline in Eniseisk *guberniia*.[136] In addition to telling the center what it wanted to hear, these reports show neither Murav´ev nor Padalka shared the center's persecutory impulse toward *Skoptsy*.

A significant number of exiled *Skoptsy* originated as soldiers or sailors. In the wake of the 1812 war sectarianism sometimes served to demonstrate practitioners' newfound patriotic beliefs. This patriotism graduated over time into chauvinism and, as such, targeted in particular the "Germans" believed to be in charge of both the military and society. The Romanovs were widely rumored to be German, which was true in the sense of ancestry; but more importantly, to call Nicholas I a "German" meant establishing one's *bona fides* as a true son of the Fatherland. Hence such Russians as Arakcheev were considered "Germans" while such Germans as Decembrist Andrei E. Rozen (Rosen) were accepted as "Russians."[137] Needless to say, *Skoptsy* were a fringe manifestation of Russo-Orthodox patriotism, but they clearly frightened the government. The government had been so desperate for troops that it recruited known *Skoptsy* during the 1812 war.[138] But this policy (a tsarist "don't ask/don't tell") seemed to change on 3 December 1827, when the Committee of Ministers ruled: "Henceforward, recruitment tickets for *Skoptsy* will not be issued." However, the Senate muddled the issue with a confusing ruling three years later,[139] as did Nicholas when in 1835 he ordered that only *Skoptsy* "utterly unsuitable for service" be designated for "removal to Siberia."[140]

This contradictory legislation makes it difficult in many cases to determine why individual *Skopets* servicemen were exiled. Official records show that as of 1859, among the 36 *Skoptsy* in Cheremkhovsk *volost*, Balagansk *okrug*, Irkutsk *guberniia*, ten were former solders, two former officers, and one a former sailor. Whether they and other *Skopets* servicemen had castrated themselves or (as was less frequent) others, and whether they committed either act because of religious devotion or a desire to be released from service, is uncertain. If the goal was dismissal from service, this was rarely achieved, for in most cases *Skopets* servicemen were simply transferred to other commands. In its desire to retain even castrated soldiers and sailors the military apparently believed it could comply with the emperor's 1835 order by nevertheless having them continue to serve in Siberia. Hence in 1842 the castrati Savelii Artem´ev and

Aleksei Rodionov, who had both served with the Baltic Fleet in Petersburg, were reassigned to Irkutsk's Naval Command.[141]

Skopets servicemen were purged if deemed incapable of performing their duty, though it is difficult to tell if castration itself was a basis for dismissal. In 1838, Governor-general V. Ia. Rupert sent Eniseisk governor Vasilii I. Kopylov a list of 24 "[s]oldiers from the *Skoptsy*, dismissed from service for incapacity, who are to be exiled to settlement in Turukhansk *krai* but are still in Eniseisk." Peasant Aleksandr Solodovnikov and exile-settlers Fedor Karzhev and Prokhor Shul´gin were included in this list, presumably because they were *Skoptsy* as well. All the soldiers had originally been assigned to invalid regiments in Eniseisk, Achinsk, Minusinsk, Kolyvansk, Tomsk, Kirensk, and Kainsk. Directly contravening Petersburg's orders, Rupert suggested to Kopylov that instead of assigning them to Turukhansk they be allowed to reside in locations they had earlier requested. For example, Malafei Sofronov owned a house in the city of Eniseisk and wished to remain there; Mikhailo Cherepanov hoped to return to Kolyvansk where he had a wife and son; and because they did not own homes each of the three men from Minusinsk's Invalid Command asked to join a *Skopets* community in Kazachinsk *volost*.[142] The result of Rupert's intercession on behalf of these *Skoptsy* is not known.

Despite his rank Rupert was unable to shield one Frol Efimov, a soldier who apparently practiced *skopchestvo* out of faith rather than to get out of the military. In September 1814 Efimov was sentenced to a year of fortress labor for planning to castrate fellow soldier Kiril Korneev. Later, in 1822, having been transferred to Vladikavkaz, Efimov castrated himself. Yet his only punishment was to be transferred again. In 1838 Irkutsk governor Andrei V. Piatnitskii decided "that Efimov," after he had retired into the Nizhneudinsk Invalid Command, "being dangerous because of his sect, [should] be assigned to a settlement in a distant location." Despite Rupert's request for a more salubrious region, the obstreperous Piatnitskii pithily insisted on sending the 43-year-old to a "distant location among the natives, as the Verkholensk Steppe Duma's instructions of 11 May 1838 [made] clear to me."[143] Rupert learned from this rebuff. Several years later, after Eniseisk's governor wrote him concerning one Danil Khovrin, dismissed from the military as a *Skopets* and ordered to Turukhansk *krai* by the Committee of Ministers, Rupert emphatically informed Petersburg: "... I have [already] assigned Danil <u>Khovrin</u> to settlement in Minusinsk *Okrug*, on the basis of Your list received by me on 30 October 1839...." He noted that *Skoptsy* there were building a settlement and added, "although you recommended this *Skopets* be assigned to settlement in Turukhansk *krai*, I did not assign him there because a settlement [already built] there by a similar group of people is unsuitable [*neudobnym*]...."[144] Why it was unsuitable he did not say. But like his successor Murav´ev, Rupert interceded on *Skoptsy's* behalf time and again. This put him in conflict with Piatnitskii, whose comments about the need to keep members of this "sadistic sect"[145] under surveillance corresponded with his intent to follow Petersburg's orders to the letter.

Petersburg also singled out so called Evangelists for separate treatment, though in contrast to its treatment of *Skoptsy* did not exile them systematically. On 25 August 1845 interior minister L. A. Perovskii informed the Committee of Ministers of the locations of exiled criminals with "Evangelist passports." He was particularly concerned about Letts living in the vicinity of Tobol´sk, "*Chukhony*" (a pejorative for "Finns") and other Finns near Omsk, and Germans near Tomsk. Pastors had been assigned to administer to Western Siberia's Evangelists in 1839, with one being sent to the "...Finnish colony of Ryshkovo [in Tobol´sk *guberniia*], which consists almost exclusively of exiles...." By contrast, noted Perovskii, "Eastern Siberia has only one pastor, assigned to permanent residence in Irkutsk with a responsibility to visit Nerchinsk once a year." This group's numbers were not great: Tomsk *guberniia* had an "insignificant number of such criminals now numbering close to 85..."; in Eastern Siberia "the number of criminals of the Evangelical belief located in various *okruga* of Eniseisk *guberniia* is up to 218...." Perovskii planned to concentrate the Evangelicals in order to limit their supposed influence over others, but he considered assigning each separate "tribe" (*plemia*) to a single settlement to be unwise. He proposed that in the future Ryshkovo be reserved for Evangelist petty criminals while more serious offenders be sent to Minusinsk *okrug*, where their travel would be limited to the city of Minusinsk. However, those already associated with the Irkutsk pastorate were to stay where they were, as were those assigned to Nerchinsk *katorga*. Others residing in (unnamed) locations were to have the choice of relocating to either Ryshkovo or Minusinsk *okrug*.[146] During the period 1841–43, 453 prisoners and 151 *dobrovol´nye* of Lutheran or Evangelical persuasion passed through Moscow on their way to Siberia.[147] Despite Perovskii's concern and efforts to quarantine them, nothing suggests they were punished for their religious beliefs.

Indeed, it is notable in this regard that Jews, despite being generally oppressed in Russia, were disproportionately underrepresented among Siberia's exiles. Petersburg was uncomfortable assigning them to a region over which it exerted little direct control. Nicholas I forbade the wives of Jewish convicts from accompanying them to Siberia, and in 1826 ordered Jewish exiles living near Omsk *oblast*'s frontier to be relocated because he believed they were helping smuggle gold from local mines. An 1860 regulation similarly prevented Jews from settling within 100 versts of the Chinese border.[148] All the same, Jews were never systematically deported to tsarist Siberia.

Tsarism's persecution of minorities therefore contributed to the surge of exiles that overwhelmed the exile system. A comparison of various sources demonstrates that 49,600 male exiles accounted for 5.69 percent of Siberia's total male population in 1823. These figures grew to 122,200 and 11.68 percent in 1835; 186,900 and 13 percent in 1851.[149] Figures on the number of female exiles *in situ* are lacking, but 42,309 are known to have been exiled between 1823 and 1860. Women accounted for a third (children, the rest) of the 20,000 *dobrovol´nye* who followed husbands, sons, and fathers into exile during this period.[150]

None of the abovementioned factors contributing to exiles' numbers excludes the fact that many had committed crimes both society and state wanted punished. Whereas a state that sought to purify, cleanse, and subjugate society produced many innocent victims, it is equally the case that the empire's many subcultures and regions each produced their fair share of murderers, thieves, rapists, arsonists, counterfeiters, embezzlers, and others who threatened civilized society. In memoirs published in 1900, a former commandant of Aleksandrovsk *zavod* recalled a penal laborer named Gavrilo Minaev who, each time he saw him, cheekily asked for a pinch of tobacco. Always gladly acceding to his request, the commandant one day asked Minaev why he had been sentenced to 20 years *katorga*. "For mere trifles, sir: for stabbing a couple of Yids," answered Minaev. After the commandant instructed him that killing a Jew was as sinful as killing a Christian, Minaev rationalized his crime by saying they had murdered Christ.[151]

According to figures published by the MVD 83,699 individuals were punished with exile between 1822 and 1833, the majority (42.2 percent) for *brodiazhestvo*. Another 31 percent were punished for robbery, banditry, theft, swindling, or falsifying documents, and 7.9 percent for murder.[152] During the period 1827–46, 11,552 men and 2,979 women were exiled for murder; 4,818 men and 250 women for armed robbery or brigandage; and 1,085 men and 883 women for arson. During this period 79,848 entered Siberia through judicial sentences, 79,909 through administrative procedures.[153] The Siberian Committee reported that in 1833 alone 524 male and 114 female convicted murderers, 225 male and 4 female armed robbers and brigands, and 45 male and 33 female arsonists entered Siberia.[154] In 1856, among the several thousand exiles sent to Tobol´sk *guberniia* that year, 182 were convicted murderers, 46 armed robbers, and 70 arsonists.[155] Eastern Siberia, where most *katorga* sites were located, received many more violent criminals each year. As of 1852 there were in Siberia 26,162 penal laborers and 182,299 exile-settlers—criminal convicts, that is, as opposed to lesser offenders deported administratively.[156] Aside from the link that officials, journalists, and Siberian peasants had an interest in making between immorality and crime there existed a very real link between exiles and crime, even when the prejudice and casuistry of tsarist justice are taken into account. Between 1823 and 1832 there were 207 cases of murder and robbery in Tobol´sk *guberniia* for which 326 individuals, 192 of them exiles, were arrested. Comparable figures for Tomsk *guberniia* are 184 cases, 321 arrests, and 167 exiles; and for Omsk *oblast* 34 cases leading to the convictions of 68 persons including 20 exiles.[157]

The Siberian Committee's 1837 report presents numerous crime statistics. For all Siberia, the number of murders in which exiles were considered some way involved grew from 847 in 1833 to 1,018 in 1834. For purposes of comparison, in 1833 non-exiles accounted for only 16 of Eastern Siberia's murderers, 19 of its robbers, and six of those who committed such religious offenses as "castration, sacrilege, and grave-robbing." A table for Eastern Siberia lists 30 categories of criminal offenses: in 1833 the number of exiles defined by these categories totaled 699, with women accounting for 64 of them. By far the largest number (246) of offenders fell under the category of "escapes, along with such falsifications as name changes and the hiding of exiles." The second-largest category was "stealing; theft" and accounted for 181 exiles. Several categories covered homicide or attempted homicide and together accounted for 96 exiles.[158] In 1836 the MVD recorded 69 and 41 murders in Irkutsk and Tomsk *guberniia*, respectively. This may not at first appear excessive. However, the populations in both *gubernii* were not large and so their murder rates were, respectively, seven and six times higher than for the empire as a whole. Eniseisk *guberniia*, which had the largest percentage of exile-settlers, qualified as Siberia's most violent: its 1836 murder rate was *eight and a half times* the national average. The number of murders committed "by unknown individuals" in Siberia were similarly much higher than the national average, reflecting the fact that many fugitives and *brodiagi* were literally getting away with murder.[159]

During the period 1838–47 penal laborers, exiles, other prisoners, and *brodiagi* were deemed responsible for 1,190 violent crimes in Siberia, including murders (327), acts of brigandage (19), robberies (86), and violent assaults (87).[160] In 1839 thefts in Eniseisk *guberniia* were over

24 times the national average.[161] That same year there were 52 murders in Tomsk *guberniia* alone. For the empire as a whole there were 4.98 murders for every 100,000 persons in 1839. Comparable figures were 11.74 for Irkutsk *guberniia*; 18.49 for Tobol´sk *guberniia*; 36.81 for Tomsk *guberniia*; and a whopping 47.58 for Eniseisk *guberniia*.[162] To put these figures in perspective, the United States, generally regarded as a violent society, had a homicide rate of 6.1 in 2006.[163] Eniseisk's homicide rate was only somewhat below that of 2006's most deadly country, El Salvador, which suffered a rate of 55.3.[164]

Like those for previous years, MVD statistics beginning in 1841 and continuing through 1855 indicate that on a per capita basis Siberia continued to be more crime-ridden than the empire as a whole. Yet these same figures also suggest a lower crime rate than during the 1830s. For example, in 1841 murders committed in Siberia accounted for nearly 15 percent of the national total; in 1844 those committed during the summer (when murder is always more prevalent) represented around 13 percent of the total; ten years later, murders in May and June accounted for just 10 percent of the total.[165] The drop in Siberia's murder rate was even more precipitous than these figures suggest, given that between 1833 and 1850 Siberia's male population grew from 6 to 8 percent of the empire's total male population.[166] This apparent decline in crime during the second half of Nicholas's reign may be misleading, however. It is possible that as crime became more common it was reported less often. Also, Siberian officials may have altered crime figures to protect themselves against reprisals from the center. In 1833 an article in the *Journal of the Ministry of the Interior* concluded that during the previous eight years exiles were responsible for "no more than 165 crimes in Siberia." "Such a remarkable number of crimes [relative] to the number of people for whom villainy is not alien, clearly shows that the morality of those exiled to Siberia is being successfully corrected," claimed the anonymous contributor, who nevertheless acknowledged a total of 52 murders by all parties in 1830 alone.[167]

This claim aside, Siberia's crime rate more likely remained the same or even increased during the end of Nicholas's and early into Alexander II's reign. Tobol´sk's administration reported 43 murders, 308 cases of horse-theft, and 13 armed robberies for the year 1855, during which Siberian village assemblies administratively exiled "further into Siberia" 17 state peasants and 25 exile-settlers (all males) and *guberniia* courts convicted 105 exiles of various crimes.[168] Perm *guberniia*, through which most exiles fled when escaping Siberia, reported 1,966 crimes including 60 murders during 1861.[169] This was a considerable increase over 1855, when 1,056 crimes were committed in Perm. Yet even that year witnessed 46 murders, 37 armed robberies, 154 horse-thefts, and 363 other cases of stealing.[170]

The MVD, Siberian Committee, and other agencies used these and other statistics to try to gain some leverage over the Imperial Chancery regarding exile, and so they must be approached with caution. Statistics were strategically deployed in the paradigmatic struggle between sovereign and governmental power, and as such highlighted the disparity between advocates of cogent policymaking and statecraft and those wedded to the autocrat's traditional expression of power. Both sides, however, were hampered by a view that equated criminality with immorality. This view was consonant with contemporaneous views in other countries and so it would have been anachronistic for them to look at crime differently, but its impact upon the treatment of thousands of convicts and other deportees served to dehumanize them, as the next chapter will show.

2
Administering Exile: Malfeasance, Corruption, and Failure

The financial constraints imposed upon the exile system were as detrimental to it as the surge in exiles' numbers. Despite his support for certain measures, Nicholas I was little interested in perpetuating Alexander I's reform agenda (though Alexander had been inconsistent toward it as well). Yet, even had he stood behind M. M. Speranskii's exile regulations little would have changed because of the structural problems conditioning Russian penality and Siberia's administrative apparatus. This did not stop officials in both Petersburg and Siberia from presenting plans to retool the exile system and from trying to impress upon the emperor just how bad conditions really were. The Imperial Chancery and key ministers responded with directives and proposals revealing their almost willful ignorance of the true state of affairs.

Russia's militarized regime adopted a hard-line approach toward crime and criminal exiles, yet sovereign power's persistent need to scourge the flesh undermined governmental power's utilitarian deployment of docile bodies. Indeed, Alexander I abolished mutilation in 1817 but failed to heed the Committee of Ministers' calls to abolish the knout (*knut*)—a three-tailed whip with metal talons that literally shredded the victim's back and often proved fatal. In 1830 the government secretly capped the number of blows of the knout at 50, but far fewer than this were enough to kill, and anyway this maximum was routinely exceeded in practice. Despite being officially abolished by the 1845 *Ulozhenie*, the knout continued to be used in Siberia for years afterward. The lash (*plet*)—three-tailed, like the knout, but with braided leather knots in place of metal talons—and birch rods (*rozgi*) were not officially abolished until 1903. "Rods were made out of slender switches," explains a history of corporal punishment in Russia,

each 1-1/2 *arsh[iny]* long. So that the blow be stronger and more painful the switches were not too fresh but also not dry. For this reason they were usually kept in a damp place. Rods were created from ten or fifteen such switches bound with a cord. Each rod could be used for only ten blows, after which it became useless and was replaced.[1]

Like the knout the lash and rod often killed their victims and at the very least scarred them for life. In 1845 a limit of 100 blows was placed on the lash as punishment for a single crime or as part of a sentence of *katorga*. This undoubtedly spared many lives, but numerous sources attest to executioners' ability to render almost any number of blows fatal.

All commoners sentenced to *katorga* and sometimes those exiled to settlement were flogged. A victim would be chained onto a cart and driven to the market or other public arena while children pelted him with rocks and more knowing observers tossed a few kopeks. Turned over to the executioner (*palach*) and his assistants, he was scourged to the delight (or disgust) of the assembled crowd.[2] Convicts were also tattooed by incising the flesh on the face or body with a razor-sharp metal template and rubbing black ink or gunpowder into the cuts. *Katorga* convicts were designated with the Cyrillic letters K A T (*katorzhnyi*—"penal laborer"). In Siberia, if an exile escaped and was recaptured he was tattooed with either С К (*ssyl´no-katorzhnyi*—"exiled penal laborer"), С П (*ssyl´no-poselenets*) if he was an exile-settler, or Б if he was a *brodiaga* (that is, refused to identify himself).[3] Over time these stigmata (*kleima*) took on a bluish hue. In 1897 the journalist Vlas Doroshevich met on Sakhalin old penal laborers who had either sliced them out of their faces or seared them with red-hot irons in pathetic attempts to obliterate them.[4]

After 1822 most facing deportation were not scourged, but everyone except administrative exiles had to wear iron shackles during the march, and in any case nearly all had their fitness as laborers or farmers reduced by the journey into Siberia. Shackles produced their own stigmata in the form of gangrenous wounds that often eventuated in amputation or death. Prisoners could with their own money purchase leather gators to protect their ankles, but not everyone could afford these. Then there were the filthy and dangerous conditions of the way-stations and semi-stations (*polu-etapy*) between which exile parties marched an average of 25 versts a day in all kinds of weather. If they survived what were in some cases journeys of 5,000 miles these weary exiles faced upon arrival a dilapidated prison barracks, a corner in some peasant's hut, or the necessity of clear-cutting and building their own shack.

Aside from this large-scale carnal suffering, Speranskii's plans for rationally exploiting exiles' labor also crashed against administrative realities. "Bureaucracy as a disciplined corporate body which serves defined political ends does not exist in Russia,"[5] wrote Mikhail Saltykov-Shchedrin upon resigning from the civil service. Benkendorf shared Shchedrin's frustration, reporting to Nicholas early in his reign about civil servants:

> Embezzlements, forgeries, misinterpretations of the laws—this is their craft. Unfortunately, they rule over not just their departments, but the most important of them, in essence, over everything, since they know the limits of the bureaucratic system. They fear the introduction of justice, precise laws, and the eradication of embezzlement; they despise those who investigate corruption, and flee from them like an owl from the sun. They systematically censure all government measures and train their own cadres of malcontents....[6]

Siberia's administrative apparatus was perhaps the most underdeveloped in the empire. Managing the exile system was foremost among Siberian governors' many duties, but to speak of systematic management between 1823 and 1861 would be misleading. A system existed on paper, but operated haphazardly, sporadically, and inchoately at ground-level. Most Siberian officials lacked the bureaucratic consciousness Speranskii's regulations assumed *a priori*. Patronage networks and turf battles stymied development of procedural norms; governors-general ignored the MVD's and other ministries' instructions; their own underlings lacked initiative. Even when they received the rare unambiguous order these officials were too overburdened by other duties or too distracted by embezzlement and bribery schemes to execute them. Between 1822 and 1852 five of Tobol'sk's 11 governors were dismissed for corruption.[7] Sometimes, as with some of the *Skoptsy*, Siberian administrators' counter-conduct actually protected exiles from the center's policies. In 1825 interior minister Vasilii S. Lanskoi queried Siberia's two governors-general about the possibility of exiling Dukhobors to their regions. They simply ignored the MVD's repeated queries until it gave up and, in 1828, decided to exile the Dukhobors to the Caucasus instead.[8] S. Frederick Starr's comment that "what the government was doing badly in the provinces was not as important as what it was not doing at all"[9] is particularly apt regarding Siberia.

Chaos stemmed in large part from the lack of a clearly defined vertical apparatus between regional administrations and Petersburg. Governors-general, for instance, occupied positions within separate hierarchies culminating in the MVD, Ministry of War, and Imperial Chancery, each of which often failed to coordinate policy with the others. There were also shortfalls in funding and personnel. With over 50 percent of the imperial budget being spent on the military little was left to maintain infrastructure or pay salaries. The budget grew by 172,223,000 rubles between 1840 and 1854, yet all but 9,000,000 rubles of this increase went to the military or to cover the Ministry of Finance's expenses and interest payments on foreign loans. As a consequence Russia's civil servants were notoriously underpaid, though finance minister E. F. Kankrin's belief that they deserved no more did nothing to help. There were only 1.3 civil servants for every 1,000 subjects; and during Nicholas I's reign gubernatorial staffs typically consisted of only ten clerks. The MVD generated a staggering 30 million official communications in 1850 alone, half of which consisted of reports requested from what were in turn understaffed provincial administrations. During this period each gubernatorial clerk was responsible for writing more than 20 letters a day and processing a much larger number of letters received.[10] In the midst of this epistolary deluge even those buoyed by *esprit de corps* floundered about as best they could.

Once again, Siberia faired poorly compared to the rest of the empire. Its governors earned about half that of their European Russian counterparts[11] and were especially pinched by restrictions on funding and personnel. They sometimes had to depend upon a single official, the only one for thousands of square miles, to execute their orders. In 1856 the staff of TobPS—which processed, supplied, and situated nearly every exile who entered Siberia—consisted of a director, two assessors, two book-keepers, and two reporters (*zhurnalisty*). The director had a budget of 2,500 rubles for hiring scribes and another 800 rubles to cover stationery and other office supplies.[12] The mid-century staff of Omsk *oblast*'s land court consisted of a secretary, two clerks, a registrar, and a part-time scribe, and was responsible for administering 36,000 souls (not counting exiles) and processing 13,000 documents a year.[13]

Not surprisingly, Siberia's civil servants often fell behind in their duties. Omsk's and other circuit courts delayed for years the resolution of criminal trials due to the sheer number of cases and lack of judges and other court officials. Not until six years later was the matter resolved in one case for which complaints were filed in 1840. During his 1851 inspection of Western Siberia the Committee of Ministers' adjutant-general learned of nearly 2,000 unresolved criminal cases, some dating back to 1821.[14] On 24 May 1827 the IGP related to *okrug* officials Governor Ivan B. Tseidler's warning "that [with] the arrival of springtime there is the inevitable escape and *brodiazhestvo* of exiles and other similar people," but it did so almost six weeks after the governor announced this.[15] Two years later, an investigation into TobPS's activities showed it had mishandled the assignments for at least 42 separate parties of exiles. The IGP ordered local officials to review their records with the goal of "limiting such disorder."[16] If exiles sometimes benefited from administrative mistakes and irregularities, they more often suffered from them. In the winter of 1829–30 Iakutsk officials reported that their counterparts in Kirensk dispatched six exiles to Okhotsk without supplying them with either clothes or "foraging money" (*kormovye den´gi*). They had made it to Okhotsk alive, but must have been in pretty bad shape if tsarist officials were moved to complain on their behalf.[17]

Administrative problems also stemmed from ignorance or confusion over regulations, which themselves presented a tangle of problems. There had been no codification of Russia's laws since the 1649 *Ulozhenie*, and much legislation through to the late nineteenth century was never committed to print or circulated through government channels. A larger number of legislated acts were never actuated because there were not enough civil servants to process the paperwork: by the early 1840s a backlog of some 3,300,000 decrees and similar documents had built up.[18] Moreover, in addition to the emperor several government bodies including the Senate and Committee of Ministers promulgated ukases, and so inconsistency and contradiction characterized many of the laws that were known about and actuated. Early in Nicholas's reign Speranskii, as director of the Imperial Chancery's Second Section, completed the 45-volume *Complete Collection of Laws* and the 15-volume *Digest of the Laws*. The former was in fact not complete because the emperor refused to publicize a number of secret decrees and other legislative articles, and its usefulness was further curtailed "because Nicholas regarded the collection as a historical source rather than an active code of laws...."[19] His reliance on *ad hoc* committees and plenipotentiaries to bypass government institutions undermined the usefulness of the technically more relevant *Digest* as well. Lincoln claims these collections nevertheless established "clear-cut notions of legality" as protection against bureaucratic arbitrariness. But this is unconvincing. Arbitrariness (*proizvol*) remained a persistent feature of the tsarist bureaucracy until its end and was especially pronounced within the Siberian apparatus.

The following four cases occurred before Speranskii's codification projects, but serve to demonstrate *proizvol* in action. In 1827 the IGP reported to local officials that justice minister Dmitrii I. Lobanov-Rostovskii had informed it of the State Council's decision to prohibit landowners from dispatching serfs to Siberia's metallurgical works unless they relinquished ownership over them.[20] Landowners were using the exile system as a disciplinary tool prior to reclaiming their serfs; but more importantly, the State Council's tacit support for assigning serfs to factories in the first place violated the 1822 Reforms' prohibition against assigning an individual to penal labor without a criminal conviction. Also in 1827 the IGP recalled all exiles convoyed and distributed by the Ilginsk Invalid Command because it had done so in violation of transfer regulations issued four years earlier. The exiles were returned to Irkutsk for redistribution and the IGP distributed copies of the convoy regulations to local commands.[21] Two years later, Irkutsk's governor blithely announced that he and the governor-general had decided that if a penal laborer was caught exchanging names with others he was to receive 100 birch strokes, be returned to his original location, kept under strict surveillance, and have five years added to his sentence.[22] No legislation was necessary—the governors simply considered themselves judge, jury, and executioner. Coincident with these governors' unilateral decision a rumor went around that the emperor had decided that every exile in Siberia—excluding administrative exiles but (interestingly enough in the wake of the Decembrist Uprising) *including* noblemen—be immediately enrolled in the army. The IGP circulated this news after learning it from justice minister Aleksei A. Dolgorukii, who himself heard it from another top official.[23] There appears to have been no truth to the rumor, nor is there evidence it was ever acted upon. But the episode shows how rumor and innuendo supplanted proceduralism.

Because of vertical confusion and lack of proceduralism the center periodically relied upon revisions (*revizii*, which in this context amounted to varying combinations of what in English would be termed inspections, audits, and censuses) to determine what was happening (or rather, what had been happening) and to frighten officials into becoming better administrators. "Forty-two special senatorial fact-finding missions were undertaken in the course of [Nicholas I's] reign," writes Lincoln, "and these included seven of the 11 senatorial studies of the most distant and least-known regions of the Empire that were carried out in the nineteenth century."[24] Petersburg's reliance upon revisions epitomized its approach toward managing Siberia. The era that ended with the 1822 Siberian Reforms had included numerous revisions, and there were three more major revisions of Siberia before 1862. The first, conducted in 1827 by senators B. A. Kurakin and V. K. Bezrodnyi, concerned Western Siberia and led to the dismissal of Governor-general Petr M. Kaptsevich and Tobol´sk governor Dmitrii N. Bantysh-Kamenskii. The other two, conducted in 1842 and 1851, are discussed below.[25] Revisions sometimes proved to be clarion calls for Petersburg officials as well. Not until 1827, when it was already overflowing with prisoners, did the finance ministry learn that Tel´minsk, its own textile mill not far from Irkutsk, had for decades been the sole destination of women sentenced to *katorga*. "[T]he Ministry of Finance is commissioning an investigation into whether it is possible to build a special labor home or factory to which women may be exiled, though not in Siberia," the IGP accordingly reported.[26]

The unforeseen surge in exiles' numbers combined with administrative problems doomed the 1822 Reforms. Nevertheless, Schrader's claim that officials ignored legal and administrative problems and made female exiles scapegoats for the malfunctioning exile system is a stretch at best and fatuous at worst.[27] Either way, it ignores a mountain of contrary evidence. It is true that all exiles, males as well as females, were disparaged for their supposed immorality and dissoluteness; yet officials in both Petersburg and Siberia repeatedly tried to make some cosmos out of the chaos by addressing—not ignoring—legal and administrative problems. Between 1823 and 1861 these efforts included a number of ambitious proposals and investigative reports often addressed directly to the emperor. Ekaterinburg prison, for example, was visited several times by inspectors of various ranks who sought to correct abuses there.[28] A reformist zeal existed within the area of penality similar to that Kagan has described among mid- and upper-level military personnel.[29] The proposals and reports these zealous civil servants produced indicate that Nicholas was well-informed about the exile system's problems. However, in stark contrast to his attitude towards the military he ignored them and allowed Siberian society to become criminalized and degraded.

Some reformers believed exiles' problems could be solved by developing a sounder penology. In 1828 senator Aleksei M. Karnilov (var., Kornilov), a former governor of first Irkutsk and then Tomsk *guberniia*, addressed a report to the emperor titled *Observations on Siberia* in which he presented, *inter alia*, recommendations for "the improvement of the system of administering exiled criminals in Siberia and extracting the intended use from them." Karnilov began by explaining why he believed exile was failing:

Any exiled criminal arriving in Siberia enjoys from the outset rights and freedoms such as he (excluding noblemen deprived of privileges) did not possess even before his crime: for, since he would typically have been owned by a landowner, he would have either paid *obrok* or always worked under his close supervision and control; but, having arrived in Siberia without any job, without any preparatory correction of his moral dissoluteness, he receives all necessities for setting himself up. His fortune is so great that he receives from the Government's beneficent hand such as is needed for a new life—a furnished house on good soil, a financial loan to establish a domestic economy—and he becomes a free peasant without any probationary service. Such is the transition from the state of serfdom to complete freedom that a large portion of exiles, infected as they are by their vices, succumb to idleness, drunkenness, and depravity, destroying all they own, their future, and their prospects.[30]

Whereas the state was being far too generous toward exiles, these vice-ridden reprobates would be better disciplined if they (excepting convicts from the nobility) were instead assigned to one of four categories Karnilov proposed, the first of which involved assignment to a militia command (*militsionnoe voisko*). Karnilov envisaged healthy young males serving in what would apparently be irregular detachments[31] for three years, supporting any *dobrovol´nye* who followed them, then establishing farmsteads upon their release. Those who failed to become peasants would "be returned as irregulars to militia service." Like the legislation and correctional battalions discussed in the previous chapter, Karnilov's recommendation shows the extent to which penology and military discipline were interrelated in authorities' minds: it was taken for granted that a three-year stint in this militia would transform most criminals into serviceable peasants.

Karnilov's second category exemplifies what Lindenmeyr has shown was the government's tendency to force private parties to provide social services. "Middle-aged exiles," he writes,

> will be sent to *volosti*, where they shall be distributed in the capacity of workers among large families of prosperous peasants, under such conditions that the peasant takes the assigned exile into his home, houses him, clothes him, and upon the expiry of three years labor provides him the items needed to establish his own home....[32]

Peasants' use of exiles as laborers had already been provided for in the 1822 "Regulation on Exiles," albeit in an ill-defined provision that was probably forced on Speranskii by the Siberian Committee's conservative members, for it clearly undermined his general aim of strengthening village society. Karnilov shared what was nonetheless the universal view that labor (like military service) would rehabilitate offenders: "if, *despite all the householder's efforts*, he persists in his old ways..." the exile was to be assigned to labor for the state (*kazennaia rabota*).[33] The assumption that any prosperous peasant could supervise a criminal's rehabilitation reveals how Karnilov and others operated within a penological paradigm that was authoritarian rather than professional or bureaucratic, and also highlights Durkheim's observation that the state's expropriation over punishment converts citizens into property.

For his third category, Karnilov wanted exiles who failed in the second category to be assigned to privately-owned factories. These "correctionals" (*ispravliaiushchimsia*) would be so distributed that factories "will be strengthened by such help [*posobie*] and their owners garner a significant profit...." Following their labor terms, these prisoners would still have the opportunity to become peasant homesteaders; but if they refused to till the soil they would be "employed in a position similar to that of free laborers...." "[T]hose steeped in vice and showing no ability," intoned Karnilov, "will be sent to penal labor."[34] He somehow believed that factory owners, like peasants, would not only welcome exile laborers but be able to exert a corrective influence over them; it was just that factories, with their rigid schedules and other normalizing procedures, were more appropriate for especially unrepentant deviants.

Karnilov's final category is somewhat vague but concerns the large numbers of "incapables" among the exile population. He seems to have been willing to allow this category to continue to be administered as it already was (most mentally or physically disabled exiles were foisted onto villagers and given insignificant stipends), yet stresses that their "masters" (by which he presumably meant "serf owners") should be held more accountable for proving they were actually incapacitated. If they could not do so, these masters should somewhat paradoxically be forced to pay the cost of supporting them.[35] In short, Karnilov acknowledged the widespread abuse of administrative exile to rid villages and other communities of the elderly and disabled, but offered little to redress this problem.

There is no evidence Karnilov's report was ever acted upon. But as a former Siberian governor Karnilov was more familiar than most with what was happening in the exile system, and despite his disparagement of exiles he clearly wanted to improve their management. The degree to which he depended upon peasants and factory owners to supervise exiles reveals how anemic the state's presence was in Siberia. Lack of personnel would bedevil all future efforts to improve the exile system.

Around the same time as Karnilov's report Irkutsk *guberniia*'s ruling council investigated the exile system. Proceeding in a more diagnostic fashion than Karnilov, the council identified two major factors under-mining the state settlements then being constructed in the *guberniia*. First was the absence of sufficient numbers of women for exiles to marry and establish families with; second was the *Brodiagi* Regulation, which according to the council had been responsible for the deport-ation of nearly 60,000 people as of 1828. "Without hesitation," it declared in its circulated minutes of March 1829,

> it can be emphatically stated that up to this point, sixty percent of those assigned to settlements have not settled as required. [They have not] outfitted homesteads and such a possibility appears unlikely and, as a result, exile-settlers assigned to *volosti* are surviving thanks to *starozhily* and are an extreme burden.[36]

The council predicted that morality would decline and crime increase throughout the region. Unlike Karnilov, it did not harp upon exiles' depravity, and candidly stated that the main reason for even worse prob-lems ahead was lack of funding. Under existing arrangements funds were supposed to originate from state peasants' land taxes and exiles' labor earnings, but the council describes the former as "insignificant" and the latter as insufficient due to the small number of privately-owned factories in Irkutsk *guberniia*. Tomsk and Eniseisk *gubernii* had more factories, it noted, but these were already filled with exile-workers and so there was nowhere to put those assigned to Irkutsk.

The council offered a plan it claimed would gradually relieve those "distant regions of Russia… of the crime and low morality of the people being sent there as punishment…," and cited as a precedent for it the state's transfer, in 1807, of 6,000 males from "doss-houses and drinking establishments" in Arkhangel *guberniia* and Siberia to "Vologda *Guber-niia*'s various districts [*uezdy*]…," where they now lived as sharecroppers (*polovniki*) "on the land and are assigned for the most part to *raznochintsy*, merchants, *meshchane*, and even peasants…," to whom they owed half their produce. Vologda supposedly offered a "model" for managing Siberia's exiles, and so to create the necessary landlords the council advised giving between 3,000 and 12,000 *desiatiny* of land each to officials, merchants, and lower-level *meshchane*. Sharecroppers for these *latifundia* would each be assigned 15 *desiatiny* of arable land and would be derived from two groups, the first of which consisted of state peasants, Tatars, "Bukharans," "Tashkentians,"[37] and others from the region (with the express exception of "small nomads" [*kochuiushchi*]), the second of which consisted solely of exiles. The council stipulated that after 12 years a landowner's estate should average one settler household for every 15 *desiatiny* of land and that one-third of these households should have been established in the first four years of ownership. If the landowner failed to satisfy these criteria he would forfeit his land and it would be given to someone else. If no one wanted "to fulfill the forerunner's responsibilities, then in that case the land distributed to the settlers on the basis of 15 *desiatiny* per person reverts to them and they assume the full rights of state peasants...." Settlers were to operate under the same regulations as the Vologda sharecroppers and give half their produce to their landlords. After 12 years a sharecropper could leave his owner's estate for that of another, but had to announce this intention in the eleventh year. Whether under his original or a new landlord, he was again bound by another 12-year contract. As for landowners, their rights would be similar to those in European Russia, with the exception that they would not own their sharecroppers as serfs because they were technically state peasants. For this reason, landlords could not use sharecroppers as domestics or assign them to factories on their estates unless a sharecropper was a tradesman and agreed to this. Also, the landowner could not administratively exile a sharecropper during the first 12 years of his residence.[38]

According to a summary of this report by the IGP, the Siberian Committee reviewed it but recommended a geographical survey be completed before any steps were taken. Pintner writes that Kankrin, despite supporting gentry control over the peasantry as a matter of principle, refused to finance land surveys,[39] presumably out of fiscal conservatism and a reluctance to tamper with any mechanism involving state peasants. This would largely explain why the council's plan attracted no viable support from Petersburg. Irkutsk's plucky councilors next tried to drum up support among those local officials and others identified as potential landowners. Probably because most officials were simply counting the days until their service in Siberia was over and because merchants and *meshchane* thought it safer and more profitable to remain in urban areas than try to manage an estate of hundreds of exilic or indigenous "sharecroppers," they evinced a similar lack of interest. The plan to create Siberian *latifundia* therefore died upon conception.[40]

Nonetheless, it highlights how Siberian officials shared the center's overall goal to transform exiles and other marginal groups into docile and serviceable subjects. "When the general attitude toward private serfdom became more critical" during Nicholas's reign, writes Pintner, "the state peasantry came to be regarded as a group that could serve as an example and testing ground for policies that might subsequently be applied to the privately owned serfs."[41] The Irkutsk council's plan reflects this desire to experiment with subject populations, yet it went even further by proposing to create whole-cloth a gentry from among local notables. Its efforts to co-opt merchants and *meshchane* and to establish alliances between both the official and civilian sectors and various *soslo-viia* are especially interesting, for had these efforts—themselves indicative of a consciousness at odds with hegemonic discourse—succeeded, Irkutsk and possibly all Siberian society would have been radically altered. More than anything, this very possibility probably accounts for Petersburg's lack of support.

Better reasoned and argued than Karnilov's, the Irkutsk council's recommendations, however, similarly called for civilians (albeit social elites as well as some officials) to manage the exile population. It was understood beforehand that Petersburg was not going to offer additional funding or personnel. Interest at this time in Western-style prisons was confined to a few top officials as an intellectual exercise that had yet to affect policy,[42] and so neither Karnilov nor the council proposed erecting prisons in Siberia or anywhere else. Both schemes were influenced by notions of bonded labor, and serfdom's existence goes some way toward explaining why exile and not penitentiaries epitomized tsarist penality. The conceptual linkage of penality with enserfment explains why during this period instrumentalism superseded a genuine ascetic of rehabilitation in dealing with exiles, so much so that officials expected the state would be served by its convict population without even having to maintain or supervise it.

Despite Petersburg's failure to act on Karnilov's or the Irkutsk council's proposals, certain top officials became increasingly concerned with penal administration. For instance, an ongoing debate concerned whether or not to tattoo captured fugitive exiles, recidivists, *brodiagi*, and others many believed should be tattooed to facilitate identification. Despite justice minister Dmitrii V. Dashkov's and others' objection that tattoo-ing permanently stigmatized an individual and prevented his ever being reincorporated into society, Nicholas sided with the hardliners in March 1846 and supported legislation that according to Schrader led to the immediate tattooing of "939 fugitive exiles and vagrants" and 3,553 the following year. Nonetheless, this project "proved ineffectual" and served only to create an entire stratum of permanently disfigured outcasts.[43]

Another debate influenced by developments in Siberia concerned reinstatement of the death penalty. In 1831, after visiting Irkutsk, I. I. Gogel, one of Nicholas's aides-de-camp, recommended the Siberian Committee mandate capital punishment for exiles who committed serious crimes. Led by Speranskii, the committee rejected this recommendation in May 1832, saying there was no basis for it. However, Eastern Siberia governor-general A. S. Lavinskii soon countered by calling for the death penalty for exiles who committed political crimes or whose repeated offenses proved they were incorrigible. To consider the matter the emperor this time ordered V. P. Kochubei to form the so-called Secret Committee, chaired by Kochubei and including Speranskii, fellow Siberian Committee member Aleksandr N. Golitsyn, war minister Aleksandr I. Chernyshev, finance minister Kankrin, interior minister Dmitrii N. Bludov, and Benkendorf. Historian I. Iu. Foinitskii writes that a majority was "inclined" to support the death penality but not as a general rule, and only if it was used on a case-by-case basis through "secret orders [issued] in the names of the governors-general..." because of fears exiles would revolt en masse if the ruling became public knowledge.[44] Speranskii and Golitsyn opposed the measure, claiming no evidence showed an increase in crime by exiles and, even if there was more crime, the death penalty would not deter it. They reasoned that because other nations' governments had been unable to justify their use of the death penalty, neither could Russia, and that adoption of the measure without proof of its effectiveness would justify expediency without that expediency's effects being clear.

Influencing the capital punishment debate were the cholera epidemics of 1831 and 1832. These are discussed in greater detail in Chapter 6, but it is important to note here that they terrified the leadership in a way similar to the SARS epidemic's effect on China's leaders in 2003. Some in Russia could still remember Moscow's plague riot of 1771, when tsarist officials suddenly found themselves helpless and vulnerable before the roiling masses. Hence when "the cholera" seemed a destabilizing threat, Nicholas promulgated the "Quarantine Regulation" (*Karantinnyi ustav*) of 20 October 1832. It required capital punishment for 1) crimes that, as determined by the Supreme Criminal Court established earlier to judge the Decembrists, would otherwise normally lead to deprivation of rights, the knout, and *katorga*; 2) so called "quarantine crimes" as defined by courts-martial; and 3) crimes by soldiers which, if committed during a campaign, would be adjudicated under the Battlefield Criminal Code (*Polevoe ugolovnoe ulozhenie*) that already allowed for summary executions. The regulation rendered any person liable to execution for such crimes of a "political nature" as slandering the emperor or his government; conducting an "uprising accompanied by plunder, murder, arson, destruction of prisons, and freeing of prisoners"; inciting rebellion or insubordination among local inhabitants; insubordination against military authority or *katorga* commanders; and violent actions taken to free those in *katorga* or prison.[45]

There is no evidence the Quarantine Regulation resulted in many (or even any) executions. It is important because it reflected society's militarization and the government's increasingly hard-line approach toward dealing with offenders and because it made rationalizing the use of capital punishment that much easier. Despite having at first supported the Siberian Committee's rejection of capital punishment, the emperor soon came round to the Secret Committee's majority opinion. In early December 1833 he ruled that governors-general could, for the commission of new crimes, execute penal laborers whose original sentences had been for life or 20 years *katorga* because, legalistically speaking, such sentences had anyway amounted to reprieves from the death penalty, as indicated by the standard sentencing formula: "You have been sentenced to death, which His Imperial Majesty has mercifully commuted to 20 years (or life-time) *katorga*." On 26 December 1834 and 1 September 1837 Nicholas secretly expanded upon this ruling by granting governors-general the power to try penal laborers and exile-settlers with military courts according to the Battlefield Criminal Code.[46]

During the Secret Committee's debate of this issue Kochubei formed another committee, which learned there were large numbers of unemployed penal laborers at Siberia's *katorga* sites. Kochubei's subsequent 1832 report resulted in some convicts being redistributed to mining *zavody* (necessitating double-shifts there) and others to Omsk fortress.[47] *Katorga* convicts' numbers nevertheless remained too high to employ them all.

Prior to the late nineteenth century crime in Russia and elsewhere was nearly always viewed through the prism of good and evil, and discussion of it resembled the emerging discourse on epidemiology. Governmentality's creation of "population" called for statistical production of crime rates that supposedly measured commoners' pervasive iniquity rather than political or economic factors. Opponents of Siberian exile routinely argued that exiles "infected" non-exiles with their immorality and criminal behavior. Following yet another investigation during the mid-1830s the Department of Laws (*Departament Zakonov*), a subcommittee of the Committee of Ministers, accordingly drew the following conclusions:

> [T]he number of crimes by exiles in Eastern Siberia in 1833 and 1834 shows that there is enormous depravity and an inclination toward vice in these people; these same people moreover manifest unlimited criminality among themselves and the native population. Since the

investigation into the current situation has the goal of determining these people's immoral qualities and the extent of their burdensome presence in the regions to which they have been sent, it therefore cannot be disputed that, given the proportion of crimes within the space of two years in the two large *gubernii* [of Eniseisk and Irkutsk], nothing too terrible is impossible to expect from these people owing to their criminality and failure to establish any sort of community, the death of civility, and, by objective measures, the stripping away from the majority [of Siberia's population] of its previous moral defenses.... [E]xiles' relationship to the native population is essentially almost hostile, especially towards the natives [*inorodtsy*], whom they attempt, especially secretly, to exterminate at first sight.[48]

Journalists expressed similar views and helped popularize the link between crime and immorality. In 1818 Grigorii Spasskii, editor of the *Siberian Messenger*, compared *starozhily* to exile-settlers who, he wrote, after "no more than three years without their privileges... enter the peasant class on an equal footing with *starozhily*; but all of them are as distant from this type of lifestyle as they are from morality." By stark contrast, the *starozhily* were hard-working and maintained happy, close-knit families. "In general, they are intelligent and appreciate education," Spasskii rather disingenuously added. "It may be said of their morals that they could be more trustworthy, or, so to speak, not so cunning; but this seems to come from their proximity to danger."[49] Thus, even when the *starozhily* did wrong, it was explained by the presence of exiles. In 1833 a contributor to the MVD's mouthpiece similarly reported that throughout Siberia, exiles were murdering young women who would not agree to marry them and that others "often seduce another's wife or collude with her to murder her husband. By the same token, a wife will become the victim of a jealous husband." He offered the examples of an exile-settler named Beketov, who conspired with his lover Batmasova to murder her husband, and of the civil servant Vasilii Gusevskoi, who killed exile Petr Ivanov when he came home to find him "having illegal intercourse with his wife." Relishing the venality of these crimes, the author luridly described several more cases.[50]

Supercilious disdain for those deported to Siberia was tied in with a paternalistic compulsion to protect others, the good ones, from their infectious immorality. By 1837 interior minister Bludov and justice minister Dashkov were actively promoting the Committee of Ministers' general belief that exile should be abolished for this reason. Each presented detailed plans to build a series of prisons modeled on Philadelphia's

Walnut Street Prison—the jail the Quakers had turned into the United States' first penitentiary in 1790.[51] This marked the first effort by top Russian officials to replace banishment with modern prisons.

Nicholas responded to their overtures by sending tsarevich Alexander to Siberia in early summer 1837. Alexander's tour indicates how different the *Weltanschauung* of sovereign power was from that of governmentality. It was the first visit there by a member of the royal family and lasted only a week, with Alexander visiting just four cities not far from the Urals. During this ersatz fact-finding mission he responded to petitions by dispensing "various relief to Siberian exiles, excluding those exiled to *katorga*,"[52] and issued a manifesto of 22 July 1837 that allowed 200 exiles to return home, freed another 1,244 from taxes for three years, and permitted 11 to work for city governments.[53] This solipsistic spectacle of mercifulness summed up the sovereign's notion of confronting exile. After Alexander's return the Department of Laws slowly deliberated over his report and other materials in a series of meetings that in 1840 finally rejected Bludov's and Dashkov's call for prisons. It recommended instead that exile categories be more clearly defined and that additional correctional battalions be created to relieve pressure on *katorga* sites. Tail between its legs, the Department of Laws had retreated from its earlier self-righteous call for a response to exiles' depravity.[54] Around this time the government also granted *volost* administrations the authority to punish exiles who committed new crimes. "Neither women, nor the elderly, nor crippled exiles were spared corporal punishment," writes Vlasenko. *Volost* officials could also now subject exiles to "internal exile" by sending them (within Western Siberia) to such wretched locales as Berezov *okrug* or the Pelym and Narym territories (*kraia*).[55]

One of the most detailed and damning assessments of the exile system was that by the Siberian Committee in 1837.[56] Established in 1821 to develop the Siberian Reforms, the committee had been responsible for improvements in the administration of Siberia as a whole and over its indigenous population in particular. Despite the at times ingenious and rigorously systematic "Regulation on Exiles" and "Regulation on Exile Transfer within Siberian *Gubernii*" its impact on exilic affairs was limited, however, and so before his death in 1839 Speranskii must have recalled with bitterness and regret his efforts in this area. One measure of the Siberian Committee's ineffectiveness is that its only major report came out a year before Nicholas disbanded it.[57]

The report demonstrates the uneven distribution of judicially-convicted exiles among the six categories established by the "Regulation on Exiles": 1) penal laborers assigned to *katorga*; 2) convicts temporarily assigned to factory labor; 3) skilled craftsmen; 4) domestic servants; 5) exile-settlers; and 6) incapables. As of 1835 the criminal exile population stood at 97,121: *katorga* convicts accounted for 9,667 of these; exile-settlers for 58,026; and incapables for 28,477. The other three categories—temporary factory laborers; skilled craftsmen; and domestic servants—barely existed, respectively comprising 156, 281, and 514 exiles.[58] One reason for this was that GUZS (and possibly GUVS as well) limited the number of exiles in these categories, in the first two cases so as to favor non-exilic laborers and craftsmen in a region with few manufactories. With regard to domestics, their numbers reflected the small number of government officials who owned homes in which they could work. Moreover, in 1830 GUZS ruled that no more than two exile domestics could work for a single employer[59]—a move undoubtedly intended to forestall creation of the harems and retinues Siberian officials had traditionally managed to create. Almost no additional information exists on these categories or those persons assigned to them, and little more can added here except to say that evidence from later in the century suggests most female exiles employed as domestics were actually concubines or prostitutes.

Most strikingly, the report shows that Siberia was not only an enormous prison, but the empire's almshouse. Large portions of exiles were incapacitated for reasons of age or mental or physical handicaps. Penal laborers living "on assistance (in villages near factories)" totaled 5,969, or 38.2 percent of all convicts assigned to *katorga*. A separate category of "enfeebled and incapacitated" (*driakhlye i nesposobnye*) exile-settlers totaled 22,508. In sum, 29.3 percent of all exiles present and accounted for as of 1 January 1835 were officially incapable of serving as laborers or farmers.[60] The committee presented these and other figures largely without comment, but its choice of information undoubtedly reflected a hope that Nicholas would confront the problems they represented.

Such a large population of the aged and incapacitated raised the exile population's overall death rate, which based on the committee's figures stood at 18.63 per 1,000 persons in 1833.[61] To put this rate in some perspective, in 2005 the country of Mali had a death rate of 17.23 per 1,000 persons—the seventeenth highest in the world. But even this comparison to a ravaged and impoverished African nation is misleading, since what is actually a *standardized* death rate (that is, one that accounts for just adults) for Siberia's exiles does not strictly correspond to what was, in fact, Mali's *overall crude death rate*. A country's overall crude death rate is always raised by including its much higher infant death rate, which in Mali's case was 117.99 in 2005.[62] In other words, the death rate among Siberia's exiles was considerably higher than even the worst adult death rates found in the world today. Naturally, the elderly and physically and mentally disabled among Siberia's exiles were the most likely to die in a given year, and the committee's figures accordingly yield a staggering death rate of 83.75 among the 5,970 penal laborers listed "on assistance" in 1833. Overall, penal laborers were generally more likely to die than exile-settlers, with a death rate of 24.44 versus 12.67. Also, Eastern Siberia lived up to its reputation as a harsher destination than Western Siberia by having higher death rates. The death rate for incapacitated penal laborers in Eastern Siberia was 89.50 versus 39.42 for those in Western Siberia. Comparable regional figures were 26.80 versus 12.64 for all penal laborers and 17.83 versus 7.69 for all exile-settlers.[63] Finally, male exiles' death rate was almost twice that of female exiles: 20.05 versus 11.58. Siberia was therefore a charnel house as well as a prison and almshouse.

Other data from the Siberian Committee's report relating to crime and agricultural settlement are discussed elsewhere in this book; but for anyone who took the time to scan its 83 pages the message was unmistakable: exile was proving an unmitigated failure and endangering Siberian society. Convicts tasked with eventually becoming independent peasant householders were instead ending up as dependent lodgers, fugitives and violent criminals, or in almshouses. The exile population suffered a disturbingly high death rate and (according to the prevailing paradigm) its immorality and dissoluteness were infecting non-exiles. Although the report may have belatedly influenced the 1845 *Ulozhenie* (Chapter 7), Nicholas seems to have ignored it until 1842, when he probably would have had to at least acknowledge its existence while approving another senatorial revision of Siberia.

This 1842 revision appears to have been unique insofar as it was prompted by complaints against Eastern Siberia governor-general V. Ia. Rupert from what historian V. A. Volchek writes were "Jewish exiles and state criminals." Volchek offers no further information as to who these exiles and criminals might have been, but writes that M. N. Zhemchuzhnikov, who began the revision, was replaced within weeks by senator I. N. Tolstoi who, despite no cooperation from Rupert, concluded the governor-general had forced exile-settlers to work in the gold industry, concealed famine in Eniseisk *guberniia*, illegally restricted the grain market, and favored certain local merchants over others. Senator Tolstoi certainly felt he had enough dirt on Rupert to get him removed. But not so: the emperor required only that Rupert apologize.[64] This rebuff presumably signaled Nicholas's disdain for the Senate, for the "Jewish exiles and state criminals" who apparently provoked the revision, or both. It also pointed to his increasingly militant approach to ruling Russia, an approach that by the 1840s was hostile to convicts and exiles as well as the Senate—technically Russia's highest court—because it occasionally granted them minimal legal protections. Siberian officials were split down the middle between those who sympathized with the Senate and those who shared Nicholas's contempt for exiles. In a letter of 10 November 1845 to the MVD Western Siberia governor-general Petr D. Gorchakov, having noted the wholesale failure to transform exiles into peasants, proposed that all should instead be assigned to industrial sites where they would be housed in workers' barracks under armed guard.[65] This was an ignorant proposal, since it was already impossible to find enough sites for those sentenced to *katorga* alone. Yet Gorchakov's plan was "progressive" both in seeking to abolish exilic settlement and in the dystopian sense of forecasting the twentieth-century GULag.

Despite Nicholas's cavalier disdain toward exiles and evident lack of interest in the exile system, dissatisfaction with both ran high at the ministerial level. In 1847 the Committee of Ministers issued a strongly worded call for immediate improvements. Nonetheless, several more years passed before it commissioned the revision that led, first, to establishing the second Siberian Committee in 1852, and, secondly, eventually to the most significant changes for Siberia's administration since the 1822 Reforms. "The Siberian Committee played a large role in the development of Siberia and the change in relations towards this region," writes Volchek. However, his claim that Siberia came to be regarded as a "single entire organism" and "not a colony"[66] is belied by both the committee's deliberations as well as tsarist Siberia's later history. The most obvious fact refuting this claim is the government's retention and enormous expansion of the exile system.

Between 20 January and 14 October 1851 Nikolai N. Annenkov, who had previously served in the Imperial Chancery and, in 1848, become adjutant-general of the Committee of Ministers, conducted a thorough revision of Western Siberia's administration and operations. This resulted in a report lambasting GUZS and the region's lower administrative bodies. Annenkov's most serious and frequently made charges were corruption and malfeasance; and as early as mid-November the Committee of Ministers ordered the MVD to "eradicate" corruption in Tobol'sk's *guberniia* administration in particular and to demand an explanation from GUZS. Annenkov also suggested ways to rationalize and systematize procedures at all administrative levels.[67]

Most importantly, Annenkov reviewed procedures for resettling criminal exiles in Western Siberia (and, by extension, Eastern Siberia) and aimed a spotlight on the activities of TobPS, the Exile Bureaus (*Ekspeditsii o ssyl´nykh*), *volost* administrations, and land courts, as well as on the conditions deportees faced during their march into exile. TobPS's and the Exile Bureaus' record-keeping was in complete disorder. Records for most of those exiled between 1823 and 1829 had been lost, as well as for many exiled later. During the period 1823–38 the tens of thousands of exile records that did remain were not alphabetized, so that it was virtually impossible to find a particular individual's file. TobPS had often assigned exiles irrespective of their judicial sentences, so that exile-settlers destined for peasant villages ended up in *zavody* and penal laborers destined for *zavody* ended up in villages. For the past six years TobPS had sent GUZS no information concerning the number of exiles in Western Siberia or the costs associated with maintaining them. For the past ten years it had not stricken deceased exiles from its rosters. Annenkov assigned a subordinate to re-catalog TobPS's files for the decade beginning 1838, but the combined effect of what was lost and the continued receipt of new documents resulted in this task never being completed. Exile Bureaus' records were in a similar state, with their officials having little idea how many exiles were assigned to their regions and who had died, been transferred, or escaped.[68]

As for the exile system's march-route, Annenkov reported little improvement despite Speranskii's 1822 regulation overhauling deportation procedures. All the stations built in 1820–22 between Kazan and Tobol´sk were dilapidated except those in Viatka *guberniia*, which had been remodeled. Those built in Western Siberia in 1826–28 were in only slightly better shape. Conditions overall were terrible: stations were dark and airless, too small for the parties they received, and lacked separate quarters for women. Men, women, and children, guards as well as exiles, slept beside each other on the platforms or the mucky floors beneath. Kitchens and bathhouses were typically broken or otherwise unserviceable. Convoy officers embezzled the money that was to be distributed to deportees so they could buy food from peasants en route. Guards were drunk and slovenly and allowed exiles to escape. Annenkov recommended that stations be refurbished or rebuilt, and that in European Russia exiles be transported by barge along the Volga and Kama rivers to shorten the marching distance. Barge travel eventually replaced portions of the march-route in Western Siberia, though not until the 1860s. Western Siberia's stations were fixed at a cost of 58,000 rubles during the early 1850s, but were not maintained and soon fell apart.[69]

Annenkov wrote that "neither Speranskii's previous system nor new resolutions have been sufficiently implemented in Western Siberia."[70] Crime in the region was increasing, for which he blamed convicts both directly and indirectly. Most exile-settlers failed to establish homesteads and fell behind in their taxes, and there was a lack of almshouses and other institutions for dependent exiles and exiles' orphans. He proposed that exiles be geographically separated according to the severity of their crimes, with the most serious criminals sent further east. This had in fact been the trend for some time, but his recommendation led to legislation that explicitly equated extreme social deviance with the peripheral locations of Nerchinsk, Iakutiia, and, later, Priamur *krai* and Sakhalin. Russia's most noxious elements needed to be kept at arm's length.

Nevertheless, Annenkov did not question the propriety of exile. Like so many other officials he believed the system to be sound—it just needed to be modified and certain officials replaced for it to function as intended. This purblind faith in Russia's penology reflected a similar faith in tsarism and helps explain why the Imperial Chancery resisted calls to abolish exile, for these calls threatened a primary arena in which sovereign power could demonstrate itself.

Responding to Annenkov's report—and, it might be imagined, all other reports since at least 1837—A. I. Chernyshev, in his capacity as chairman of the Committee of Ministers, acknowledged the need for quick action, but added that the committee's responsibilities were too many and various for it to assume primary advisory authority over Siberia. In a report dated 13 April 1852 that cited the Committee of the Caucasus as a model, Chernyshev therefore recommended forming a second Siberian Committee. Four days later the emperor ordered it established, but curtailed its authority by requiring it to work in consultation with relevant ministries.[71] Here, then, was an instance where Nicholas seemed to have his cake and eat it, too: a plenipotentiary body that appeared to function within ministerial government. The new Siberian Committee met for the first time on 24 April and continued to do so regularly until its dissolution in 1864. Throughout its tenure it addressed nearly 3,000 separate matters related to Siberia. Chernyshev chaired its first meeting, at which the other members present were P. D. Kiselev, D. N. Bludov, L. A. Perovskii, V. N. Panin, P. F. Brok, and Annenkov; absent were members tsarevich Alexander and Count A. F. Orlov. Annenkov read at this first meeting a statement from the emperor detailing the committee's responsibilities and how it should organize itself to meet them. Later that year Nicholas ordered that Grand Prince Konstantin and Prince V. A. Dolgorukii be included as members. There were numerous personnel changes over the years. For example, as of late 1861 the committee consisted of Konstantin, Annenkov, Dolgorukii, Panin, Bludov, S. S. Lanskoi, A. M. Kniazhevich, K. V. Chevkin,

N. O. Sukhozanet, M. N. Murav´ev, V. F. Adlerberg, A. M. Gorchakov, V. P. Butkov, and D. N. Zamiatnin (whose membership he shared along with his other duties with the terminally ill justice minister Panin).[72]

The presence of leading ministers as well as figures from the Imperial Court once led Soviet historians to assert that the second Siberian Committee was characterized by "conservative reactionaries." Volchek argues that it was more progressive than they gave it credit for, and notes that even the emperor told the committee in his initial brief: "In no case should Eastern Siberia be seen as a colony, but rather this part of Siberia, just like the Western part, should be subsumed under the general rules of the civilian apparatus and administration."[73] In fact, the committee was divided over what the center's policy should be *vis-à-vis* the eastern territories. Some members simply wanted to be the emperor's yes-men, others wanted to grab the bull by the horns and solve the problems confronting them. Neither side was helped by the emperor's ambivalence toward Siberia, for in the same brief that seemed to welcome its full-fledged incorporation into the empire he also reminded the committee that Siberia's uniqueness must be accounted for. This proviso, as well as his reluctance to move against the governor-generalships and those who occupied them, laid the basis for a disparity between word and deed. Whereas Western Siberia had for some time already been increasingly incorporated into the empire's administrative apparatus and, as a result, had its role as an exilic destination ameliorated, Eastern Siberia continued to be treated like a colony until tsarism's collapse. Beginning in the 1850s the government publicly characterized the Amur region and Sakhalin as colonies, and explicitly compared the latter to Australia;[74] and in any case Western Siberia always remained a destination for administrative exiles and small numbers from other exilic categories. That said, the Siberian Committee showed, regarding exiles, a concern hitherto largely absent from official discourse. In 1855 it succeeded in having reduced to 1,000 the maximum number of blows given by the gauntlet, a traditional military punishment penal laborers were subject to. However, this legislation was kept secret. That same year saw a lessening of punishments for those captured after escape from *katorga* sites.[75]

Volchek is eager to credit the committee with other measures improving exiles' conditions. But in trying to make his case he cites much legislation that was initiated before 1852 and points to proposals that, although they reflected committee members' good intentions, failed to have an effect. For example, in 1857 Tobol´sk governor Viktor A. Artsimovich ordered a revision which found that since 1854—that is, two years after the Siberian Committee was established—TobPS had failed to forward over 8,500 rubles budgeted for exile locations. TobPS's assessor was immediately fired, but problems continued. A year later, Western Siberia governor-general G. Kh. Gasford learned that TobPS was distributing exiles unevenly throughout the region. This time more substantive measures were taken. Gasford transferred 600 exile-settlers to Bergmatsk *volost* in Tara *okrug*; reduced the number of rosters TobPS had to maintain; systematized its procedures yet again; and alleviated it of the need to deal with administrative exiles (whose management seems to have devolved to *volost* administrations). Volchek writes that Siberian officials' salaries and budgets increased early in Alexander II's reign; nonetheless, TobPS employees remained impoverished. "If one were to judge them by their clothes, they would not at all be taken for bureaucrats," observed M. L. Mikhailov, a poet and publisher of *The Contemporary* who passed through Tobol´sk in 1861. "Such pathetic costumes are to be encountered—and then not even always—in a barracks among the poorest strata of exiles."[76] TobPS therefore remained a hotbed of corruption and malfeasance that negatively affected exiles. Finally, many of the improvements and constructions of new prisons that Volchek credits to the Siberian Committee actually resulted from local prison committee initiatives (see Chapter 7).[77]

The following illustrates the resistance the committee's progressive members faced from more powerful decision-makers. Soon after its formation the committee recommended exile-settlers be assigned to where the climate was more conducive to farming, but that they also be separated from non-exiles. As we shall see, the conditions dictating settlement rendered this second recommendation virtually impossible to fulfill, and so at first glance it would be tempting to conclude the committee shared the emperor's cognitive dissonance toward Siberia. However, at the same time it also felt compelled to add that exile had done virtually nothing to promote settlement, but was in fact undermining the very society it was designed to further develop. In September 1852 Kiselev, in his capacity as minister of state domains, responded to this. Abolishing exile was impossible, he wrote, because the absence of locations in the "interior" rendered Siberia's broad expanses the only places to which exiles could practicably be assigned. He acknowledged the dangers and difficulties with assigning violent criminals and *brodiagi* to settlements, but recommended that such convicts be more consistently assigned to correctional battalions or industrial sites. In other words, Kiselev trotted out the same arguments that for decades had served only to avoid the problems of exilic settlement. Interior minister Dmitrii G. Bibikov seconded Kiselev, writing "it should not be forgotten that exile to settlement in Siberia is one of the only punitive measures established by our criminal legislation, and that all attempts up to now to replace it have been unsuccessful."[78] Despite having earlier called for exile to be abolished, D. N. Bludov, now in charge of the Second Section, recommended the construction of a new series of state settlements and that exiles should be assigned to indigenes' villages. Justice minister V. N. Panin similarly defended government policy and blamed lower officials for failing to implement it correctly. He also recommended that governors-generals' supervision over exiles extend to the *volost*-level. On the one hand, these men capitalized on Annenkov's and others' reports that exposed Siberia officials' venality so as to deflect attention from state policy; on the other, they blithely made proposals the state would never offer sufficient funding or personnel for. These often well-intentioned officials suffered from what might be called the Nicolaevan *Weltanschauung*: they conceived of Siberia and the exile system only in the abstract; replaced reality with figures, forecasts, and annual reports; and offered no workable solutions whatsoever.

To its credit, the Siberian Committee remained undeterred by these rebukes. In its minutes of 7 December 1852 it stated that if exile's abolition were not forthcoming, "this important issue" would have to continue being raised, because most members agreed that criminal exile was "an object of terror and danger for commoners."[79] It recommended that all exile categories be reviewed and that at least the use of exile be limited. (Between 1852 and 1860 the annual exile rate did fall below the average for the period 1823–60.[80]) However, the committee also now drew a distinction between Western and Eastern Siberia that refuted Nicholas's earlier proposition to regard them as one, claiming instead that whereas the former had been sufficiently integrated into the empire for it to resemble European Russia, the latter, "given its distance and natural environment, should perhaps be seen as a colony."[81] The committee hoped through this concession to salvage something of its call for abolition by suggesting that at least Western Siberia formed part of that "interior" Kiselev had defined as off-limits to exilic settlement. If exile was fated to continue, at least criminals would be as far removed from this interior as possible. But Nicholas ignored even this concession.

Alexander II abolished the committee on the final day of 1864. Volchek suggests a combination of personal ambition by committee members as well as reaction to the 1863 Polish Uprising played determining roles. But if there was ever a time a committee on Siberian affairs was needed it was when 20,000 Polish exiles began pouring across the Urals.[82] The abolition of the second Siberian Committee is one more reason why, as I have argued elsewhere, a characterization of the Great Reforms as "liberal" is mistaken.[83] Though largely ineffective, the committee nevertheless strongly opposed exile and as such threatened a central pillar of sovereign power. The autocracy's decision to prop up this pillar and ignore this opposition was irrational from the perspective of *raison d'état*, but not inexplicable from that of *raison de le roi*. Indeed, Alexander could not so easily disavow his inheritance. To better understand why, it is helpful to consider the situation in the Germanies where, writes Lindenfeld, the emerging view that the ruler's authority was neither unlimited nor arbitrary "led to the recognition of the police law as a way of setting boundaries to that power. The emphasis shifted from techniques of administration to rules thereof."[84] In the Germanies, bureaucratic consciousness supported an entire regime of counter-conduct activities that privileged governmental power over that of the princes and, eventually, the kaiser. In Russia, bureaucratic consciousness remained sufficiently undeveloped to impose the same kind of constraints upon the tsar.

However, during most of the period covered here ultimate responsibility for Siberia's woes fell squarely on the shoulders of Alexander's father, who so publicly declaimed his devotion to service and discipline. By having avoided the two greatest challenges facing society—serfdom and exile—Nicholas I comes to resemble his namesake Nicholas II more than any other Russian ruler. Yet it would be incorrect to imply that he made a conscious decision to avoid these challenges, since sovereign consciousness itself prevented him addressing problems only a governmental approach could arguably have solved. Nicholas was (as Nicholas II would even more so be) an anachronism before he succeeded the throne, a fossil left behind by developments that no longer yielded to traditional forms of power. Despite wanting to strengthen the autocracy Nicholas, who so starkly revealed his own powerlessness that even devotees ignored his orders, ended up doing just the opposite. Yet if the emperor was seen to have no clothes, the bureaucracy remained too timid and weak to do much without him.

"Everything here is fine and peaceful," Nicholas wrote I. F. Paskevich from Tsarskoe Selo in 1832, using a phrase common throughout his private correspondence.[85] A year before this letter, the Ministry of Finance and first Siberian Committee had debated which device to use to punish Nerchinsk's penal laborers: should it be the lash or the gauntlet?[86] A decade after this expression of tranquillity, GUVS would report the murder of "almost an entire family" in the village of Kuskunsk in Krasnoiarsk *okrug*, where an estimated 70 fugitives were at large.[87] For the emperor, Siberia simply allowed for convicts to be removed out of sight and out of mind—he was not unduly concerned with what happened once they were gone from European Russia. But he had a much different attitude toward the Decembrists.

3
Political Exile and the Martyrdom of the Decembrists

Political repression already had a long history in Russia before 1823, and though the term "political exile" (*politicheskaia ssylka*) did not appear in juridical legislation until the nineteenth century, exile for political reasons commenced no later than Ivan IV's reign. The deporting of political opponents gained rapid pace during Anna Ionnovna's and Elizabeth Petrovna's reigns, when a number of "secret prisoners" (*sekretnye arestanty* or *uzniki*) were assigned to fortress jails (*ostroga*), monastic dungeons, or literally holes in the ground in Siberia. Later, Catherine II's Secret Office kept busy dispatching a number of undesirables beyond the Urals, most notably Aleksandr Radishchev.[1] The findings of an investigation conducted early in Alexander I's reign suggested the Secret Office was even more active during Paul I's brief reign, when more than 700 people were incarcerated through "personal rulings," though the number exiled for expressly political reasons during that period is unknown. Despite Alexander's immediate abolition of the office, wartime exigencies and other concerns gave rise to subsequent secret police departments such as the Committee of Public Safety (1807) and the Ministry of Police's Special Chancery (1810). Military police were first introduced in 1815,[2] and the secret investigation unit created after the Semenovskii Mutiny was mentioned in Chapter 1.

Therefore, when Aleksandr Kh. Benkendorf recommended to Nicholas I the creation of an internal security administration he could cite several precedents. Given what was by then the MVD police's unsavory reputation, Nicholas wanted the new Third Section and its subordinate Corps of Gendarmes to be visible models of probity, and thus ordered to be dressed in baby-blue uniforms those "to be chosen from serving or retired officials known for their excellent service, efficiency, enthusiasm and especially their good moral qualities."[3] The eye-catching prominence of these guardians of order did not prevent the Third Section simultaneously employing spies, informers, and undercover agents. Moreover, during the late 1840s the MVD, Russia's largest ministry, expanded its brief to include political crimes. Nonetheless, there were more political police in the city of Paris under Napoleon III than in all Russia under Nicholas I.[4]

Political exile to Siberia has been characterized as playing a significant part in Nicolaevan repression. Soviet historians in particular contributed to this shibboleth, which their foreign counterparts accepted as historical fact. Hence claims that Nikolai I. Nadezhdin was exiled to Siberia for publishing Petr Ia. Chaadaev's famous "Philosophical Letters," and that Taras Shevchenko was "sent to hard labour in Siberia" for writing poems critical of the royal family.[5] Actually, Nadezhdin was sent to Ust´-Sysol´sk (present-day Syktyvkar)—a desolate location to be sure, but one west of the Urals. As for Shevchenko, he was assigned to Orenburg *guberniia* as a private in the Siberia Corps—an assignment considerably milder than *katorga*. For the simple reason that political crime was still not a widespread phenomenon, between 1823 and 1861 few were exiled to Siberia for "state crimes" (*gosudarstvennye prestupleniia*). Determination of a crime as "political" and one directed against the state lay with the prosecutor, who in virtually every case would have taken direction from the Imperial Chancery.

Unfortunately, both contemporary literature (official and unofficial) and subsequent accounts confuse and loosely apply the terms "state criminal" (*gosudarstvennyi prestupnik*) and "political exile" (*politicheskii ssyl´nyi*) such that it is often difficult to untangle who exactly was exiled for state crimes *per se*. According to statistician E. N. Anuchin, 439 men and four women were exiled for state crimes between 1827 and 1846.[6] However, these figures include neither the Decembrists who were mostly deported in 1827, the Poles and others exiled as political exiles following the 1830–31 Polish Uprising, nor the Petrashevists. Anuchin's figures seem even less convincing in light of the Siberian Committee's 1837 report, which for 1833 *alone* lists 129 persons exiled "for crimes against the government," including 85 "for rebelling against established authorities," 35 "for refusing and disobeying a command," and nine for "illegally crossing the border."[7] That said, the Siberian Committee apparently used much broader criteria than Anuchin and, in any case, 1833 was a year when many were exiled for their roles in the Polish Uprising.

Another bad year for dissidents was 1849—the year following the outbreak of mass unrest across much of Europe. Sixty soldiers among the Russian troops sent to quell the Hungarian Revolution that year rebelled in what became known as the "Hungarian mutiny." Eight were eventually exiled.[8] Then, on 16 November 1849, a military court convicted 23 individuals (all nobles except one) of involvement in the so-called Petrashevskii Circle, which actually comprised several different discussion groups (*kruga*), at least one of which was probably conspiring against the government.[9] Fifteen Petrashevists were sentenced to death, though Nicholas immediately commuted all their sentences. Eventually, nine were exiled to *katorga*: five to the mines, two to Omsk fortress, and two to *zavody*.[10]

The two most renowned Petrashevists, Mikhail V. Butashevich-Petrashevskii and Fedor Dostoevskii, went to Nerchinsk and Omsk, respectively. Dostoevskii is discussed in Chapter 7. Petrashevich, who before his arrest was a titular councilor, immediately began petitioning high officials about his rights, citing by chapter and verse various tenets of the law code. This did nothing to endear him to administrators. Released from *katorga* by Alexander II's manifesto of 26 August 1856, which allowed nearly all Decembrists to return to European Russia, Petrashevskii was nevertheless denied permission to leave Siberia. Those who have studied this issue blame this on the whims of Governor-general Nikolai N. Murav′ev and his successor Mikhail S. Korsakov, yet also note that Petrashevskii did nothing to mollify these powerful executors. "Fearing the local administration," explains one, "Petrashevskii strove for legality and expressed in his *idée fixe* an almost sick, maniacal conviction that in this way he could achieve some positive results."[11] Indeed, his letters resemble the convoluted petitions prisoners on death row sometimes send to anyone who will listen: they cite a mountain of legal clauses and sub-clauses but fail to shape them into any coherent narrative. Petrashevskii's addressees were convinced they were dealing with a madman (which in a sense they were) and became even more reluctant to permit him to return to European Russia. The conclusion by sympathetic historians that officials tried to drive him insane is, however, somewhat misplaced, for the real insanity was bureaucratic arbitrariness, that Kafkaesque nightmare in which compassion and common sense are displaced by wan indifference and pointless formality. Faced with this, Petrashevskii—who lambasted Murav′ev as a "tyrant" in an article published in an émigré London newspaper[12]—had little choice but to die in exile, which he did in 1866.

After all that Petrashevskii, Dostoevskii, and other political victims went through, Nicholas's death in 1855 and Alexander II's manifesto the following year offered hope to many that a turning point had come and the suffocating repression was lifting. Early in Alexander's reign the total number of political exiles compared favorably to even the surprisingly small number under his father. In 1862 Tobol´sk's unfortunately named and mathematically challenged governor Aleksandr I. Despot-Zenovich reported:

> Kept under special police surveillance during the year 1861 were 1 state criminal, 11 for participating in the [1830–31] uprising in the former Kingdom of Poland and for other political crimes, 1 for proselytizing the *Skoptsy* sect, 1 exiled from Abkhazia for bad behavior, 1 from Chechnia for inflicting a serious wound, 35 sentenced by the courts for suspicion of murder, 1 by order of the Eastern Siberia Governor-general, 2 by order of the Governor-general of St Petersburg and Grodno for making false reports and for robbery, and 2 [Catholic] priests [*ksëndzy*] for exciting people to confusion with sermons—in total, 58 [*sic*] people.[13]

Despite all being under surveillance, only 11 of these exiles had apparently been convicted of state crimes.

One of the first political dissidents exiled by Alexander II was also one of Russia's most famous: Mikhail A. Bakunin. Already in Austrian police custody for his revolutionary activities in Prague and Dresden, Bakunin was repatriated in 1851 only to face several more years' incarceration in the Peter-Paul and Shlissel´burg fortresses, where scurvy claimed all his teeth. In 1857, after many petitions, Bakunin was allowed to relocate to Siberia, where he was assigned to Neliubinskaia *volost* in Tomsk *guberniia*. "Neliubinskaia" means "unloved" and this sums up Bakunin's attitude to the place. Feigning illness, Bakunin received permission to relocate to the city of Tomsk, where he worked as a government clerk and married 18-year-old Antonia Kwiatkowska, the daughter of a Polish merchant. Bakunin's good fortune was to have as a second cousin governor-general Murav´ev, who secured him a position with the Russian-American Company in Irkutsk. Bakunin relocated as this company's employee to Zabaikal´e, but soon quit and began working for a gold magnate named Benardaki. During his time in Siberia, Bakunin sparred with Murav´ev's detractors Petrashevskii and Dmitrii I. Zavalishin in the pages of Alexander Herzen's émigré publication *The Bell*. This rivalry, combined with his unique political experiences in Europe, led to his feeling isolated in Eastern Siberia, especially after Murav´ev resigned and returned to Petersburg in 1861. Murav´ev and Bakunin's mother petitioned for him to be allowed to return to the capital, but without success, and so he began planning his escape. In June 1861, having obtained permission from the new governor-general Mikhail S. Korsakov to travel to the Amur region, Bakunin took as either a gift or a loan a thousand rubles from a merchant named Sabashnikov, sent his wife Antonia to Irkutsk, and traveled to Nikolaevsk-na-Amure where he boarded a Russian warship bound for De Kastri. During a stop at the port of St Olga along the way, Bakunin convinced the American captain of the *SS Vickery* to spirit him away to Japan, wherefrom he eventually returned to Europe to resume his revolutionary career.[14]

Few exiled political dissidents managed to escape as spectacularly; but then, few escaped at all because there were so few to begin with. As of 1863 only two such exiles were in all of Eniseisk *guberniia*. One was Petrashevskii, who as a lonely bachelor was clerking for the city of Krasnoiarsk in return for a yearly stipend of 114 rubles. The other was Simon Mazuraitus, age 31 from the Western Provinces, exiled for his role in the Hungarian Mutiny. Mazuraitus was living under permanent surveillance in Minusinsk *okrug* where, like Petrashevskii, he was a bachelor, though surviving as a peasant without government assistance.[15]

During this period those prosecuted as state criminals tended to be exiled judicially rather than administratively. The government only began systematically using administrative exile against state criminals after 1878, when a jury refused to convict Vera Zasulich for her attempted assassination of Petersburg's governor-general. The examples of the Decembrists and Petrashevists prove this rule: the only two major groups prosecuted as state criminals during Nicholas's reign, they were sentenced by criminal, military, or specially-convened courts. In both cases many of the accused were acquitted. Of the nearly 600 put on trial for the Decembrist Uprising half were released without punishment. Had these defendants been exiled administratively, that is, without judicial proceedings, they could only have been "acquitted" by imperial decree. Nearly all those who were convicted saw their terms shortened. Decembrist Sergei P. Trubetskoi later recalled, "A reduction of the terms to which we had been sentenced occurred several times: the first during [Nicholas I's] coronation."[16]

It is not beyond the realm of possibility that the regime secretly or administratively exiled political dissidents who went unnoticed by Anuchin and other sources. Historian Aleksei Bolkovskii writes that upon completion in 1830 the entire third floor of Ekaterinburg Prison was specifically reserved "for secret prisoners."[17] Nonetheless, given Nicholas's interest in proving through courts of law that the Decembrists and others were guilty and deserved their sentences (however predetermined these may have been), it seems fair to say that Anuchin's numbers, while not complete, are accurate, and that when account is taken of the groups they exclude it becomes clear that between 1823 and 1861 the use of Siberian exile as a tool of political repression was neither systematic nor widespread.

This and the next chapter concern the Decembrists; Chapter 5 concerns Polish exiles. Yet first to be considered are some less prominent figures who either committed political crimes or were perceived as capable of doing so. Late in Alexander I's reign the MVD reported to Eastern Siberia governor-general A. S. Lavinskii on "the Pinsk Jew Leib Klodon." "Of the crimes of this Jew Klodon there were many" it asserted without elaboration, though these crimes had been serious enough to warrant a sentence from the Committee of Ministers. Klodon was first assigned to a village in Irkutsk *guberniia*. But in 1835 officials learned that for several years his relative Moisei Blankov had been coming to give him donations collected for him in his *shtetl* back home. This violation of the terms of his sentence led to Klodon being ordered "removed for settlement to Nerchinsk *okrug* [and] kept under strict police surveillance...." The transfer was delayed when Klodon fell ill, according to a June 1836 letter by Nerchinsk commandant Ivan Govorov, who nevertheless assured superiors that as soon as possible "this dangerous Jew will be put under strict surveillance."[18] Similarly accorded special attention was the Cossack Petr Bratchiko, convicted and sentenced by Poltava *guberniia's* Periaslavl Land Court for defaming the emperor. In 1841 Benkendorf asked GUVS to assign this "vicious person" to the city of Irkutsk so he could more easily be watched. Officials monitored his progress until he arrived there the following year.[19] Finally, there is Timofei Filipov, knouted and sentenced to *katorga* in 1822 by a so-called Royal Committee (*Komitet Vysochaishe*) for, "among other [crimes], plotting against the life of... Emperor Alexander Pavlovich...." In 1826 officials reported difficulty locating Filipov, whom they eventually learned "exchanged names in Tomsk with the prisoner Ivan Kovalev, who was being exiled to a settlement, and under this name he remained in settlement in Achinsk *uezd*." Benkendorf ordered Filipov sent to Petersburg, presumably to face new charges.[20] Such were the quotidian political threats the regime combated with exile.

*   *   *

Few nineteenth-century actors have attracted more attention from Russian historians than the Decembrists. The literature grows annually, with studies of their activities before, during, and after the 1825 uprising suggesting an unquenchable thirst for information about what many regard as Russia's first socially conscious revolutionaries. Studies of the Decembrists in Siberia are typically biographical in nature and laud individuals' intellectual and philanthropic activities there. "An almost legendary romance surrounds like a halo the exile of the Decembrists and the few brave women who followed them to Siberia," Constantin de Grunwald, who himself did not stint hyperbole, acknowledged as early as the 1950s.[21] A quasi-hagiographic canon credits Decembrists with revolutionary intentionality and elides their often less admirable but all-too-human behavior in exile. The similarity of Soviet-era accounts that manage to blur all Decembrists into a single admirable personage call to mind the literary tradition of the "princes' lives" (*kniazheskie zhitiia*) whose *topoi*, writes Margaret Ziolkowski, presented "an idealized portrait, a verbal icon" rather than an historically accurate portrait of a living being. Indeed, there is an interesting genealogy in all this, since the *kniazheskie zhitiia* tradition early on influenced the nationalist historian Nikolai Karamzin, who despite his philism for autocracy influenced Kondratii F. Ryleev and other Decembrist writers.[22] What with Aleksandr A. Bestuzhev-Marlinskii considered by some to have been "the 'instigator' of the Russian Romantic historical tale in the 1820s,"[23] the stage was set for Decembrists to contribute to their own mythification. Bearing in mind Andrei Siniavskii's critique that Socialist Realist writing accords with a neo-Classical esthetic,[24] and applying this critique to Soviet historiography, it may be observed that the Decembrists' place in historical memory owes more to literary genealogy than to any ideological genealogy eventuating in Leninism. The prevailing historical literature also tends to obscure administrative factors relating to their exile, though recent exceptions to this rule exist. For instance, A. D. Margolis has detailed Nicholas's deportation procedures as well as the exceptional treatment accorded "soldier-Decembrists" (*soldaty-dekabristy*); and A. V. Sobolev has analyzed the cooperatives (*arteli*) that Decembrists established among themselves.[25]

Despite Anglophone historians' generally high regard for the Decembrists, surprisingly little has been written about them in English and virtually nothing about their time in Siberia. Moreover, what accounts there are focus solely on those sentenced by the Supreme Criminal Court (*Verkhovnyi ugolovnyi sud*) and ignore the just mentioned soldier-Decembrists. Anatole Mazour's and Marc Raeff's accounts are vague or misleading about the Decembrists in exile, though better descriptions (albeit based solely on Decembrists' memoirs) can be found in studies by Mikhail Zetlin and Glynn Barratt. Separate articles by Barratt and Jeanne

Haskett on the celebrated Nikolai A. Bestuzhev include useful information about Decembrists' conditions generally.[26]

The Decembrists' banishment therefore remains swathed in martyrdom's Romantic folds. John Keep has suggested "demystifying the officers' reform movement" by treating it "as an early instance of Praetorianism,"[27] and this seems a worthwhile goal. However, we are most concerned here with what happened to these officers and others exiled to Siberia as a result of the Decembrist Uprising. Compared to political dissidents both before and after, their treatment was indeed unique in the annals of Siberian exile, but there is little to support S. V. Kodan's and P. L. Kazarian's separately made claims that the exile administration expressly designed for them established a precedent or even a model for dealing with subsequent political exiles.[28] Throughout the tsarist era administrators in both Petersburg and Siberia dealt with political exiles variously and confusedly. It was only the privileged status of most political exiles that established a continuum to their treatment, insofar as this treatment was usually distinct from that meted out to non-privileged exiles. Thus almost all senior officers and noblemen among the Decembrists were explicitly convicted of state crimes by the specially convened Supreme Criminal Court, while the more numerous foot-soldiers and junior officers were convicted of mutiny by military courts. For clarity's sake, "Decembrists" will hereon refer to the former; "soldier-Decembrists" to the latter.[29] Also, although my goal is to de-mythify the Decembrists' exile, this should not be read as an effort to diminish the physical and mental anguish many of them suffered. What follows is intended not to trivialize their experiences but rather to contextualize and thus better understand them.

It must first be acknowledged that five Decembrists (Mikhail P. Bestuzhev-Riumen, Petr G. Kakhovskii, Sergei I. Murav´ev-Apostol, Pavel I. Pestel, and Kondratii F. Ryleev) were hanged—which fate enshrined them forever in the capacious halls of Russian martyrdom. Yet characterizing the suffering endured by the remaining 124 convicted Decembrists is problematic.[30] "The [Decembrists'] sufferings were, in the main, not physical at all," writes Barratt, "... but rather moral and emotional."[31] Concerning their lives in Chita, in Zabaikal´e, where most ended up for longer or shorter periods of time, Haskett writes, "There was little to do except talk, brood over their failure, and work on the senseless tasks devised by the prison authorities. These tasks were not difficult or lengthy, just ridiculous."[32] With the exception of the three who lingered for years in fortresses or prisons,[33] the Decembrists' physical sufferings never approached those of criminal exiles. Moreover, the soldier-Decembrists—i.e., those least responsible for the uprising—suffered far greater hardships than did their commanders. A history of the Decembrists in exile is therefore one about class relations in early nineteenth-century Russia.

It was during their trials and incarcerations before deportation that many Decembrists suffered most. "I don't know, perhaps with age or depending on cast of mind and character, I may in the end get accustomed to the situation I've now been in for five years in Siberia," wrote Petr N. Svistunov to his brother in 1832:

> But I confess that something has been weighing on me since the day of my incarceration in prison. I cannot yet speak of the moral torments which came to bear in the fortress and especially during trial. Since then the whole of my life consists of deprivations, uneasiness, discontent, and gloomy mental tension. The melancholy I experienced mulling over the wrecking of my future has actually abated, but the peacefulness that has followed it is only a mournful convalescing after spiritual torments.[34]

Those involved in the bloody stand-off in Petersburg's Senate Square were after arrest squeezed into Peter-Paul fortress, where by all accounts conditions were barbaric. Some were distributed to other fortresses in early August 1826. Nicholas ordered isolation cells and food deprivation to be used to elicit confessions and denunciations, though nothing suggests physical torture was ever used. The technique worked well, however, particularly in the case of Trubetskoi, would-be "dictator" of the regime some conspirators planned would replace the Romanov dynasty. Collapsing in tears at his emperor's feet and begging for mercy the evening of the uprising, he dishonored himself as thoroughly as he had earlier that day when he deserted his troops,[35] though it should be added that Trubetskoi especially suffered later in prison: Ivan D. Iakushkin wrote that he was "spitting blood in plate-fulls" the day before leaving for Siberia.[36]

Following incarceration, the second most trying period for some Decembrists was their journey into exile. A total of 89 departed for Siberia between 22 July 1826 and 17 November 1827. Another group of four left several months later, on 24 April 1828 (see Table 3.1).[37]

Owing to Nicholas's paramount fear that Decembrists would escape, Ivan I. Dibich, chief of His Imperial Majesty's General Staff, ordered every two prisoners accompanied by a special courier (*fel´d˝eger*) and four gendarmes. In instructions issued to war minister Aleksandr I. Tatishchev several days before the first group's departure Dibich specified that each "should be taken in a *telega*, and not in his equipage." The prisoners

Table 3.1   Decembrists' Departure Dates from Petersburg to Siberia

Date	Names
7/22/1826	V. L. Davydov, A. Z. Murav'ev, E. P. Obolenskii, A. I. Iakubovich
7/23/1826	A. I. Borisov, P. I. Borisov, S. G. Volkonskii, S. P. Trubetskoi
7/24/1826	P. P. Konovnitsyn, A. A. Fok, N. P. Tsebrikov
7/25/1826	A. N. Andreev, S. G. Krasnokutskii
7/26/1826	N. P. Okulov (Akulov), M. I. Pushchin
7/27/1826	N. F. Zaikin, F. P. Shakhovskii
7/28/1826	A. N. Murav'ev
7/29/1826	Ap. V. Vedeniapin, N. A. Chizhov
7/31/1826	V. M. Golitsyn, A. I. Shakhirev
8/2/1826	N. S. Bobrishchev-Pushkin, M. A. Nazimov
8/4/1826	V. I. Vranitskii, N. O. Mozgalevskii, I. F. Fokht
12/10/1826	I. A. Annenkov, A. M. Murav'ev, I. M. Murav'ev, K. P. Torson
1/18/1827	D. I. Zavalishin, A. A. Kriukov, N. A. Kriukov, P. N. Svistunov
1/21/1827	N. V. Basargin, F. B. Vol'f, M. A. Fonvizin, A. F. Frolov
1/24/1827	I. I. Ivanov, A. O. Kornilovich, P. D. Mozgan, P. I. Falenberg
1/27/1827	P. V. Avramov, P. S. Bobrishchev-Pushkin, N. I. Lorer
2/2/1827	A. P. Beliaev, P. P. Beliaev, M. M. Naryshkin, A. I. Odoevskii
2/5/1827	M. N. Glebov, M. K. Kiukhel'beker, N. P. Repin, A. E. Rozen
2/7/1827	A. V. Ental'tsev, N. F. Lisovskii, V. N. Likharev, Iu K. Liublinskii
2/10/1827	S. I. Krivtsov, V. K. Tizengauzen, V. S. Tolstoi, Z. G. Chernyshev
2/15/1827	I. V. Abramov, A. F. Briggen, P. F. Vygodovskii, A. I. Cherkasov
2/17/1827	N. A. Zagoretskii, V. P. Ivashev
3/5/1827	A. F. Furman
6/17/1827	V. A. Bechasnov (Bechasnyi), I. S. Povalo-Shveikovskii, V. I. Shteingel'
6/21/1827	N. A. Panov, A. N. Sutgof, D. A. Shchepin-Rostovskii
9/28/1827	A. P. Bariatinskii, M. A. Bestuzhev, N. A. Bestuzhev, I. I. Gorbachevskii
10/2/1827	Ia. M. Andreevich, A. S. Pestov, M. M. Spiridov, A. P. Iushnevskii
10/5/1827	A. P. Arbuzov, A. I. Tiutchev, I. D. Iakushkin
10/8/1827	P. A. Mukhanov, A. V. Podzhio, I. I. Pushchin
11/17/1827	F. F. Vadkovskii
4/24/1828	P. F. Gromnitskii, I. V. Kireev, M. S. Lunin, M. F. Mit'kov
Total	93

were to be fettered and their parties to travel "not only during the day but around the clock" except for every third day, when they were allowed to recuperate in a post-station, though certainly not a city or town. They were to leave Petersburg at night along a secret route bypassing Moscow and following the Iaroslavl road. To purchase food, couriers were provided with 50 kopeks per prisoner per day. According to instructions, their meals "should be sufficient only to maintain their strength and health, while avoiding all such extravagances and indulgences as: large dishes, and the consumption of champagne and other wines." The prisoners were not allowed to write letters or speak to anyone, and no one was allowed to give them gifts or money. On 13 August, during a pause in the deportations, Dibich informed regional officials that the emperor had ordered identification tags (*primety*) made stating each prisoner's age and height.[38]

The first two groups of Decembrists experienced particularly harrowing journeys, the breakneck pace set by the couriers of the first delivering them to Irkutsk a mere 37 days after leaving Petersburg, those of the second taking only slightly longer. Men and horses were exhausted and several of the animals were run to death. For many, their journeys were psychologically harrowing as well. Following the removal of these first two parties a gendarme captain named Miller reported that the shackles all prisoners wore had caused "thin cuts" on Artamon Z. Murav´ev's shins. He and other prisoners begged to have them removed, to no avail. In various locations along the way Murav´ev's escorts found waiting for him his wife, uncle, and a serf who "brought him a canvas and a hat." They as well as the throngs of onlookers who gathered in towns to catch a glimpse of the Decembrists had somehow been made wise to the "secret" route. "Gendarmes report that all the prisoners, especially while passing through the [European] Russian *gubernii*, were very sad and for the most part silent and often crying...," wrote Miller:

> Murav´ev mostly cried and reproached himself for his stupidity and the very cause of his misfortune. Along the way [Evgenii P.] Obolenskii often blamed himself, at first saying he was there by mistake and knew of no law whatsoever for why he should now be suffering. [Aleksandr I.] Iakubovich was also sad, but seemed in better spirits compared to the others, and sometimes gave them courage. In general, they spoke little with the gendarmes, and had almost no conversations concerning their crimes. Between themselves, when they were together in the stations, the prisoners always spoke French....[39]

Miller claimed they brightened after crossing the Urals, which seems rather odd both to report and if it was true. Subsequent removals were less frantic. Iakushkin, who departed on 5 November 1827 with Anton P. Arbuzov and Aleksei I. Tiutchev, later recalled, "For us, the journey from Petersburg to our place of confinement was a pleasant ride."[40] "[A]ll our state criminals are alive and healthy," Aleksandr F. Briggen, *en route* to Chita, cheerfully wrote his sister, "and some are even happy—therefore, don't believe the false rumors you'll hear."[41] Nonetheless, Mikhail Bestuzhev, who departed in September that year, barely managed to escape serious injury or worse when he was thrown from his wagon and got his shackles caught in the wheels.

Nicholas's indecision over how to dispose of the Decembrists was another reason they were not exiled *en masse*. He dispatched earliest those he considered to be the eight major conspirators still alive, but then allowed them two leisurely months in Irkutsk before ordering them assigned to Blagodatsk, an ugly iron-ore pit 12 versts from Nerchinsk Zavod. Arriving on 25 October, the "Blagodatsk Eight" were later immortalized by Aleksandr Pushkin's "Message to Siberia" ("Poslanie v Sibir"[42]):

> Deep in the Siberian mine,
> Keep your patience proud;
> The bitter toil shall not be lost,
> The rebel thought unbowed.
>
> The sister of misfortune, Hope,
> In the under-darkness dumb
> Speaks joyfully courage to your heart:
> The day desired will come.
>
> And love and friendship pour to you
> Across the darkened doors,
> Even as round your galley-beds
> My free music pours.
>
> The heavy-clanging chains will fall,
> The walls will crumble as a word;
> And Freedom greet you in the light,
> And brothers give you back the sword.

This poem invites the mythification of the Decembrists' exile to be examined from a different angle than above. The romanticizing actually began even before the first Decembrists entered Siberia, thanks to a public relations campaign conducted by friends, relatives, and the Decembrists themselves. Twenty-year-old Mariia Volkonskaia (who distracted herself in the hours following husband Sergei G. Volkonskii's arrest by singing the "Don Juan" duet[43]) so convinced Petersburg's aristocracy of his and the others' heroic tribulations, that when Nicholas agreed to let her join him in Siberia it was probably more for his sake than hers. There is some evidence the Third Section, acting upon Nicholas's fears of residual sedition, condoned or even spread the rumor the Decembrists were being worked to death so that potential conspirators would know the fate that awaited them.[44] Several Decembrists were poets and contributed mightily to their mythification. Fedor F. Vadkovskii, in a poem titled "Wishes" ("Zhelaniia"), describes the Decembrists as the "good children" of "blessed Rus, our mother." In addition to wishing for "the chains of the people to be broken" and for "schools to be founded throughout Rus," Vadkovskii evinced the concern of many Decembrists that they not be forgotten.[45] Similarly, "blessed Rus, our mother" is invoked in an anonymously written song dated 1836 and credited to the Decembrists. This formula is followed by a long chronology of their sufferings beginning on Senate Square through various prisons and exile. The far-flung locales named in this song (one line goes: "We languished in irons, suffered in prisons, perished in Georgia, in Suzdal, on the Lena's shores") exemplify the development in Russian literature of what Paul Austin has called the "exotic prisoner."[46]

The Decembrists considered Aleksandr I. Odoevskii their best poet. Ziolkowski has shown that his narrative poem "Vasil´ko," written in 1829–30 and based on a story from the *Primary Chronicle* about Prince Sviatopolk's blinding of Terebovl's prince, contains elements that are "a stock component of the *prince's lives*."[47] Odoevskii's reliance on historical symbolism and martyrology is similarly evident in another poem written as a response to Pushkin's "Message to Siberia":

> The sound of your prophetic harp,
> Impassioned, came to us at last.
> Swiftly our hands reached for the sword,
> But found that shackles held them fast.
>
> Yet, singer, fret not: we are proud
> Of these our chains as of our fate.
> Locked in our prison cells, we scoff
> At the rulers of the State.
>
> Our grievous toil will not be lost,
> The spark will quicken into flame;

> Our people, blindfolded no more,
> A new allegiance will proclaim.
>
> Beating our shackles into swords,
> Liberty's torch we will relight,
> And she will overwhelm the Tsars,
> While nations waken in the night.[48]

Combining images and themes from antiquity (harp, sword, fate) with those of contemporary concern (liberty's torch, the people *v.* monarchy), this poem is archetypically Romantic. Like other Decembrist poems Odoevskii's evinces "the concept of poetic *utilitas*," by which Classics scholar Gareth Williams has explained Ovid's motivation for exaggerating the difficulties he faced during his exile in Tomis, on the Black Sea. Ovid sought diversion through verse, yet "[poetic *utilitas*] also denotes the functional use of his poetry as a means to an end, as Ovid can hope to influence his friends to work for his transfer from Tomis."[49] Odoevskii's poetry helped him achieve this same goal to a certain degree: despite "scoffing at the State" he accepted, in 1837, the emperor's offer to enlist as an ordinary soldier in the Caucasus, where two years later he died of malaria.[50]

Poems, rumors, and hearsay nevertheless contained a gram of truth with regard to the Blagodatsk Eight. Timofei S. Burnashev, commander of Nerchinsk *zavody*, waited until 11 February 1827 to assign Trubetskoi and his companions to the mine, but nevertheless expected them to engage in hard labor.[51] They worked as a group from five o'clock to 11 o'clock in the morning, separate from the criminal convicts, and each had to extract 23 pounds of ore per shift. "The work was not onerous," Evgenii P. Obolenskii however later recalled, "it is generally fairly warm below ground, but when it did prove necessary to warm up I would take a hammer and quickly grow warm."[52] This suggests the labor may even have been voluntary, possibly except for a brief time when the Decembrists had to work double-shifts transporting ore (about which Obolenskii writes: "But for all this, our position was a fairly tolerable one…"[53]). In any case, criminal convicts often completed their quotas for them. Blagodatsk presented Decembrists sentenced to *katorga* with the greatest physical challenges they ever faced in exile.

However, the petty authoritarianism of a junior officer named Rik presented the Blagodatsk Eight with one of their greatest psychological challenges. Each small cell in which two men were placed was uncomfortable for just a little while, but in Burnashev's absence Rik locked the men in these cells for 18 hours a day. His reign lasted only a few days because it provoked a hunger-strike. A tense stand-off between guards and prisoners was only defused by Burnashev's timely return.[54] Another incident is described in a letter of 15 April 1827 to Burnashev from an Ensign Riuzakov, reporting the Decembrists had been discovered planning to escape. Had they seen their plans through, he explained, they could have gotten weapons from the soldiers' barracks. Riuzakov took unspecified "necessary measures" to disrupt the conspiracy and requested four additional soldiers to guard the state criminals.[55]

Riuzakov may just have been angling for a promotion. Nevertheless, his and others' fears had some basis in reality. In late March 1828 an official at the nearby Zerentui mine foiled a plot involving some 20 penal laborers and Decembrist Ivan I. Sukhinov, who was accused of planning to seize the guards' magazine and artillery, free the Decembrists then at Chita, and spark a mass revolt. The following November a military court, citing legislative actions between 1754 and 1817, sentenced Sukhinov and nine other defendants to 400 blows of the knout. This was a death sentence, as everyone knew. Others were sentenced to the lash. After two failed attempts Sukhinov managed to hang himself before he could be flogged. During the punishment of his fellow penal laborers the commanding officer urged executioners to flog them as hard as they could then ordered five summarily shot. One was still alive when he and the others were dumped into a pit. Sukhinov's body was dragged outside and thrown on top of them.[56] At one point Mikhail S. Lunin also planned a prison riot and mass jailbreak, but after finding no support chose instead to begin depriving himself of food in preparation for a solo escape attempt.[57] Other Decembrists later claimed to have devised escape plans, though how genuine these were is questionable. All the same, periodic riots among Siberia's seething mass of disaffected elements made officials queasy with fear at any hint the Decembrists were hatching plots. Gangs of fugitive exiles pillaged settlements in the Nerchinsk Mining District during 1827; and shortly before the Decembrists transferred to Petrovsk Zavod penal laborers there staged an uprising, "the legend of which lasted a long time among the local population."[58] Later, riots among convict and non-convict miners rocked Tomsk's gold mining industry between 1831 and 1833.

Although Burnashev's labor assignment conformed to the Blagodatsk Eight's sentence of "Nerchinsk *katorga*," it was merely provisional. Nicholas knew Blagodatsk could not accommodate the other 76 Decembrists sentenced to *katorga*. As with the 15 Decembrists sentenced to exile to settlement he was unsure where exactly to send them. This indecision, besides undermining the image of an iron-willed emperor, explains the caesura between the deportations of 4 August and 12 October 1827 shown in Table 3.1 above. Andrei E. Rozen later concluded that Nicholas halted the deportations because he feared that if all the Decembrists were sent to Nerchinsk rebellions would take place in the larger *zavody*.[59] But the tsar's decision to distribute Decembrists and soldier-Decembrists still in Peter-Paul fortress to other fortresses in Petersburg and Finland[60] paradoxically indicates a lack of concern with spreading the revolutionary bacillus.

In late August 1826, after as many as 27 Decembrists had already left for Siberia, the emperor settled upon what eventually proved a temporary location. Prior to his coronation ceremonies that same month he named Stanislav R. Leparskii, a russified Pole and major-general, to head what was soon officially called the Nerchinsk Commandant Administration. This ad hoc unit would exist until 1839, when the last Decembrists completed their *katorga* terms. Nicholas asked Leparskii to choose a site east of Lake Baikal that would serve for "the construction of a durable spacious prison based on the American solitary or penitentiary system."[61] Leparskii suggested Chita, a settlement of 300 residents midway between Verkhneudinsk and Nerchinsk founded during the late seventeenth century when the fur trade was booming. "Chita's residents were few and poor, like all *zavod* peasants," writes Rozen. "They lived in 20 huts and survived by farming and fishing the Ingoda River and Lake Oninsk, which abound in especially large and plump crucians." A local mine commander named Smol'ianinov made sure that residents fulfilled their duty to produce charcoal for Nerchinsk's smelteries.[62] Chita's dilapidated *ostrog* would serve as a prison until the American-style penitentiary, this state-of-the-art representation of Nicholas's dynamic response to a new breed of state criminals, could be built. The prison would ultimately prove as chimerical as his ability to repress dissent.

Rozen's apocryphal account of this discussion between the emperor and Leparskii is supported by the 31 August minutes of the first session of the "Special Committee for Determining the Legality of the Decembrists' Exile to *Katorga*" (*Osobyi komitet po opredelenuiu zakonodatel'nogo statusa ssylki dekabristov na katorgu*).[63] Dibich put together this assemblage that besides him included Benkendorf, Lavinskii, Leparskii, and Speranskii. Nicholas had already forced Speranskii to serve on the Supreme Criminal Court that tried and sentenced to death or lesser punishment many of his friends.[64] Now, out of a sadistic desire to further test this extraordinary and much-needed bureaucrat's loyalty, he was making Speranskii organize the details of their confinement. The minutes confirm that Chita *ostrog* was to be a temporary location for Decembrists still *en route* or in fortresses "if the sovereign emperor decides it will soon be appropriate to order their removal to Siberia." Nicholas had already ordered "special barracks" (*narochtye kazarmy*) built in Chita, but the Decembrists' ultimate destinations remained as yet undecided. A special force of 150 soldiers would guard them at Chita, and Leparskii would supervise the construction of a new prison wherever it would be located. Despite his lingering uncertainty, the minutes show Nicholas had decided to keep all those Decembrists sentenced to *katorga* in a single location, presumably to facilitate supervision, though he may have also worried about their influence if dispersed among various sites. Whatever his reasoning, this decision allowed the Decembrists to form counter-conduct communities in both Chita and Petrovsk Zavod.

Nicholas may have at first intended the Decembrist prison to be built in Akatui, a silver smeltery and prison near the Chinese (now Mongolian) border whose poisonous fumes reputedly caused birds to fall from the skies within a hundred-mile radius. But Leparskii and E. F. Kankrin's wife, who was the sister of Decembrist Artamon Murav´ev, dissuaded him from what would have been tantamount to a death sentence, and Leparskii suggested the prison be built in Chita, where the Decembrists were going to be anyway. Despite its small coalmine and lack of a *katorga* administration Nicholas agreed, though the delay until mid-December 1826 in ordering construction materials to Chita suggests he still retained second thoughts. Nonetheless, despite the delivery of rotten timber a stockade prison (though certainly not an American-style penitentiary) was completed there by August 1827.[65]

But if Nicholas was by August 1826 resolving what to do with the Decembrists exiled to *katorga*, he remained forever undecided about those exiled to settlement. In instructions to war minister Tatishchev dated 17 July Dibich listed the destinations for 13 Decembrists as follows: Apollon V. Vedeniapin—Viliuisk; Nikolai A. Chizhov—Olëk; Valer´ian M. Golitsyn—Kirensk; Mikhail A. Nazimov—Verkhne-Kolymsk; Nikolai S. Bobrishchev-Pushkin—Srednekolymsk; Nikolai F. Zaikin—Gizhinsk; Fedor P. Shakhovskoi—Turukhansk; Ivan F. Fokht—Berezov; Nikolai O. Mozgalevskii—Narym; Andrei I. Shakhirev—Surgut; Vasilii I. Vranitskii—Pelym; Semen G. Krasnokutskii—Verkhoiansk; Andrei N. Andreev—Zhigansk.[66] Verkhoiansk and Zhigansk, both inside the Arctic Circle, epitomize the severity characterizing all these locations, some of which had long been destinations for political exiles, others of which served this function after the Decembrists. However, "because certain of these places, according to the governor-general of Eastern Siberia

[Lavinskii], were found to be unsuitable for the settlement of exiles…" the Special Committee "made certain alterations to the list and informed the Chief of His Majesty's General Staff [Dibich] to bring them to the attention of the sovereign emperor."[67] Though most of these Decembrists were delivered to the designated locations, nearly all were permitted to relocate almost immediately.

*   *   *

Having sent the first two parties of Decembrists to Blagodatsk, Petersburg began deporting the rest to Chita. The new prison consisted of several barracks that enjoyed only indirect sunlight due to the surrounding stockade wall. Several Decembrists therefore paid workers to build them private huts inside the grounds.[68] Leparskii did nothing to prevent this. In September he ordered Trubetskoi's and Volkonskii's wives transferred from Blagodatsk to Nerchinsk Zavod because he could not guarantee their safety in the wake of recent escapes by criminal exiles.[69] Similar worries may have led the following month to the transfer of the Blagodatsk Eight to Chita, where the men's wives soon rejoined them and the Decembrist population rose to 47.

Whatever the reason for these transfers sources agree the Decembrists would have faced worse conditions without Leparskii, under orders to report bi-weekly to Nicholas about "how they conduct themselves, the disposition of their moods, whether they engage in labor, and everything that concerns them."[70] They were not to consort with other exiles and were forbidden to write letters to relatives or friends. There was, however, some inconsistency to these epistolary restrictions, with the Special Committee stating that Decembrists' wives could write letters on their behalf, while Nicholas demanded to see any letter personally written by a Decembrist. As it turned out Leparskii, through mistake or design, ignored most of his orders. His interest in the Decembrists was not keen enough for him to report on their moods or even their labor assignments, which he anyway never enforced; and not only did he allow contact with other exiles, but even allowed them to hire convicts as personal servants. Decembrists managed to send letters in ways that should not have been difficult to prevent. Writing from Petrovsk Zavod, Svistunov explained to one recipient that a Polish female domestic was helping him smuggle letters out by secreting them in book bindings and candles.[71]

In their memoirs most Decembrists recalled Leparskii fondly. According to Rozen he was an educated man who "knew Latin and was fluent and wrote in French and German, and read the great writers in these languages, but most importantly—he was a completely honorable man and had a kind heart."[72] However, Zavalishin had a more jaundiced view, contending that although kind he had not the courage of his convictions and primarily defended his own interests.[73] This view was shared by Svistunov, who secretly wrote his brother from Petrovsk Zavod: "Our commandant can be summed up in two words—he's a kind of Chinese mandarin, whose sluggishness, indecisiveness, and cowardice exceed all acceptable boundaries." Svistunov admitted that Leparskii was a "good man" who enjoyed a "reputation for incorruptibility," but believed he was hobbled by old age and fear. "He cannot say either yes or no." Some historians have suggested that Leparskii feared the emperor's spies. But according to Svistunov everyone understood he had "the right to ease our conditions."[74] Indeed, Nicholas did not want these men turned anymore into martyrs. Writing many years later the academician Mikhail V. Iuzefovich quoted Leparskii as having tearfully told him:

> The Sovereign called me to Petersburg and told me: "Stanislav Romanovich, I know that you love me and so I want to demand a huge sacrifice from you. I have no one else I can appoint in this instance. I need a man such as you, in whom I have complete faith; and who has a heart such as you. Go to Nerchinsk as commandant and ease the lot of the unfortunates there. I authorize you to do this. I know that you will agree to fulfill this duty with Christian compassion."[75]

Whether or not Iuzefovich's story is true, it remains that Nicholas prohibited some Decembrists' wives from joining them and demanded that others give up their children before doing so. In September 1826 the Special Committee ruled that children born to Decembrists in Siberia would be enrolled as state peasants and prevented from entering European Russia.[76] In 1833 the emperor ruled that for as long as their husbands were alive those wives who had joined them would be considered "the wives of penal laborers" and have their rights accordingly restricted. If they remained in Siberia after their husbands' deaths their nobiliary privileges would be returned; but if they returned to European Russia their rights would be restricted in ways he left unspecified.[77]

Yet Nicholas was also generous by turns. Historian M. A. Rakhmatullin has noted that Soviet historiography offers a lopsided and ultimately caricatured portrayal of him with regard to the Decembrists.[78] Western historians have been somewhat more evenhanded, noting, for example, that he gave not only permission but also 3,000 rubles and other assistance to the Frenchwoman Pauline Geueble after she asked to follow and marry Ivan V. Annenkov; and that after Mariia Volkonskaia and other wives arrived in Siberia and began petitioning him, he granted many of their appeals to improve prisoners' conditions. It should also be recalled that Nicholas reduced the sentences of nearly every Decembrist convicted by the Supreme Criminal Court, including those who were hanged (though of course it mattered little in the end): originally, the five sentenced to death were to be beheaded and quartered like Pugachev had been 50 years earlier. As a result of commutations and reductions both before and after the Decembrists were exiled, 31 escaped the gallows and nearly all those sentenced to *katorga* were released early.[79] Nicholas also assisted Decembrists' relatives to compensate for his punishment of their loved ones and breadwinners. In September 1827 Dibich gave him a long list citing relatives' ages, occupations, financial situations, and other information. After each entry Nicholas wrote his "resolution" of their cases. Thus he learned that the 68-year-old father of Andrei and Petr I. Borisov had reached class eight in the Table of Ranks, "has a sick wife, two daughters, and one [other] son, lacks in his impoverished condition any fortune whatsoever, and supports himself on only the pension of 200 rub[les] he receives each year." Nicholas's response: "Give him 400 rub[les]." Vladimir I. Shteingeil's deportation had left "[h]is wife and nine children in a disordered state, and his mother-in-law—wife [and apparently widow] of state councilor Vonifat´ev—in extreme poverty." Nicholas allowed Shteingeil's sons to be enrolled in the Cadets.[80]

None of these emoluments render Nicholas a saint. But when judging his punishment of the Decembrists historians seem to forget that he was a 29-year-old man who faced a revolt on his first day on the job—moreover, a revolt later shown to include plans to murder him and his family. Pavel Pestel had at one point tried to persuade Polish revolutionaries to assassinate the tsarevich.[81] Whereas Peter I has been lionized for crushing the rebellious *strel´tsy* (musketeers) who killed his relatives and sought his own death, Nicholas has paradoxically been demonized for doing the same to his nemeses, albeit with far less cruelty and bloodshed.

However one qualifies his treatment of the Decembrists, his easements regained the allegiance of many, as he intended they would. Despite having originally been sentenced to the "6th Category," that is, six years *katorga*, Aleksandr N. Murav´ev somehow became convinced the emperor had spared his life. In December 1826, during a stop in Irkutsk as part of his transfer from Iakutsk to the more salubrious Verkhneudinsk *okrug*, he wrote the tsar:

> Your Imperial Highness!
> All-Merciful Sovereign!
>   ... According to the Supreme Criminal Court's original sentence I was condemned to death [*sic*]; Your mercifulness granted me life! After that, dishonor and labor were the fate assigned me; but You, august sovereign, saved me from this horrible calamity! Finally, having pitied me, You, O sovereign, looked with a fatherly eye at one who was suffering, and instead of my distant exile mercifully ordered me assigned to a nearer and dearer place, and once again extended the thread of my life![82]

Writing during the late 1860s Aleksandr V. Podzhio reasoned that "[Nicholas] was not the culprit for all scurrilous Russia, the culprits were precisely those judges before whom I stood...." The emperor, he continued, "was no more, no less, than a brigade commander...."[83] This from a man Nicholas kept in prison for eight years.

Thanks to a combination of the emperor's and Leparskii's largesse, then, their sojourns at Chita and Petrovsk Zavod proved halcyon days for many Decembrists. With labor assignments completed by guards or criminal convicts who either volunteered or were paid, the exiles had time to play chess, read, and organize discussions and lectures. Some of the wealthier had relatives ship them their personal libraries, which at Chita totaled as many as 30,000 volumes, and so there was no shortage of reading material. Many learned foreign languages (Zavalishin reportedly learned 13) and produced "translations of favorite writers, including Gibbon, Caesar, Pascal, Montesquieu, Franklin, and many others."[84] Creation of a public library and school for local children by what became known as "The Academy" established a legacy which, despite the Decembrists' departing with the economic resources that had lifted Chita's natives and Cossacks out of poverty and alcoholism, helped the town later emerge as both Zabaikal´e's administrative center and home to a small but active elite who in the spirit of their predecessors promoted plays, balls, lotteries, and other cultural activities during the 1880s to raise funds for a shelter for exiles' children.[85]

The wealth of many Decembrists was indeed enormous. The Special Committee imposed strict limitations on the amount of money each was allowed. An individual could bring no more than 2,000 rubles to Siberia and receive from relatives no more than 1,000 a year. Governors of those *gubernii* to which they were assigned were to dispense these funds every month "or as they [saw] fit."[86] *En route* to exile, several Decembrists were forced to hand over the money they were carrying, though others managed to conceal theirs. Decembrist wives were not under the same monetary restrictions and brought their husbands more than they were allowed and received added funds from relatives. In the end financial rules like other rules were not enforced. "In the ten years they spent as state convicts, that is, until 1836," writes Barratt, "the Decembrists received from home almost 355,000 roubles in cash, and their wives another 778,000 roubles. And this was through official channels only."[87]

Yet many Decembrists were not as well off as the Trubetskois or Volkonskiis. Nicholas ordered those not receiving money from home be given a private's salary and "peasant-style winter and summer clothes."[88] Recipients may have looked this gift horse in the mouth, for it reeked of Nicolaevan humiliation. Nonetheless, 34 Decembrists accepted a subsidy of 114 rubles 23½ kopeks each. This impoverished group suffered at first; but in true Russian fashion the Decembrists soon formed cooperatives (*arteli*) that allowed everyone to live comfortably enough. Some took up handicrafts that in addition to being useful diversions earned money for the cooperatives.[89]

As of late January 1830, 72 Decembrists were living inside Chita's stockade.[90] "[W]e were packed in cells like herring in a box," Mikhail Bestuzhev later claimed.[91] Given that the Decembrists either lived separately with their wives or with two or three others in private quarters, Bestuzhev was exaggerating. Nonetheless, overcrowding was a problem and thus provokes the question: Why had the new prison not been designed to accommodate all the Decembrists assigned to Chita? There seems no good answer. Also something of a mystery is when Nicholas decided to transfer them because of this overcrowding to Petrovsk Zavod. Nikolai V. Basargin wrote that long before their transfer in September the prisoners became aware that another prison was being built at Petrovsk Zavod.[92] The emperor may have feared that Chita's deteriorating conditions would provoke them to escape. But if so, this foreboding superseded his earlier evident concern about placing them in the midst of a large population of criminal convicts, for unlike Chita Petrovsk Zavod was a *katorga* site *bona fide*.

Two hundred and fifty miles west of Chita in a shallow valley in what was then Verkhneudinsk *okrug*, Petrovsk Zavod is today called Petrovsk-Zabaikal´skii and is a 20-minute stop on the Trans-Siberian line. The exterior wall of one trackside building sports a huge mosaic showing several Decembrists and their wives seated round a table. When I briefly stopped in 1999 there was a life-size statue of Lenin that looked like it was made out of dough atop a small monument bearing bas-reliefs of eight of the revolutionaries. Despite being a full 1,089 versts from Nerchinsk Mining Bureau headquarters in Nerchinsk Zavod, Petrovsk Zavod fell within its administrative ambit. Founded in 1788 as both a metallurgical and *katorga* site by Nerchinsk's commandant Barbot de Marni, it began producing iron five years later. As of 1823 the *zavod* was yearly generating 18,000 to 30,000 poods of cast iron and 9,000 to 18,000 units of iron products like kettles and axes.[93] When the Decembrists arrived in 1830 Petrovsk's population was around 2,000. "A quarter of this population was comprised of officials, mining hands, serving and retired men of various classes, soldiers of the Department of Mines, old men who had served out their terms of labour, and so forth," observed Basargin:

> The rest, that is, three quarters of the population, were exiled workers or convicts deported for serious crimes, who had been punished with the knout and bore brand-marks—people, in short, excluded from society forever by their crimes and, more especially, their punishment, and therefore society's natural foes.[94]

These convicts built the prison the Decembrists were now being sent to. On 7 and 9 August two groups comprising 71 Decembrists, three of the five wives already in Siberia, Buriat retainers, guards, and Leparskii left Chita to walk to Petrovsk.[95] The parties covered between 20 and 30 versts a day and rested every third day. The women rode in carriages and if the men got tired they climbed into baggage carts. At one point the road was washed out and Leparskii ordered another one built so the ladies' carriages could proceed.[96]

Before leaving the Decembrists had viewed this journey with foreboding. But years later many nostalgically recalled the month and a half spent walking through Zabaikal´e's landscape as their best time in Siberia, if not their entire lives. Iakushkin:

> Fairly pleasant weather prevailing, this journey was, generally speaking, a delightful walk for us.... The Buriats were at our service, and carried our greatcoats, pipes, and so forth.... It was simply a pleasure for us, in comparison with our earlier life, to spend the greater part of the day in the open air....[97]

"Of our journey..., it can only be said that it was extremely pleasant for us and beneficial for our health," Mikhail Bestuzhev similarly recalled. "Indeed, it gave us new reserves of strength for many future years."[98] His brother Nikolai, who became among other things an artist while in Siberia, painted landscapes during the trek. One painting shows Decembrists leisurely gathered round campfires near yurts the Buriats had erected a month in advance.[99] The meadows, brooks, and gentle hills impressed everyone. Many felt like Basargin, who wrote, "So magnificent, so astoundingly beautiful is the countryside of Eastern Siberia, and of Transbaikalia in particular, that one cannot—and could not—help standing in wonder and rapture and gazing [*sic*] at the objects and scenery about one...."[100] The journey was infused with fresh air, a general sense of release, and even mirth:

> We ourselves practically died of laughter looking at our costumes and our comic procession, which almost always began with Zavalishin in a round hat with a monstrous brim and a kind of black coat of his own design that resembled a Quaker's caftan. Being small, he held a stick far taller than himself in one hand, and in the other a book which he read. Besides him came Iakushkin in a little jacket *à l'enfant*, then Volkonsky in a short, fur-trimmed jacket; then some in long-skirted sacristans' frock-coats, others in Spanish cloaks, others again in blouses—in such comically motley attire, in other words, that had we met some European fresh from the capital he would most certainly have thought that here was a mental asylum, and that the inmates were being taken for a walk.[101]

Comic relief was needed when on 21 and 23 September respectively, the two parties climbed the last ridge to gaze upon their destination, for "Petrovskiy Zavod was a real prison, not a makeshift reinforced strongpoint like Chita. It looked forbidding and depressing."[102] A large stockade surrounded a series of 12 one-story clapboard barracks, which at that time had no windows. Though the intimidating barracks appeared straight and true, convicts had in fact slapped together shoddy buildings that later proved fire hazards unable to withstand the cold. Nonetheless, life at Petrovsk would prove even easier than at Chita. For one thing, the new prison was large enough so that almost every man had his own private quarters.[103] For another, Leparskii grew ever more lax and allowed the following living arrangements: wives without children lived in husbands' quarters; some with children lived part of the week in private huts on prison grounds and part of the week in husbands' quarters without their children; and then there were those nuclear families that, according to what some Decembrists claimed was the "pretext" of illness, lived in the huts full-time.[104]

The Decembrists had plenty of free time to transform Petrovsk Zavod as they had Chita. In winter they paid guards to fulfill their assignment to grind rye; in summer, when assigned to level the prison grounds, "our principal responsibility," explained Svistunov in a letter home, "is to turn up, and this is quite enough."[105] Much time remained to focus almost exclusively on intellectual and cultural pursuits. Aleksandr P. Beliaev recalled participating in a "marvelous school of learning, in moral and intellectual as well as religious and philosophical terms."[106] They established a preparatory school to help local children get accepted to Nerchinsk's Mining Academy or, if especially talented, Petersburg's Mining Corps.[107] By the time the last prisoner left in 1839[108] they had amassed a library of as many as half a million volumes, founded a school for Buriat children, and so thoroughly altered the settlement through collective and individual pursuits that writer and diplomat Semën I. Cherepanov, who paid a visit in 1834, wrote, "It is possible to say that Petrovsk Zavod comprised for me none other than an academy or university with 120 [sic] academicians or professors."[109]

The Decembrists' activities at Petrovsk have been well-documented.[110] However, a largely unexplored issue is the safety of them and their families among so many violent offenders. Only one bit of evidence suggests they were ever in danger. On 9 March 1831 Leparskii ordered penal laborers Anfii Lobanov, Leontii Terent′ev, and Ivan Voroshilov transferred from Petrovsk because, several nights earlier, they broke into the home of Aleksandra Davydova, wife of Vasilii L. Davydov, and, reported Leparskii, "committed… a crime against the household…, wounding the legs of Davydova's Servant Girl [*Devka Sluzhanka*]…." Due to what seems to have been the attempted or accomplished rape there was "no hope they might continue to labor in the future at the local zavod…."[111] It is unclear if Davydova herself or anyone else was home at the time; but as many as seven of her children, including a two-year old boy, are known to have been with her at Petrovsk. Moreover, she was then pregnant with a daughter who would be born in July. Whatever did happen inside her home it must have disconcerted her as much as it did Leparskii.

Nevertheless, overall there seems to have been genuine communion between Decembrists and the criminal convicts who sometimes attended lectures at the Academy, made use of its library, worked as personal servants, and voluntarily fulfilled their labor assignments. "In all our time at Petrovsk," Mikhail Bestuzhev later recalled,

> not one servant ever sinned against us in either word or deed; and though there were hundreds of criminals serving the first years of

their prison sentences, never did we hear of property belonging to us missing—and there were thousands of opportunities for theft.[112]

Basargin similarly recalled that beginning in July 1831, when Nicholas allowed windows added to the barracks, convicts worked for two months in Decembrists' rooms performing this and other repairs. "And notwithstanding this not one of us lost even a pin. How was this to be explained?"[113]

How indeed? Most Decembrists penned their memoirs years later and so might simply have forgotten any petty thefts. Then again, these noblemen gave convicts money and were kind to them and so perhaps the latter felt they should not take anymore from them, and anyway they knew that if they did they would be severely punished. But more than anything, Basargin's and others' accounts reveal the powerful role class played in conditioning relations between these two groups. Obolenskii describes a convict leader at Blagodatsk named Orlov who let it be known the Decembrists were to be assisted, not molested,[114] in stark contrast to the way convicts often dealt with each other. The apparent lack of incidents like the Davydova break-in further indicates how the convict community's honor code, which Orlov invoked, commanded more fear than did executioners' blows. Yet if class conditioned relations *a priori* it also seems that the Decembrists, imbued as they were by Romantic ideals and moral altruism, adopted an approach that caused criminal convicts to genuinely respect them as fellow human beings. For the Decembrists *noblesse oblige* amounted to a form of subconscious cognitive behavior that contextualized and gave meaning to their predicament, and so their establishment of schools and lecture series carried deep emotional relevance that furthered their larger goal of enlightening the *narod*. This self-reinforcing behavior countered the traditional conduct of nobles and convicts alike and for a brief time generated communities the likes of which had never been seen in Russia. Therein lay the greatest threat to tsarism.

4
Extraordinary Decembrists: Chizhov, Lutskii, and Lunin

Decembrists began completing their *katorga* terms soon after arriving at Petrovsk Zavod, usually years ahead of schedule thanks to the successive reductions of their sentences. Take Petr N. Svistunov, originally sentenced to life but who ended up serving only nine years. In July 1826 Nicholas immediately reduced his term to 20 years followed by settlement; then, with his Coronation Manifesto of 22 August 1826, to 15 years; then an imperial ukase of 8 September 1832 reduced this to ten; finally, an imperial ukase of 14 December 1835 allowed Svistunov to be released to settlement.[1] Most Decembrists left Petrovsk between 1835 and 1837, the year S. R. Leparskii died. After some initial hesitation Leparskii's successor resumed his predecessor's lax attitude toward the Decembrists and, in this paternal guise, saw the last of them off two years later.[2]

The influx of dozens of known revolutionaries into the vast Siberian countryside set many officials' nerves on edge. Originally, no more than three Decembrists were to be assigned to a single settlement. But officials from top to bottom ignored this rule because of the paucity of locations with police forces large enough to provide adequate surveillance. Semën B. Bronevskii, governor-general of Eastern Siberia from 1834 to 1837, recommended they be assigned to distant regions of European Russia or even banished abroad because "little by little they will disseminate their ideas and, misconstruing the government, may be harmful."[3] Nicholas ignored Bronevskii. According to Barratt, "Some twenty-one Decembrists settled in or near Irkutsk, nine in the settlement of Minusinsk [in Eniseisk *guberniia*] and eight more in Kurgan, in... Tobolsk [*guberniia*]. There were groups of four or more men in Tobolsk itself, Turinsk, and Yalutorovsk."[4]

Release from the security of Petrovsk's community compelled Decembrists to confront individually the full impact of their banishment from European Russia. Some, like Zavalishin and the brothers Bestuzhev, prospered.[5] Others valued for their education and intellectual abilities managed to find work clerking in government offices.[6] But many others—despite the Third Section allowing extended visits to both other Decembrists and even the Turukhansk mineral springs[7]—found Siberia's provincial cities and towns more psychologically harrowing than prison. I. D. Iakushkin grimly noted the difference between life in prison and "release" to settlement:

> Out of fifty men, two went insane in Petrovskiy—[Iakov M.] Andreyevich and Andrey Borisov. However, settlements proved even more harmful in this respect than actual imprisonment. Of thirty men living in settlements, five went insane: [Fedor P.] Shakhovskoy and Nikolay Bobrishchev-Pushkin in Yeniseysk, [Andrei F.] Furman in Surgut, and [Vasilii I.] Vranitskii and [Andrei V.] Ental'tsev in Yalutorovsk.[8]

Besides the awareness they were always being watched, slander and random denunciations, writes O. S. Tal'skaia in her analysis of the relationship between administrators and Decembrists in Western Siberia, probably explain why Ental'tsev and others went mad. In 1830 authorities received an anonymous letter claiming that Ental'tsev, then in Ialutorovsk, had maintained an illegal correspondence with local clergymen during his earlier sojourn in Berezov. An investigation amounting to a "mass interrogation" of local residents was begun, though most attested to Ental'tsev's innocence. A year later, Osip V. Gorskii wrote Benkendorf that Ental'tsev and two other Decembrists were spreading sedition throughout the region. Gorskii had been arrested on Senate Square and convicted and exiled by the Supreme Criminal Court but always maintained his innocence, and so was probably trying to ingratiate himself with Benkendorf, whom he was also petitioning for permission to leave Berezov. (With the help of Tobol'sk's governor Gorskii had already managed to wangle a 1,200-ruble annual stipend out of Petersburg, ostensibly for having served in the military.[9]) Another investigation ensued but concluded only that Gorskii was "a terrible man whose name frightens children." Nonetheless, Ental'tsev was by now a marked man. Was he really infecting Ialutorovsk's residents with seditious ideas? It is impossible to know for certain, but after Ialutorovsk's mayor made a similar claim Nicholas ordered Ental'tsev and fellow Decembrist Vasilii K. Tizengauzen sent to Iakutsk if they were found guilty. Fortunately for them another mass interrogation established their innocence. Ental´tsev's problems still did not go away. In 1837 police raided his home after learning he was stockpiling weapons in preparation to assassinate tsarevich Alexander during his visit to Siberia, but found he had simply bought some old gun carriages to salvage their iron fittings. Tobol´sk governor Khristofor Kh. Povalo-Shveikovskii nonetheless launched another investigation, and war minister A. I. Chernyshev and Western Siberia governor-general Petr D. Gorchakov, who, writes Tal´skaia, was "distinguished by his especial intransigence towards the Decembrists," added to the harassment. Ental´tsev eventually lost his mind and died in 1845.[10]

Attestations by police, constables, mayors, governors, and governors-general show that surveillance over the Decembrists was extensive. Petersburg received a monthly report on each prisoner, whose activities were also regularly reported to local officials. In 1852, for example, Oëk *volost*'s clerk reported to Irkutsk *okrug*'s land constable about Aleksandr L. Kuchevskii, who had been assigned to the village of Tungututskaia in 1839. Kuchevskii was an oddity among the Decembrists. According to Zavalishin, who clearly loathed him, Major Kuchevskii was arrested for planning to torch Astrakhan with the goal of looting the city. It is not clear when this happened or whether he considered himself a revolutionary, but Kuchevskii ended up being incarcerated and then exiled to Petrovsk Zavod with the Decembrists, who by then had nicknamed this "enigmatic personality" and would-be arsonist "Fire-Major." Also known as "Bump" for the welts he raised on his forehead during religious prostrations, Kuchevskii had alienated cellmates in Peter-Paul with his sanctimonious proselytizing. Nikolai Bestuzhev usually called him "Lukich," after his patronymic, but also "Lukach" or "Kulich" because he would request large amounts of onions (*luk*) during religious fasts or similar quantities of cakes (*kulichi*) during Easter Week. When he begged for donations for a non-existent wife Kuchevskii did nothing to enhance his stature. After release from Petrovsk he purchased and married a young girl from the local peasantry. Zavalishin claims that he renounced piety and routinely beat the girl, though the Oëk clerk's 1852 report describes him as living a "quiet life" and "engaged in the reading of spiritual books."[11]

Long before most of those sentenced to *katorga* were released, the small group of Decembrists originally exiled to settlement was enduring isolation in locations much harsher than those to which Petrovsk's residents were now being sent. Andrei I. Shakhirev, a lieutenant in the Chernigov Regiment that "mutinied" in the Ukraine, was the first Decembrist exiled to settlement. Assigned to Surgut, a remote city (*gorod*) of just over 500 inhabitants in Tobol´sk *guberniia*, he lived with two Cossacks who watched his every move. Shakhirev arrived without a kopek to his name, and until he began receiving funds from home survived for over a year thanks to a small stipend from Tobol´sk governor D. N. Bantysh-Kamenskii. In May 1828 Shakhirev unexpectedly died. Because the nearest official authorized to autopsy the body was 1,700 versts away, it was buried without determining cause of death. Shakhirev's estate was valued at over 2,000 rubles in money and property at that point, but not until 1832 did relatives receive just 59 ruble-*assignats*. The rest was apparently embezzled. Like Shakhirev, Andrei F. Furman, a captain from the same regiment, was assigned to the far north, to the village of Kondinsk in Berezov *okrug*. To conceal it from Petersburg, Bantysh-Kamenskii paid him a stipend out of an emergency food fund for natives. Furman later received several hundred rubles from his father and sister. He died in Kondinsk in 1835, two years after his request for a transfer to Tobol´sk was refused and after he had sired two children with a young peasant named Mar´ia Shchepnina, who inherited his hundreds of rubles of debt. At Benkendorf's and Tobol´sk's deputy governor's instigation Furman's relatives gave Shchepnina 4,360 ruble-*assignats* which, even after the debts were paid, left her with a windfall of 3,426 rubles.[12]

Iakutsk *oblast* was the harshest location to which Decembrists were assigned. Ten arrived there between 1826 and 1828, including Aleksandr A. Bestuzhev and Matvei I. Murav´ev-Apostol, each of whose sentence had been reduced from *katorga*. Seven of the ten were soon relocated to Irkutsk or Eniseisk *guberniia* or to the Caucasus. In June 1829 Murav´ev-Apostol obtained a transfer to Omsk *oblast*. This left only two Decembrists in Iakutiia. In August 1831 Governor-general A. S. Lavinskii gave Andrei N. Andreev permission to transfer to Irkutsk *guberniia* to live with Nikolai P. Repin, who had completed his term at Petrovsk Zavod a month earlier and acquired a house in Verkholensk. Tragically, both men perished in the fire that consumed their home in late September, which hints at these noblemen's difficult transition to rural life.[13] There was now just one Decembrist in Iakutiia: Nikolai A. Chizhov.

Analysis of the Chizhov case reveals much about the relationship between administrators and Decembrists. Sentenced by the Supreme Criminal Court for "[h]aving belonged to a secret society and acknowledging and agreeing to the goal of mutiny,"[14] Lieutenant Chizhov was stripped of his rank and privileges and assigned to the village of Olëk (later renamed Olëkminsk) on the Lena River 400 miles southwest of Iakutsk, where he arrived on 1 September 1826.[15] Originally a stockade blockhouse (*ostrozhok*) established in 1635 as a fur collection depot, Olëk boasted all of 54 people as of 1823—mostly civil servants, merchants, clergymen, and their families.[16] A more desolate place would have been hard to find. Sometime in early 1832 Irkutsk governor Ivan B. Tseidler (who administered Iakutsk *oblast*) received a petition from Chizhov mysteriously dated 2 June 1826, that is, before his arrival in Olëk. The date is all the more curious because Chizhov wrote that he had been there for some time, but was having difficulty finding permanent lodgings because locals found him suspicious. Despite his apparent confusion Chizhov lucidly appealed for a transfer to "Iakutsk, or some other place, where medical help might be located...."[17] Chizhov's malady is not known, but after putting a question mark beside the date Tseidler dutifully forwarded the letter to Lavinskii. On 2 August 1832 Lavinskii relayed Chizhov's request to Benkendorf, noting, "For my part I have no objection to transferring Chizhov to Iakutsk, where at present there are no State criminals [i.e., Decembrists]...." That same day Lavinskii also replied to Tseidler. Most interesting about this second letter, in light of his just having tacitly acknowledged Chizhov's right to petition for a transfer, is Lavinskii's comment that "the right of travel granted to other exile-settlers by his Highness... certainly does not extend to State criminals...." The incompatibility of these statements is somewhat mitigated by his next line to Tseidler, emphasizing that Decembrists already assigned to settlements near Petrovsk Zavod were absolutely forbidden to change locations, for if this happened just once "such news will inevitably carry over to those held in Petrovsk Zavod."[18]

Besides not wanting to fuel Volkonskaia's and the other Decembrist wives' relentless petitioning, Lavinksii was probably then concerned by events that would eventually culminate in the so-called Omsk Affair, which will be discussed in Chapter 5. For now, it is sufficient to note that Petersburg had transferred 2,000 Polish soldiers to Omsk following suppression of the Polish Uprising, and by late 1831 fears were spreading that these soldiers had brought with them the cholera that played a role in the uprising. This in turn sparked rumors of a mass exodus of exiles. Rumors were also circulating that Konstantin Pavlovich, Nicholas's brother who had been in charge of Poland and died from cholera, was not dead but living in Siberia and would soon lead a popular rebellion. At the time of Lavinskii's 1832 letter to Tseidler Siberian gendarmes also found that "state criminals" were exchanging letters;[19] and there were reports that O. V. Gorskii, then assigned to Tara in Western Siberia, was conspiring with Polish exiles. These and other rumors influenced decisions affecting all the Decembrists.

Irrespective of these goings-on, Lavinskii's contradictory responses to Benkendorf and Tseidler reveal his fulcrum-like role in developing policy *vis-à-vis* Decembrists. He had already exerted considerable influence over the center's policy decisions, as his participation in both the Special Committee and Secret Committee shows. Now, in his letters, he was suggesting a liberal approach to Benkendorf while insisting to Tseidler that such an approach was impossible. This allowed him, as necessary, either to yield to Benkendorf if the latter insisted on a hard-line approach or to reverse himself and simply allow Tseidler to do what he proposed. As it turned out Benkendorf agreed Chizhov could leave Olëk but forbade Iakutsk as a destination. He failed to name a substitute, however, which gave Lavinskii all the leeway he needed to order Chizhov to Aleksandrovsk Zavod, a state distillery near Irkutsk "where there may be… medical aid… and where he may be kept under surveillance as a state criminal…." (Lavinskii really liked this phrase "state criminal.") In January 1833 subordinates reported Chizhov's successful transfer.[20]

However, within a year officials moved Chizhov yet again to a small nearby village called Mota.[21] Why is not clear. Documents show the transfer occurred without Benkendorf's knowledge, though it is uncertain whether Lavinskii or Tseidler were in the dark as well. As for Chizhov, Mota appealed to him no more than had Olëk. He wrote his mother back in Russia about his displeasure and, in mid-1833 and sharing Benkendorf's mistaken impression that her son was still in Aleksandrovsk, she petitioned state officials to assign him to a Siberian Line Battalion (a request incidentally at odds with Chizhov's earlier claims of illness). Chizhov simultaneously wrote Tseidler on 20 June to complain he did not have the skills needed to survive in Mota because "agriculture is almost non-existent, and all of the industry consists of preparing lumber and firewood for the city of Irkutsk…." He asked to be moved to the village of Smolenskoe, where he knew there to be a flour mill along the Olëk River and believed it possible "to build another useful establishment…," for places along the river "are all good, as I've learned from questioning the locals." He even asked Tseidler for "the necessary means" to help start his venture. Tseidler forwarded the request to Lavinskii, who ignored Chizhov's entrepreneurial dreams but did fulfill his mother's request by assigning the 30-year-old to Irkutsk's 14th Siberian Line Battalion. Chizhov served in the Siberian military until 26 February 1843, when he retired and returned to European Russia, where he died five years later.[22]

The Chizhov case demonstrates the degree to which the Decembrists, despite being convicts, believed they could exercise personal initiative to improve their lots. In addition to the well documented petitions from Petrovsk, Chizhov's petitions resemble those by Ivan F. Shimkov, who was assigned to the village of Baturinskaia near Verkhneudinsk and asked to join other Decembrists living in Minusinsk.[23] The Chizhov case exhibits another feature common to Decembrists' efforts to change their circumstances: the intercession of a family member or other benefactor. Decembrists' wives were instrumental in obtaining concessions from both Leparskii and Nicholas; but relatives back home were also important. For instance, after release from Petrovsk Zavod Svistunov was assigned to the small village of Kamenka, 110 versts downriver from Irkutsk. Thanks to an appeal from his brother-in-law Count Aleksandr A. de Bal´men, a major-general in the imperial suite, Svistunov relocated to Kurgan, Eniseisk *guberniia*, where there were already a considerable number of Decembrists.[24] Indeed, individuals used petitions and family connections to shield individuals even before the Supreme Criminal Court began its proceedings. P. V. Il´in found that proximity to the royal family and other fortuitous connections, rather than degree of guilt, primarily determined individuals' sentences. He notes, for instance, that Nicholas ordered charges dropped against Lev P. Vitgenshtein, despite his membership in the Southern Society and "obvious closeness to P. I. Pestel."[25] Vitgenshtein's father sat on the State Council and commanded Russia's Second Army, whereas it was Pestel's misfortune to have as a father Ivan B. Pestel, one of Siberia's most corrupt governors ever who was put on trial by Alexander I. Pestel senior never legally paid for his crimes, but he saw his son hanged by Nicholas. Proximity to power therefore cut both ways. However, petitioning—an important ritual of political exile—often yielded positive results. Like petitioners before and after Chizhov's mother managed to alter decisions within a political environment wherein arbitrariness superseded regulatory procedures. Moreover, emperors' and top officials' frequently favorable responses suggest they craved the acknowledgement of their authority that petitioning provided. By granting or withholding mercy (*milost*) even *okrug* commanders could exercise an exquisitely sovereign form of power.

The Chizhov case also demonstrates how bureaucratic procedures linking Petersburg to *guberniia* administrations broke down or were simply ignored. Lavinskii personally made most decisions regarding Chizhov, though appears to have sought Benkendorf's approval in nearly every instance, after which he would order Tseidler to implement his instructions. But the chain of command was ignored at least once, as made clear by the report showing Chizhov was in Mota, not Aleksandrovsk, as generally believed. It is unclear whether Lavinskii or

Tseidler knew of Chizhov's actual whereabouts before Benkendorf found out,[26] but intentional or not (and despite one historian's claim that only the emperor or Third Section could act on petitions[27]), circumvention of chains of command occurred at all levels, largely because the hierarchical relationship between governors-general and the center was not clearly established. For instance, due to his "corrupting influence on the probity of the administration," Governor-general Gorchakov at one point categorically refused Benkendorf's recommendation that Vladimir I. Shteingeil be transferred from Tara to Tobol´sk.[28] If governors-general believed they knew better than the Third Section chief, subordinates sometimes held the same opinion of them. After extended indecision due to a transition in governors-general, the commander of Verkhneudinsk *okrug* unilaterally ordered I. F. Shimkov sent from the village of Baturinskaia to Fort Tsurukhaituevsk on the Chinese border. After he became the new governor-general, Nikolai S. Sulima granted Shimkov's petition to return to Baturinskaia because, he agreed, Tsurukhaituevsk was too "harsh" a location.[29]

Finally, an abstract but no less important theme emerging from the Chizhov case, as well as those of Shimkov, Nikolai I. Lorer,[30] and other Decembrists, is that any personal cruelty Nicholas exhibited towards the Decembrists pales in comparison to the institutionalized cruelty characterizing exile during Stalin's rule, when assignment as a state criminal to the GULag approximated a death sentence. It is true that after the Decembrists conditions for political exiles in tsarist Russia worsened, as Dostoevskii's and the *narodovol´tsy*'s situations make clear, but even then nobles enjoyed privileges and protection that would have been inconceivable for commoners. After 1917 the relationship between social privilege and protection became inverted, so that the deaths of Osip Mandelstam and other social elites occurred as a matter of course.

The benefits of class privilege were made even starker by the case of the soldier-Decembrists—a group that for the most part comprised junior officers and foot soldiers sentenced by courts-martial rather than the Supreme Criminal Court. Despite ascertaining their lead roles in the conspiracy to topple him from the throne, Nicholas, as we have seen, often made allowances for Decembrist noblemen; but against their underlings he vented his wrath to the full. This difference in treatment turned on questions of class and domestic politics: after hanging five Decembrist noblemen Nicholas restrained himself against the others out of consideration for their social standing. To have actually seen through to the end the original 36 sentences of death would have been a reckless act he probably could not have survived, and he undoubtedly thought of his father Paul, murdered by courtiers for his despotic behavior. But when it came to punishing junior officers and foot soldiers Nicholas felt no such compunction. Indeed, to do so was his solemn duty.

The as many as 1,000 innocent bystanders killed on 14 December are in some ways better remembered than the lower-ranking insurgents fired at by loyal troops. In the days following the revolt 702 soldiers and sailors were arrested and incarcerated within Peter-Paul's casements. The following summer most were sent to penal battalions in the Caucasus, where disease and warrior tribesmen killed them like flies. Nicholas ordered especially severe punishments for soldiers of the Chernigov Regiment, which under Sergei I. Murav´ev-Apostol had rebelled on 30 December and maneuvered pointlessly around Kiev for a few days until being decimated. Military courts sentenced Murav´ev-Apostol's subordinate officers Mikhei Shutov, Prokofii Nikitin, and Alimpii Borisov to 12,000 blows via the gauntlet and to *katorga* for life. Another 52 junior officers and 102 soldiers received sentences of between 1,000 and 6,000 gauntlet blows followed by assignment to the Caucasus. Three other regulars received sentences of 12,000 blows for having also participated in the Semënovskii Mutiny five years earlier.[31]

Soldiers in the gauntlet used the *prut´ia*, a long flexible switch, which Peter I learned of during his tours of Europe and introduced to Russia. Nearly every army in Europe employed the gauntlet, but in Russia the "street" victims had to tread like Jesus to Calvary was considerably longer, and so they were more likely to die there than elsewhere. The victim was stripped to the waist and had each arm tied to a musket. Each musket was held by a soldier who dragged him through two columns numbering up to 1,000 soldiers, each charged with delivering a sharp blow across the back. Officers watched from outside the gauntlet to ensure every soldier fulfilled his gruesome duty. Victims who collapsed were put on carts and pulled through the gauntlet so the procedure could continue. "The punishments often resulted in the offender's death," writes Bruce Adams. "In Nicholas's reign the number of strokes was reduced to 600 during peacetime, but this was still more than enough to kill."[32] After doctors were assigned during Nicholas's reign they could halt proceedings if they sensed the man was about to die. He would be sent to hospital for the time it took him to recover then subjected to the blows still due him. Soldier-Decembrists sentenced to many thousands of blows would have experienced this mind-bending to-and-fro several times, for which they had their "Little Father" the tsar to thank, since he had to personally approve any punishment over the norm.[33] The gauntlet was eventually proscribed by the 1863 military reforms.

After nearly all the soldier-Decembrists were punished Nicholas ordered the 14 still in Peter-Paul further interrogated to expose what he believed were their key roles in the conspiracy. In July 1826 minister of war A. I. Tatishchev asked Ivan I. Dibich to pursue their cases. In November, the emperor ordered six of the 14 assigned to border units and the rest court-martialed.[34] On 22 January 1827 the Moscow Guard Regiment's military court sentenced two of these men—Junior Officer Aleksandr N. Lutskii and Private Nikolai Povetkin—to death. Four months later, the emperor reduced their sentences to 20 lashes of the knout and *katorga* for life, but then amnestied both from the knout. Lutskii and Povetkin began marching to *katorga* in Siberia the following June. That same month a military court sentenced Peter-Paul's last few soldier-Decembrists to between 6,000 and 8,000 blows in the gauntlet and *katorga* for life. A. D. Margolis writes that these six men walked the gauntlet at the end of June, though for the reason just indicated, they could not have received all their blows at once. They seem to have left for Siberia in late summer or early autumn 1828.

Unlike the Decembrists, who rode into Siberia in sleighs or wagons, the soldier-Decembrists marched on foot, connected to common criminals by a long chain of manacles and enduring hardships and humiliations no aristocrat-Decembrist ever suffered. Ironically, proximity to these commoners was what allowed Lutskii, and later, fellow soldier-Decembrist Semën Rytov, to exchange names during the march. Facilitated by poor record-keeping and official nonchalance, this practice was common among Siberian exiles and often allowed experienced recidivists to trick first-time offenders into serving their own, usually much harsher, sentences. But this practice was exceedingly rare among Russia's early political prisoners, and Lutskii's adoption of it is our first indication of what an extraordinary individual he was. Moreover, he used it to *his* advantage, not that of the other convict.

Lutskii and Rytov were as a consequence delivered to settlements in Eniseisk *guberniia* instead of to Nerchinsk *katorga*. As for the soldier-Decembrists deported later, Gavril Mezentsov was redirected to the Caucasus and the other five arrived in Irkutsk no later than November 1828. Of these, Povetkin, sentenced alongside Lutskii, was debilitated by either his imprisonment, punishment, or the march, and remained in Irkutsk City Hospital until 1832, when he left to commence his *katorga* term at the Aleksandrovsk distillery. Nicholas amnestied him in March 1849, after which he settled in the region and died in 1855, the same year as the tsar. In March 1829 the four other soldier-Decembrists arrived with a party of criminal convicts at Petrovsk Zavod, where Leparskii kept them under strict supervision and in far different circumstances than those the

Decembrist noblemen would soon enjoy. In June 1830, to forestall any meeting between these two groups, he transferred them to Nerchinsk Zavod where they were reunited with Rytov and Lutskii, who had since been recaptured. Lutskii will be discussed momentarily; but for now it should be noted that with the exception of Trofim Fedotov, who was released from *katorga* in 1841 due to illness, the soldier-Decembrists labored at Nerchinsk Zavod like regular convicts until 1849, when an imperial amnesty released them to settlement. On 26 August 1856 Alexander II freed all the Decembrists and gave them the option of returning to European Russia. But he rejected the soldier-Decembrists' petitions to return, and so each finished his days in Nerchinsk *okrug*.[35]

Because he exchanged identities and was mistakenly assigned to Eniseisk *guberniia* Lutskii did not arrive in Irkutsk with the other soldier-Decembrists in 1828. The Lutskii affair warrants attention because it contrasts decidedly with the circumstances facing most Decembrists and, like the Chizhov case, highlights certain features of the exile system. Whereas Lieutenant-Captain Nikolai Bestuzhev—whose role in the conspiracy was central[36]—positively flourished in exile as a kind of Renaissance man, Junior Officer Aleksandr Lutskii—"who was in all probability not a member of the secret Decembrist societies"[37]—felt smothered by his banishment. Both shared a passionate desire for freedom, yet this led to very different outcomes because of their contrasting stations in life. Scion of an aristocratic Petersburg family, Bestuzhev turned exile to his advantage, becoming among other things a painter, craftsman, ethnographer, and teacher. With his brother Mikhail he built a home in Selenginsk, in Zabaikal´e, their place of settlement after Petrovsk, operated a farm and other business concerns, and tutored local children. Nikolai became one of the first ethnographers of the Buriats, married a Buriat woman, and traveled throughout Eastern Siberia. A commercially successful landscape and portrait painter, he died in Siberia in 1855. Burial in Siberia was about the only thing Lutskii shared with Bestuzhev. Born in or around 1804 in Bobricha village, Novgorod *guberniia*, Lutskii was the son of a petty official who had gained noble status through military service and owned no serfs. In 1821, a year after he joined the army, Lutskii achieved the same junior officer rank he held when arrested. In the army he befriended Nikolai Bestuzhev's younger brother Aleksandr.[38]

Lutskii paid one Agafon Nepomniashchii 60 rubles to exchange names during their march together into Siberia. *Brodiagi* routinely used the pseudonym *Nepomniashchii* ("I-don't-remember") to hide their identities. However, we know that Agafon was a state peasant from Kiev *guberniia* who was sentenced for *brodiazhestvo* and destined for the village of

Bol´shekemchugskaia in Eniseisk *guberniia*. This is where convoy guards left Lutskii while Nepomniashchii continued on, offering no protest and passing through Irkutsk on 26 January 1829 on his way to Nerchinsk.[39] Officials did not learn about the real Lutskii's whereabouts until June 1829, thanks to a letter he addressed to relatives asking for help. They arrested and incarcerated him in Krasnoiarsk's city jail that same month.[40] Given what would have been the difficulty of living in Bol´shekem-chugskaia, this letter surely reflects Lutskii's desperation rather than fool-ishness. No later than September, officials transferred Lutskii to Irkutsk's city jail so Governor-general A. S. Lavinskii could keep better tabs on him.[41] On 1 October the emperor ordered a "painstaking investigation" into the Lutskii affair. GUVS did conduct an investigation, though how painstaking it was is another matter. In any case, by mid-November Nicholas had learned enough to order Lutskii punished for this new crime and sent to Nerchinsk as originally intended. Benkendorf ordered Lutskii be given 90 birch blows and Tseidler had him punished on 23 January 1830.[42] Less than a month later Lutskii—who accord-ing to his rap sheet stood five-and-a-half feet tall and had red hair and gray eyes—arrived at Novozerentuisk mine to begin his *katorga* term.[43]

In addition to red hair and gray eyes Lutskii was distinguished from other prisoners by his determination. The following May, as soon as the thaw set in, he fled Novozerentuisk and returned to Eniseisk *guberniia*, this time traveling to Minusinsk *okrug* where a small num-ber of Decembrists lived. Officials found him there nine months later and returned him to Irkutsk in early June. For this second escape he received 16 lashes of the *plet* and was again imprisoned, albeit this time chained to a wheelbarrow.[44] There is some indication Lutskii escaped again in 1831, returned to Eniseisk *guberniia*, and worked under a pseu-donym in the Kamenskii distillery. If so, he seems to have been there only a month before being rearrested. Whether or not this escape act-ually took place, records show that GUVS officials were confused about his location that year.[45]

In late February 1831, in response to criticism for losing track of Lutskii, chief of Nerchinsk *zavody* Stepan P. Tatarinov addressed a letter to both Lavinskii and Leparskii:

Keeping watch over all such exiles gathered from almost the entire Empire and held here [in Nerchinsk *okrug*] in confinement is an impossibility because there are no special buildings. Hence the mines and factories are used as prisons and filled with exiles confined pending decisions, with many chained to wheelbarrows for brief periods because of escape attempts.[46]

Tatarinov pointedly added that people originally sent to Nerchinsk *katorga* "for escapes and insignificant crimes" were escaping and going on to commit "murders, robberies, and other serious crimes...." Much more familiar with *katorga* than his superiors, Tatarinov warned that besides silver and lead, Nerchinsk was producing a new criminal class that threatened the region.

Following his 1831 capture Lutskii disappears from the documentary record until September 1835, when a letter from EOGU to GUVS reported that he was "sent with a Cossack from Eniseisk's city regiment to Irkutsk to cut timber" and miraculously escaped yet again. Lutskii had before this been reassigned to Nerchinsk *katorga*, and so the fact that he was allowed to leave on a timber-cutting expedition suggests he had earned administrators' trust. He was soon captured and delivered once more to Irkutsk jail. Upon reviewing Lutskii's record, Governor-general Bronevskii informed Petersburg he intended to reassign him to the north Pacific coast, "to Okhotsk, to the Saltworks, under strict guard...."[47] Okhotsk was one of Siberia's grimmest *katorga* sites and its conditions could not have contrasted more with those of Petrovsk. Fortunately for Lutskii Petersburg countermanded Bronevskii and ordered him kept in Irkutsk jail, where administrators thought he was until early March 1837, when Tatarinov learned he had exchanged names with a prisoner named Semën Elkin and under this name tried to escape during transfer to the Kuenskie gold fields in Nerchinsk *okrug*. Lutskii was now in Nerchinsk Zavod's jail, reported Tatarinov: "He personally asked to remain in Nerchinsk Zavod, though in the prison, otherwise there will be no hope of keeping him from escaping during assignment to the Kuenskie works." In December GUVS's Governing Council reached the same conclusion, deciding that with Lutskii securely in jail it was best to keep him there.[48]

In 1838 Lutskii married a barber's daughter named Mariia Portnova. He completed his *katorga* term in May 1850 and was released to settlement. He attempted no more escapes. Aleksandr and Mariia later settled near Nerchinsk *okrug*'s Kultuminsk mine and eventually had a total of eight children. Lutskii reportedly became a farmer, though Margolis adds that he received a remarkably generous government stipend of 300 silver rubles per year. If so, this dispensation suggests Petersburg was trying to placate this trouble-maker with funds for his large family. Alexander II's 1856 amnesty initially excluded Lutskii as it did the other soldier-

Decembrists.[49] However, on 1 December 1857 Lutskii received permission to leave. Like the stipend, this probably owed much to Lutskii's relentless determination and to petitioning as well. Intending to return to Bobricha, Lutskii and his family departed Zabaikal´e in 1859 but got no further than Irkutsk because some of his children fell ill. He remained in Irkutsk for nearly a year, during which he exhausted his travel allowance. With no money to continue, the Lutskiis returned to Zabaikal´e. Whether he felt defeated by circumstance or was content to remain in his humble surroundings we do not know, but the lash-scarred man lived to be 78 years old, dying on 24 February 1882 in Nerchinsk Zavod.[50]

The Lutskii affair in particular and the soldier-Decembrists in general show that both Nicholas I and Alexander II regarded them, in their own way, as more offensive than Trubetskoi, Obolenskii, or others convicted by the Supreme Criminal Court. Birthright and rank as well as the tsars' need to demonstrate sovereign power explain this difference in treatment. The punitive line drawn between aristocrats on the one hand and petty nobles and commoners on the other reflected an essentialist view of human nature. The former were relieved of corporal punishment and manual labor: their punishment boiled down to banishment from society and as such reflected Nicholas's didactic intent to instruct the mind rather than the body. But the sensibilities of soldier-Decembrists who had at best been on the edges of society were unfamiliar to the Romanovs, and so all that remained was to punish their bodies in the traditional manner of scourging. This simultaneous enforcement of rehabilitative punishment on the one hand and retributive punishment on the other also highlights a duality inherent to sovereign power. Nicholas initially ordered Lutskii knouted; spared the knout, Lutskii was nonetheless flogged with the birch rod and *plet*. The Decembrist noblemen did not suffer corporal punishment. It may be objected that five were hanged—yet even this was a psychological punishment directed primarily at Russia's elite. The division between punishing the mind and the body was further reflected by the agency of the Decembrists themselves: whereas aristocratic Decembrists could escape their confinements via the intellectual activities they collectively pursued at Chita and Petrovsk Zavod, Lutskii never had the same luxury (and may not in any case have availed himself of it). His only recourse was to physically distance himself from his exilic locations.

Although extraordinary, Lutskii's numerous escapes highlight two general themes. First, escape from *katorga* was neither uncommon nor especially difficult. Administrative circulars from the 1820s routinely listed fugitives wanted by officials. "[With] the arrival of springtime there is the inevitable escape and *brodiazhestvo* of exiles and other similar people," IGP reported in May 1827. In November that year the Tomsk administration reported: "exiles Aleksandr Dunaev, Fedor Masal´skii, and Vasilii Syshchenko have escaped...."[51] These and numerous other circulars indicate the poor maintenance of the exile system's physical plant as well as Siberian officials' notoriously low pay, which in turn led to corruption and systemic dysfunction. That said, Lutskii's escapes were so numerous as to raise the possibility that some officials helped him, perhaps out of sympathy or simply because he bribed them. Second, Lutskii so challenged the integrity of the system that he seems to have wrangled what was essentially the pay-off of a 300-ruble stipend in return for his tacit acceptance of his status as an exile. Tatarinov's letter complaining about petty offenders being turned into serious criminals indicates how Lutskii's escapes stimulated a host of fundamental concerns. If Nerchinsk's chief was questioning Petersburg's policies, what might other officials have been thinking? Tatarinov's very line of questioning may actually have led to the decision—which the emperor would almost certainly have had to approve—to grant Lutskii the stipend. As next chapter's discussion of the Omsk Affair shows, Nicholas could not tolerate an examination of authority, and so he may have thought it best to hush up the Lutskii affair rather than allow it to expose the fragility of his entire apparatus.

Lutskii therefore emerges as a quite different type of Decembrist from those generally written about. His open contempt for authority involved an almost Christ-like passion that denied the pain of the flesh so as to retain the ideal of freedom. At one point he even planned to follow the Amur River to Sakhalin Island, presumably in hope of boarding a foreign whaler and escaping Russia altogether. His statement to Tatarinov that if released from prison he would simply escape again amounted to an absolute disavowal of the regime. His ability to effect name exchanges and escapes suggests an ability to relate to both common criminals and key-locks. Only marriage and family rearranged Lutskii's priorities, to the extent that he was willing to sacrifice even his return home to attend to the needs of his children. In the end, Lutskii was a most noble Decembrist indeed.

*   *   *

Mikhail S. Lunin was another Decembrist distinguished by his devotion to freedom, though in a way different than Lutskii. Glynn Barratt's is the definitive Anglophone biography, and he conjectures that Lunin's

Catholic faith contributed to his becoming a dissident. Be that as it may, Lunin's own writings show him influenced by other ideas that were idiosyncratic within Nicolaevan Russia. Born in 1787 to a landowner who served in the military and was unrepentant about using the knout on his serfs, Lunin's rebelliousness was also undoubtedly directed at a tyrannical father he could not abide. Lunin distinguished himself during the Napoleonic Wars, winning special renown for a daring charge he led at Austerlitz. Like many eventual Decembrists he became enamored of Freemasonry, but unlike most gave it up when it conflicted with his religious beliefs. He was versatile in several languages, including Greek and English. Assigned in 1824 to Warsaw, Lunin was arrested there on 9 April 1826 as a result of interrogations that confirmed he belonged to Decembrist secret societies, though he apparently had few, if any, links to Polish revolutionaries and certainly did not support an independent Poland. According to Zavalishin, "together with [Vladimir D.] Novosil´tsev and others, [Lunin] wanted to make Konstantin Pavlovich take the throne, vouchsafing him a blessed reign if alongside his expressed liberal reforms he prepared the groundwork in Russia for liberating reforms."[52] Lunin was sentenced to 20 years *katorga* (immediately reduced to 15), but instead of going directly to Siberia he was incarcerated in Sveaborg prison between October 1826 and October 1827, then Vyborg fortress, before finally departing on 24 April 1828.

After a couple of years in Chita, Lunin went to Petrovsk Zavod in September 1830 with the other Decembrists but maintained a certain distance from them. At Chita he had neither participated in the Academy's activities nor contributed to the general welfare fund; for the journey to Petrovsk he purchased a covered wagon and hardly exited it during the entire trip; and once in Petrovsk, writes A. E. Rozen,

M. S. Lunin lived in the most curious manner. He lived in No. 1, a totally dark cell in which no window had been pierced.... He did not share our common table, and kept his fasts after the custom of the Roman Church, which he had joined some years before in Warsaw. One third of his cell was shut off by a curtain behind which, elevated on some steps, was a large crucifix blessed by the Pope, which his sister had sent him from Rome. All day long, loud Latin prayers would be audible in his cell. He was no ascetic in his ways, however; and when he strolled among us he was invariably witty and agreeable. Whenever we called on him in his cell we always found him ready to converse in a secular and often jocular strain. He was greatly provoked by Victor Hugo's *Notre-Dame de Paris*, I recall, which penetrated even our wilds and was read avidly; he had the patience to burn the whole book with a candle....[53]

Despite (or perhaps because of) his aloofness and devout fastidiousness, Lunin was probably the most respected among the Decembrists. Zavalishin, despite ridiculing Kuchevskii-the-Bump's religiosity, says nothing negative about Lunin in his memoirs, but instead consistently praises him.

The amnesty of 14 December 1835 freed Lunin for settlement, but he waited until early June 1836 to go to Irkutsk. Five months later he moved with Aleksandr and Nikita Murav´ev, the Volkonskiis, and Ferdinand B. Vol´f to the village of Urik. This favorable location a mere 18 versts from Irkutsk reflected intercessions on his behalf by his beloved sister Ekaterina S. Uvarova. Lunin built in Urik a large cabin with a chapel and several outbuildings, cleared the surrounding grounds, and operated a serviceable though intentionally unprofitable farm. An elderly servant affectionately called Vasilich also lived there with his family, as did four horses and six borzois. Lunin compiled a personal library of 397 books on law, Classics, and history and even subscribed to the Ministry of Education's monthly journal. A Catholic priest arrived once a week from Irkutsk to deliver him the sacraments.

After his release from Petrovsk Lunin received the right to correspond with his sister, to whom he mailed his first letter in September 1836. I. A. Zhelvakova and N. Ia. Eidel´man reproduce and analyze these letters in an excellent annotated edition that was published in 1987.[54] The editors divide his letters into two series covering 1836–38 and 1839–40 because (as we shall see) Benkendorf banned Lunin from corresponding for a year beginning in August 1838. Lunin's first few letters lack clearly defined political aims and, as such, counter Barratt's contention that his was a continuous and systematic act of protest. Barratt is closer to the mark in noting that as time went on "Lunin had increasingly little to lose"[55] given his age and lack of dependents, and this gave him free rein to take increasingly radical stands.

Lunin instructed Ekaterina to copy and circulate his letters among Petersburg society; enlisted the Volkonskiis and other Decembrists to reproduce them in French and circulate as many copies as possible; and sent to his sister a "reissue" of the letters in two "booklets" with added comments. He supplemented these proto-*samizdat* publications with an essay entitled "A Look at the Russian Secret Society from 1816 to 1826," which he sent to Ekaterina in September 1839. By the time of his arrest in March 1841 Lunin was wielding his pen like a mighty sword against the government. The Third Section intercepted almost all these letters and noted their contents before forwarding them to Ekaterina. Its archives are all that confirm the existence of some letters and the subsequent booklets Ekaterina never received.

Touching mostly on innocuous personal matters, Lunin's early letters nevertheless suggest a fragile mental state. "I live with people who see but do not understand me," he writes on 29 September 1836, "or with an invisible one [*s nevidimym*] I cannot comprehend"; and on 1 May 1837: "After long seclusion in casemates the memory recalls only vague, color-less forms, [just] as planets reflect without heat the sun's light." These phrases and the tone of many of his letters show that his incarceration affected him long after his release from prison, and also speak to a common tendency among prisoners and exiles to experience religious ecstasy and transformation. Malcolm X as well as many on death row offer recent examples of those who have received revelations while in confinement or under duress. The seventeenth-century schismatic exile Avvakum Petrovich found confirmation of his religious mission while in Siberia; and Peter I's disgraced and exiled lieutenant Aleksandr Menshikov became renowned for his piety during his final years in Berezov. Lunin's experience was therefore not unique—even among Decembrists. Writing to Benkendorf in 1837, Governor-general Bronevskii sympathized with his charges:

> [S]everal have become very devout and lead strict lives. Though much of what is noticeable may be called mysticism, as it is known in Russia and all Europe, devotion to incessant praying may lead to the repentance and consolation they are searching for in the terribly shocking fates they have consigned themselves to.[56]

Lunin's letter of 27 June 1837 seems at first mundane. However, in con-trast to his previous letters it contains a veiled reference to Mariia Volkon-skaia, "whose name is already in our patriotic chronicles." This phrase is known to have attracted Benkendorf's attention. Similarly eye-catching was Lunin's letter of 28 April 1838, which asserts that between 1700 and 1826 the government had done nothing to positively develop Russia's legal code. On 19 May 1838 he reports, "I am now analyzing the friendly Socrates's idle talk before his death." On 30 July he writes that his 70-year-old servant Fedot Shablin's "former master, in a moment of bad temper, exiled him to Siberia without a court or certificates [of permission]."

In Nicolaevan Russia such words, especially when written for posterity by a state criminal, amounted to sedition. On 5 August 1838 Benkendorf's assistant Aleksandr N. Mordvinov informed Eastern Siberia governor-general Vil´gel´m Ia. Rupert:

> From the time of his settlement in a village the state prisoner Lunin has often, in his letters to his sister, allowed himself to enter into discussion of matters that do not concern him, and, instead of repentance, has shown how deep-rooted are his profligate ideas. Count Benkendorf, bearing in mind that state prisoners have the [sovereign's] authority to write to relatives *only* to inform them of their health and of family matters, has indicated to his sister the impermissible mould of his thoughts and suggested that she warn him, so that he may escape unpleasant consequences. This notwith-standing, letters have once more been forthcoming from Lunin—letters containing impudent ideas and judgments not in keeping with his position.[57]

Rupert was furthermore told to inform Lunin he was banned from writing letters for a year.

During this enforced hiatus Lunin appears to have worked on his essay "A Look at the Russian Secret Society." This reacquainting of himself with his past, combined with his advancing age, solitude, and the muzzling of his epistolary voice, seems to have led him to throw caution to the wind. On 15 September 1839 he celebrated the end of his ban by writing two incendiary letters, one to Ekaterina, the other to Benkendorf, whom he addressed as "Chief of Gendarmes." To his sister, he writes, "I have shown that in the Caucasus the delay of success is resulting from people of dated sensibilities: within military ranks people with new understanding have appeared and made an important step." This struck at the heart of the Nicolaevan military establishment, and incidentally supports John Keep's argument that Decembrism should be considered a form of Praetorianism. In this letter Lunin added that his decision to free his serfs back home was a "responsibility... to humanity." These were loaded words intended for the authorities he knew were reading his correspondence.

In his letter to the "Chief of Gendarmes" Lunin combined a lugubrious with a mocking tone. After noting that his sister "has no other except me" and therefore misses his letters, he writes:

> The order to interrupt my period of correspondence was regrettable for me. To avoid similar misfortune anew, I take the liberty to ask: would it be inconvenient for Your Highness [*sic*] to provide instruc-

tions so that my letters, which I try to compose with exactitude, are preliminarily looked at, altered, or retained if certain of them are found to be incorrect? These instructions will deliver me from burdensome responsibility[58] for unwonted deviations or misplaced candor: and the effect of prohibitive measures depriving my sister of my needed consolation and assistance will fall no more upon the innocent. As is apparent, by avoiding neither justice nor judgment [*rassudok*], I am asking for siblings' correspondence no more than what the laws offer writers destined for publication.

The remaining letters Lunin wrote before his arrest amounted to an uncompromising indictment of Russia's government and society. In his letter of 22 October 1839 he returns again to the theme of law, or rather lawlessness, which since the mid-seventeenth century had deprived peasants of legal protection and imposed crushing tax burdens on them and served to institutionalize "slavery" (*rabstvo*)—a word he uses several times. Lunin does not blame the government as being solely responsible for these evils, noting (as would Aleksandr Solzhenitsyn many years later when writing about the GULag) that society was complicit in allowing them to continue:

> We suffer death on the field of battle but dare not say a word for justice and humanity in the State Council. Because of this we are deprived of the lamp of a sober minded opposition which, illuminating the government's path, would enable its benevolent purposes to be fulfilled. The fruitlessness of our literature comes from the same reasons. Our books, devoted to the goal of commerce, are filled with witlessness or absurd fabrications and produce no consequences whatsoever. Morning publications are forgotten by evening.

Lunin attacks serfdom from several angles, writing that it commodifies human beings, undermines the judiciary's reputation, limits development of a civil society, and disgraces both Russia and Russians:

> The Code of Laws includes a table, where the price of people is designated according to age and sex; where a one-year-old child costs less than a calf. Human meat is traded in our courts of law, where buying and selling take place as in a bazaar…. Slavery, incompatible with the spirit of the times, is supported only by ignorance and comprises a source of manifest contradictions insofar as the people are progressing towards the world of citizenship. The American States, where slavery is

affirmed by law, offers a regrettable but useful example of this truth.... Liberation of the peasantry... was accomplished in the Kingdom of Poland and the Baltic regions without the slightest upset. Are we really worse than the Poles, Liflanders, and Courlanders?

Lunin's next letter discusses the growing number of Polish exiles in Siberia, as well as Warsaw's secret revolutionary societies. His specific comments about Polish exiles will be discussed in the next chapter; but for now it may be observed that the Third Section possibly allowed Lunin to correspond for as long as he did because he was providing valuable information. With no free press in Russia, Lunin's candid letters gave Benkendorf an insight he would not otherwise have had. This was true of Nicholas as well, since he undoubtedly also read these letters.

That said, Lunin's letter of 21 November 1839, though returning to the more reflective style of his earliest letters, also let Benkendorf and Nicholas know that they were dealing with a zealot who, like many throughout history who have felt themselves drawn to a higher calling, was prepared if necessary to sacrifice his life:

> In fulfilling my existence there is no sense of danger. I have so often met death on the hunt, in singular combats [*v poedinkakh*], in battles, in political struggles, that danger has become a habit, a requirement for developing my abilities. There's no danger here. I paddle the Angara in a canoe, but its waves are placid. I meet robbers in the woods; they ask for alms.

In a letter the following month he addressed Ekaterina's legal difficulties in obtaining her inheritance. "In 1828 the Senate's Eighth Department ruled that your adversaries held the disputed land illegally (*'illegal possession'*) and decided the case on your behalf," he writes, again clearly addressing third parties,

> but in 1838 the same Senate finds that the adversaries' possession was legal (*"conscientious possession"*), and decides the case against you. Your request to transfer the case to the General Assembly was rejected by the Petitions Commission, contrary to all existing legislation.

This letter was important not only because it exposed the government's duplicity and arbitrariness but also shone a spotlight on women's lack of legal rights. Having parenthetically defined legal terminology and identified judicial bodies and procedures, Lunin offered a brief primer to encourage readers to seek redress through what legal avenues were available. However, his main point was to criticize the absence of legality under tsarism. After briefly alluding to the existence of Common Law in England, he contrasts proceedings there with

> [o]ur legal proceedings, [which] begin in the dark, furtively drag on in silence, often unbeknownst to one participating side, and conclude with an enormous pile of muddled paperwork. There is no advocate to speak on behalf of the case, no one available to swear to the event, and especially no transparency [*glasnost*] to illuminate, support, and direct the judicially-empowered authorities. Their decisions, even if correct and legal, become the bases for new lawsuits conducted illiterately and in the dark.

Lunin's final letters before his arrest once again became more personal, but also demonstrate through feigned ignorance of the danger facing him a kind of fatalistic resignation. For instance on 20 December 1839 he wrote about his dog Laetus, named after the fifteenth-century Italian humanist Julius Pomponius Laetus, tortured by Pope Paul II for heresy but who refused to confess and survived to continue teaching in Rome until his death in 1498. His pet had been missing for some time, but Lunin delightedly informs Ekaterina that he has returned and, moreover, "The beautiful creature, like a living letter, informs me: that your feelings after 14 years have not changed; that you love your outcast as you loved the hussar and, 7,000 versts away from him, wish him luck." It seems that coincident with Laetus's return Lunin received a letter from Ekaterina, for he writes that his dog has let him know she is worried about the subject matter of his letters, about which he replies:

> [T]hese days it's almost impossible to say hello without this word itself containing a political implication. However, it seems you're crediting too much significance to an outcast's ideas, [which are] not expressed for publication. They may only deserve the government's impartial and well-founded attention later, when, and in that case, the evolution and self-realization of the above-named [dog, Laetus] can be sooner expected than prohibitive measures. Where it would not be, truth always becomes precious. If it's expected from the Ruling Senate, then much water will flow before this happens. Be that as it may, but I'm much contented by the comradeship of [my] new outcast, who every minute reminds me of the best and most loving of sisters.

This letter documents the beginning of Lunin's rather gleeful and almost giddy embrace of a devil-may-care attitude towards fate. His protestations of immunity cannot be taken seriously, especially when at the same time he unfavorably compares the government's development to that of his dog's mental abilities.

However, a letter he wrote two days later regarding the Investigatory Commission's (*Sledstvennaia komissiia*) pedantic criticism of one of Pavel Pestel's writings calling for a constitution is more serious. "The niggling over words almost visibly demonstrates that there is nothing to say about the well-established point or the forbidding of an investigation into it due to some extraneous reasons." "Extraneous reasons" mocked the phrase Benkendorf used to characterize Lunin's discussion of forbidden topics in his letters to Ekaterina. Lunin also turns the tables by noting the commission's inaccurate terminology regarding Decembrist societies:

> When the government—our lantern and guide—fails to notice similar anomalies in its official acts, then its bureaucrats should, it seems, show greater tolerance towards carelessness or mistakes that have slipped into political essays.

As earlier, Lunin obviously wanted to provoke Benkendorf with this satirical one-upmanship. He had in previous letters already made the profound points he wanted to; now, in these final brief letters, he was pushing Benkendorf (and by extension Nicholas) to fulfill the designated role of Pontius Pilate to his Jesus Christ. Lunin's identification with Jesus and martyrdom in general is made more apparent by his next letter dated 1 January 1840, a rare example of tragedy in Lunin's epistolary canon. He movingly writes of being in Peter-Paul fortress and listening through the walls to a prisoner, who later turned out to be the soon-to-be-hanged Sergei Murav´ev-Apostol, reciting the following lines:

> I, a solitary man,
> Pass through the world unknown by anyone;
> Only at my end
> Does the world,
> Suddenly illuminated, recognize whom it's lost.

In his final letter from Urik, dated 10 January 1840, Lunin informs Ekaterina that he has just received a warning to desist writing if, quoting Benkendorf, "the impermissible judgments about extraneous matters deviating from the realm usually concerning letters between relatives does not change." Lunin first tells his sister he will stop writing altogether since he cannot determine which matters are extraneous, but then writes, "I will limit my correspondence to you to expressions, now and then, of my scholarly pursuits, by which you may know that your brother exists still in the depths of banishment and always maintains a devoted friendship toward you." However, Lunin apparently wrote no more letters to Ekaterina until after he was arrested. He may have been too busy with such essays as "The Russian Secret Society," "An Historical Investigation," and "An Examination of the Secret Investigatory Commission's Reports to the Sovereign Emperor in 1826." Each discusses matters primarily concerning the Decembrists before their arrests and deportations and so all that need be said here is that, even more than his letters, they broached topics Nicholas did not want broached.

Barratt writes that the Third Section somehow learned of the first of these essays' existence in early 1841, and so it, rather than the letters *per se*, prompted Benkendorf's order of 25 February to arrest Lunin. All the same, the letters had created the static for this lightning strike. "His Excellency Count Benkendorf," Mordvinov once again informed Rupert,

> ... has ordered that Lunin be taken immediately to the Akatui mine, but not set to work, but kept in the *strictest* isolation away from other prisoners, so that he may have no contact whatsoever, personal or written, with anyone, and be kept in that fashion until further instructions.[2]

Years later, after Alexander II amnestied the Decembrists and they had come to be considered patriots, Rupert claimed the emperor initially ordered Lunin shot but that he saved him by claiming he had gone mad. This claim should be taken with a grain of salt. Nonetheless, a report written by Vasilii I. Kopylov, Rupert's deputy governor, within hours of Lunin's arrest the night of 26 March does show he was acting strangely. Lunin offered no resistance during the gendarmes' five-hour search of his cabin, though he was greatly agitated, which is understandable when armed men invade your home. Yet even after being taken to Irkutsk he continued rambling incoherently about religion, to the extent that at least Kopylov became convinced he was insane. Barratt doubts Kopylov's diagnosis, but admits that his "comments give a clue to the way in which Lunin's thoughts were developing in his last few months in Urik."[60]

Whatever Lunin's actual mental state at the time of his arrest, it is impossible to agree with another of Barratt's conclusions: "To be an effective politician or 'member of the opposition,' he seems to have held by the time of his second arrest, it was not merely useful or desirable to be a Catholic—it was necessary."[61] Lunin certainly wanted to be martyred, and this desire dovetailed with his messiah complex—both conditions were either symptomatic of, or at least found expression through, his religious dogmatism. But nothing written by him indicates he believed effective political opposition required faith in Catholicism *per se*; and in making this suggestion Barratt overlooks what he also celebrates as Lunin's humanism, liberalism, and knowledge of history. The most that can be said is that this erudite saintly revolutionary was, by virtue of his contradictory influences, a thoroughly modern man whose appreciation of "the spirit of the times" revealed his opponents to be anachronistic.

After Volkonskii managed to slip him a thousand rubles before the gendarmes took him away Lunin was never seen again by friends or family. In early June 1841 some Decembrists finally learned he was in Akatui—the place where birds fell from the sky. Having been inter-rogated in Irkutsk for several weeks he was delivered there on 11 April. Lunin had named only one accomplice, and he was dead. This refusal to cooperate earned him no favors, but by then he was too far along his path to give a damn. Police squeezed considerably more information out of a certain V. Zhuravlev, a teacher of Latin at the Irkutsk *gimnaziia* who, unlike his fellow Classicist, identified several living accomplices.

Lunin's letters from Akatui—where he was kept in a low-ceilinged cell dripping with moisture and separate from regular inmates, some of whom were chained to walls—are remarkable for their consistently courageous and even frequently upbeat tone.[62] On 30 January 1842 he wrote with acerbic wit in a mixture of French and English to the Volkonskiis and their young son Mikhail:

> Akatui prison's architecture is certainly an inheritor of Dante's imagination. My earlier casemates were boudoirs compared to what I now occupy. I have no view. Guards are at the door, the windows, everywhere. I have for companions in captivity a group of 50 murderers, assassins, leaders of brigands and forgery-counterfeiters. Moreover, we get along with each other perfectly. These brave men have a liking for me. I am trustee of their little treasures acquired God knows how, and confidant of their petty secrets, which decidedly belong to a galvanized literature.

This latter phrase is borrowed from Pushkin and indicates, along with much else, that if Lunin had indeed lost his mind at the time of his arrest he recovered it in prison. "To give you an idea of my current situation, you would have to read *The Mysteries of Udolpho* or another novel by Madame Radcliffe,"[63] he writes in another letter to Mariia Volkonskaia dated no earlier than May 1843. After thanking her for her letters, he continues:

> I am deep in the darkness, without air, space, or nourishment, surrounded by brigands, assassins, and counterfeiters. My only distraction is to attend to the application of the knout in the heart of the prison. Amidst this dramatic situation, intended to foreshorten my days, my health is maintaining itself wonderfully and my strength, far from being diminished, is augmented. I can easily lift nine poods with one hand. My present experience has absolutely convinced me that happiness is possible in all circumstances in life, and that in this world there are fools and beasts of unhappiness.

Was this last sentence a riddle? Were there only two kinds of people in the world, and were the only ones who were happy the fools? If so, did this make Lunin a fool? Lunin was also fooling about his strength, since nine poods equal almost 325 pounds. From his Dantesque inferno Lunin was serializing his own *Divina commedia*.

Along with this letter to saint-like and motherly Mariia, Lunin included a separate letter to ten-year-old Mikhail Volkonskii written in English and encouraging him to keep studying this language:

> It is not so very easy, and requires a good deal of attention and diligence: but you are no more a child, and will, I hope, overcome all difficulties as a man. Remember, my dear, that your progress in knowledge is the best proof you can give me of your friendship.—Do not read all sort of books that may fall in your hands. You must know that the world is full of foolish books, and that the number of useful books is very small.

Lunin's last known letter was also to Mikhail. Undated, unsigned, and written in Latin, it was probably composed sometime after October 1844. He praises the boy's studiousness, which he tells him he has learned of from his mother. "Concerning me, I'm healthy, studying much, [and] I love you and wish the best for you, but have also received more precise news about what you'll be doing," writes Lunin. "Everything else is in the best way for me."[64]

Lunin was probably disguising the true state of his health in all these letters from Akatui. Nicholas certainly intended that this oubliette's terrible conditions would hasten his death, and by not straightforwardly executing his unbowed opponent he revealed himself for the coward he was. No letters exist for Lunin's final year in prison and so it is impossible to know if he was unable or just forbidden to write, or for how long he suffered before dying on 3 December 1845 from what was officially described as internal bleeding of the lungs—a description suggesting chronic pneumonia. Many Decembrists upon learning of his death did not trust the official explanation and started rumors that he was deliberately murdered. However, no evidence for this exists. In the end Lunin suffered to death as both he and the emperor wanted.

5
Paranoia and Conspiracy: Polish Exiles and the Omsk Affair

Throughout its existence tsarist Russia exiled various national and ethnic groups, yet Poles accounted by far for the largest non-Russian cohort among Siberian exiles. The relationship between Poles and Siberia dates to the early seventeenth century, when as prisoners of war they were among the first persons exiled there, mostly to be assigned to Cossack detachments. The Seven Years War and successive partitions of Poland resulted in new rounds of exiles, so that by the late eighteenth century several exilic Polish communities existed in the Altai and Zabaikal´e. Following defeat of the Confederation of Bar in 1772 Catherine II deported 5,000 Poles who served in the Siberian military before being allowed to return home.[1] Poles captured from Napoleon's *Grande Armée* were assigned to Kazan, Samara, Saratov, Ufa, and Orenburg.[2] In 1813–14 some 900 captured Polish cavalrymen were assigned to the Siberian Cossacks. When Alexander I allowed them to return home in 1815 only "160 men were still voluntarily serving in the Cossacks," writes S. V. Maksimov. As for the rest,

> [t]he city of Omsk had served as a significant temptation for many of these Poles; yet General [Semën B.] Bronevskii's Cossack orchestra offered them the best haven at the time. Czechs, Germans, and Poles amazed Omsk, which had been without music since the dawn of time.[3]

Maksimov claims few in this group chose to return home.

Prior to the 1863 Polish Uprising the largest group of Polish exiles originated as a result of the uprising of 1830–31, sometimes called the November Insurrection. Like those before, this group was an ethno-linguistic mixture: during the Polish-Lithuanian Commonwealth's existence Poles formed only the largest portion of a population that also included Germans, Belorussians, Ukrainians, and Jews as well as smaller numbers of Roma, Wallachians, Tatars, and others. Analysis and description of those deported from the territory absorbed by the Russian Empire between 1772 and 1795 is further hindered by the historically complicated notion of "Polishness" and the inapplicability of present-day national signifiers.[4] Convenience rather than specificity therefore explains my use of the catch-all term "Polish exiles."

What began on 29 November 1830 (new style) as a *coup d'état* by Polish army lieutenant Piotr Wysocki and others eventually transmogrified into full-fledged war between Poland and Russia, with both sides fielding the largest armies seen on the continent since the Napoleonic Wars. By March 1831 Poland's frontline troops totaled 68,000. Nicholas correctly regarded the uprising as a significant threat, not only because it involved his deposition as king of Poland but because it spread to the so-called Western Provinces (*zapadnye gubernii*), which had formed much of the erstwhile Polish-Lithuanian Commonwealth and are roughly equivalent to today's countries of Lithuania, Belarus, and Ukraine. Upwards of 30,000 partisans there were tying down thousands of Russian troops and cutting supply lines. Moreover, this conflict brought the emperor face-to-face with the manpower shortage that made Russia vulnerable to attacks anywhere along its enormous foreign border.[5] He also feared *agents provocateurs* were sowing the seeds of revolt still deeper in Russia. In March the MVD warned, "people from the Kingdom of Poland are being allowed to pass completely unsuspected into our internal *gubernii* to gain support," and ordered that individuals unable to produce appropriate residence permits and identification be arrested as *brodiagi* and remanded to military courts.[6]

Nevertheless, the insurrectionists' base of support remained narrow. A certain number of Byronesque young men from Austria, Italy, and France fought to defend the ideal of liberty. But neither peasants nor Jews did so to any great extent, primarily because class, economic, and religious tensions distanced them from the Polish *shliakhta* (in Polish, *szlachta*[7]). Jewish leaders told followers to refrain from joining the insurrection out of a justified fear of Russian reprisals. Despite initial support from Warsaw's artisanate the insurrectionists originated for the most part from the military and *shliakhta*. The *shliakhta* had made up nearly 10 percent of the Commonwealth's population, and though consisting principally of ethnic Poles, was a multifarious estate that included even converted Jews. By virtue only of the legal rights and privileges it acquired over the centuries the *shliakhta* was roughly analogous to the Russian nobility (*dvo-*

rianstvo), but more economically diverse, ranging from colossally wealthy magnates who owned *latifundia* with thousands of serfs to impoverished farmers who rented shacks from these magnates. Most *shliakhtichi* ("noblemen") were actually subsistence farmers; a significant portion were despised as "the rabble" (in Polish, *holota*), a group that included both tenant farmers and penurious city-dwellers.[8]

Soldiers and *shliakhtichi* therefore bore the brunt of Russian retaliation. A decision of 15 March 1833 reassigned 11,653 Polish officers and soldiers to penal battalions, fortress labor, or residences elsewhere within the empire. "However," writes A. S. Nagaev, "the basic mass—9,346 members of the lower ranks—were assigned to various military detachments for continued service." The large use of Polish soldiers in the Caucasus between 1835 and 1846 suggests that most from this earlier group were likewise sent there.[9] R. F. Leslie notes that the few peasants detained were either assigned to the Siberia Corps or simply released.[10] By contrast to Poland, the Western Provinces were more integrated into the empire, and so Nicholas regarded as especially traitorous those *shliakhtichi* and others who had rebelled there. He ordered many tried by field courts-martial and summarily shot, though also approved of lesser sentences that were nonetheless generally harsher than those given residents of the kingdom. "The tsar personally saw to it that Prince Roman Sanguszko (1800–81), one of the Polish magnates in the Ukraine, traveled on foot to his exile in Siberia," writes Piotr Wandycz, for example.[11] The partial amnesty Nicholas later granted to combatants was not extended to those from the Western Provinces; and documents found in Siberian archives and discussed below show that after it crushed the uprising the government pursued them for many years. Indeed, Nicholas seems to have wanted to eliminate *shliakhtichi* from the Western Provinces altogether. New regulations issued in 1836 deprived many of their social rank and abetted the deportation of what Wandycz claims was "some 54,000... between 1832 and 1849 from Lithuania, Podolia, and Volhynia to the Caucasus, Siberia, or beyond the Volga."[12] Remarkably little seems to have been written about this displaced mass, despite the fact that it dwarfed the 7,000 to 8,000 insurrectionists who escaped across Congress Poland's western and southern borders to form the renowned "Great Emigration."[13]

Before those exiled because of the November Insurrection arrived, few Poles were in Siberia with the exception of Catherine II's victims and their descendants. Moreover, writes one historian, "the number of Polish *political exiles* in Nerchinsk *katorga* numbered in the single digits...."[14] Calculating the number exiled thereafter is made difficult, however, in part because several government agencies were involved. Insurrectionists "were exiled by the judiciary to settlement in Siberia, but also by administrative procedure to residence [*na zhitel´stvo*] and to civil and military service in Siberian garrisons," explains S. V. Kodan.[15] Nonetheless, nothing supports Norman Davies's claim that "[f]ield tribunals condemned all rebels and their families to penal servitude in Russia, and some 80,000 Poles walked in irons to Siberia."[16] Exiled Poles' numbers were large, but nowhere near 80,000; and only a handful were sentenced to *katorga*. "Siberia has been inundated by new deportees for some time," M. S. Lunin wrote his sister on 5 November 1839:

> They are of a political character, though in actuality they're victims of an irrational fervor or credulity related to ignorance. We're talking about the Poles exiled after the 1830 revolution. There are several thousand of them. [In a previous draft Lunin writes: "There are around 20,000 men."] One portion is in *katorga*, another in settlement, and a third has been assigned to garrisons.
>
> They're both revolutionaries and agitators [*kosvennye volnovateli*].
>
> They consist of *shliakty* [*sic*], former soldiers, townsmen, tenants, and peasants. Among them are children [deemed] guilty before their majority; elderly cripples who've relapsed into childhood; and religious who can barely read their prayer-book[s]. You ask each and every one: what was their goal? None can think of an answer for you.[17]

In light of Kodan's archivally-based figure showing *circa* 900 "political exiles" for the period 1831–35,[18] Lunin's estimate of "around 20,000 men" would seem nearly as rash as Davies's. In this context it is germane to note that by collating the rosters routinely maintained on "state criminals" F. F. Bolonev and other historians have identified only 250 Poles being assigned to Eastern Siberia between 1830 and 1858. While continuing to exclude those like Aleksander Mozalewski and Stepan Arszewski exiled prior to 1830, this figure might be conservatively increased to only 300 at most.[19] Yet here again one encounters the semantic confusion described in Chapter 3 between "state crimes," "state criminals," and "political exiles." It appears that Kodan's and Bolonev's figures refer only to those judicially convicted of state crimes.

By comparison, historian A. I. Shinkovoi estimates similarly to Lunin that "no fewer than 10 thousand" Poles were exiled to Eastern Siberia during the 1830s.[20] Partially supporting this estimate is a key archival document. In a letter of October 1831 to Eastern Siberia governor-general A. S. Lavinskii, EOGU reported its response to an earlier order from finance minister E. F. Kankrin that land be set aside for a group of exiles destined for Achinsk, Krasnoiarsk, and Kainsk *okruga* where, two years earlier, the government had begun constructing a series of exilic settlements (see Chapter 6). Accompanying this letter was a chart showing that surveys completed in July identified more than 90,000 *desiatiny* of arable land, and so at 15 *desiatiny* per soul the *okruga* would theoretically accommodate more than 6,000 exiles, whom EOGU identified as "*shliakhtichi*" but for some reason described as people "who do not keep a settled way of life...." This and its reference to a "Polish *Guberniia*" reveal considerable ignorance about central Europe; but the documents more importantly show that as the Russian army was pursuing victory in Poland Kankrin and others were planning a mass deportation.[21]

From Petersburg's point-of-view the sudden availability of thousands of exiles was fortuitous, since Eniseisk *guberniia* had a yawning need for agricultural settlers. A massive territory covering 2,885,000 square versts populated by only 173,898 males and females, this "Siberian Switzerland" was extolled in the MVD's journal that same year of 1831: "The districts most suitable for growing grain are: *Achinsk, Kansk, Minusinsk, Krasnoiarsk*, and part of *Eniseisk*." The author claimed "the variety of climate and quality of soil" made it possible to grow "rye, spring wheat, [indecipherable], barley, oats, buckwheat, millet, and poppies." The only thing lacking was people, and so Minusinsk *okrug*, for instance, despite its 88 villages and 7,035 male peasants, had only 13,663 of its 565,873 *desiatiny* of arable land under cultivation. Ratios were similar in the other *okruga*.[22] As with the very first people punished with Siberian exile in 1593 there was in the case of the Polish exiles a fortuitous convergence of the state's punitive and economic goals.

Based on available evidence, then, at least 10,000 and as many as 20,000 residents of Congress Poland and the Western Provinces were exiled to Siberia in the decade following the November Insurrection. Those judicially convicted of state crimes numbered in the hundreds. Due to semantic confusion and because officials routinely ignored judicial, criminal, and exile regulations, determining more precise identities for most of these exiles is impossible. Finally, nearly 2,300 Polish soldiers captured by the Russian army are known to have been reassigned to the Siberia Corps headquartered in Omsk.

Unfortunately lacking as well is information concerning how this large deportation was conducted, for it must have greatly stressed an already overburdened exile system. What evidence does exist is discussed below. But for now it will simply be noted that in August 1831 the MVD arranged for Department of Social Services funds to cover the cost of burying prisoners who died in its hospitals. Such legislation had first been tabled in late 1829, but the sudden deportation of thousands of Poles so raised the exile system's body-count that the government finally had to act.[23]

*   *   *

Before analyzing those exiled as a direct consequence of the 1830–31 uprising it is important to note that Poles were exiled throughout the period 1823–61 as a result of Russian oppression, which also took the form of a large police presence in Congress Poland and involved the politicization of its semi-autonomous judicial system. Poland's judiciary operated according to a separate law code created in 1818. But in the aftermath of the 1830 uprising it was forced to incorporate the punishments of exile and correctional battalions into its sentencing guidelines, and in 1847 was forced to adopt the Russian penal code, though it retained separate criminal procedures.[24] "Deprived of the assistance of legal counsel, not understanding the language in which they were prosecuted, the guilty, wishing to vindicate themselves, often strengthened their guilt," wrote Lunin of those Poles he met or learned of in Siberia. "Either through ignorance of legal procedures or through zeal the judges, for their part, increased this chaos by judging them erroneously. A large portion of the convicts are demanding verifications of their sentences." He added that "many of the unfortunates were exiled without trial."[25]

Between 1822 and 1847 Polish courts became increasingly busy, such that criminal trials grew from 422 to 914 per 100,000 persons. The largest figure (1,193/100,000) occurred in 1833, two years after the uprising began.[26] The 1848 revolutions similarly later influenced policing in Poland: arrests for "crimes against public order" rose from 78 to 187 per 100,000 persons between 1848 and 1852—a 140 percent increase. This figure subsequently fell; but as of 1860 it was still almost 100 percent over that for 1848.[27] Of course, not every arrest or trial was politically motivated. But MVD data further indicate that Poland's courts were being politicized. Between 1830 and 1839, 1,965 Poles were brought to trial for crimes "against religion and legal order," with the 1833 figure of 319 (7.9 per 100,000) marking a 56 percent increase over the previous year's figure of 205 (5.2 per 100,000). MVD data however also suggest Polish judges resisted their imperial masters, since they convicted only 509 of those brought to trial during this period. This conviction rate of 26 percent was less than half that for Poles tried for criminal charges during the period 1830–39.[28] Courtrooms thus became battlegrounds in the centuries-long struggle between Poland and Russia.

When convicted, Poles faced confinement (*zakliuchenie*) or, in rare cases, capital punishment. In 1838 seven were sentenced to death and 4,918 to one of three confinement categories the MVD labeled as follows: fortress (*krepostnoe*), heavy (*tiazhkoe*), and correctional (*ispravitel´noe*).[29] The lack of a consistent legal lexicon at that time renders these terms unclear, but the first probably designated either fortress labor (*krepostnaia rabota*) or fortress *katorga*, each a traditional punishment in Russia. The latter two categories—to which 1,856 and 2,634 convicts were sentenced, respectively—may indicate prison and/or assignment to a correctional battalion. If indeed any Poles were sentenced to *katorga*, their numbers appear to have been quite small, judging by Siberian sources. For example, as of October 1837, Piotr Jankowski, Josef Zubricki, and 26 others were the only "state criminals" in Nerchinsk *katorga*.[30]

Given such frankly confusing and imprecise terms and figures, it is difficult to establish links between, on the one hand, persecutions and convictions in Poland and, on the other, figures on "state criminals" and "political exiles" retrieved from Siberian archives. Suffice it to say that after 1831 Petersburg used exile as a prophylactic against secret societies and suspected conspirators disseminating throughout Congress Poland, Bessarabia, and the Western Provinces, as Maksimov makes clear:

> Of the 59 cases of exile for mutiny and high treason in 1839: 31 pertain to Kiev *guberniia*, 11 to Vil´no *guberniia*, 1 to Grodno *guberniia*, and 16 to the city of Warsaw; in 1846, of the 28 cases, 23 pertain to the city of Warsaw; in 1847, 23 of 24 pertain to Warsaw (i.e., the Kingdom of Poland [*sic*]).[31]

In addition to mutiny and high treason Petersburg classified "abandoning the fatherland" (*ostavlenie otechestva*) as a state crime. Between 1838 and 1846 Warsaw accounted for the largest number (26) of those exiled under this charge, whereas another "12 [came] from Bessarabia, 7 from Vil´no *guberniia*, 3 from Podol´ia *guberniia*, and 1 each from Kovno, Grodno, and Vitebsk." Between 1827 and 1846 those exiled for state crimes from the nine Western Provinces equaled two-thirds the number similarly exiled from the 39 Russian *gubernii*. Within the Western Provinces the largest numbers of exiled state criminals came from the *gubernii* of Vil´no (from which 49 were exiled for unspecified state crimes and 30 for "abandoning the fatherland"), Grodno, and Kiev and from Belostok *oblast*.[32]

When exiled, Poles were assigned to both Western and Eastern Siberia. Because the latter was reserved for those prisoners considered most dangerous, a greater amount of official data useful to historians exists on them. At any one time between 1830 and 1863, 100 to 250 Polish exiles identified as "state criminals" were present in Eastern Siberia. In August 1842 GUVS official Aleksandr Zaborovskii reported a total of 125 "political exiles" resident in Irkutsk *guberniia*, including Ignati Necunski, a former Catholic priest and member of the Grodno *shliakhta* exiled to settlement for conspiracy, and Jan Rakicki, exiled to *katorga* for his role in a "gang" led by one Jan Rekka.[33] As of January 1846, 20 state criminals were in the Nerchinsk Mining District, 92 in Irkutsk *guberniia*, and, as of May that same year, 58 in Eniseisk *guberniia*.[34] The following entry exemplifies the information recorded about these prisoners in official rosters:

> Wojcjech Bimenski, 25 yrs. [old] from Podol´ia *guberniia*, from the entitled *shliakhtichi*, [sentenced] to settlement in Siberia because of unsuitability for military service by the Podol´ia *Guberniia* Administration for participation in the mutiny. [Arrived] 28 May 1833 at a settlement in Badaisk *volost* in Irkutsk *uezd* [*sic*].[35]

Some rosters offer greater detail. Medical doctor Josef Antoni Bopre (Beaupré), a 38-year-old resident of Kremenets, Volynia *guberniia*, is described in a roster of prisoners who all hailed from Kiev, Volynia, or Podol´ia *gubernii*. Sentenced together in 1839 they were referred to as the *konarshchiki*—that is, the followers of partisan Szymon Konarski, whose Association of the Polish People had formed "a sizable underground network"[36] and who unlike his followers was executed. According to his roster, Bopre, after joining the organization in 1836, found employment as the Volynia Land Assembly's chief secretary under the pseudonym "Tojad." He used this position to gather statistical data "for carrying out a partisan war… with the goal of preparing minds [*umy*] for the revival of Poland," and sent money, letters, and books to other conspirators. Following his arrest a military court sentenced Bopre to death on 21 February 1839, but the sentence was reduced to 20 years *katorga* and confiscation of his estate. He began marching to Siberia several weeks later.[37] We learn from another roster that Bopre reached Irkutsk in October and was assigned to the salt works there. In early 1840 GUVS transferred him to Nerchinsk Zavod's Vozdvizhensk mine, where as of 1844 his behavior was considered "good."[38] Despite this, as late as February 1847 the Third Section refused his request for release from *katorga* on the grounds of "the seriousness of Bopre's crimes."[39]

Another roster of Poles assigned to Eniseisk *guberniia* as of 1844 reports that Jan Butkiewicz went twice through a thousand-man gauntlet before being exiled to settlement for having abandoned his military unit during the uprising; and that *shliakhtich* Josef Klaner was first exiled to Narym, in Western Siberia, for not reporting an unspecified conspiracy, but then had his sentence reduced to "exile to residence" by the tsar, who allowed him to settle in Minusinsk.[40] Other rosters show 92 state criminals assigned to Irkutsk *guberniia* as of January 1846 and 58 assigned to Eniseisk as of May that year. Despite having been leader of a "gang," *shliaktich* Ignati Arpiszewski was exiled as a state criminal to Boguchansk *volost*, Eniseisk *okrug*, where he arrived in early 1835. He subsequently transferred to the village of Sotnikov in Maklakovsk *volost*.[41]

Arpiszewski's case supports Kodan's claim that in the aftermath of the uprising the state often made no distinction between violent criminals and insurrectionists and exiled both as "political criminals,"[42] albeit without necessarily convicting them of state crimes. Numerous documents' references to banditry and gangs and the tendentious connections drawn between them and secret societies demonstrate how Russian officials conflated criminal with political offenders. Two not mutually exclusive explanations suggest why. First, given the low conviction rate for defendants charged with state crimes in Polish courts, Russian authorities bypassed the courts and simply used administrative and police powers to exile captives to Siberia. In other words, during a national emergency the labeling of criminal offenders as "political criminals" facilitated their deportation. Second, military hostilities caused a general breakdown of law and order that some in the region took advantage of for personal gain. After hostilities formally ended many soldiers and *shliakhtichi* who were still at large turned to banditry, either from a refusal to abandon their political goals or simply to survive. Like Colombia's FARQ guerillas or Peru's Shining Path Maoists they walked a fine line between freedom fighter and *bandido*. Their activities coincided with the guerrilla war being waged by Konarski and others. Officials decided not to split hairs and simply lumped them all together under the category "political criminals."

In the short term, deportation reduced the threat posed by dedicated revolutionaries. On 13 February 1832 a Special Criminal Court (*Osobyi ugolovnyi sud*) exiled the uprising's instigator Piotr Wysocki to *katorga*. He crossed the Urals sometime between late 1834 and early 1835.[43] In 1839, 35 *konarshchiki*, most sentenced to 20 years *katorga*, arrived in Irkutsk.[44] Subjected to a level of surveillance and scrutiny hitherto reserved only for the Decembrists, the *konarshchiki* were "proven criminals," GUVS subsequently warned local officials, "[and] should be kept under strict observation and not allowed to escape into criminality, and should in early January be immediately transferred over Lake Baikal's ice sheet to Irkutsk's General City Office for forwarding to the proper quarter."[45] Despite the importance placed on these prisoners, governors often employed them to translate and censor the letters other Polish exiles mailed home.

In his sprawling history of Siberian exile Maksimov divides the mass of Polish exiles into four categories. The first, "to settlement" (*na poselenie*), accounts for those who were administratively as well as judicially exiled to the countryside and consisted mostly of *shliakhtichi* whose property was confiscated and who would, it was imagined, form a new stratum of agricultural settlers. Petersburg tried to make this a reality by supporting each householder with an annual stipend of 57 rubles (114 for the elderly or otherwise incapacitated), but provided exiled townspeople and peasants no support whatsoever, even though they had also lost their property and were expected to become permanent settlers. Their numbers were admittedly few, but such class discrimination undermined a relocation policy ostensibly designed to serve the state's interests. Similarly counterproductive was a restriction that prevented Poles assigned to Western Siberia from straying more than ten versts from their locations and as such made earning a living that much more difficult. Poles in Eastern Siberia enjoyed greater freedom of movement, even if they were state criminals, and could live virtually anywhere with official permission. This distinction shows the arbitrary rulings of Siberia's two governors-general. Polish exile-settlers were freed from taxes for two years; and after a period of ten years, if not involved in any activities rendering them "undependable" or leading to additional punishment, could join the peasantry or merchantry (*kupechestvo*); their children were assigned to the state peasantry but absolved of taxes and military service.[46]

Penal battalions stationed in fortresses along Western Siberia's border with China constituted Maksimov's second category. Several Polish exiles, including Szymon Tokarzewski, were with Dostoevskii at Omsk, for example. Given their education and language skills, most worked as chancery clerks. Moreover, they were not legally classified as penal laborers (*katorzhnye*), as was Dostoevskii.[47]

The third category was the Siberia Corps, to which both soldiers and civilians were assigned. Maksimov illustrates the fate of many forced to serve 15- to 20-year terms in the military:

> As a result of their pointless life, without hope or a future, Polish soldiers in Siberia gave themselves over to unbridled drunkenness.

Many reached such a level of demoralization and drunkenness that, just as they lost all sympathetic and human qualities, so too did they lose their noble bearing and expressive features.[48]

Like Maksimov, Lunin believed these reluctant men made poor soldiers and were as a result often punished.[49] Given the dismal reality of tsarist military life in general, Poles must have been singled out for especially unpleasant treatment by Russian soldiers and officers.

Maksimov's final category was *katorga*. At first, Poles were not assigned to the Nerchinsk Mining District for fear of putting them in contact with the Decembrists still at Petrovsk Zavod. But this policy was reversed after the 22 June 1835 escape of seven from the Aleksandrovsk distillery near Irkutsk. Piotr Wysocki led the group, which despite being captured within two days provoked serious concern among officials, in large part because they were found with maps of Europe and Asia and were reportedly planning to go to India, where they would board an English ship and return to Europe. This fueled speculation they intended to resume the rebellion against Russia. In October 1835 Governor-general Bronevskii informed war minister A. I. Chernyshev that all Polish state criminals were being distributed among various Nerchinsk *zavody* with the exception of Petrovsk Zavod, where a large number of Decembrists were still present. Soon afterward Bronevskii allowed no more than two "Polish criminals" per week to be transferred between Irkutsk and Zabaikal´e.[50] In January 1836 Commandant S. R. Leparskii convened a military commission in Nerchinsk that sentenced his countryman Wysocki to pass twice through a five-hundred-man gauntlet. After this Wysocki was sent to Akatui, where he was chained to a wheelbarrow and put in solitary confinement. He nonetheless managed to befriend Lunin, whose letters he posthumously smuggled out of prison upon his release in 1857. Wysocki returned to Poland, where he died in 1875.[51]

Bronevskii's order assigning all Polish state criminals to Nerchinsk remained in force throughout the rest of Nicholas's reign, albeit with some exceptions. For some reason Bronevskii himself assigned a priest named Michailo Starzinski to the Ilginsk distillery, for example. Moreover, exiles from the Western Provinces were somewhat less likely than those from Poland to go to Nerchinsk. In 1839 TobPS assigned Valerian Shchepkovskii, a nobleman convicted of participating in a Kiev secret society, to the Irkutsk salt works.[52] However, most state criminals served their *katorga* sentences at Nerchinsk regardless of origin. There was never a large number of Poles assigned to *katorga*. Table 5.1 shows the distribution of the 27 assigned to the Nerchinsk Mining District as of November 1837. By December 1839 the district had 31 such prisoners. According to

Table 5.1 Distribution of Polish Political Exiles in Nerchinsk Mining District, November 1837

Nerchinsk Zavod	Ducharsk Zavod	Kadainsk Zavod	Kutomarsk Zavod
Piotr Jankowski	Teofil Kownacki	Wikenti Chlipicki	Napoleon Wysocki
Waleri Wereg	Kazimir Kisilewski		Waleri Jewdokimow
Michailo Gedoic	Maksimilion Parznicki	**Shil'kinsk Zavod**	
Jan Bogunski Josef Czanberg	Norbert Lewandowski	Anton Luboracki	**Kutuminsk mine** Felix Kasperski
Ignati Sicki	**Klichkinsk mine**	**Klotomarsk Zavod**	
Juri Dowyt	Josef Jankewic	Franc Iwaczewski	**Akatui mine**
Anton Asamitowski		Leonard Urbanowicz	Stanislaw Marciewski
Josef Palczicki	**Akatui jail**		Jan Dobrowolski
Josef Zubricki	Piotr Wysocki	**Location unknown**	Ewtafei Zaczicki
		Wladislaw Kralicki	

Source: GAIO, f. 24, op. 3, k. 14, d. 352, ll. 5–7.

Nerchinsk's commander Stepan P. Tatarinov each was receiving 24 rubles annually and "the agreed upon victuals."[53]

What was life like for Poles sentenced to *katorga*? Maksimov claims that although Nerchinsk administrators treated the first arrivals somewhat roughly, for the most part "relations towards the Poles were gracious, delicate, and easy." To support this claim he quotes a number of individuals, from Bronevskii to Polish memoirists Agaton Hiller and Rufim Piotrowski. In at least one *zavod* "Poles lived in special large houses built expressly for them." Several including Bopre had their personal libraries delivered to Siberia, so that Nerchinsk Zavod eventually had a library of some 3,000 Polish-language volumes.[54] I. V. Efimov, commandant of the Aleksandrovsk distillery from September 1848 to 1853, recalled five Polish prisoners under his command who had been "exiled during the revolutions in 1848…"—Dr Aniceti René, Wadislaw Kleczowski, and three others named Ciwinski, Slobodzinski, and Weiztort. Efimov separated them from the regular penal laborers; allowed René to work for the prison buying foodstuffs from local peasants; Kleczowski to help the smiths and other prison tradesmen; and Ciwinski to work at the prison rye mill four versts away.[55]

Szymon Tokarzewski, exiled twice to Siberia and who was the first time incarcerated at Omsk fortress for seven years beginning in 1849, gave a very different picture of *katorga* in the memoirs he wrote in 1857. He describes Omsk's penal battalion commander Major Vasilii Grigor´evich Kryvstov as "Lucifer himself..., a card sharp and a drunkard: almost an embodiment of evil." The prison was a "satanic abyss" where prisoners were routinely dragged out of wards for savage beatings. Tokarzewski claims that Aleksander Mirecki, who came to Omsk three years before he did, was forced to work as a *parashnik*:

That meant that he had to clean pit toilets at night. The work would start at 10:00 PM and end at about midnight. On several occasions the fateless [*sic*] Mirecki had to be lowered on ropes into the very depth of these pit toilets. While doing his "work" he lost his sense of smell and never regained it.[56]

This passage does not withstand scrutiny. Vats (*parashi*) were the standard for collecting septic waste in Russia's prison wards, not pit toilets. Even had pit toilets existed at Omsk they could not have been used during the long winters, and would have been not only pointless but impossible to clean, since pit toilets are simply filled with soil when they are no longer serviceable. Nonetheless, Tokarzewski's account indicates that some officials adopted a less gentlemanly approach toward Polish prisoners than Maksimov describes.

Upon initial assignment or eventual release to settlement Poles nonetheless acquired privileges similar to those enjoyed by the Decembrists. For example, the founder of the Society of Military Friends, Konstantin Igelstrom, exiled to the small town of Stretensk on the Amur River, felt within his rights to request that he and his brother be allowed to send clothes and money to fellow exile Antoni Luboradski, "a young Pole [who] any day should be arriving at Shilkinsk Zavod."[57] A body of petitions filed between February 1837 and June 1844 shows Polish exile-settlers requested work releases and transfers and permission to send and receive parcels.[58] In 1843 Aleksander Kraewski, who had been exiled to the village of Tsurukhatui in northern Eniseisk *guberniia*, complained to authorities:

In a package sent me from Warsaw by my mother... I did not receive [two items she included]..., namely, a *Geographical Atlas* in French, consisting of 27 maps and 65 pages of descriptions, published by Ambrose Tardé in Paris in 1842, and the *1843 Calendar*, in

> Polish. I therefore respectfully request the administration take measures to send me the aforementioned publications.[59]

Could Kraewski not imagine why officials might not want him to possess these publications?!

Many Polish exiles found the surveillance over them immoderate and intolerable. Konstantin Walicki, exiled to settlement in the early 1830s as one of Juri Zaliwski's partisans, complained that people did not visit his home but only met with him in public because they did not want the gendarmes who always watched him to suspect they were conspiring together. The surveillance personally ordered by the emperor, whose interest in the Poles was nearly as obsessive as that in the Decembrists, was indeed intense. Thirty of Walicki's fellow partisans "were assigned to a special category and assessed every month in a 'list of Polish residents residing in Nerchinsk *zavody* who have been exiled to *katorga* for political crimes,'" writes Kodan. Three times a year, Irkutsk's gendarmerie would send summaries of these monthly reports to MVD headquarters. Censors able to read both Polish and French scrutinized every letter the Poles sent home.[60] After the *konarshchiki* arrived in Eastern Siberia Governor-general V. Ia. Rupert mandated that letters by "Polish criminals" discuss only their health and avoid describing their surroundings. Each was to be sent to Irkutsk's governor (who between 1839 and 1848 was Andrei V. Piatnitskii) who would then approve or disapprove its forwarding to Europe. The Poles could address petitions to the emperor, but each was first read by Rupert. Certain *konarshchiki*, like some Decembrists, found all this so oppressive they opted for military service in the Caucasus.[61]

Nonetheless, officials often sympathized with the Poles and did what they could to ease their conditions. Many shared Lunin's view that "it should not be forgotten that ties of kinship and friendship exist for them as for us; but perhaps more than for us, as such ties are stronger and more long-lasting according to that social life wherein they find themselves."[62] In 1839 Jan Oraczewski was exiled by a "supreme directive" assigning him "to one of the distant locations in Siberia that has been placed under strictest surveillance." Such rhetoric redolent of the sentences contained in the 1649 *Ulozhenie* could only have come from Nicholas, who eventually dropped the histrionics and reduced Oraczewski's punishment to exile to residence (*ssylka na zhit´ë*). This allowed Rupert to assign him to Kirensk, "because," he informed Chernyshev, "it is lightly populated, there are absolutely no other cities within 1,000 versts of it, and Oraczewski may be put under strict surveillance there." It was undoubtedly for these very reasons that Oraczewski immediately put in for a transfer. After some delay he was permitted to relocate to Verkhneudinsk, where he opened a medical practice. As a "doctor" in a region sorely in need of doctors Oraczewski won renown sufficient for him to join GUVS's medical division. However, this boon came with a catch, for he was soon told he would have to ply his trade in Verkhoiansk, the outpost in the Arctic Circle where temperatures drop to –90° F. In the end, the imperial amnesty of October 1843 that reduced all the *konarshchiki*'s sentences also spared Oraczewski, and paved the way for his return to Poland.[63] What is known about the emperor's toying with other exiles suggests it was he, and not Siberian officials, who was jerking Oraczewski's chain.

Rupert's successor Nikolai N. Murav´ev helped some Polish exiles. In 1848, soon after he took office, Murav´ev received a petition from Franc-ziszka Michalska, whose husband, the *konarshchik* Friderik Michalski, had just died:

Merciful Sir, Nikolai Nikolaevich!

My husband Friderik and son Lukan Michalski were exiled to *katorga* labor for participation in a secret society, received in good condition by an office of the Bureau of Exiles, and assigned to Aleksandrovsk Zavod. Wishing to fulfill my duties as wife and mother, I asked permission to follow them. No rigorous conditions whatsoever could alter my steadfast intention; death alone could have deprived me of the contract I undertook to share my husband's fate entirely. I took it as a repetition of my sacred vow of marriage!

I have had the misfortune of outliving my husband, who died at work, though by His Majesty's Order my son is now returning to Vologda, to residence [*na zhitel´stvo*, i.e., a mild category of exile]. By virtue of the contract I undertook, my lot in Siberia is coming to an end. I asked [Irkutsk's] Gentleman Civilian Governor to give me the means to return to Russia with my son, but he verbally refused. I am turning to Your Highness with a most humble request to grant me Your protection. You will please see that I came to Siberia not by order of the Court but voluntarily, for fulfillment of the duties of wife and mother, and I now have no reason at all to remain longer in Siberia. My request is completely lawful, as established in Articles 1310 Volume XIV and 169 Volume XV of the Code of Laws, and it is difficult for me to see why my innocent Mother should remain in exile when her Most Mercifully Pardoned son is returning to Russia [*sic*].

> I will await Your Highness's decision over my petition, but in the meantime I humbly request my son's removal to Vologda be delayed. I have the honor to be, with complete respect, Merciful Sir, Your Francziszka Michalska, Widowed from Friderik Michalski 7 May 1848. Irkutsk[,] in the home of Princess Volkonskaia.[64]

Michalska's references to the law code and final line suggest she was being advised by Mariia Volkonskaia, and this undoubtedly helped her case. Murav´ev sent a formal letter to Irkutsk's governor in which he cited Article 1310 for his "having no opposition whatsoever" to granting her petition.

Michalska's letter points to the relationships formed between exiled *shliakhtichi* and Decembrists. The Trubetskois and Volkonskiis, along with Artamon Murav´ev, Iakubovich, and many others, knew of the Poles' arrival beforehand and offered individuals both monetary and emotional assistance after they arrived. The Volkonskiis and Odoevskiis briefly guested several *shliakhtichi* before they could find private lodgings. Despite frequent meetings and discussions the two parties failed to agree on what Poland's political status should be because almost all the Decembrists opposed its independence. Nonetheless, they found common ground in artistic and educational pleasures. Several Poles were talented musicians and joined their Decembrist counterparts for evening recitals. Others taught French and German to local children. And there was sthe legendary friendship between Lunin and Wysocki at Akatui.[65] These mutually beneficial relationships resemble others in exile, for example among those who fled revolutionary France and among today's worldwide exilic communities. As for other exiles, the shared experience of displacement allowed Poles and Decembrists to bridge cultural and ethnic divides.[66]

Relations between these two groups were close enough for many officials to fear they were hatching plans for an uprising. "God save us from a second conspiracy similar to the Omsk [one] but more successful,—that it will not destroy Siberia or Russia for a long time," Tomsk's postmaster M. M. Gedenshtrom, himself an exile, wrote in a shambolic letter to Benkendorf on the 1834 anniversary of the Decembrist Uprising, "[and that] the clever and hateful Poles and 80 t[housand] debauchees—[for] the most part homeless exile-settlers (Kolyvansk, Nerchinsk, and violent Ural *zavod* peasants and up to 29 t[housand] penal laborers)—will be incapable of uniting into a dangerous mob....["]67

Soviet-era historians drew upon documentation showing suspicions of a Polish-Decembrist conspiracy to argue that where there was smoke there was fire. But their tendentious elaborations owed more to efforts to bind Communist Poland more closely to the USSR than they did to historical reality.[68] We shall see below that officials had good reasons to believe certain Poles were plotting everything from mass escapes to full scale rebellions; yet B. S. Shostakovich, a present-day expert on Siberia's Polish exiles, discounts claims of conspiratorial links to Decembrists by pointing to the lack of solid evidence. And without such evidence there is merely speculation.

After 1840 the number of state criminals exiled from Poland and the Western Provinces declined. There were only 17 political exiles in all Nerchinsk *zavody* as of February 1843.[69] In January 1844, 24 political exiles were distributed among Nerchinsk's *zavody*. The administration had taken pains to distribute them carefully, because no more than three were at any one *zavod*. Similarly low figures characterize Nerchinsk rosters for other months that year. There were only 85 political exiles in Irkutsk *guberniia* as of January 1844. As of January 1846 there were only 92 assigned to either *katorga* or to settlements in the same *guberniia*; and in May of that same year there were only 58 assigned to settlements in Eniseisk *guberniia*.[70]

Because they were the "most dangerous of criminals" few were ever assigned to Western Siberia. Despite Tokarzewski's highly charged account, Poles exiled towards the end of the period 1823–61 generally received more lenient treatment than their predecessors. In 1861 the priest Ignati Zakrzewski was convicted for delivering a "scandalous" sermon and exiled to Krasnoiarsk, where he continued his religious duties on a stipend of 6 rubles a month. After one year he was allowed to relocate to Saratov.[71] A significant number of Polish exiles were paid for services they alone could provide, not the least of which was literacy. The Nerchinsk Mining Administration hired several, including Wladislaw Cholodowski and Osip Peskowski, paid annual salaries of 288 and 228 rubles, respectively.[72] Not all were so fortunate, however. In 1855, after completing a three-year *katorga* term, Sewerin Meczkowski, a nobleman from Warsaw, was first removed to a settlement in Ilim *okrug* then later transferred to the only slightly less desolate village of Oëk, near Irkutsk.[73] For an urbanite from Warsaw there would have been little to do in either place other than contract cabin fever.

As he did the Decembrists, Nicholas routinely modified individual Poles' judicial sentences. In 1838 he reduced Konstantin Sawiczewski's and Aleksander Kraewski's sentences from *katorga* to exile to settlement "in consideration of [their] youth."[74] In 1851 he released early to settlement a total of 26 Poles serving *katorga* terms.[75] This and other meliorations culminated with Alexander II's amnesty of 26 August 1856, which allowed along with the Decembrists virtually all state criminals from Poland and the Western Provinces to return home. Twenty-seven opted to remain in Siberia.[76]

*   *   *

S. V. Kodan and P. L. Kazarian contend that the special administrative systems created for Decembrists and Poles marked not just a turning point in dealing with political exiles, but a turning point in Russia's overall administrative development. Nicholas created *ad hoc* bodies to interrogate, try, and sentence many of them; issued new regulations and established special prisons and special regimes to administer them; and oversaw the creation and activities of both the Third Section and the Gendarmerie to monitor them. It is reasonable to conclude that the procedures created for exceptional prisoners on the periphery came to be applied to average persons living in the Russian interior, in a kind of reverse fertilization by which frontier culture conditioned that of the motherland. Mere possession of Siberia therefore played a role in determining certain characteristics of imperial society, for had the realm ended at the Urals, Russia would probably have emulated Western Europe and the United States and constructed a prison system rather than depend for as long as it did on exile as a penal and retributive strategy. Nonetheless, reverse fertilization and Siberia's determinant role were evident long before 1825. By the early seventeenth century the autocracy was already freely using the charge of "state crimes" to exile people to Siberia; later, Peter I's Preobrazhenskii *prikaz* established a template for secret police forces created by his successors. An analogy also exists between the Polish soldiers, insurrectionists, and partisans deported during the 1830s and 1840s and the so called *Litva*—war captives exiled during Muscovy's seventeenth-century border wars. The deportation and treatment of Decembrists and Poles therefore did not catalyze overall trends in the way Kodan and Kazarian argue they did. Rather, they symptomatized the struggle between governmental and sovereign power in Russia. It also needs to be stressed that the surveillance these historians point to as being catalytic initially involved only several hundred exiles, and even then Siberian administrators were at their wits' end trying to account for their whereabouts and activities. In other words, the autocracy's "All-Seeing Eye" was far more imposing as an image than as a reality.

The most telling examples of the security apparatus's practical limits relate directly or indirectly to the Omsk Affair (*Omskoe delo*). This imbroglio partially involved those Polish soldiers captured during the November Insurrection and later transferred to the Siberia Corps. Founded in 1816, the corps consisted of infantry, cavalry, and Cossack regiments and a horse-artillery brigade. As of 1833 its roster listed 27,655 Russians and 2,296 Poles. More than 4,000 of these Russians had been assigned to the corps by criminal or military courts and so it was already a destination for recalcitrants, malcontents, and ne'er-do-wells. Military courts may have been used to assign these captured Polish soldiers to the corps as well; yet this is unlikely because none seem to have been enrolled in penal battalions. Instead, they were apparently simply removed by administrative fiat. Polish soldiers were also assigned to units in the cities of Orenburg, Krasnoiarsk, Eniseisk, and possibly elsewhere, but their numbers were small given that Krasnoiarsk, for example, had only 2,000 troops in total. As of 1833 Poles accounted for nearly half the 4,000-man garrison at Omsk fortress—headquarters of the Siberia Corps and principal defense for Western Siberia's vulnerable southern frontier.[77]

The city of Omsk itself had a prior history as a destination for criminals, with exiles laboring in the linen factory that was built there in 1822. Aside from the garrison, Omsk had a medium-sized civilian population: an 1825 census lists 5,455 males and 3,041 females, as well as four pubs, a public garden, and 990 wooden houses.[78] In 1838 GUZS relocated to Omsk from Tobol´sk; incorporated Omsk *oblast* into Tobol´sk *guberniia*; and renamed its regional government the Border Administration (*Pogranichnoe upravlenie*). This change was partly intended to better manage the Kirgiz and Kazakh nomads still migrating through their ancestral grounds. The Border Administration failed to perform as intended, however, and so in 1854 was divided into Semipalatinsk *oblast* and the *oblast* of Siberian Kirgiz, both still part of Tobol´sk *guberniia*.[79]

Yet all this was in the future, and so it need only be observed that in 1833 one and the same man commanded both the *oblast* and the Siberia Corps: Major-General Semën B. Bronevskii. Bronevskii had served in the Siberian military since 1808. While just a captain he attracted the attention of Mikhail M. Speranskii, who in his capacity as Siberia's governor-general promoted him to colonel and commander of Omsk *oblast*. Bronevskii personally met and similarly impressed Nicholas, who in 1834 would name him to the Eastern Siberian governor-generalship.[80] The strange circumstances surrounding the Omsk Affair suggest the emperor had mixed reasons for doing so.

Those writing on the affair do not explain why Petersburg relied so heavily on Polish prisoners to garrison Omsk; nor is it clear who decided to assign them there. If it was Bronevskii, perhaps he believed he could keep an eye on the insurgents better than could his subordinates in diverse locations; if it was Nicholas, then he was probably copying the policy used for the Decembrists out of a similar fear the Poles would spread sedition among Siberian civilians. Whatever his motive, the man who made the decision could not have better facilitated a mutiny.

An appreciation of the tendency for rumors to spread through tsarist society contextualizes the Omsk Affair and its aftermath. A superstitious and illiterate peasant population combined with official censorship made for a rumor mill always in full grind. Factors particularly conditioning the situation in Siberia include undependable communications; a small, disparate, and frequently isolated population; and a susceptibility to both paranoia and grandiose delusions by those living in a naturally harsh environment rendered more brutal by its diaspora of desperate castaways. Until 1857 Siberia had no regularly published newspapers or journals,[81] and so the absence of even a quasi-dependable news source meant word-of-mouth had to suffice. News about what was actually occurring in European Russia therefore often mutated into Biblical prophecy by the time it reached Siberia.

In late 1831 officials panicked that cholera was spreading through Siberia. This was a legitimate source of concern. Personified by contemporary writers as Morbus, pestilential demon of Roman antiquity, cholera had the year before started on the northwestern shores of the Caspian Sea and raced along the Volga and other rivers into Russia's heartland. By mid-July 1830 as many as a hundred people lay dying in the city of Astrakhan alone.[82] Petersburg's response was limited and so primary responsibility for dealing with the epidemic fell upon local officials, who responded in various ways. Not until early 1831 did the MVD publish an article describing how to prevent, diagnose, and treat cholera and how to dispose of its victims.[83] The interior ministry also reported that the emperor had heeded the advice of Petr M. Kaptsevich, commander of the National Guard Corps (*Otdel´nyi Korpus Vnutrennei Strazha*), and ordered that prisoners *en route* to Siberia be kept away from Moscow so as to limit spread of the disease.[84] However, Morbus had by this time claimed most of his victims. Poltava *guberniia*, for example, suffered grievously, largely because its administrators restricted information in a misguided attempt to forestall panic: between July and November 1830, 48,826 of its residents contracted cholera and 14,552 of these died.[85] Lincoln writes that during the 1830–31 Polish Uprising "cholera… claimed more Russian lives than did the Polish bullets."[86]

Moscow fared comparatively well. Cholera reached the city of 300,000 in mid-September; by 27 November 7,625 residents had been stricken, of whom 4,101 had perished. The historian who published these findings in 1893 could find no figures for after this date, but noted that by then the epidemic had pretty much run its course. Moscow's death rate would have been higher were it not for a well-coordinated effort by city leaders and medical professionals. Yet these same authorities initially chose not to inform the emperor of the epidemic because they did not want him to cancel his much-anticipated visit to the city. Thus Nicholas arrived the evening of 29 September, a full week after Moscow authorities first learned of at least seven cholera deaths, and, blissfully unaware of the risk, performed his ceremonial duties before an adoring public.[87]

Well-served by local authorities or not, imperial subjects everywhere spread rumors about a disease that even medical experts understood poorly; and sometimes panicked and rioted in response to these rumors. Writing later about the riots that engulfed several military colonies in Novgorod *guberniia* in July 1831, when Morbus again stalked the empire, two of the senior officers who managed to survive recalled they were sparked by the hygienic fumigation of a military engineers' barracks near Staraia Rusa. With rumors already rife that officials were exterminating residents by *poisoning* them with cholera, Arakcheev's cantonists and sympathetic townspeople went on a two-day rampage, sacking the police department and pharmacy and lynching, shooting, or beating to death more than 60 military and civilian leaders.[88]

By the time Siberian officials began panicking in late 1831 these events in European Russia were in the past; nonetheless, they still gave officials nightmares because the officials were all too aware of their tenuous hold over a largely hostile population. Many undoubtedly believed that the Poles then arriving by the thousands were bringing cholera with them. In November 1831, following the escape into his jurisdiction of eight exile-settlers from what they insisted was a death zone in Tomsk *guberniia*, Orenburg governor Aleksandr S. Osipov frantically wrote Irkutsk governor I. B. Tseidler, "I personally interrogated the eight aforementioned persons and all assured me that several thousand exile-settlers have left Siberia and are in Kazan *Guberniia*...," where they were supposedly besieging officials with demands to be transferred to other locations. As word spread that exiles were flooding Kazan and Orenburg *gubernii* officials east of the Urals began hyperventilating that the dam had finally burst, that Asiatic Siberia was about to wreak vengeance on Rus by submerging her gentle steppes beneath his blackest tides. This nightmare seemed all the more real when Tseidler learned through other channels that Cheliabinsk *okrug*'s land constable had discovered, north of Orenburg, another group of exiles fleeing the cholera they believed was spreading through Tobol´sk *guberniia*.[89]

Upon receiving this news Eastern Siberia governor-general A. S. Lavinskii, to his credit, kept a level head. He realized that if Eniseisk *guberniia*'s 22 exile settlements (see Chapter 6) caught wind of the rumor there would be a mass of terrified exiles fleeing during the middle of a Siberian winter. The results would be catastrophic. He immediately ordered Eniseisk's constables "to take secret but most energetic measures, so that lies may by no means be spread amongst the exile-settlers...."[90] But fear had already gripped Eniseisk governor Ivan G. Kovalev. On 13 November he relayed to Lavinskii news similar to that from Osipov, that a "large number of runaway exile-settlers from Siberia have arrived in the city of Kazan, where they are expecting the administration to settle them in Saratov and Astrakhan *Gubernii* in order to save them from the cholera." These locations suggested the masses were pouring westward and so, reported Kovalev, Osipov had urged him to somehow stem the flow.[91]

Despite Osipov's and others' presentiments, Eniseisk police soon determined that "a significant escape of exile-settlers outside the *Guberniia* has not occurred." It appears that with the exception of those fugitives questioned by Osipov and those detained by Cheliabinsk's land constable, virtually no exiles anywhere in Siberia were fleeing because of cholera. The rumor obtained what credence it had from Osipov's belief that what the eight exiles he "personally interrogated" told him was true. Eniseisk police were now more concerned with the rumor's potential impact, and therefore reported taking "secret, but most energetic measures" to suppress it.[92] Like their commander Lavinskii they left unwritten what exactly these measures were.

Another, quite different, example of what the rumor mill could produce concerned a chest of gold supposedly buried—one official emphatically underlined—"deep in the ground under a tree <u>in a garden</u> named <u>Panshinyi</u>."[93] Stories about pots of gold were not especially rare, and reflected the desperate toil of many Siberians. In this case a worker named Ermil Maslenikov[94] had reportedly told one Vasilii Gubkin, a 70 year-old former Moscow merchant, that when he labored at the Demidov metallurgical works in Tobol´sk *guberniia* he buried for safekeeping a chest of stolen gold. For some reason Gubkin informed officials that Maslenikov repeatedly told him this story during their march together into Siberia in 1833. The following year this news prompted a wide-ranging search that drew in both Siberia's governors-general to find a cache rumored to be as much as 180 pounds of pure gold. After a few fruitless months TobPS's procurer reported that in 1829 Maslenikov had been flogged and sentenced to Nerchinsk *katorga* for the theft of a mere 125 grams of Demidov gold. This happened four years before Gubkin supposedly met him.

There was no opportunity to solve the riddle because Maslenikov had since escaped. The search for the buried lucre was canceled.[95]

Hence wariness toward rumor-mongering was what probably caused Bronevskii to discount a letter he received in July 1832 from Vitsentii Grudzinskii,[96] who had been a nobleman in the Polish army before his exile to Omsk, where he was an artillerist in the horse-artillery brigade's 10th Company. Grudzinskii informed Bronevskii the Polish soldiers were planning to mutiny, pillage Omsk's armory, and escape to Bukhara, where they intended to strengthen their numbers with other fugitive Polish and Russian soldiers and return to Siberia to incite a mass uprising among exiles and peasants. Grudzinskii cryptically identified as the conspiracy's ringleaders a trio named "Markevich, Servidovich, and Kviatkovskii." Bronevskii responded by informing subordinates "it is well known that Private Grudzinskii is a depraved and inconsistent character"[97] and transferring him to a Cossack regiment on the border near Kolyvansk. He nevertheless ordered subordinates to report any suspicious activity.

A year later, on 6 June 1833, the mayor of Tara, an *okrug* city in Tobol'sk *guberniia*, received a letter from a local exile named Ivan Vysotskii. Vysotskii claimed that Osip V. Gorskii, the louche Decembrist we met in Chapter 4 and who was now living in Tara, was plotting a rebellion that would commence on 12 June, when a party of 360 Polish exiles was scheduled to pass through Tara. Similar to the scenario Grudzinskii outlined for Bronevskii, Vysotskii claimed that Gorskii and the Poles intended to pillage Tara's armory, torch the city, liberate exiles and laborers in the nearby Ekaterininsk distillery, then spread rebellion among the "many exile-settlers" in neighboring Kainsk *okrug*. An army that Vysotskii prophesied would eventually consist of many thousands of exiles, Tomsk and Barnaul factory serfs, and "*arakcheevtsy* and *semenovtsy*" (i.e., exiles resulting from the Semenovskii Mutiny and the cholera riots in Arakcheev's military colonies) would eventually descend upon Omsk, seize its munitions, and rampage through the rest of Siberia and Central Asia liberating all the exiled and disfranchised. Vysotskii even provided the name of Gorskii's fellow conspirator in Omsk: Ian Serotsinskii.[98]

Tara's mayor immediately forwarded this news to higher authorities, who ordered Gorskii's arrest and put the Tara Invalid Command on high alert. Bronevskii sent two Cossack squadrons with cannon to Tara and even armed several hundred peasants. The Polish exiles scheduled to pass through Tara were split into two groups and diverted elsewhere. At some point, Western Siberia governor-general Ivan A. Vel'iaminov found time to reward Vysotskii with a medal and permission to return home. Police arrested several Poles including Serotsinskii, whom investigators linked to Ian Ianitskii, a Pole first exiled to Omsk as a result of the 1812 war and who had since moved to Tara. Serotsinskii was found in possession of materials used to counterfeit official stamps as well as letters that connected him to two more exiled Poles, one in Tara and another in Tobol′sk, who were also arrested. Prosecutors would later use these letters to prove Serotsinskii had established a network of Polish conspirators throughout Siberia.[99]

After these arrests officials recalled Grudzinskii's letter of the previous summer to Bronevskii. While they were scrutinizing it for clues Bronevskii received another letter from Grudzinskii containing still more details, including that conspirators planned to make common cause with the Kirgiz and even seek France's support in conquering Siberia. But his most surprising revelation was that the conspiracy's principal leader was not just anyone named "Markevich" but none other than Colonel F. P. Markevich himself, one of Omsk's top officials.

In 1806 Markevich, an ethnic Pole, had voluntarily left Grodno to join the Siberian military, where he earned a number of distinctions. He served for seven years as Omsk *oblast*'s chairman (lit., *predsedatel*—equivalent in this case to "vice-governor") but had taken a sudden furlough in summer 1833. Despite his decorations and prominence the widower Markevich shared a very private life with one Francziszka Lopatova, who was still married to the Vil′no judge advocate she abandoned (along with six of her children) in 1826 when she and a young daughter joined Markevich in Omsk, where she lived without a passport and passed herself off as his sister "Elena." Locals knew her true identity and dismissed her as "Markevich's Polish woman" (*pol′ka Markevicheva*).[100]

According to the conspirators already under arrest Markevich, "but especially *pol′ka Markevicheva*," were, along with his Polish orderlies Onufrii (a.k.a. A. Verzhbitiuk) and especially A. Kviatkovskii, the true ringleaders. With Serotsinskii also under arrest it now seemed the trio first identified by Grudzinskii—"Markevich, Servidovich [*sic*], and Kviatkovskii"—had been apprehended. When governor-general Vel′iaminov learned that Markevich might be a traitor he forwarded this extraordinary news to Petersburg and requested instructions. Nicholas's response is evinced by the arrival on 10 August at Markevich's home of a cavalry battalion with orders to arrest him and Lopatova. Later, in response to Petersburg's demand for information on the couple, an official characterized Markevich as "foreign, simple, and lazy"; but of Lopatova he wrote: "His sister is smarter than Markevich, and cunning."[101]

Nicholas ordered all those caught in the dragnet tried according to the Battlefield Criminal Code. But this order ended up being delayed for two years to allow a commission, initially in Tobol´sk, to investigate Gorskii and the 16 Poles arrested there. The commission soon cleared Gorskii of all charges but confirmed there were connections between Tobol´sk's Poles, Markevich, and 26 lower-ranking Poles who had been arrested in Omsk. At Markevich's request the commission, apparently deferring to his rank and position, transferred proceedings to Omsk. Once his trial began, Markevich claimed he and Lopatova were innocent and that his orderlies Onufrii and Kviatkovskii and the other defendants had framed them. After the commission rejected this defense he and Lopatova refused to answer any more questions, and so attention turned to three others who by then had become most suspect: Ian Serotsinskii, Ksaverii Shokal´skii, and Vladislav Druzhilovskii.[102] Serotsinskii and Shokal´skii were from Kiev *guberniia*; Druzhilovskii from Volynia *guberniia*. Serotsinskii and Druzhilovskii were *shliakhtichi*; Shokal´skii had been a physician in Vil´no and was officially registered as a nobleman (*dvorianin*). Each had been assigned to the Siberia Corps for his role in the uprising, though at the time of his arrest Serotsinskii was teaching in Omsk's Cossack School and apparently not on active duty.[103]

Investigation into the Omsk Affair would not conclude until 1836. But in the meantime other disturbances involving Polish exiles occurred. We will return to the affair after first discussing these disturbances, for they influenced the commission's verdicts and sentencing as well as the emperor's handling of the affair.

*   *   *

The same year authorities uncovered the Omsk conspiracy a woman named Maria Szimanskaja walked from Krasnoiarsk to Irkutsk proclaiming herself Mariia Pavlovna, daughter of Emperor Paul and sister of Nicholas. She told villagers and exile-settlers that her other "brother," Konstantin Pavlovich, who had died of cholera, was in fact still alive. Not only this, but he was living incognito in Siberia and would soon "ascend to power." Szimanskaja foretold that upon Konstantin's second coming, so to speak, he would free the peasants from their oppressors.[104] Around this same time Achinsk *okrug*'s constable reported that another Pole, Ian Barszewski, was spreading a similar story, telling anyone who would listen that Konstantin was alive and would soon lead exile-settlers in a *jacquerie*.[105]

The Konstantin rumor began circulating within months of the man's death in June 1831 and gained especial currency in Eniseisk *guberniia's* handful of settlements for Polish exiles (see Chapter 6). One version held that Konstantin would emerge from his disguise to lead an uprising among Poles and other exiles, then march west with this army to destroy Russia's landowners and, with France's help, liberate Poland. Another had him already in France gathering forces for an eastward assault. Based on Russian and Polish demotic liberation myths, these and other versions were immediately comprehensible and quickly spread. Writing in 1878, a contributor to the journal *Russian Olden Times* recalled meeting a credulous believer in Akkerman, Bessarabia, as late as 1836, by which time the rumor had won converts across Moldavia and in Odessa, Sevastopol, and Kostroma in addition to Siberia. It had also mutated and was now linked to forestalling a purported Jewish plot to exterminate Russians, Poles, or "all Christians in general."[106]

Why did exiled Poles in particular consider Konstantin their savior? Some progressive Russians had considered Konstantin preferable to Nicholas or even Alexander as a ruler. This view filtered into the popular consciousness, such that the Decembrists were able to embolden their foot soldiers during the stand-off in Senate Square by having them chant "Konstantin-Constitution!" Konstantin's *de facto* vice regency over Poland, which began in 1814 when he took command of military forces there, did involve aspects of traditional Romanov despotism. Despite blissful union with the Polish princess Lowicza and a growing affection for her country and its people, he reputedly tyrannized Polish officers to such an extent that several preferred suicide over being subjected any longer to his whims. However, it was largely through his efforts that Poland's lower ranks were better compensated and provisioned than their Russian counterparts; and whereas the latter still had to serve 25 years the former had only eight. Probably contributing most to Konstantin's popularity was his refusal, out of a reluctance to shed blood and a genuine belief that Poland was the sovereign state its constitution said it was, to use force against the November insurrectionists. He even withdrew his troops from Warsaw to avoid provoking a showdown.[107] Following the brutal suppression and russification by his successor Ivan F. Paskevich, many exiled Poles recalled nostalgically, if not idyllically, Konstantin's 15-year rule.

Siberian officials were well aware of the Konstantin rumor by the time the Omsk Affair broke. This and their growing realization of the extent of the conspiracy caused them to react as they did to a report received in September 1833. One Shlomo Kozlinski, apparently during his march into exile, told Krasnoiarsk officials about two Poles who were spreading the Konstantin rumor throughout Siberia with the goal of fomenting rebellion. Kozlinskii identified 25 May 1834 as the date for an uprising and identified the two Poles as "Kol´chevskii and Molodetskii."[108] Nikolai S. Sulima, Eastern Siberia's governor-general at that time, warned officials about this pair, adding that they were traveling under false passports and possibly disguised as women. Tseidler somehow conceived from this the pregnant conclusion that they were planning to contact the Decembrists in Zabaikal´e. This in turn prompted Leparskii to warn Nerchinsk's commander Tatarinov that the mysterious duo had entered his mining district.[109]

The various activities accredited these two Poles were not necessarily mutually exclusive, and the very imagining of such disastrous scenarios suggests the hysteria that gripped officials over a pair of *agents provocateurs* no one could find. Tatarinov put his police on high alert and informed officials at Petrovsk Zavod (where the Decembrists mostly still were) of the danger. In mid-December 1833 Leparskii's office sent Tatarinov another warning, this time giving physical descriptions and identifying the Poles as "Kolychevskii and Count Molodetskii." With a minor variation on the spelling of the first these were the same names Kozlinski had given three months earlier. One week after Leparskii's letter Tatarinov wrote in frustration to a subordinate: "[V]illains similar to the descriptions provided—using various aliases and false disguises—have not been found."[110] In late January 1834 Eniseisk governor I. G. Kovalev, responding to Sulima's demand for more information, could only report that whereas many witnesses spoke of "two young men" traveling by horseback or wagon along the postal route, police still could not find them. The story was the same six weeks later.[111]

Despite the *provocateurs* beginning to prove to be phantoms, other signs suggested something was afoot. On 26 October 1833 a certain Starikov, a townsman being held in Orenburg's jail, informed the warden that a soldier named Ludwig Meyer, also in the jail, had told him about an uprising, planned by local Polish troops "grieved by the unfortunate events of the Polish revolution," that they had scheduled for either 27 or 28 October. According to Starikov, the conspiracies' ringleaders were "Zan, the Military School Museum's curator; Suzin, the Frontier Commission's accountant; Witkewicz, a junior ensign in the cavalry; junior officers Iwaczkewicz and Kowalski; and unknown ranks of various Polish officers." Meyer had said the rebellion would eventually include all Polish troops in the empire as well as 30,000 Russian soldiers, and that Zan and a group of *provocateurs* disguised as botanists and mineralogists had for some time been sowing dissension throughout Orenburg *krai*. Also, that Zan had contact with an unnamed "Tatar" who promised him Bukhara was ready to explode. After military governor Vasilii A. Perovskii heard Starikov's story he ordered the ringleaders arrested and their homes searched. Despite some incriminating documents an investigatory commission decided there were insufficient grounds to press charges, and instead punished Meyer and another man for spreading rumors.[112] As we shall see, its decision was not dissimilar from those of the Omsk commission.

There were still more alarming signs. During that same autumn of 1833 Poles assigned to the Eniseisk Invalid Command openly rebelled because of living conditions. Then, in early 1834, two incidents caused further anxiety. The first took place in Krasnoiarsk, where Polish soldiers freed inmates from the city jail with the intention of marching on Petrovsk Zavod to free Decembrist A. I. Iakubovich.[113] The second was really a series of incidents that apparently began in January or February, when military and civilian authorities learned that Polish soldiers stationed in Eniseisk were planning an uprising. How many were involved is unclear, but police arrested several suspects including the supposed ringleader named Boczarski. While they were being arrested other Polish soldiers verbally abused the mayor. Perhaps because the only casualty was the mayor's dignity Major Morozov, who commanded the Eniseisk troops, ignored his request to punish the offenders. A more serious offense occurred on 4 March when four Polish soldiers broke into the home of Eniseisk resident Pechenkin and savagely beat his son. There is no record of the assailants' motives, largely because Morozov once again failed to honor city authorities' requests for punishment.[114] Having received news of these incidents from the mayor, Governor Kovalev informed GUVS on 19 March:

> I instructed the Commander of the 12th Siberian Line Battalion, Major Frantsov, immediately to take appropriate measures to restrain the aforementioned Polish servicemen from illegal actions in the future, for which purpose Mr Frantsov has been dispatched on this date to the city of Eniseisk.

He then curiously added:

> [Morozov] of the Eniseisk Command told me there are Polish soldiers in the local invalid command who are plotting various uprisings, and that the local military Command [i.e., Morozov himself] can do nothing about this.[115]

Did Morozov's claim that he could "do nothing," in addition to his earlier rebuke of the mayor, simply amount to a lazy official unwilling to discipline his men? Or was he (like Markevich at Omsk) involved in a conspiracy? There is not enough evidence to conclude either way, but soon after Kovalev's letter he was dismissed from his post.[116] Whatever his motives, Morozov had sufficiently emboldened Polish soldiers to tell investigator Frantsov that if indeed they were guilty of what they were accused of, this was only because their superiors were "foolish and a joke." Frantsov later reported that relations between them and Eniseisk residents remained tense and so he ordered the Poles quartered with "older, well-behaved soldiers" who would keep "strict watch" over them. He also imposed a curfew on the Polish soldiers enforced by Cossacks.[117]

Siberian officials saw a pattern, if not evidence of an outright conspiracy, in these separate events. It is impossible to determine if their suspicions were more than just that. Because they were already on pins and needles over the Omsk Affair and the Konstantin rumor they were more than ready to read ulterior motives into any altercation involving Polish soldiers. Yet it is hardly surprising that men forcibly deported thousands of miles from home repeatedly quarreled with authorities and others.

Siberia's officialdom therefore entered with apprehension the month of May, the final days of which, Koz´linskii told them, Kolychevskii and Molodetskii had scheduled for their uprising. The Siberia Corps was taking no chances and concentrated troops around Tomsk and Krasnoiarsk. So called undependable persons were rounded up and given labor or military duties in distant locations. In the end no uprising took place, though contretemps involving exiled Poles sporadically erupted for several more years. For example, officials uncovered a conspiracy involving Polish soldiers, Russian exiles assigned to the Ilginsk distillery, and "a certain Anna, daughter of a laborer at the Irkutsk workhouse." As for "Konstantin," he finally appeared in Krasnoiarsk *okrug* in 1835 and proved to be a *brodiaga* identified as N. Prokop´ev, a soldier exiled for desertion in 1814. Prokop´ev managed to attract a large enough following that peasants helped him escape his exile convoy after his arrest, but he was soon recaptured and marched off into obscurity.[118] In Siberia truth remained stranger than fiction, however, as the commission investigating the Omsk Affair would learn.

*   *   *

The leading figures in the conspiratorial circles that were formed in Omsk and Tobol´sk had all originally been exiled together for partisan activity after the November Insurrection. Some belonged to those secret societies that made contact with Pavel Pestel and the Southern Society.[119] Given this background, the Omsk conspiracy's true leader appears to have been neither Markevich nor Lopatova but Ian Serotsinskii, the Cossack School teacher, who worked indefatigably to form a network of various individuals east of the Urals. Most remarkable were his attempts to include the Kazakh sultans Tursun Chingisov and Chingis Ablaikhan Valikhanov, who together commanded tens of thousands of mounted warriors. Valikhanov was a well educated young man and aesthete who studied eastern languages and was the least likely of the two to have actually joined the conspiracy.[120]

The commission also identified a Dr Petr Moshinskii as having formed a discrete circle in Tobol´sk that nevertheless had connections to Serotsinskii. Moshinskii had met with one of the sultans as well, though there was less evidence he actively sought the sultan's support and the two were probably just friends. More credible evidence showed he tried to contact the small group of Decembrists in Western Siberia. This raises the question of Gorskii's involvement, despite the fact that charges against him were dropped. It will be recalled that Gorskii manipulated both Petersburg and the governor-general of Western Siberia so as to gain preferable treatment. Also, according to Nagaev, of the two conspiratorial societies the one in Tobol´sk professed a more "revolutionary-democratic ideology," which further hints at a connection with Gorskii or other Decembrists.[121] But no concrete evidence exists to link these groups.

As for Markevich and Lopatova, the commission initially sentenced the former to death. During their trial evidence was presented that Markevich asked Sultan Chingisov during one of his visits to Omsk to travel to Tobol´sk with a Russian exile named Foma Petrzhitskii. Prosecutors argued this proved Markevich was part of the conspiracy. Yet despite this and other incriminating evidence the commission waived Markevich's sentence, and eventually all he received was an irrevocable mark on his service record. Why this happened for a man initially sentenced to death is unclear. As for Lopatova, the commission handed over the final decision on her fate to Petersburg, which ordered her removed to house arrest in Vil´no.[122]

In the final tally, between 1833 and 1836 the investigatory commission prompted the arrest of 464 Poles and several Russians in Omsk, but only 41 were ever sentenced: 17 to *katorga* for life and the rest to either "fortress arrest" or the Caucasus Corps. An indeterminate number ran the gauntlet for between 500 and 6,000 blows, leading to the deaths of Serotsinskii, Druzhilovskii, and three lesser figures.[123]

Despite these killings the government's response was clearly muted. At first glance it is surprising Nicholas did not order all Poles in the Siberia Corps exiled to *katorga* or at least to settlements. But his treatment of them mirrored his overall attitude toward the Omsk Affair: he wanted it hushed up. As John Keep writes about Nicholas in general, "The tsar's main concern was less to dispense justice even-handedly than to preserve the army's image."[124] And so in 1837 he ordered the commission's records placed in a secret archive kept by the war ministry. Not until 1863, when Alexander Herzen published a redaction of a minor participant's memoirs in *The Bell*, did Russian readers learn of the affair's existence. Knowledge of the event grew more widespread following Maksimov's account of it eight years later in *Siberia and Katorga*.[125]

"[The Polish conspirators'] plot did not possess a radical program of struggle"—so the USSR's official history of Siberia explains their failure to ignite a rebellion.[126] But Nagaev's detailed study shows that Serotsinskii's was about as radical (and grandiose) a program as anything that could be imagined at that time. Had the sultans' 100,000 horsemen along with disaffected elements from the military, exile, and peasant populations rallied behind the conspirators as planned, the Russian government would have faced a revolt larger than Pugachev's. But the very absurdity of this proposition indicates the real reason the conspirators failed, for such an army could never have been formed, let alone commanded or supplied. The possibility that some Decembrists might have joined does not alter this assessment in the least. Hopes that France would become involved were simply pipe dreams. The incidents in Eniseisk and Krasnoiarsk show that mutinies in specific locations were possible; but there remained little chance they could have coalesced in the way conspirators hoped and authorities feared.

In conclusion, a certain number of Polish exiles undoubtedly engaged in conspiratorial activities during the 1830s; and it is remotely possible that some Decembrists joined them. More importantly, however, responses by officials to both legitimate evidence and unsubstantiated rumor demonstrate the extent to which they knew their control over Siberia stood on a knife edge. Nikolai N. Murav′ev expressed this anxiety as late as the 1850s, when he noted that the vulnerability Siberians felt as a result of the mass exile of Poles had fomented secessionist ideas among Siberia's residents.[127] The extent to which exiles presented administrators with a volatile and nearly insoluble problem will become clearer in the next chapter, when we turn attention to the countryside.

6
Exile to Settlement

Late in Nicholas's reign the government began settling members of the self-castrating *Skoptsy* sect in two of Siberia's most remote regions. Laura Engelstein, in her study of the *Skoptsy*, notes that between 1849 and 1861 Iakutsk *oblast*'s population of *Skoptsy* grew from 24 to almost 600 people.[1] Turukhansk *krai*, Eniseisk *guberniia*'s bitterly cold northern wilderness, saw its population grow similarly. It is difficult to imagine a more forbidding place than this, where summer lasts two months, grain cultivation is impossible, and the Turukhan River, a tributary of the mighty Enisei, remains ice-bound until early June. As of 1831 the city (*gorod*) of Turukhansk consisted of 52 houses sheltering 366 men and women. Post-horses were not stationed anywhere along the 1,000-verst road between Turukhansk and Eniseisk because they would have frozen to death. Dogsleds were the principal means of travel for most of the year. The *krai*'s rural population totaled 811 male and female Russian peasants and 5,336 indigenes, mostly Tungus who, like their ancestors, provided their imperial masters an annual fur tribute know as *iasak*.[2] It is tragically poetic that *Skoptsy*, most of whom were barren of their sexual organs, were consigned to one of Siberia's most barren regions, the utter bleakness of which matched their vision of the future. They embodied a scarred, flattened landscape within whose geographic reality they were swallowed whole, like Jonah in the whale. Yet both remained within the boundaries of the sovereign's cartographically-iterated body-realm and therefore were necessarily to be used.

As of 1857, 242 of the 425 *Skoptsy* assigned to Eniseisk *guberniia* lived in separate *Skopets* communities within Turukhansk *krai*, whose population was nearly five times that of 1851, when just 51 *Skoptsy* were there. The vast majority (155) had been assigned to the region after 1853, coincident with the outbreak of the Crimean War. Forty-seven percent (113) were female—a disproportionately high figure compared to those for *Skopets* populations in the rest of Eniseisk and all of Irkutsk *guberniia* (23 and 25 percent, respectively). *Skoptsy* generally lived long lives. Turukhansk's 1857 male/female *Skopets* population was younger than the rest of Eniseisk's *Skopets* population; but all the same, over half (147) were over 40; 44 percent (103) over 50; and 24 percent (59) over 60. Yet the age difference between the sexes was significant: 80 of the 140 males living outside Turukhansk *krai* in Eniseisk *guberniia* were 60 or older. Within Turukhansk, 53 percent of males were over 50 and 30 percent over 60; comparable figures for females were 30 percent and 18 percent. The difference was still wider at the lower end of the scale: 72 percent of females were under age 30, but only 11 percent of males. Such a high proportion of female *Skoptsy* of child-bearing age was to be found nowhere else in Eniseisk or anywhere in Irkutsk *guberniia*: only three of the 42 women elsewhere in Eniseisk were age 30 or younger; while all 23 women in Irkutsk were over age 30.[3]

The government may have believed, or at least hoped, that sending younger women to Turukhansk would propagate its tiny Russian population. But if this was the plan it was not working: only three of the women there were married. A quite different explanation may be that it wanted to protect males in the Siberian heartland from so called "*Skopets-virgins*" (*skoptsy-bogoroditsy*)—Sirens who retained their sexual organs reputedly only to seduce men into eventually being emasculated. Whatever its motivations, the Committee of Ministers assigned 64-year-old Agrafena Baiksilova and her three adult children—Kseniia, Mariia, and Ivan, each deprived of Cossack status because of *skopchestvo*—to the city of Turukhansk; and similarly removed from Minusinsk *okrug* the 26-year-old peasant Mar´ia Soimonova "for showing the scars on her breasts and exposure of her adherence to *skopchestvo*" and assigned her to the Turukhansk countryside. Not all women sent to Turukhansk were young. Anna Zabnina and Avdot´ia Kuznetsova, ages 54 and 51 respectively, were exiled "for castrating themselves." Nonetheless, Kuznetsova was accompanied by her daughter Ekaterina.[4]

Siberian officials sometimes resisted Petersburg's orders regarding *Skoptsy*. Some of Governor-general Vil´gel´m Ia. Rupert's efforts on behalf of *Skoptsy* were noted in Chapter 1. He also responded to petitions that *Skoptsy* sent him and other officials. In 1839, after being rebuked by the Eniseisk Land Court, four men put their case before Rupert:

> For our crimes—namely, castrating ourselves—we were exiled without [corporal] punishment to settlement in Siberia and assigned to

> Tobol'sk *Guberniia*. But now, by the government's will, the Eniseisk Land Court has for these crimes ordered us all settled in a distant region of Siberia and assigned with others to Turukhansk *krai*....[5]

The petitioners—Ignatii Anan´in, Afonasii and Andrei Abrosimovyi, and Erofei Chenakov—were aged 81, 69, 67, and 42, respectively. Anan´in was feeble and sickly and believed he would not survive being transferred. They explained that fishing and hunting were the only means of survival in Turukhansk, but confessed they knew nothing about these things and therefore predicted "we will perish." Rupert forwarded their petition to V. I. Kopylov, his nominal inferior to whom he seems to have deferred in all these matters, but the outcome of this particular case is not known.

The notion that *Skoptsy* deserved harsher punishments than other schismatics persisted after Nicholas's death. In 1857 Governor-general Nikolai N. Murav´ev ruled that all schismatics should be settled in "suitable locations," but excluded *Skoptsy* from this provision. The Senate confirmed his decision in 1860. Three years later the *bezpopovets* Old Believer Ananii Prokop´ev, despite having been convicted of *brodiazhestvo*, receiving 30 birch blows, serving ten months in a correctional battalion, and now facing eight years resettlement (*na vodvorenie*) in Siberia, was nonetheless explicitly exempted from the kind of harsh locations to which *Skoptsy* were to be assigned.[6] In 1862 the Irkutsk MVD reported that Old Believer exile-settlers Ivan Kholostov and Pavel Malyshkin, captured after fleeing their assigned location of Menshikov *volost*, Kurgan *okrug*, Tobol'sk *guberniia*, had been punished excessively, not because Kholostov, as an "incorrigible," was given ten lashes and tattooed with "С П," but rather because both had been reassigned to "distant locations." Supporting the convicts' petition for relocation to Verkhneudinsk *okrug*, the MVD respectfully reminded Eastern Siberia's new governor-general Mikhail S. Korsakov of his predecessor's ruling assigning all schismatics "except *Skoptsy*" to "suitable locations."[7]

Skoptsy were therefore treated unusually harshly and differently compared to others exiled to settlement. Their persecution increased late in Nicholas's reign, by which time the exile system had collapsed and his political agenda lay in tatters. Along with other minorities *Skoptsy* formed part of a growing number of internal enemies for the regime.

Though especially severe, *Skoptsy*'s treatment symptomatized larger developments involving the control and use of subject bodies toward statist ends. Between 1823 and 1858 the judiciary sentenced nearly 200,000 people to exile to settlement.[8] They were almost evenly divided between Western and Eastern Siberia, with the largest group of over 70,000 assigned to Eniseisk *guberniia*. Unlike *Skoptsy*, other exile-settlers were not assigned to Iakutiia, Kamchatka, or similar locations where agriculture was virtually impossible because Petersburg genuinely wanted to turn them into productive peasants. That it failed to do so[9] testifies to its misguided notions but certainly not lack of will. More-over, given their numbers and the length of time involved, Petersburg's effort to use exiles to colonize Siberia did indeed make for a *Sonderweg* that distinguishes Russia's expansionary experience from those of other states.[10]

Initially, primary responsibility for finding land for exiles and creat-ing settlements fell on the MVD. The Third Section took over the first task after its establishment in 1826, whereas the Ministry of State Domains assumed the second after it was established in 1838. The latter ministry eventually assumed the first task as well, and even undertook to encourage exiles to marry and have families.[11] One factor rendering the transformation of exiles into peasants as futile as squar-ing a circle was the absence of land known to be fertile. The operative word here is "known," for as of 1838 less than 1 percent of Russia's estimated 90 million *desiatiny* of state land had been surveyed, and so the government literally did not know where to assign exile-settlers. Moreover, much of the surveying done after 1838 was sloppy[12] and probably not focused on potential exilic sites. Even when information about land quality was available the lack of data on the number of exiles or others assigned to it hindered its rational distribution. For example, in August 1832 Tomsk governor Evgraf P. Kovalevskii could find no data whatsoever on exiles assigned to Tomsk *okrug*.[13]

Siberia's geography and northern latitude anyway limited the amount of land that could be farmed. In 1810 a traveler to Western Siberia stated the problem unequivocally:

According to current observations, it is necessary to state as irrefutable: 1) that the northern part of Siberia, beginning from the 58° parallel, does not produce grain, even for local consumption; 2) that the south-ern part itself, from the r[iver] Kama to the east, is subject to inevitable bad harvests for reasons of rocky humus and the resultant coldness of the shallow soil; 3) that the southern half of Tobol´sk *guberniia* also produces bad harvests, correspondent with similar ones in Perm *guberniia*; and 4) that these regions' western and eastern populations have to be fed in poor harvest years with production from a single cornfield in southern Tomsk *guberniia*. From this follows the question,

How much of the population can be supplied by yields from Tomsk's lands?[14]

Conditions in Eastern Siberia were even worse, with Eniseisk *guberniia* a partial exception. One historian argues that in Western Siberia, "the problem of providing land suitable for agriculture was severer than in Eastern Siberia" because it had a larger and longer-established peasant population that managed to prevent some regions being opened to exilic settlement, and because the climate in Tobol´sk *guberniia*'s northern *okruga* of Berezov and Surgut and Tomsk *guberniia*'s Narym *okrug* made it impossible to assign exiles there.[15] However, Eastern Siberia's admittedly smaller peasant population exerted the same effect over what was at the same time a smaller amount of suitable land.

Nonetheless, between 1823 and 1861 the state continued deporting exiles to remote areas for the purpose of agricultural settlement. Although exiles formed a significant proportion of the large number of subjects the government relocated during this period, they have been overlooked by historians writing on migration.[16] Though certainly not blind to the challenges these faced, officials believed they could be superseded by intervening in the countryside more forcefully than in the past and adopting a disciplinary approach to managing agriculture. The countryside's impoverishment was due to an absence of both protection and supervision, believed Pavel D. Kiselev, who wrote in 1836, "Because of the lack of protection the peasants are burdened with illegal requisitions and personal taxes. Because of the lack of supervision debauchery and drunkenness destroy the basis of rural well-being at the very source."[17] Kiselev was addressing these comments to M. M. Speranskii, who as head of the Siberian Committee was at that time very much concerned with better managing both peasants and exile-settlers.

Before turning to these involuntary agriculturalists, however, it should be recalled that as required by the 1822 Siberian Reforms small numbers of nominal exile-settlers were assigned to factories or workhouses. Moreover, those who were assigned to the land sometimes obtained tickets of leave that allowed them to relocate to cities and towns to work as tradesmen, domestics, or industrial laborers. In this way exile-settlers came to be employed alongside both freemen and penal laborers in Western Siberia's distilleries, for instance. In July 1840 Tobol´sk's and Tomsk's exile bureaus began transferring small numbers of those deemed unsuitable for agriculture (a classification that could have accounted for nearly all exile-settlers) to the cities of Tobol´sk, Tomsk, and Omsk. At the same time, so as to limit the number of exiles competing for urban jobs, they forbid *volost* administrations from issuing tickets of leave on their own. In the late 1840s GUZS established quotas defining by city the number of exiles who could work in them: Tobol′sk—300; Tiumen—120; Ialutorovsk—30; Kurgan—30; Ishim—30; Omsk—300; Tara—30; Turinsk—25; and Petropavlovsk—40. Exiles worked for and were housed by private entrepreneurs, though the exile bureaus retained jurisdiction over them and even designated their pay scales: chefs, drivers, and gardeners, for example, could earn up to 3 rubles a week; cooks, kitchen staff, laundresses, maids, and charwomen between 1 ruble 50 kopeks and 4 rubles. Exiles therefore contributed to Siberia's urban development, but their numbers were small. As of 1841 the 4,763 exiles assigned to cities and towns in Western Siberia made up 5.1 percent of its urban population. But these were atypically high figures for the period ending in 1861, during which they normally accounted for only around 1.5 percent. Officials were sometimes exceedingly pedantic in enforcing laws that limited exile-settlers' urban employment. Nonetheless, exiles played major roles within certain regions and specialties. For example, in 1850 they accounted for 380 of the 960 tradesmen in Tomsk and were also numerous among tradesmen in Omsk.[18]

Nonetheless, exile-settlers were overwhelmingly assigned to the land. They were divided into two categories: those assigned to so called *starozhil* villages and those assigned to state settlements (*kazennye seleniia*) designated exclusively for exiles. As of 1835 the first category accounted for 30,243 exiles in Western Siberia and 14,769 in Eastern Siberia. Women represented one-seventh of this cohort.[19] Exile bureaus were supposed to assign overseers to each *okrug* and *volost* where exiles were settled; and Cossacks' duties included watching over exile-settlers. But the acute lack of personnel meant these tasks usually fell to *starozhily* or headmen chosen from among the exile-settlers themselves. In 1830 the Siberian Committee lambasted Siberian officials for not doing enough to administer exile-settlers:

> *Volost* administrations... devote not the slightest attention to their behavior [to see that they are] employed in work and trying to establish homes. For the most part these settlers lead an idle life, being neither forced to work nor taken to the land for farming. Having retained their free time they are, as insolvent residents of that village of which they are a part, rewarded with food brought to them for the most part by *starozhily,* and as such the newly resettled become a burden upon native residents.[20]

That same year the MVD's journal published an article on Zabaikal′e's population that blankly stated: "There are not many good householders among the exile-settlers: their principal vice is drunkenness."[21] The article's second installment focused on state settlements in Irkutsk and Nizhneudinsk *okruga*, where one out of every four exile-settler families was reportedly living on state subsidies.[22] The following year GUZS appointed overseers for Tomsk and Kainsk *okruga*. Nonetheless, in 1833 gendarme colonel A. P. Maslov, following his inspection of Western Siberia, concluded, "Tobol´sk *guberniia*'s administration is not devoting sufficient attention to the Exile Office's [i.e., TobPS's] distributing of exiles to settlements in Siberia." Maslov complained that TobPS was largely staffed by Jews who accepted exiles' bribes to assign them to better sites or provide them conditions easier than those required by their sentences. He singled out a certain Brilliant (*Briliiant*—almost certainly a pseudonym) who, despite being both a Jew and an exile, was the office's "chief agent... providing the Office director Popov with a good revenue." Like other underpaid tsarist bureaucrats TobPS's probably accepted more bribes than they refused, as Decembrist A. N. Murav´ev found during his brief employment in Tobol´sk's administration, but despite Maslov's insinuations their ethnicity had nothing to do with this.[23]

For the most part, then, administrators washed their hands of the exiles they assigned to villages of *starozhily*, who loathed giving any of their valuable cleared land to them. In Siberia more land was needed to yield the same harvests as in European Russia because growing seasons were shorter. For instance, while he was in Petersburg in September 1831, Governor-general A. S. Lavinskii received a letter from an assistant back in Irkutsk, who suggested an average of 50 to 60 *desiatiny* per exiled family and 15 *desiatiny* per exiled "soul" were necessary for sustainability and productivity.[24] Another source reports that around this time 15 *desiatiny* per soul became the norm until the end of tsarism, though this norm was not always met.[25]

No matter where they were assigned exile-settlers were absolved of taxes for their first three years. If during that time they established a home and followed standards of good behavior they were freed from taxes and obligations (*povinnosti*) for another three years; if they did not, they had to pay a yearly tax of 50 kopeks or 15 silver kopeks to the exile-settlers' fund, yet still remained free from obligations. Rulings passed in 1835 and 1836 also freed exile-settlers' children under age 17 from taxes. Exile-settlers who entered into a first-time marriage with another exile received an outright gift of 15 silver kopeks as well as a ten-year loan for another 15 kopeks.[26]

Despite these incentives most found themselves subject to taxes they had no way (or intention) of paying. For instance, of the 15,600 exile-settlers assigned to Tobol´sk *guberniia* as of 1 September 1832, a mere 2,323 owned their own homes and only 1,053 others were employed as agricultural laborers. Tomsk *guberniia*'s numbers were somewhat better: for example, 2,981 of Tomsk *okrug*'s 12,702 exiles were "set up with homes." But Siberian officials used generous definitions to determine what constituted a homeowner and farmer and so even these figures are deceptive. As of 1832 Omsk *oblast* had only 593 exiles: 32 operated their own farms; another 51 owned houses but were not farmers. Many Omsk exiles worked instead as tradesmen, yet counterproductive bans both there and elsewhere restricted their ability to do so legally. In 1841, 24,606 of Western Siberia's exiles did not own homes. During the period 1846–53 only 1,574 of these exiles met the requirements needed to enter the peasant *soslovie*.[27] In 1862 Tobol´sk reported that only 10,007 of its 38,578 exiles could be "regarded as householders"; noted this situation was "far from satisfactory"; and added that most were in towns doing various jobs "or moving from one village to another, having in this way gotten used to a wandering life." It suggested employing some in the fishing industry in the far north in Berezov *okrug*, but acknowledged there were still not enough jobs for the exiles assigned to the *guberniia*.[28]

Deported to a region most were unsuited for and where little help could be found, exile-settlers faced dire situations. Even when assigned to *starozhily* villages exiles tended to be used to buttress lightly populated and underdeveloped *okruga*, particularly Tiukalinsk, Tara, and Ishim, all in Western Siberia. As of 1840 exiles accounted for 31.9 and 38 percent of the populations of Western Siberia's Kainsk and Mariinsk *okruga*, respectively.[29] Abandoned by officials and shunned by peasants, these societal deviants forcibly removed to Siberia felt doubly outcast. One indication of this is Siberia's high suicide rates. In 1836 around 20 per every 100,000 males in Tomsk and Irkutsk *gubernii* killed themselves, whereas the rate for the entire empire was 8.10. Three years later the figure for Eniseisk *guberniia* (which had especially large numbers of exile-settlers) was 24.61, whereas that for the empire had fallen to 7.74. Seven people in Tobol´sk *guberniia* killed themselves in June 1850 alone.[30] These figures account for Siberia's overall male population, and so how many exiles killed themselves cannot be precisely determined. Nevertheless, they seem to have accounted for a disproportionate number of suicides. For instance, it is known for certain that 59 exiles killed themselves during 1855–56 in Tobol´sk *guberniia*.[31]

The grand-scale failure to turn exiles into peasants was also enormously costly in financial terms. Simply put, exile to settlement was an economically irrational policy, a losing proposition that in no way justified the amounts the state invested in it. As of 1836 tax arrears for Western Siberia's exile-settlers totaled 1,830,000 rubles.[32] In 1841 Ishim *okrug*'s exiles paid only one-third of the taxes they owed. During the second half of 1851 Tobol´sk's male exile-settler population accumulated arrears totaling 116,243 rubles; the comparable figure for Tomsk was 246,342. In addition to costs associated with maintaining and administering its own exiles, GUZS also bore the costs of maintaining and supplying all those convoyed further to Eastern Siberia. In 1838 these costs totaled over 96,000 silver rubles; ten years later, almost 103,000 silver rubles. Because of physical or mental infirmities large numbers of exiles could do no work whatsoever and thus further drained government coffers. In 1842 Tomsk *guberniia*'s administration reportedly spent 71 silver rubles 51 kopeks to maintain each such disabled exile who was unmarried and a whopping 712,933 silver rubles to support all needy exiles together.[33]

*   *   *

State planners tried more diligently to insure success for the second, smaller, category of exile-settlers assigned to state settlements. Nominally created and operated according to the 1822 Regulation on Exiles, these settlements actually perpetuated a tradition that began when Empress Anna used convicts to establish agricultural colonies on Kamchatka Peninsula and in Orenburg *krai*. Under Elizabeth Petrovna and Catherine II the *poselenii*, as these settlements were then called, proliferated, particularly in southwestern Siberia's Baraba Steppe, where thousands of hapless administrative exiles died building and settling a forlorn stretch of the Great Siberian Road. Yet even these tribulations were superseded by Paul's and Alexander I's botched efforts to colonize Zabaikal´e with a mix of administrative and criminal exiles. M. M. Speranskii, who had no qualms about exploiting convict labor, nevertheless found the camps erected by Irkutsk governor Nikolai I. Treskin so inhumane that he disbanded them immediately upon becoming Siberia's governor-general in 1819. The state's long-term interest in maximizing agricultural production lay behind this use of exile-settlers. From its very beginnings in the late sixteenth century exile had as its primary goal the economic development of Siberia; retribution and punishment were important but thoroughly secondary goals, at least as far as the state was concerned.[34]

During the early nineteenth century, colonization everywhere within the empire "became increasingly bureaucratic, routinized, systematized, and distinguished by… the micromanagement of settlement," writes Willard Sunderland. "[T]utelage thus became an essential modus operandi of state colonization policy."[35] Aleksei A. Arakcheev's military colonies epitomized this tutelary micromanagement. Described by Walter Pintner as "a curious mixture of barracks, concentration camp, and utopian community"[36] and lasting until the 1860s, they were a transmogrification of the military colonies established earlier in Siberia under Catherine II.[37] Arakcheev's creations involved the peacetime assignment of soldiers to the countryside to supervise and boost state peasants' production; as well as the training of soldiers' and peasants' sons as potential recruits, or cantonists. By 1825 nearly 150,000 servicemen lived in these colonies, "mainly in the gubernii of Novgorod in the north and Khar′kov, Kherson and Ekaterinoslav in the south," isolated from surrounding communities, administered under an extralegal regime, and aptly forming what one British visitor called an "Imperium in Imperio."[38] The colonies' early years were fraught with disorder and tyrannical management, though conditions improved as time went on. John Keep estimates that by 1850 their combined population of peasants, soldiers, reservists, and cantonists (wives and dependents included) probably totaled over a million.[39]

Less is known about the state settlements for exiles, but they seem to have been modeled on the military colonies. Finance minister Dmitrii A. Gur′ev used the military colonies to experiment with new agricultural techniques; his successor Egor F. Kankrin extended this experimentation to the state settlements in Siberia. Both institutions reflected the idyll of an economic pastorate requiring supervision by sovereign authorities. The emergence of Nicholas's exilic settlements also reflected the series of legislative acts that ended the use of foreign colonists to settle the frontier as of 1830.[40] The assigning of convicts to realize what Sylvia Schafer has in a different context called *l'imaginaire d'état*[41] altered Russia's penal landscape. As the settlements grew, *katorga*'s population shrank: whereas 1,351 men and women were exiled to Siberian *katorga* in 1825, this figure declined to just 728 in 1854.[42] Funds for maintaining *katorga* prisons appear to have declined as well.

All state settlements for exiles were in Eastern Siberia.[43] Western Siberia's leaders began opposing establishing settlements in their zone as early as March 1825, and despite repeated injunctions from Petersburg and GUVS they avoided implementing this provision of the 1822 Reforms. This was consonant with their larger effort to curb exile to Western Siberia altogether and which led to legislation such as that of 2 April 1826 that prohibited settling exiles along the Omsk frontier. Exile to the Altai region, which included the *okruga* of Biisk, Barnaul, and Kuznetsk, had been banned since 1808.[44] Eventually, legislation passed in 1859 and 1862 freed all Western Siberia from convicts sentenced to exile to settlement or exile to resettlement. From then on, the region served with some exceptions as a destination for administrative exiles only.

As of 1835 there were 13,014 exiles in Eastern Siberia's state settlements, a third of whom were women. The exact number of settlements is unclear but they appear to have totaled 40–50 by the late 1830s. The substantial amount of archival and secondary material related to a series of 22 settlements built in Eniseisk *guberniia* suggests these were the largest among them, and were also considered by Petersburg as models for future development. On 25 August 1827 the Siberian Committee budgeted 479,000 ruble-*assignats* for the Eniseisk settlements' construction. Ten years later the committee reported that "resettling began in March 1829... in the *okruga* of Kansk, Achinsk, and Minusinsk, where 5,955 exiles have been assigned... at a cost of 490,000 ruble-*assignats*."[45] Despite Petersburg's investment in these settlements, local officials viewed them jadedly. In 1827 Eniseisk governor Aleksandr P. Stepanov explained to Governor-general Aleksandr P. Lavinskii:

> The new settlements in Eniseisk *guberniia* do not consist of those colonies that are designed for propagating agriculture and strengthening the population, but have a singular goal—the collecting of exiles scattered throughout all the *gubernii* into residences established only for them, so as to conveniently surveil people who disturb the general peace.[46]

The cost to deport these disturbers of the peace was 100 to 150 rubles each. Administrators billeted them in villages near their designated sites while they built the settlements over the course of ten years. A standard plan was used for them all: each house was two stories with a four-window façade and placed close to its neighbor along a single main street, as in a traditional village. Living arrangements for each house consisted of a collective (*artel*) of "four brothers" led by an "elder brother," or a so-called "family" of two married couples. The first exile-settlers arrived later than planned, and so instead of living off their own produce had to depend on government rations their first year. Moreover, each received only four *desiatiny* of land—extremely small considering that 15 *desiatiny* became the norm four years later.[47] The poor planning revealed by this insufficiency of land and exiles' late arrival was probably not as keen for later arrivals, described in the Siberian Committee's 1837 report as being "chiefly married and suited to agricultural practices [*uprazhneniiia*]," and whose "resettlement" was "carried out with financial assistance and the treasury's provisioning of agricultural tools, livestock, and grain for sowing and sustenance."[48] Yet even the earliest arrivals' first harvest was deemed sufficient enough for officials to "tax" 25 percent of the grain and store it for future emergencies. Thirteen years later, to compensate the government for its outlays and to provide funds for other exiles, this tax in kind was replaced by a poll tax on each exile-settler of 2 rubles 50 kopeks.[49]

Each settlement tended to have a uniquely homogeneous population. For example, Sagaisk consisted mainly of *brodiagi* who had escaped from fortresses, and Tigritsk of local exiles who had for several years been assisting the settlement of new arrivals. At least two and possibly three settlements had predominantly Polish populations.[50] Each possessed an assembly (*skhod*) and headman (*starosta*) whose authority, however, was limited to dispensing minor punishments and communicating instructions from government officials. Female exiles served in the assemblies and also separately nominated their own *starotitsy*, whose job it was to inspect houses where women lived and censor those who neglected their domestic duties. Two senior officials, separately headquartered in the *okrug* cities of Minusinsk and Kansk, commanded the overseers (*smotriteli*) and Cossacks assigned to each settlement. These overseers micromanaged the exiles: Sagaisk's specified the type of trees ("short and stout") to be cut for firewood and the precise number of bricks to be used for building a jetty along the Amyla River.[51]

Besides the Eniseisk settlements, several smaller settlements totaling 104 men and 67 women are known to have been built during 1831 "between Irkutsk and Maltinsk Station [110 versts west of Irkutsk]" at a cost of 25,000 ruble-*assignats*.[52] However, these settlements immediately failed to meet expectations. In early 1830, as the Eniseisk settlements were coming into existence, Benkendorf noted in his annual report on public opinion the disregard interior minister Arsenii A. Zakrevskii was showing toward convicts' conditions generally, and also cited the deplorable state of foreigners' colonies where, he wrote, "things are going poorly—colonists are given no protection whatsoever owing to the minister's strange hatred for foreigners and incomprehensible prejudice that colonies in Russia are useless."[53] If Zakrevskii was disregarding convicts and colonists alike, then it is likely the exiles in state settlements were doubly suffering.

The Siberian Committee's report shows that Petersburg's agricultural agenda was not being realized through the assignment of exiles to either *starozhil* villages or state settlements. As of 1835 there were

58,026 exile-settlers in Siberia. The vast majority (45,012) resided in *starozhil* villages, and most (30,243) of these were in Western Siberia. The failure of exiles to become productive farmers was made clear by the fact that only 8,168 male and 1,601 female exiles in Western Siberia had "settled down with homes and full domestic economies." The remaining 20,474 were lodgers in peasants' or other exiles' homes. In Eastern Siberia, the 14,769 exile-settlers assigned to *starozhil* villages reportedly possessed "over 4,890 houses, significant privately-owned business establishments, and livestock and agricultural enterprises." But despite the committee's parenthetical comment that these exile-settlers harvested 97,000 poods of winter grains and 313,000 poods of spring grains in 1834, these numbers could not disguise the fact that only one-third of these exile-settlers had, in fact, "settled down." The committee did not identify the proportion of exiles assigned to state settlements who had "settled down," but noted they had built only "1,405 houses and outbuildings." [54] Most worked as laborers for others or simply crowded together into what amounted to flophouses and did nothing. As we have seen, significant numbers were dying; nonetheless, exiles' excessively high death rates account for only a small portion of those who did not establish households. The overseers of the state settlements were no better than *starozhily* at turning exiles into farmers.

The committee also reported that over the period 1823–32, 11,482 exile-settlers graduated into either the state peasantry or *meshchane soslovie*. In 1833 and 1834 alone, 995 and 3,211 had respectively done so.[55] The disparity between these two figures is difficult to explain. Perhaps an amnesty or administrative decision reduced sentences across the board and suddenly made a large number of exiles eligible for these *sosloviia*. The latter figure may alternatively reflect the sudden influx of Polish exiles deported as a result of the November Insurrection. Given that 67,139 exile-settlers are known to have been deported to Siberia between 1823 and 1832,[56] the Siberian Committee's figures nonetheless show that only one out of every seven was graduating to the peasantry or *meshchane*. Regardless of overseers, Cossacks, and the introduction in November 1835 of bi-monthly rosters, many exile-settlers were abandoning their assigned locations. They simply did not want to take up farming, and there was little else to do in these places but steal horses—an especially lucrative "industry" particularly in Eniseisk and one punished as severely as in the American West.

Officials tended to explain exiles' proclivity to escape on the lack of women who were traditionally believed to exert a domesticating influence over criminal and non-criminal frontiersmen alike.[57] Despite Abby

Schrader's claim that in so doing officials wanted "to deflect blame from themselves and the Russian penal system,"[58] these officials were simply expressing what was commonly accepted wisdom without the ulterior motives she suspects. Between 1823 and 1860 TobPS processed 38,842 females punished with exile, 7,467 of whom were sentenced to *katorga* for particularly serious crimes. Altogether they accounted for 13.6 percent of those forcibly deported during this period. Whereas females accounted for a small percentage of convicts and administrative exiles, they represented virtually every one of the spouses who accompanied exiled husbands, as well as half the children these women brought to Siberia. Between 1823 and 1860 these *dobrovol´nye*, women and children together, totaled 22,764 and accounted for 7.3 percent of all deportees combined. Data on *dobrovol´nye* before 1854 do not distinguish between the sexes or between adults and children, but comparison with later figures shows that women accounted for nearly 40 percent of all *dobrovol´nye*, which means that around 9,000 would have been deported between 1823 and 1860. More precise data show that between 1854 and 1860, 1,526 women and 2,407 children accompanied exiles to Siberia, with the former accounting for 3.2 percent of the 47,623 deported during this period. Men accounted for only eight of the *dobrovol´nye* during this period.[59]

Conditions for *dobrovol´nye* were especially dreadful during the march into Siberia. Women and children were raped and molested in transit prisons and way-stations and sometimes exchanged sex in return for rations, protection, or favored treatment by guards. One indication of their fate is reports detailing the number of exiles hospitalized with venereal diseases, which officials invariably blamed on exiles' "dissoluteness." According to Tobol´sk *guberniia*'s medical inspectorate, of the 72 exiles found to be infected with incurable venereal diseases between 1823 and 1827, 68 died. A higher overall number is suggested by a finding showing one out of every hundred exiles was infected. To combat the couplings that inevitably occurred the government ordered in 1826 that separate groups for women follow those for men by two days. However, this applied only while exiles were traveling through European Russia and not Siberia, where the lack of personnel made it impossible to split up convoy parties. A regulation did prescribe that within the same party men and women be kept apart, but like others this was routinely ignored, and in any case convoy officers could always be bribed.[60]

The government took various steps to procure females for male exiles. In 1825 the Senate authorized the purchasing from indigenes of female children as wives for exiles. G. S. Fel´dstein calls the 150 rubles paid for each of these girls a "bounty" (*premiia*), which hints at probable excesses by indigene males providing the goods for this market.[61] Slavery had a long history in both Russia and Siberia. In 1647 the Iakutsk commander Martin Vasil´ev petitioned Tsar Alexis for permission "to have the young woman I bought to do my work for me [a Iakut named Bakaian] baptized into Orthodox Christianity and have the priest teach her prayers," since he evidently wanted to marry her. A 1679 document details the successive sales of a "young Tungus woman named Lavruk," bought first by a Cossack then sold after his death to a Tungus named Kevani, who then sold her to a fellow tribesman named Inkan.[62] Such sales and the purchasing of indigene children by Russians had long been common when Empress Anna formally legalized the latter. In 1767 Catherine II authorized the purchasing of natives specifically designated as slaves (*raby*). While serving as Siberia's governor-general Speranskii tried to curtail slavery by offering natives 150 rubles for each slave they *freed*. His 1822 Regulation on the Administration of Natives (*Ustav ob upravlenii inorodtsev*) expressly prohibited slavery. The Siberian slave trade persisted a while longer but eventually died out, and there is no evidence the Senate's 1825 program to purchase native girls was successful in providing sufficient numbers of exiles with wives.[63]

During the 1820s (though probably beginning earlier) Siberia's male peasants sold female relatives to exiles for 50 rubles each; yet after such a deal they would, as tradition demanded, give the groom a dowry of 30 rubles. The overseer of the Sagaisk settlement encouraged exiles to kidnap local women, who then often became prostitutes rather than wives. In 1831 Eastern Siberia governor-general A. S. Lavinskii initiated a program to reward a peasant 150 rubles if he took an exile-settler into his home and provided him a wife. The woman could be his daughter or any other female relative, and after consummation of the arrangement the exile-settler was allowed to enter the peasantry. Nonetheless, these exiles remained under limitations by virtue of their criminal sentences, and so in 1837 Lavinskii revised his scheme to allow them to leave the village anytime, as long as they had the means to establish their own households. He simultaneously forbade peasants from ejecting exiles for three years after they had taken them into their homes, but now offered them 100 to 200 rubles for each additional exile they adopted. Nonetheless, only a hundred peasants acquired sons-in-law through Lavinskii's program, because they considered exile-settlers "rotten good-for-nothings," explains Maksimov.[64] Western Siberia's governors-general offered similar incentives to encourage marriage and procreation. A ruling of 20 May 1831 allowed penal laborers, if joined by their wives, to be released from *katorga* for the purpose of settlement, even if their terms were not yet completed. Free women who entered into a first-time marriage with an exile received a one-time cash payment of 50 silver rubles. The couple was freed from taxes and duties for three years and had both their poll-tax and *obrok* halved during the following seven, after which they could join the peasantry. In 1840 the Holy Synod relaxed its rules regarding marriage so that one's inability to repeat prayers and the absence of confession no longer barred a man or woman from marrying an Orthodox partner; and priests could no longer demand fees from exiles to perform weddings.[65]

None of these measures prevented exile-settlers from escaping in droves. Nor did police measures. Fugitives were occasionally captured and returned for resettlement: 497 in 1833, for example.[66] But as of 1834, 2,883 exile-settlers were considered "at large,"[67] despite the MVD having several years earlier offered soldiers and gendarmes a bounty of 10 rubles for each fugitive they captured.[68]

Bowing to the inevitable, administrators sometimes gave exiles permission to leave settlements and villages to find employment elsewhere. Exiles were permitted to leave for work in the gold mining industry, as fishermen, or as urban artisans. Individuals needed a pass (*pechatnaia bileta*) approved by the land court and *volost* overseer in order to work for up to a year as a gold miner. They could work as fishermen for only six months at a time, and only as far down the Lena River as Iakutsk, and as artisans for the same time-length, albeit no farther than 30 versts from their place of exile. Fishermen, like gold miners, needed a pass from their *volost* overseer; artisans needed an identity card (*pismennyi vid*) from their village headman. Other exiles worked as wood-cutters providing fuel and timber. This allowed some exiles to find steady and lucrative employment in areas outside agriculture, but also created administrative confusion and abetted escapes. In 1841 the IGP issued restrictions on work permits expressly to prevent "disorder and *brodiazhestvo* among exile-settlers."[69]

Whether they left with permission or not exiles were key to the development of Siberia's gold industry, which began in Western Siberia in the late 1820s. Between 1840 and 1849 the 9,091 poods of gold mined in Siberia represented nearly all that for the empire generally. In 1861 Siberia's private gold industry employed nearly 31,000 laborers.[70] As of 1834 exiles accounted for 82 percent of all Siberia's gold miners; and in 1847 made up 68 percent of Eniseisk *guberniia*'s gold miners. According to historian V. I. Semëvskii, bosses valued exile-settlers because they were not only more "compliant workers" than free laborers but also "competent people."[71] During the 1840s the Eniseisk *okruga* where the state settlements were situated contained few gold mines, so exiles traveled to such other *okruga* as Eniseisk, Krasnoiarsk, Irkutsk, Nizhneudinsk, Verkhneudinsk, Olëkminsk, and, in Western Siberia, Tomsk and the Kirgiz steppe. They could theoretically earn much more as gold miners than as farmers: during the mid-1830s contracts in Tomsk *guberniia* offered miners 10 to 13 rubles a month. By 1846 more than 30,000 men and women, exiled and free, were laboring in Siberia's gold industries. The prominence among them of exiles explains what happened to many of the 70,000 deported to Eniseisk *guberniia* between 1823 and 1858 but who left the plantation.[72]

All the same, working for the gold bosses was hardly a panacea. According to the 1833 labor contracts of bosses Riazanov and Balandin, the workday began at 4 am and did not end until sundown, with the usual one-hour lunch break halved between 20 June and 1 August. Mining usually ceased in winter. However, in Olëkminsk *okrug*, where the gold lay near the surface and private owners mostly used penal laborers provided by the state rather than freebooting exile-settlers, mining continued year-round. Working outside at –60° must have claimed many a convict's life; but conditions were terrible throughout the industry. Miners were crowded into hastily-constructed shanties; forced to buy all their food, provisions, and tools at extortionate rates from company stores; and were often killed or maimed in accidents, or died of typhus, influenza, or scurvy. The government recognized gold mining as being so debilitating that in 1838 it prohibited individuals from working in the industry for longer than a year. But the huge demand for miners meant this law was rarely, if ever, enforced.[73]

Legislation gave mine bosses enormous power over all who worked for them; and because most sites were isolated they could ignore what legal protections workers had and, with the help of Cossacks and goon squads, tyrannize them, break their contracts, and force them to accept meager pay and rations. Bosses typically withheld workers' pay until their contracts expired so as to prevent them from leaving; and when the charges for what these workers had purchased on credit from company stores were applied against their earnings, many ended up with practically nothing. Contracts during the 1850s permitted foremen to administer corporal punishment "as they saw fit," despite the law giving only mining constables (*gornye ispravniki*) this authority. An 1845 law limited to 50 the number of birch blows a constable could give a laborer; but legislation during the next decade subjected those exile laborers caught escaping to the much harsher punishment of 20 lashes of the *plet*, and in

1858 constables obtained authority to punish such individuals with 100 birch blows followed by a year in either a factory or a correctional battalion. Given such repellent conditions and draconian punishments it is no wonder exiles and non-exiles alike often broke their gilded shackles and fled. During the period 1830–35 the escape rate among Tomsk *guberniia*'s mines ranged between 6 and 9 percent. More than one out of ten laborers in all of Western Siberia escaped in 1847.[74]

In September 1833 the commander of the Kolyvansk *zavody*, E. P. Kovalevskii, toured the region's gold mines to learn why so many were fleeing. Shortly beforehand there had been a mass escape of 500 laborers from the Rozhdestvensk and Burlevsk mines, both owned by the notoriously abusive Khristofor Popov. Kovalevskii found these men working at the nearby Birikul´sk works. Despite the fact that they told Kovalevskii they intended to remain at Birikul´sk and that Popov, when apprised of their location, told Kovalevskii he no longer needed them, the commander wanted to set an example. Guards marched all 500 laborers to the nearest Popov-owned mine, from which 129 immediately fled again. Kovalevskii next appealed to the Ministry of Finance to supply guards for all Kolyvansk's mines. Military guards were soon assigned to mines in Dmitrievsk *volost*, though E. F. Kankrin informed Kovalevskii that he neither authorized this nor acknowledged their authority. Escapes from Western Siberia's mines continued, with 52 percent of the workforce fleeing in 1834 and 43 percent in 1835. The next year the governor-general created a force of 200 Cossacks charged specifically with hunting down fugitive gold miners in Tomsk *guberniia*.[75]

There are other instances of gold miners' resistance during this period. A dispute erupted the following summer at Voznesensk mine over officials' expectations that laborers should meet production quotas despite most of the wheelbarrows being broken. A fight began and five miners beat up a clerk and attacked the foreman. The next day 41 miners walked off the job. The four who rather foolishly remained were arrested and thrown into Tomsk jail. Miners often prospected on their own, and so when one day at Tomsk *guberniia*'s Mitrofanovsk mine the exile Afanasii Nepomniashchii informed his commander Grebeshchikov that he intended to do just this, 50 of his mates decided to join him. Soon there was a full-scale revolt, with miners imprisoning Grebeshchikov and assaulting a clerk and foreman with birch rods and tool handles—evocative symbols of their oppression. However, enthusiasm waned after several hours and the miners returned to work. Nepomniashchii and two others were arrested.[76]

These and similar disturbances fueled an ongoing dispute between mine owners who wanted constables to help capture escapees and Benkendorf, who as chief of gendarmes was reluctant to use his constables this way. But with the government becoming increasingly enamored of the tax revenue gold mining was generating, the owners eventually prevailed. By 1838 both the MVD and Ministry of Finance had moved to subject gold miners to all military justice punishments save the death penalty. One of the many acts of legislation regulating the industry that year required individuals to obtain a special stamp in their passports before they could become prospectors; if found without, they were now liable to criminal prosecution. In summer 1838 the Ministry of War assigned nearly 500 Cossacks to capture fugitive miners in Tomsk and Eniseisk *gubernii*.[77] In 1841 Nicholas appointed a special gendarme staff-officer, charged with "overseeing order in Siberia's private gold mines" and reporting to Western Siberia's governor-general and the commander of the Corps of Gendarmes' Siberia district. Gendarmes were also to be rewarded 10 ruble-*assignats* for each fugitive they captured.[78]

*   *   *

For the reasons already discussed, the depopulating and general failure of Siberia's state settlements for exiles eventually compelled the regime to admit defeat. In 1842 Petersburg took steps to convert its 22 Eniseisk settlements, all of which now "presented a picture of utter poverty and dissolution," into "ordinary government villages [*obyknovennyia kazennyia sela*]." Those exiles still remaining had all restrictions over them removed and became subject to the same taxes as state peasants.[79] Aside from the significant exception of the Sakhalin penal colony that was established in the 1870s and 80s,[80] the Eniseisk settlements represent tsarism's final attempt to create exilic colonies. From 1842 on, convicts sentenced to exile to settlement were simply assigned to *starozhily* villages, where they were left to their own devices among hostile peasants. The overseers and Cossacks were no more and so these exiles, despite being criminals, were simply told not to leave their locations and not to engage in commerce. Yet even these restrictions were often waived, such that many left to find work in cities and towns. After a certain period of time those who remained in the villages were supposed to begin paying taxes like state peasants, but only a tiny fraction became sufficiently well established to do so. Exile-settlers far more commonly survived on paltry state subsidies or through robbery, prostitution, and other activities that undermined Siberian life.

How this new policy affected the exiles themselves is suggested by an 1843 report concerning conditions in Ishim *okrug*, Tobol´sk *guberniia*. The report's author, N. Cherniakovskii, identifies himself as an Ishim city merchant, and was in all likelihood the Nikolai Cherniakovskii known to have given a substantial donation to the Tobol´sk Prison Committee in 1845 (see Chapter 7). Irrespective of its status as an *okrug* city, Ishim was a provincial but nevertheless growing town: its population increased from 1,211 in 1823 to 2,147 in 1843 to 2,365 in 1851. In 1843 Ishim *okrug*'s population of 146,078 included only 2,303 exile-settlers.[81] Besides showing how the government failed to administer the exiles it assigned to *starozhil* villages, Cherniakovskii's article captures peasants' prejudices toward them. Despite their small numbers he claimed "[r]esearch reveals that it is a rare crime in which a '*poselshchik*,'[82] as they are called here, is not involved." Cherniakovskii writes that peasants referred to exiles as "outsiders" (*nechastnye*) and shunned them. This partially explains why only 217 of Ishim *okrug*'s exile-settlers actually worked the land, whereas many were tradesmen instead. (Of course, many others would have escaped or been idle, but Cherniakovskii's data do not account for these.) Cherniakovskii's figures show an increase over time in the number of cases handled by the *okrug* court, yet simultaneously undermine his claim that exiles were primarily responsible for crime: exiles were indeed disproportionately overrepresented among (new) criminals; but peasants and other non-exiles accounted for the majority.[83]

Refutation of Cherniakovskii's claim does not absolve exiles of what was indeed their disproportionate responsibility for crime, but does serve to highlight the extent to which *starozhily* considered all exiles guilty, not necessarily for committing new crimes *per se* but for *being* "criminal." This essentializing and binary perspective contributed to the irremediable rift between these groups. "The exile-settler is a child that steals what it sees," went a peasant saying.[84] And so Cherniakovskii complained that after delivering them to the countryside, officials simply left exiles without overseers to send them into the fields. Nonetheless, their widespread employment as tradesmen suggests their ostracism may not have been as profound as Cherniakovskii insisted, and that *starozhily* anyway benefited to some extent from this fringe society. But even if this was the case, Cherniakovskii correctly sensed what Petersburg already knew thanks to the Siberian Committee's and MVD's statistics: exile to settlement was a catastrophic failure.

7
Katorga and the 1845 *Ulozhenie*

Forty-four thousand men and over 7,000 women entered Siberia bound for *katorga* during the period 1823 to 1860, during which they accounted for just over 18 percent of all deportees.[1] Administrators faced a continual problem of what to do with them all. "C[oun]t Speranskii's projected jobs for exiles were not practically realizable," reads a brief history of *katorga* published in 1910, "and work for penal laborers was even more unrealizable."[2] The problem was particularly acute in Western Siberia, where the only *katorga* sites were Omsk's fortress and textile mill as well as several state distilleries. The fortress could accommodate only about 200 prisoners; the textile mill much fewer (only seven convicts were assigned to it in 1835,[3] though more were assigned later). Siberian distilleries produced vodka through the so-called steaming method, which required less manpower than other methods, and so Tobol´sk *guberniia*'s Uspensk distillery required a maximum of only 200 penal laborers. As of April 1831, 496 and 526 penal laborers were assigned to Tomsk *guberniia*'s Bogotol´sk and Krasnorechensk state distilleries, respectively, and each of these figures superseded the designated maximums.[4] After the government sold most of its distilleries to private entrepreneurs the number of *katorga* sites in Western Siberia declined. Nonetheless, the judiciary and TobPS assigned more than 11,000 penal laborers to the region between 1823 and 1858.[5]

GUZS and its subordinate *guberniia* administrations therefore had few options. They eventually redirected many penal laborers, despite their sentences of *"zavod katorga,"* to Omsk fortress in a technical violation of the law. *Katorga* convicts were also illegally assigned to the workhouses mandated for exile-settlers by the 1822 Reforms. In 1829 the MVD circulated a memo issued four years earlier listing spaces available in fortresses throughout the empire where criminals and problem soldiers could be reassigned. Several of the 19 fortresses, like Kherson with 356 spaces and Riga with 100, could accommodate a fair number; others such as Gangaud with six and Neitlot with five resulted in the number of available spaces totaling only 1,073.[6] Moreover, this figure was four years out of date. Several years later, Petersburg allowed so-called "Tatar" penal laborers already in Western Siberia to be formed into special correctional battalions and transferred to fortresses in Finland.[7] These and other *ad hoc* measures failed to correct the problem, and officials in Omsk and elsewhere faced such overwhelming numbers of penal laborers that they actually began turning them away. As of 1835 only 1,613 penal laborers were "at work" in Western Siberia, despite nearly 5,000 having been exiled there during the previous decade.[8]

Eventually there was some respite. Beginning in 1829 more penal laborers were assigned to Eastern than to Western Siberia each year. Between 1846 and 1853, 2,956 males and 278 females were assigned to *katorga* in Western Siberia, an average of just over 400 per annum, though there was a spike during the final year of this period in response to the outbreak of war.[9] Nonetheless, there were certain years between 1829 and 1858 when over 90 percent of penal laborers were assigned to Eastern Siberia.[10] In addition to Western Siberia's limited number of *katorga* sites, its growing civilian population and closer integration with European Russia explains this shift. As of 1839 it had a male population of 341,351 (200,073 in Tobol´sk *guberniia*; 141,278 in Tomsk *guberniia*), compared to Eastern Siberia's 256,912 (60,948 in Eniseisk *guberniia*; 195,964 in Irkutsk *guberniia*).[11] Although its cities were only moderately larger than Eastern Siberia's, the proportion of females in both them and the countryside was greater, except in its more sparsely settled southern regions.[12]

During the period 1823–58 around 30,000 penal laborers were assigned to Eastern Siberia,[13] where *katorga* sites were more numerous but nonetheless insufficient to accommodate all these convicts. During the late 1840s GUVS obtained permission to transfer convicts from its Ust´-kamenogorsk factory to fortresses in Ukraine and along the Baltic.[14] But such transfers were rare and involved small numbers. Even more than its western counterpart Eastern Siberia suffered the burden of exile, largely because its status as a colony was less in dispute.

Within Eastern Siberia by far the largest *katorga* site (collectively speaking) was Nerchinsk Mining District, which encompassed a series of mines and metallurgical works in Zabaikal´e owned by the Imperial Cabinet and operated by the Nerchinsk Mining Administration, whose jurisdiction extended to the Petrovsk ironworks in Verkhneudinsk *okrug*. In 1823 a visitor reported 5,041 "servitors" working in the mining district, though identified only 1,534 as penal laborers.[15] However, numbers grew. As of 1859 the mining administration reckoned it had 3,458 penal laborers actually on site with another 531 "temporarily relocated" to other jurisdictions.[16] Penal laborers were also assigned to Eastern Siberia's state distilleries, salt works, and Tel´minsk textile mill outside Irkutsk. Two of the distilleries were in Irkutsk *guberniia*: Ilginsk was nearly 400 versts from Irkutsk, produced 250,000 vedros a year, and employed around 600 penal laborers; Aleksandrovsk was 64 versts from Irkutsk and much larger, producing twice as much vodka and employing over 1,000 convicts. Both distilleries used penal labor exclusively.[17] Eniseisk *guberniia*'s Kamenskii distillery also served as a *katorga* site, but seems to have had a mixed workforce that included freemen and less than half the number of convicts as Ilginsk. Salt works employed similar numbers. For example, in 1822 Zabaikal´e's Selenginsk salt works employed 317 penal laborers, a figure reduced to 180 by decade's end. Eniseisk *guberniia*'s Troitskii salt works employed 38 penal laborers in 1821 and around 120 during the late 1830s.[18] Tel´minsk had few penal laborers, a large portion of whom, if not most, were women.

Individual *katorga* sites within the Nerchinsk Mining District and elsewhere in Eastern Siberia were typically defined as "*zavody*." In the case of Nerchinsk especially, this appellation designated the presence of a number of separate factories or works; but its real significance rests in the type of administration and social arrangement it designated. In essence, a *zavod* was an autarkic industrial penal labor site organized along military lines. The best description of this institution during this period comes from I. F. Efimov, who commanded the Ilginsk distillery until 1848, when he took charge over the Aleksandrovsk distillery. Each site was officially a "*zavod*." Describing Ilginsk, Efimov writes that the administration was divided between an industrial and a police office. The former consisted of the "warden [*smotritel*], as chief commander of the *zavod*, and a paymaster, who in his absence fulfilled [the warden's] responsibilities as well as his own." There were also a clerk and an accountant. The only official staff member of the police office was the police chief (*politsmeister*). Each office also made use of two assistants, "a pair of penal laborers, cantonists assigned to the service." Penal laborers similarly accounted for all the guards (*karauly*), soldiers (*nariadchiki*), and "so-called *desiatniki* ['tenners'— possibly a reference to the length of their sentences]" who made up the police force. *Desiatniki* were directly responsible for watching convicts at worksites and in barracks, whereas a battalion of either invalided servicemen under the command of a senior officer, or Cossacks under a Cossack officer (*uriadnik*), protected warehouses and other installations. Finally, there were a priest, a doctor, and "one or two" medics (*fel'dshera*).[19]

The prison itself was a large wooden building with a tin roof located in the center of a stockade fort (*ostrog*). It was divided by a corridor on either side of which were two wards (*kamery*). One ward contained the kitchen and mess hall; the other three were "very narrow and able to hold no more than a hundred persons," writes Efimov. "The crowdedness of the lodgings was tellingly difficult, especially in winter, when passage across Baikal was halted until the ice formed over it and the penal laborers destined for Nerchinsk's mines and *zavody* overflowed Irkutsk prison's jailhouse." During a span of two to three months a party of these exiles would arrive each week for temporary detention in Ilginsk. These unwelcome guests who did no work "caused confusion in the distributing of assignments and difficulty in the relocating of transferees." Other prisoners lived in the old building that housed the hospital; still others such as "dependents and youngsters" who tended the horse stable occupied apartments and houses outside prison walls. Very young children either remained with their fathers in prison or were housed with local peasants. Prisoners who completed their terms but were enfeebled or incapacitated were likewise either foisted on peasants or sometimes allowed to remain in prison, where at least they were assured of a meal and comrades. In addition to serving as laborers and guards many convicts worked as smiths, cobblers, and in the other trades. "In a word, penal laborers' hands made everything needed for the *zavody* to function," explains Efimov. "The weakest or the chronically ill were assigned as night-watchmen, guards, and to other easier jobs."[20]

Conditions for prisoners varied considerably depending on their numbers, condition of the physical plant, and the attitudes and behavior of commanders and guards. Positive changes at individual locations tended to be short-lived. "Instructions to the Warden of the Irkutsk Prison Jail, 1832," prohibits prisoners from owning any writing implements as well as musical instruments and cards. According to Article 50, "Stubbornness, quarrels, bad language, salacious discussions, drunkenness, loud laughter, and similar behavior shall have no place among the Prisoners," who were also forbidden to engage in any type of "horseplay" (*rezvost*).[21] Needless to say, wardens and guards routinely failed to enforce these and similar regulations; and prisoners often lived on their own terms.

Overall, the period 1823–61 was a bleak one in Russia's penological trajectory, as many realized at the time. Nerchinsk Zavod conjured up images of Dante's inferno to the abovementioned visitor. "Walking toward the *zavod*," he writes, "you descend six versts, as if it into a deep pit. Inside this pit, dilapidated structures are scattered without order along the slopes, so that when you get to the main street, you cannot see anything."[22] The atmosphere was suffused with smoke, soot, and noxious fumes from the *zavod*'s six smelteries and many coke ovens and furnaces; the banging of metal on metal, huge bellows oxygenating coal and wood fires, and shouts from penal laborers' blackened branded faces and the grim tradesmen and officers who commanded them made for constant clangor. It was as if a crack in the earth had opened to reveal the demonic workings below.

Since the eighteenth century, however, the most distant and forbidding *katorga* sites were located along the north Pacific coast. In 1803 a hundred penal laborers were transferred from Irkutsk to help establish salt works in four locations on Kamchatka Peninsula, which became a destination for "incorrigibles" (*neispravimye*, which often designated convicts who committed murders in prison). As of 1831 there were 48 "incorrigibles" on Kamchatka out of a total population (Russians and natives) of 2,523 males and 1,928 females.[23] The salt works at Okhotsk, about 220 miles south of present-day Magadan, was founded sometime after 1803. "Okotsk [*sic*] is situated in the north-east part of a bay formed by the rivers Okota and Kouktui," according to the memoir of John Dundas Cochrane, the Englishman who walked across Eurasia and visited Okhotsk in 1821,

> and is approaching to more respect and consideration than it ever did before, owing, I believe, principally to the active and honest exertions of the present chief.... [Yet] even at present the new site contains but the government buildings, and those belonging to a few of the Cossacks and sailors....
>
> ...The people are employed in building vessels and storehouses, in rigging and sailing the former, and filling the latter with flour and stores. The receiving and sending away of flour is a serious and laborious duty, and open to much abuse and pilfering. Besides these works there is a salt concern, under the charge of an officer who commands the convicts, at present ninety in number, the maintenance of whom, including provisions, clothing, and pocket-money, is about a thousand pounds per annum. These extraordinary expenses are occasioned by the allowance of double rations, in consideration of their hard work. The allowance to a convict is as follows:—eighty pounds of rye flour for each man per month, one hundred and twenty pounds of the same flour for each man who has a wife, and forty pounds in addition for each child, male or female. Each man is allowed ten

pounds of oatmeal, or rice, and twenty pounds of butter per month. They are also allowed two complete suits of clothing, and about twenty shillings per annum in money. Such an allowance of provisions is commendable and liberal; indeed it is so great, that the poor wretches are enabled to sell one half of the bread for the purchase of tea, sugar, and meat; and of the latter there is not so much necessity, when the superabundant quantity of fish is taken into consideration, which is so great that I believe from twelve to fifteen hundred dogs are fed with it during the greater part of the year.

The quantity of salt made by the convicts is about two thousand five hundred poods, or one thousand six hundred bushels, which is sold alike to rich and poor, at the rate of three shillings a-bushel, equal to two hundred and fifty pounds for sixteen hundred bushels; so that the salt, although a necessary, is a losing establishment of seventy-five percent. The liberality and consideration of the emperor upon this head cannot, therefore, but be duly appreciated....

Such are the official returns of Okotsk. Of the state of society little can be said, no merchants residing in it, and the chief being the only married man belonging to the navy, and but three or four, who have wives, that belong to the civil service; in short, there is very little society, and less education, although a school has been established by the present chief, which may hereafter do well if the existing discipline be kept up.[24]

In 1818, shortly before Cochrane's visit and, it seems, the new chief's arrival, a certain naval officer was assigned to Okhotsk. He lived there several years, apparently had supervisory authority over the convicts, and 60 years later anonymously described his experiences for the journal *Russian Olden Times*. Despite embellishment with the dialog and dramatics readers then expected, his account appears veracious.[25] Okhotsk's penal laborers ("the cream of the convicts [*katorzhniki*[26]]—almost all had been dispatched from Nerchinsk and other *zavody*, and so were incorrigible and guilty of more than one murder in the *zavody*") used large salt-pans to distil salt from seawater. There was no prison *per se*: 250 convicts lived in a barracks guarded by 50 sailors. The wives of some convicts lived in "20 or 30 small houses" nearby. The officer found among the prison population six Poles about whom none of the other convicts knew a thing. "The Tatars, Persians, Germans, etc., all comprised a single mass, but everyone disdained the Poles," he writes. All the convicts including bachelors were allowed at the end of the workday to repair to the wives' quarters, where they could remain until nine o'clock at night. "Penal laborers are... a people with greater passion and, perhaps, strength, than us," explains the author, as if describing for readers a separate species. It was supposedly these qualities that enabled a convict to sit through 30 games of cards for which bricks and coal substituted as chips. "[A] game for 30 kopeks is more heatedly contested than if we were playing for a thousand [rubles]." Within these houses sex and violence raged: "For the dirty, beaten women of disfigured fortune there is passionate love afire; rabid jealousy, the envy of the predilections of a beauty, frequently causes fights and factionalism [*partiia na partiiu*]." The officer learned of a convict named Lëvka who had been caught with another's wife and beaten up by his mates. When asked to identify his attackers the black-and-blue adulterer refused to say anything for fear of being murdered.

After some time there the officer believed he had sufficiently earned the prisoners' trust to risk entering their barracks, or "the lion's den." He did so with six armed men and felt he might be attacked at any moment as he gazed into "a terrible collection of distorted, savage faces... in each of which could be read: murderer!" Maintaining his composure, he noticed "the sleeping platform seemed half-alive: various insects were skipping and crawling over it." A murder had taken place in the barracks and he found the prisoner responsible:

The murderer was named Ivan Mediantsev; he was 44 years old..., lean, very well-built, red-haired, remarkably strong, and agile—he held himself erect. Well educated, he was from the Iaroslavl *meshchane*. He had been knouted and sent for murder to the Nerchinsk mines, where he committed several murders and, as an incorrigible, was sent to the salt works in Okhotsk. While speaking with several others I noticed Mediantsev with a Bible in his hands—after committing a murder, he always loved to read the Bible. Speaking with Mediantsev, I urged him not to commit murder; besides [noting his liability to] subsequent punishment, I tried to appeal to his intelligence and suggested that crimes committed irrationally, according to the weakness characteristic of man, may be atoned, but that the taking of life, either for revenge or to punish a crime, is forbidden. Man, as a creation of God, belongs to Him; his forgiveness is not here but there, and so on. Mediantsev answered me with a sigh: "I'm so unhappy—do you think I murder a man gladly?" But you committed a murder, and for a long time have murdered! "There comes a time when a man becomes so unhappy with himself that such evil occurs he doesn't notice the light; you don't look at it—everything seems reddened by the very blood of the living; you're so melancholy that everything lacks joy, and without this, a man can't be himself. Yet then comes along some sniveler to bother you; and you don't remember how you crushed his skull with your manacles, but you see that you've killed him. Suddenly your shell falls away, anguish departs, and the redness clears from your eyes. You pity the man, but there's nothing to be done."[27]

Despite this sanguine vignette the absence of data makes it is difficult to know how dangerous prison life really was. Large communal wards and lack of prison staff imposed upon Russian prisoners a degree of cooperation that was quite different from what was being required of prisoners in England and America assigned to single-person cells. As did peasants, prisoners formed cooperatives and nominated headmen and in this way maintained basic levels of order and civility. At the Aleksandrovsk distillery they even created a short-lived orchestra. Civility was a necessary mode of protection against psychotic inmates who might suddenly turn violent. That being said, *katorga* sites concentrated together men and women hailing almost without exception from the most exploited segments of society who had been brutalized still further. Prison as well as upbringing and lack of education had rendered them coarse, violent, vulgar, and rude. Many expected to end their days in *katorga* and felt little compassion for fellow human beings. "Hell is other people," observed Sartre.

Top positions in the prison pecking order went to those most feared, that is to penal laborers known as "Ivans" (*ivany*). Later sources agree the pre-Emancipation era constituted Ivans' halcyon days, when they ruled *katorga* the way gang leaders rule American prisons today. Elderly convicts provided Vlas Doroshevich an oral history of the "Ivan" that will have to do in the absence of contemporary accounts:

He arose in Kara during the "Razgil´deev era," now remembered with horror [discussed below]. At that time, in the "cut" where they extracted gold, the mare [execution bench] was always set up and the executioner always on duty. Birch strokes were then divided into tens and were counted on "one side" only, that is, if a man was sentenced to, say, ten strokes, the executioner gave him ten on one side, then went to the other side and administered another ten. Moreover, the second ten wasn't included in the total: two strokes counted as one. They flogged not with the birch rod but with the "butt-ends," that is, they held the rod by the thin end and struck with the thick. Blood was drawn at the first blow, rods broke, splinters pierced the body. The "tasks," that is, the daily work quotas, were difficult, and the smallest "task" left unfinished drew immediate punishment.

Back then, any violation was punished. The least impertinence, the minutest opposition by exiles to a lowly guard, occasioned brutal torture.

During those especially hard times, under the hiss of the birch rod, butt-end and lash, the "Ivan" was borne into the world. A desperate cutthroat, a longterm penal laborer with nothing to lose and nothing to hope for, he manifested protest for the whole of this beaten, worn-out, shattered *katorga*. He protested laughingly and insolently, protested against the unjust punishments, excessive "tasks," bad food and those absurd, childish little jackets issued to prisoners by way of "clothing according to legislated design." Ivan didn't pass silently before such authority but at every step protested laughingly and insolently.

Ivans were chained to the wall and the wheelbarrow, their wrists and ankles were fettered, they were flogged with the butt-end and the whip. Towards the earning of their name in *katorga*, Ivans often had to receive over 2,000 lashes of the three-tailed whip—birch strokes didn't count at all. All this earned respect and conferred upon them an aureole of manliness. The administration flogged, but somewhat feared, them. These were people who any minute could stick a knife between the ribs, people who would bash in an offender's skull with their manacles.[28]

There were, then, "career criminals" alongside the mass of hapless others convicted for an ill-conceived one-off robbery or homicide resulting from a drunken brawl. Whatever their crimes, *katorga* did nothing to rehabilitate any of them, but mostly only dehumanized men and women alike. When he took charge over the Aleksandrovsk distillery Efimov found men chained to walls and soon learned that one of his prisoners killed another over a loaf of bread. Despite portraying himself as humane and generous (he rarely administered corporal punishment and allowed prisoners to go without fetters and unshaved heads in spite of government regulations), Efimov unwittingly evinces the brutalizing conditions prisoners faced when he describes his reaction to repeated escape attempts by a prisoner called Ivan Tsupenko ("Ivan-the-Punishment-Scarred"). "I went up to him and wanted to hit him right there," writes Efimov, "but saw in his eyes such a hateful, it might even be said, bestial expression that, having restrained my hand from the blow, I began, close to his face, to threaten and reprimand him for escaping." This did nothing to moderate Tsupenko's attitude, who before he could be knouted during another instance managed to assault a guard and kept resisting so violently that Efimov ordered a straitjacket brought from the infirmary so he could be held down to receive his punishment. Tsupenko later transferred to another prison, was sentenced to 4,000 lashes in the gauntlet and, Efimov writes, probably died as a result.[29]

Efimov comes across as a positive humanitarian compared to what has been written about Ivan E. Razgil´deev, the mining engineer Nikolai N. Murav´ev appointed commander over Nerchinsk *katorga* in 1849. Until his removal 13 years later Razgil´deev ruled over a hell-hole of cruelty and malfeasance, degradation and despair. Overcrowded, unsanitary conditions and lack of provisions and medicines led to a typhus epidemic that killed over a thousand penal laborers as well as a deadly scurvy outbreak several years later. "Razgil´deev was very severe," writes one historian. "It is said that as a simple administrative punishment he ordered 300 lashes of the birch rod applied using both hands."[30] The Kara mines' sovereign ruler inspired many *katorga* songs, one of which went:

> In years not so long ago,
> In the Kara works,
> There ruled a certain Ivan.
> Not Ivan Vasil´ich the Terrible!
> But an engineer from the mines
> —Razgil´deev himself![31]

Reports confirm that Razgil´deev's and other Russian carcerals were lethal indeed. For example, the MVD reported that in 1839 Tel´minsk's labor force totaled 270 people and included besides penal laborers and other exiles nine "workers' children" and 16 women "taken from villages for marriage." All lived together in a single barracks. That year alone 15 women, 12 men, and three children died—in other words over 10 percent of the population.[32] Similarly, the empire's 168 district-level prison aid societies reported that during 1840, of the 19,017 prisoners hospitalized, 1,706 (9 percent) died. The largest concentrations of hospitalized prisoners were in Moscow, Kazan, and Perm—each a major staging area for exiles destined for Siberia.[33] In 1844 a member of Tobol´sk's prison committee reported his findings after a tour of six of the *guberniia*'s prisons: Tiumen, Turinsk, Ialutorovsk, Kurgan, Petropavlovsk, and Ishim. Turmoil characterized all except the last two. "In Tiumen especially," which was another staging area for exiles, "I found not a Prison Jail, but an actual school [*uzilishche—sic*] of death for destroying humanity," wrote the representative. Sometimes more than 2,000 prisoners were held in this jail, in conditions so crowded that "I cannot understand how these criminals move in such constriction, worse than in a filthy den." He concluded such conditions were primarily to blame "for the high death rate."[34]

A major reason *katorga* sites and prisons were so bad was lack of funding. Despite its reliance upon the judiciary to convict and sentence offenders, the Nicolaevan government did not regard itself responsible for maintaining prisons where those sentenced to exile were processed and temporarily or permanently incarcerated. This did not make Russia unique. In the United States and England, for example, prisons were privately-funded affairs operated by charitable organizations that depended upon philanthropy to cover maintenance costs. Foremost in prison reform and in establishing the modern prison were the Quakers, who replaced traditional jails and dungeons with penitentiaries in which they believed offenders would be rehabilitated through strict regimes involving the Bible and hours of solitude.

Bruce Adams has described Russia's prison reform movement and English Quaker Walter Venning's role in establishing, in 1819 with Alexander I's support, Petersburg's Prison Aid Society (*Obshchestvo popechitel´nago o tiur´makh*—OPT). OPT's first president was the humanitarian Freemason Prince Aleksandr N. Golitsyn. However, OPT's changing presidency charted the ascendancy of conservatives in Petersburg. Golitsyn was soon replaced in 1822 by Baron Baltazar B. Kampengauzen, who advocated a hard-line penology. Military hero Prince Vasilii S. Trubetskoi replaced Kampengauzen, apparently in 1829, and held the position until his death in 1841, when Chief of Gendarmes A. Kh. Benkendorf took over. Benkendorf died in 1844 and was succeeded by Aleksei F. Orlov, his successor as chief of gendarmes and a member of the State Council.[35]

Space does not allow for a full discussion of OPT's activities, though several general points need be made to better appreciate its role in Siberia. First, despite the influence of Venning and other foreign religious reformers, the organization was designed primarily as a policing tool "to combat begging in the capital," writes Lindenmeyr.[36] Like the *Brodiagi* Regulation several years later OPT's founding represents the intensification of this struggle. Second, in 1826 the Imperial Philanthropic Society, which had been established in 1816 by Golitsyn, reportedly began influencing OPT's activities. Although liberals no longer held the presidency, they were active in opposing conservatives' use of OPT as a police organ rather than a charitable and social welfare organization. The Philanthropic Society's patronage was a boon for OPT. It had already created seven subordinate *guberniia* committees as of 1826, yet between 1826 and 1837 it created 38 new committees; and as of 1844 there were 49 *guberniia* committees and 217 district (*uezdnye*) committees. All donations collected by these regional committees were forwarded to the Petersburg committee, which then distributed monies throughout the empire.[37]

Third, despite its growth and Golitsyn's and other liberal reformers' temporary influence OPT accomplished relatively little. The district committees usually had no more than eight members, and "philanthropy in the provinces was not at all what it was in the capital upon the emergence of the society and *guberniia* committees."[38] Fourth, Benkendorf when he took over had long been dissatisfied with OPT, and so on 17 March 1841 he recommended to the emperor a more rigid administrative structure to better coordinate district committees' activities with those of the center. This recommendation is interesting insofar as it reflects a more bureaucratic approach toward managing OPT's activities, albeit from a top decision-maker whose Third Section operated according to plenipotentiary powers that bypassed other organs of government. In any case, its practical effects were more reflective of sovereign rather than governmental power, for they amounted to a decision "to invite" representatives of the nobility to establish committees in every one of Russia's district cities. In effect, Petersburg urged civilian authorities to fill the breach left by the government's inactivity in penal affairs by creating an empire-wide prison administration. Within ten months Benkendorf's proposal had led to 23 new district committees. However, the nobility's response was ephemeral and soon quite desultory. Committees did less and less as time wore on; and in 1846, after Orlov had taken over, OPT's central committee reported that even its board members were not fulfilling their responsibilities. At the district level, members were apathetic, contributions nil, and committees closed. In 1849 Petersburg took "energetic measures" using "police and even the courts" to collect the dues members owed from as far back as 1842. Whether they joined OPT or not, local officials were assessed a yearly tax for the upkeep of prisons: 5 rubles for a marshal of the nobility; 2 for the district judge; 2 for the land constable; 1 ruble 50 kopeks for the rural dean (*blagochinnyi*); 1 ruble for the district clerk; 1 ruble 25 kopeks for the district physician; and 10 kopeks for the city mayor. However, these officials almost never paid these dues.[39]

Finally, by the early 1850s OPT's regional committees had lost their noble constituents and consisted almost entirely of government officials whose membership was required. OPT's new charter of November 1851 defined staff positions for district committees and rendered them *de facto* government bodies. "[M]ore than anything, the 1851 regulation designated the society's role in the administration of prison affairs and imposed upon it a completely predetermined structure," an official history sourly notes. "The regulation gave a bureaucratic character to the society's administration."[40] OPT's bureaucratization and official status were formalized by its incorporation into the MVD in 1855.

Because OPT committees existed throughout the empire it would be misleading to suggest that prisons dealing with exiles were their primary focus. Most arrestees in district jails were incarcerated only briefly and never went across the Urals. Nonetheless, OPT committees in Petersburg, Moscow, Kazan, and other cities where large transfer prisons were located did influence exiles' conditions. OPT had little to no influence over *katorga* sites *per se*, but its Siberian committees raised funds to build and repair transfer prisons and jails that housed exiles. In 1830 the emperor and Committee of Ministers ordered Governor-general A. S. Lavinskii to establish an OPT committee in Krasnoiarsk to manage the prison there. Lavinskii did as he was told; but in 1842 Eniseisk governor Vasilii I. Kopylov reported to Benkendorf that the committee existed in name only and had done virtually nothing throughout its existence. Despite Kopylov's assurances that he would be more assiduous in trying to raise funds for a committee over which he would personally take charge, the committee had fizzled out of existence by the 1850s.[41] By the end of Nicholas I's reign Eastern Siberia still had no functioning committees.

Western Siberia was another story, however, and could boast of OPT committees in Tobol´sk, Tomsk, Tara, Tiumen, Ialutorovsk, Berezov, Kainsk, Barnaul, and Kuznetsk. Its more robust civil society, which in 1801 long before OPT's appearance established committees to oversee female prisoners,[42] accounts for the difference with Eastern Siberia. Working directly with OPT president V. S. Trubetskoi, Tomsk's governor established a *guberniia*-level committee sometime during the 1830s. This committee improved Tomsk's city jail, which acquired a church in 1839 thanks to a gift of 5,000 rubles from honored citizen (*pochetnyi grazhdanin*) Nikolai Filimonov.[43] Tobol´sk established its committee around the same time as Tomsk. Records for the years 1844–46 show it actively sought to improve prisoners' conditions. Committee members reported on *guberniia* prisons' dire conditions and solicited contributions. For example, Ishim merchant Nikolai Cherniakovskii donated a gift of 715 rubles, though it is important to reiterate that this money went directly to OPT's Petersburg headquarters, which disbursed all funds, and so it is questionable whether Cherniakovskii's gift had any effect locally. The Tobol´sk Prison Committee nonetheless interceded on behalf of one Ivan Chistiakov concerning his son Grigorii, who had been exiled from Kiev but never arrived in Tobol´sk. Committee members wrote TobPS asking if Grigorii had died along the march-route, though if they received an answer it has been lost. As to the larger issue of OPT's influence over exiles, there is some evidence that during the early 1840s Moscow's Prison Committee interceded on behalf of exiles belonging to the Lutheran church and Evangelical sects, expressing concern they were being kept separate from other exiled co-religionists.[44] This well-intentioned gesture apparently led interior minister Lev A. Perovskii to fear their influence over Orthodox exiles (see Chapter 1).

Western Siberia's residents' largesse continued into the 1850s. In 1855, at a cost of 131,492 rubles, a new stone prison was completed in Tobol´sk after 12 years' construction. According to Tobol´sk governor Viktor A. Artsimovich it was "a comfortable location for prisoners and all prison staff" and was funded by OPT and the local St Aleksandr Nevskii Church. That year also witnessed completion in Turinsk of a stone prison with capacity for 75 inmates at a cost of 26,000 silver rubles, which came "from a sum left over by the Omsk *oblast* administration." Artsimovich reported that a transfer prison with capacity for 350 inmates was on schedule to be completed in Tiumen the following year; and a prison for 250 in Omsk by 1858. OPT had also provided funds to repair other prisons in Western Siberia. "The activities of the Prison Committee and its divisions in Tiumen, Omsk, Tara, Ialutorovsk, Berezov, Ishim, and Kurgan, the latter two of which were created in 1855 to please His Highness, have been appropriately diligent," wrote the governor.[45]

Despite increasing alarm at the decrepitude of Siberia's prisons, especially those in Eastern Siberia, the imperial government steadfastly refused to devote the funds needed to improve them. In December 1851 it specifically assigned the maintenance of all the empire's prisoners to OPT's prison committees. The inducements it offered residents in Siberia and elsewhere to join or form such committees reveal the almost pathetic hollowness of the regime by that point. Membership was opened to both men and women from any *soslovie* so long as they were not "wards of the court" or religious sectarians (ironic, given that OPT was founded by Quakers and Freemasons). In return for paying annual dues of 10 rubles, members would receive a certificate from their region's governor-general attesting to membership in these prestigious committees and adding said fact to their formal ranks and titles. Members would also receive a ticket, signed and bearing the seal of the governor-general himself, allowing them untrammeled access to prisons. Indeed, Petersburg wanted it understood that it was a member's duty to visit prisons, observe conditions there, note any insufficiencies of food, clothing, etc., and report these to city and regional authorities. "Based on such reports members, if they are worthy of the honor, will receive as possibilities allow the means to repair or improve [the prison] according to the law," noted GUVS's ruling council.[46] Despite this and further prodding, and in contrast to those in Western Siberia, officials and civilians in Eastern Siberia steadfastly ignored calls to establish prison committees. The result was that conditions for prisoners there only worsened. In 1852 a certain Mikhail Lemu sent GUVS privy councilor Sergei S. Lanskoi 85 silver rubles the now deceased peasant Elena Mamushkina had willed for the support of prisoners in Kansk's city jail. Lanskoi returned the money to Lemu, explaining he could not accept it because Kansk did not have a prison committee to disperse donations.[47]

As Nicholas I's reign drew to a close the MVD expressed frustration that Eastern Siberia's officials were not following its orders. Prison committees "comprising persons from the clerical, military, and civilian sectors and the merchant class" and supported by regional officials had been established in Western Siberia "without especial difficulty," the Department of Police complained to interior minister Orlov in January 1854. Why were GUVS's officials not getting with the program?[48] Murav'ev, who took over Eastern Siberia in 1847, waited until mid-1854 to express support to Orlov for committees he believed could be created in Irkutsk, Krasnoiarsk, Chita, Kiakhta, and Iakutsk. Murav'ev explained he had already corresponded about the subject with these cities' authorities.[49] Yet by that point OPT was a dead letter.

The following year, when OPT became an official branch of the MVD, Sergei S. Lanskoi replaced Orlov as both interior minister and OPT president. From this date onward OPT failed to perform as originally intended, mainly due to its bureaucratic responsibilities.[50] Yet Eastern Siberia once again followed its own course, though briefly in this regard. By 1860 at least one committee, the third incarnation of the Krasnoiarsk Prison Society, was up and running and proving the adage that "three times makes a charm." That year, in a letter to OPT headquarters requesting 140 rubles to pay the medical apprentice Il'ia Putsenko for his ongoing work at the local prison, Krasnoiarsk noted that its current capital fund derived "from various sources" totaled close to 11,000 rubles. Two months later it reached 12,700 rubles.[51] Krasnoiarsk was apparently finally doing right by its prisoners, albeit on the eve of a deluge of exiles that would tax the resources of the entire exile system and nearly every branch of Siberia's government.

In conclusion, between 1823 and 1861 Eastern Siberia received too many exiles and too little money to adequately maintain its prison population. Investigators sometimes discovered prisoners completely naked because they had not been issued clothes. With regard to the exile system, the history of OPT is most significant for what it says about the autocracy's refusal to finance a penal infrastructure that was seriously degraded by the 1850s. Yet at the same time it demonstrates efforts by private individuals to improve exiles' and other prisoners' conditions.

*   *   *

In 1826 Nicholas established the Second Section of His Imperial Chancery with the explicit purpose of reviewing and codifying Russia's laws. The Department of Laws' meetings and other deliberations described earlier represent a furthering of the Second Section's activities under Speranskii's leadership. Speranskii died in 1839 and former interior minister Dmitrii M. Bludov eventually took over the Second Section in 1840. Three years later Bludov initiated what would eventually be called the Code of Criminal and Correctional Punishments (*Ulozhenie o Nakazaniiakh Ugolovnykh i Ispravitel´nykh*), though for some reason Nicholas transferred responsibility over this project to the State Council on 30 March 1844. The council created for this project a Special Commission chaired by Count Vladimir V. Levashev and including Prince Petr G. Ol´denburgskii, Bludov, Dmitrii P. Buturlin, Prince Frantsik-Ksaverii Drutskii-Liubetskii, Viktor N. Panin, Baron Modest A. Korf, Viktor P. Kochubei, Count Matvei I. Palen, and Ignatii L. Turkul. The heavy German contingent (Palen's birth name was Karl Magnus Pahlen) assured that the hard-line approach the regime had been pursuing against offenders would continue. A series of 50 meetings held between 26 April 1844 and 29 March 1845 produced a draft that the entire State Council then discussed over the course of eight meetings before sanctioning it on 15 August 1845. The *Ulozhenie* went into effect on 1 January 1846.[52]

Two of the code's ukases concern criminals exiled to Siberia. Another dealing with "strait-houses" will be noted just briefly, since for all practical purposes these institutions never came into existence. In 1845, at the emperor's request, interior minister L. A. Perovskii submitted a report recommending creation of 75 prisons modeled on Pentonville— England's state-of-the-art prison that had opened in 1842. Each would hold 520 inmates and cost 300,000 rubles to build. The MVD went so far as to form a committee that called for using a special fund, created in 1834 from the poll tax and merchant duties, to cover the 22.5 million rubles in loans for the prisons' construction over 37 years. Despite this ambitious plan almost nothing was done in practice. I. Ia. Foinitskii writes that as of 1848 only 31 prisoners were assigned to strait-houses in all of Russia, which suggests that at most only one had been built by then and even that was not modeled on Pentonville. Adams asserts that a handful of prisons were in fact built; but in any case Alexander II shared Bludov's belief that the project could never be realized at the costs budgeted and therefore canceled it in June 1862.[53]

Despite the conservatism of the men who devised it, the *Ulozhenie* contained several progressive elements. For instance, it specified strict punishments for rape, abolished all use of the knout, and exempted certain groups—foreign visitors, men-of-letters (*literatory*) and their wives, persons over age 70, lower-ranking servicemen with merits of distinction, and the Imperial Court's active-duty station masters and livery drivers—from corporal punishment.[54] Use of the *plet* was retained, though maximum numbers of blows in specific instances were now legally defined and in many other instances birch rods were now substituted. The tattooing of criminals was to be done only by a medic and according "to a physician's satisfaction, in the presence of police officials, and the district secretary and physician, who would be answerable for the tattoo's correct application."[55] This latter provision smacks more of bureaucratic than humanitarian concerns, but did pave the way for this horrible practice's eventual abolition.

Yet notwithstanding the knout's abolition and, later in 1863, more widespread limitations on corporal punishment,[56] exiles like peasants[57] continued to be flogged and beaten until the end of tsarism. With regard to conditions in nineteenth-century Russian prisons, Bruce Adams and Jonathan Daly have each sought to demonstrate they were not much worse than those of their French or English counterparts.[58] However, both overlook conditions in Siberian prisons, which were so bad as to defy imagination. "When in early 1848 I entered the *zavod* administrations the *Ulozhenie* was something new and hardly, hardly, indeed only just gradually, being introduced in the *zavody*," writes Efimov, who readily acknowledged that in violation of the new laws convicts were knouted and forced through the gauntlet an excessive number of times.[59] Corporal punishment within the exile system was not abolished until 1903. Yet I have found evidence as late as 1912 that prisoners were routinely beaten in Orel's central prison and other sites where *katorga* sentences were served.[60]

The *Ulozhenie* reiterated the use of capital punishment for state crimes and for crimes as defined by the 1832 Quarantine Regulation (Chapter 2) "irrespective of what types of courts were to have been adjudicating such cases."[61] Moreover, untold numbers of Russia's convicts died as a result of *corporal* punishment. Figures on capital executions before 1866 are lacking; but later figures and the factors conditioning them indicate that Nicholas I's militarization of society paved the way for increased use of the death penalty. During the period 1866–90 only 44 of the 134 persons sentenced to death for state crimes were actually executed, but 31 of those who were executed were sentenced by military courts, which also sentenced the 211 persons (172 of whom were civilians) executed for regular crimes (*obshchie prestupleniia*) between 1876 and 1890. During the period 1891–1900 military courts were responsible for the executions of 126 people; civil courts for none. These figures reveal a trend at odds with those in Austria and France, which respectively averaged 6 and 3.3 executions per annum during the decade 1881–90.[62]

Due to the absence of prisons, the *Ulozhenie*'s many provisions substituting incarceration for corporal punishment led to a surfeit of convicts necessarily assigned instead to correctional battalions, which according to the MVD "reached especially significant dimensions."[63] More importantly with regard to Siberia, the *Ulozhenie* greatly expanded the use of exile and *katorga* by prescribing them as punishments in literally hundreds of cases. Article 362 alone lists 18 instances in which exile was the punitive response. Many articles confusedly reference exile and *katorga* as options among various punitive responses for which, writes tsarist law scholar N. S. Tagantsev in reference to the strait-houses, "no technical conveniences whatsoever had been implemented at that time."[64] As early as 1863 jurist V. D. Spasovich complained:

The new codicils... abjure any schematic, any systematic divisions and subdivisions of crimes according to rights offended, class, rank, family, origin, or type. They separately place one crime after another, presenting them in a certain graduated way according to their internal relationship. The truth is that these codicils deal with criminality in the abstract, with theoretically belabored concepts, and that such concepts are all too few.[65]

As a result of the *Ulozhenie*'s contradictions and lack of clarity, confused judges often had no other practical choice but the traditional sentences of exile and *katorga*.

The *Ulozhenie* also laid the groundwork for exile's expansion by codifying both exile by administrative procedure and exile to residence—in other words, the administrative use of exile that Speranskii had tried to obliterate with his 1822 Reforms. Administrative exile has already been discussed, particularly in relation to the *Brodiagi* Regulation and exile for "bad behavior." Like these punishments "exile to residence" gave official sanction to a pre-existing trend, though it was now explicitly reserved for "persons of privilege" who were to be exiled to either Siberia or such peripheral *gubernii* as Perm, Archangel, and Olonets. Those assigned to non-Siberian *gubernii* were banished for a maximum of two years. Those exiled to Siberia were classified according to a five-tier scale, whose two most serious levels demanded assignment to Eastern Siberia, whereas Western Siberia was designated for the others. Offenders in the first four tiers were to spend up to four years in a Siberian prison before being released "to residence." But there is no evidence this measure was ever enforced given the lack of prisons, overflow of common offenders in those which did exist, and the social status of those exiled to residence. Offenders in the first two tiers were also forbidden to relocate to another Siberian *guberniia* for a period of up to 12 years.[66] Yet this and the general prohibition against leaving Siberia were routinely ignored by exiles who thanks to Siberian administrations' lack of police and laxity toward them could usually leave assigned locations whenever they chose.

With its ukase titled "Supplementary Resolutions Concerning the Distribution and Application of Those Sentenced to *Katorga* Labor,"[67] the 1845 *Ulozhenie* defined *katorga* much more clearly than had earlier legislation. Based on measures previously proposed and partially implemented by Bludov during his tenure as interior minister between 1832 and 1839,[68] this ukase distinguished three types of *katorga*: mine, fortress, and *zavod*. They nominally represented a descending scale of punitive severity; but in practice, local conditions often rendered labor in a *zavod* or fortress no less difficult than in a mine. The ukase specified that convicts sentenced to one type of *katorga* could not be assigned to another except as a temporary measure—but this proviso left open a crack the regime routinely exploited to the full. All penal laborers were to be sent to Siberia, though here again exceptions applied. Those sentenced to fortress *katorga* could be sent to fortresses in Orenburg, for example, or along the Baltic; whereas those sentenced to *zavod katorga* could be assigned to state distilleries in Perm *guberniia*. Moreover, "Tatars" from Kazan, Simbirsk, and Orenburg *gubernii* were to be assigned *only* to fortresses in Finland. Like the Senate ukase of 1827 this provision was blatantly discriminatory, since no other ethnic group faced similar restrictions. Male convicts sentenced to mine *katorga* were to be assigned to Nerchinsk Mining District; those to fortress *katorga* to military engineer corps; and those to *zavod katorga* to salt works and distilleries (both of which were alternately referred to as "factories" [*fabriki*] or "*zavody*" in another example of the *Ulozhenie*'s imprecise and confusing terminology). Female convicts could not be assigned to mines or fortresses, and so those sentenced to the judicial equivalent of mine *katorga* were to be assigned to Eastern Siberia *zavody*, whereas those with lesser sentences were to be placed in Western Siberia *zavody* or textile mills anywhere in Siberia. As this distinction makes clear, Eastern Siberia, due to its greater distance from European Russia and comparative lack of development, was consonant in lawmakers' punitive imaginations with harsher punishment.

When penal laborers arrived at either a mine or a *zavod* they entered a division termed the *ispytuemye*, which may be translated as "probationers." Time spent as a probationer was determined by the length of a convict's court-ordered sentence, as shown in the schedule below:

Court Ordered Sentence	Probationary Sentence
First Category (Mine)	
Life (*bez srochnaia*) = 8 yrs	
15–20 yrs = 4 yrs	
Third Category (*Zavod*)	
6–8 yrs = 1–1½ yrs	
4–6 yrs = 1 yr	

Strict conditions applied to probationers, with those serving life sentences kept in both manacles and leg-irons at all times. Lightweight chains were put on women sentenced to life. All other penal laborers wore leg-irons only, but like more serious offenders had half their scalps shaved. The ukase specifies that all were to be engaged in labor and, if necessary, punished according to military regulations.

After completing their terms as probationers convicts graduated with permission from their commanders to the division of the *ispravliaiush-chikhsia*, or "correctionals," where they would complete their labor sentences unless they committed other crimes or violations that returned them to the probationers. Correctionals enjoyed a much easier regime than probationers. They received more holidays and, upon the expiry of two-thirds of their sentences, might have their irons removed. Ten months as a correctional counted as a year towards completion of one's sentence. Those in the first (mine) and third (*zavod*) categories could, after three years and one year, respectively, petition to live outside the prison in a rented apartment or a house they might build within their local *katorga* administration's jurisdiction. At this juncture they obtained the right to marry. Those living outside the prison were eligible for financial assistance based on their "earnings" (that is, what their productivity earned the state, as distinct from the small amounts the state actually paid them). Bachelors received 25 percent of their earnings; married men 50 percent. Those who built their own homes received an additional 25 percent of their earnings and were also eligible for loans from the administration to improve their homesteads.

As enlightened as these measures seem, very few penal laborers ever managed to benefit from them. First, due to the bureaucratic muddle characterizing all levels of exile administration many probationers never graduated to become correctionals. Lower officials who often did not understand regulations lost the records on convicts who themselves were even less likely to understand the regulations. Second, survival as a homesteader in Siberia typically required one to sustain oneself through agriculture. Yet because most sentenced to *katorga* had existed at the fringes of society to begin with, few knew the first thing about farming. Most were anyway too physically or emotionally broken upon conclusion of their labor terms to maintain a farm and sometimes a family. As a result many asked to remain in prison, where they at least understood how things worked and received daily rations. Finally, once they were released from the barracks and got a taste of fresh air, many did not give farming a second thought and fled to become *brodiagi*.

Only two terms were possible for convicts sentenced to fortress *katorga*: 10–12 years or 8–10. After three years in the first category and two in the second convicts could transfer to the division of military-term prisoners (*razriad voennosrochnykh arestantov*)—roughly equivalent to the correctionals division and where every ten months likewise counted as a year toward completion of one's sentence. If a criminal sentenced to fortress *katorga* committed a violation serious enough to be punished by running the gauntlet, then he was disqualified from ever returning to the division of military-term prisoners.

Upon completion of their labor sentences, convicts in all three *katorga* categories were to become exile-settlers and, as such, could never leave Siberia. Penal laborers with life sentences could become exile-settlers only with permission of the governor-general of Eastern Siberia, and only then after having completed at least 12 years of their sentences. Convicts who completed their labor terms outside Siberia were convoyed there to begin existences as exile-settlers and thus faced the harrowing march route after having already endured the conditions of *katorga*. It is probable that mortality rates were higher among them than among those who commenced labor terms *after* arriving in Siberia.

The ukase orders that convicts who arrived at destinations unable to work or who become incapacitated during their labor terms be released early to become exile-settlers or, if unable to maintain themselves, be remanded to "almshouses or other charitable institutions, where they are held under special rules established for them, but only in those cases when their behavior is not disruptive and they can be anticipated not to cause any trouble."[69] This provision begs the question what in fact was done with convicts whose mental or psychological illnesses rendered them dangerous or unmanageable. The *Ulozhenie*'s vaguely defined rules, so similar to earlier ones that failed to prevent the neglect of such persons, offer no clues, but it is likely that responsibility for the regime's wretched and unwanted continued to devolve upon Siberian peasants.

The *Ulozhenie*'s "Statute on Civilian Correctional Penal Battalions"[70] details a sphere of imperial penology for the most part distinct from exile, but is important here for several reasons. First, as with the management of exiles generally, that of the correctional battalions required cooperation between several agencies. At the imperial level these included the MVD and the Main Administration of Communications and Public Buildings (*Glavnoe Upravlenie Putei Soobshcheniia i Publichnykh Zdanii*); at the *guberniia* level, the main administration (*Nachal´stvo*) of the region concerned, the Building Commission and Building Committee (*Stroitel´naia Komissiia, Stroitel´nyi Komitet*), and the local Prison Committee (*Tiuremnyi Komitet*). *Guberniia* governors exercised considerable leeway over prisoners in this category, but nevertheless had no authority over central agencies, and so cooperation was often lacking.

Second, the battalions exemplified like so much else Petersburg's tendency to transfer responsibility for maintaining and supervising convicts to society. The ukase repeatedly asserts that battalions are the responsibility of the "civilian sphere" (*grazhdanskoe vedomstvo*), which is to supply, maintain, incarcerate, and assign to various worksites those sentenced to correctional battalions. So as to better supervise their charges the battalion commanders (*rotnye komandiry*) appointed by *guberniia* administrations should also be expert masons, smiths, carpenters, road-builders, etc. In essence, Petersburg put into *guberniia* administrations' laps a public works program for which they had to bear all costs and most of the supervisory and maintenance responsibilities, yet over which they exerted little control. Petersburg further hemmed in governors by determining which criminals would be assigned to the battalions and for how long; specifying a five-and-a-half day work week; and ordering these convicts to be housed in district jails that were in most cases dilapidated and overcrowded.

But the greatest nuisance for Siberian governors especially, and the third reason for these battalions' importance here, was Petersburg's acknowledgement of village communes' right to refuse to re-accept convicts after their release from the battalions, in which case an individual who had already served four, six, or even 12 years would now find himself "removed for resettlement to Siberia, according to the regulations established for exile-settlers, only without deprivation of status rights." The same fate awaited those incapacitated by their labor: if the Department of Social Services could not return such persons to "their previous residences or assign them... to cities or state settlements," and if no other communes accepted them, "they [were] to be removed for resettlement in Siberia." This effectively ignored earlier legislation prohibiting the deportation of the elderly and physically or mentally disabled and, as such, condemned many to death. *Brodiagi* who after release still refused to identify themselves were to be removed "to distant *gubernii*" for resettlement; and indigenes were to be similarly removed "for settlement to distant *gubernii* or to Siberia."[71]

Along with legislation that had been issued in 1842,[72] the *Ulozhenie* specified who was to be assigned to correctional battalions. The following categories demonstrate that notions informing these battalions were similar to those influencing exile and *katorga*:

1) persons convicted by the courts;
2) persons identified as *brodiagi* or fugitives, as well as those "proving to be from the taxable class [i.e., serfs and state peasants] or from the *raznochintsy*," who may be assigned via administrative procedure to correctional battalions "until the resolution of their cases";
3) persons sentenced by city and village communes for purposes of working off debts or "reforming their morality";
4) "vicious people" sentenced by village communes or landowners for the purpose of reforming their behavior.[73]

Those in the fourth category could be sentenced to correctional battalions no longer than six months, whereas *brodiagi* who refused to identify themselves were to serve 12 years followed by resettlement in a "distant *guberniia*." The ukase predicts an average sentence of 1–2 years for those assigned to correctional battalions, but this was patently unrealistic.

It will be remembered that correctional battalions first emerged during the late 1820s. The *Ulozhenie* not only refined their functions but led to greater stress being placed on all Russia's *guberniia* administrations as well as the exile system. Foinitskii writes that as of September 1847, 5,580 men were enrolled in correctional battalions—that is, a thousand more than what official records showed at that time.[74] By allowing communes to refuse the return of formerly convicted members who had served their sentences, the regime created an entirely new and eventually very large category of deportees officially known as *nepriniatye* ("unacceptables"). Having been punished twice for the same crime, many *nepriniatye* undoubtedly reasoned that there was little difference between the fate of a criminal *brodiaga* and that of a tsarist subject who had paid his debt to society, and therefore chose the life of the former.

The effects of the 1845 *Ulozhenie* were mixed. On the one hand, it sought to define more clearly and to regulate better practices that were already staples of tsarist penality. On the other, it demonstrated continued reliance upon practices that were clearly not working. For instance, even the revamped correctional battalions amounted to a version of *katorga* since many, if not most, existed in Siberia. Moreover, if a convict sentenced to a correctional battalion eventually became a *nepriniatyi*, he was exiled with thousands of others to Siberia. The gap between what the new laws called for and what could be done in practice highlighted the center's cognitive dissonance regarding the periphery, and in this case the periphery means any spot farther than a hundred miles from Petersburg. During the years that followed, exile and *katorga* continued to be mismanaged and correctional battalions similarly failed to achieve the goals set for them, not least because many of their prisoners simply wandered away without being caught.

*   *   *

The most valuable descriptions of Siberian prison life under Nicholas I come from the pen of Fedor Dostoevskii. It is well-known that a defining moment in the great writer's life was the 20 minutes he spent on 22 December 1849 awaiting what he believed would be his execution for participation in the Petrashevskii Circle. The abrupt and curt delivery of the sentence, the priest giving last rites, the firing squad, the readied coffins, and the last-minute reprieve by a harried courier, were all part of a diabolical play written, staged, and directed by Nicholas himself. It was enough to drive one of his victims, Nikolai Grigor´ev, irreparably insane. In *The Idiot*, Prince Myshkin at one point relates a similar story told him by another man:

> [H]e said that the thing that was most unbearable to him at the time was the constant thought, "What if I had not to die! What if I could return to life—oh, what an eternity! And all that would be mine! I should turn every minute into an age, I should lose nothing, I should count every minute separately and waste none!" He said that this reflection finally filled him with such bitterness that he prayed to be shot as quickly as possible.[75]

Scarce moments following this prayer, the real-life 28-year-old writer—whose small output had impressed critic Vissarion Belinskii but nonetheless remained derivative of others—learned that, instead of death, his sentence had been commuted to four years *katorga* to be followed by five years military service.

As powerful a psychological impact as those few minutes standing before the void were for Dostoevskii, it was the years that followed which truly transformed both man and writer, proving that great artists are made, not born. "What happened to my soul, my beliefs, my mind and heart in those four years—I can't tell you. It would take too long to tell," he later wrote his brother Mikhail.[76] Yet one change had happened immediately that day of his mock execution. After he was returned to prison, he dashed off to Mikhail a letter in which he exclaimed, "Brother, my dear friend! all has been resolved! I've been sentenced to four years labor in a fortress (Orenburg, it seems) and then to the ranks." After briefly detailing that morning's remarkable events, he erupted with philosophical platitudes ("Brother! I am not despondent and have not fallen in spirit. Everywhere life is life, life is within us, and not outside us."), then lapsed into a request for books and inquiries about his relatives' health, before closing with additional exclamations:

> Life is a gift, life is good fortune, each moment may be an eternity of good luck. *Si jeunesse savait!* Now, altering my life, I will be reborn in new form. Brother! I swear to you that I will not lose hope and

will preserve my spirit in my heart and in purity. I will be reborn for the better. This is my greatest hope, my greatest consolation![77]

Prince Myshkin's story therefore faithfully portrays Dostoevskii's state of mind just before his reprieve, though this reprieve led to his being sent to Omsk and not Orenburg, as he originally surmised.

Dostoevskii also managed, through metaphor in his other novels, to express much of what he experienced that day and in the years that followed. Yet before launching the magnificent series of novels that transmuted a prison sentence into plots and characters of profound psychological depth and drama, he produced a more concretely representative work titled *Zapiski iz mertvogo doma*, which is usually translated as *Notes from the House of the Dead* but is more accurately read as *...Dead House*, since its contents make clear its author considered his former fellow inmates to be anything but men whose souls had departed. Among those he would otherwise never have consorted with during his previous life as a petty nobleman, Dostoevskii witnessed mankind at its most brutalized and depraved but also at its most admirable, fostering his later creation of Janus-faced characters whose behavior distils the irrationality of human nature.

Dostoevskii the existentialist cannot be accounted for without first taking note of Dostoevskii the prison inmate. "There is, for example, one type of murderer that is quite often encountered," he writes.

He lives quietly and humbly, enduring the vicissitudes of fortune. He may be a peasant, a house serf, an artisan or a soldier. Suddenly, without warning, something within him snaps; his endurance runs out and he plunges a knife into his enemy and oppressor. Something strange now begins to happen: the man seems to go temporarily berserk. He began by murdering his oppressor, his enemy; this, although criminal, is understandable; here there is a motive. But then he starts murdering people who are not his enemies, but just those who happen to cross his path, and he murders them for amusement, because of an insult or a look, for the sake of a string of beads, or simply, as [a] way of saying "Out of the way, don't let me catch you, here I come!" It is as if the man were drunk, or in a delirium. As if, having overshot some sacred limit within himself, he begins to exult in the feeling that there is no longer anything sacred in him; as though he felt an irresistible longing to overshoot all law and authority in one go, and to delight in the most unbridled and boundless freedom, to delight in the sinking sensation in his heart which is caused by his own apprehension of himself.[78]

Besides exploring the human psyche Dostoevskii philosophizes in *Dead House* on the institutionalization of evil. Such evil was for him most brutally manifested at Omsk by corporal punishment. He gives several examples of floggings and their effects and the desperate measures convicts took to avoid them, before observing more generally what corporal punishment revealed about Russian society:

> There are people like tigers, who thirst for blood to lick.... Tyranny is a habit; it is able to, and does develop finally into a disease.... The human being and the citizen perish forever in the tyrant, and a return to human dignity, to repentance, to regeneration becomes practically impossible for him.... Put briefly, the right given to one man to administer corporal punishment to another is one of society's running sores, one of the most effective means of destroying in it every attempt at, every embryo of civic consciousness, and a basic factor in its certain and inexorable dissolution.[79]

Something about tsarist society was indeed pathologically ill. The joy many elites took inflicting pain upon commoners was not simply a reflection of Russia's uneven development but of a tradition of cruelty whose roots extended deep into history. Tsarist Russia was a *Schadenfreude*-culture.[80]

Dostoevskii left Omsk fortress in March 1854; *Dead House* first appeared six years later.[81] It is unique in his oeuvre not least for portraying a universe in which there is practically no possibility for redemption, because all the protagonists are already in Hell. Interpretations of this remarkable book— which Dostoevskii begins through the voice of a fictional narrator who is soon almost completely abandoned[82]—are of course mixed, with some critics arguing that certain passages evince Dostoevskii's quasi-mystical notion of the Russian *narod* as embodying the nation's soul. In a much-cited passage near the end of the book Dostoevskii writes of his fellow inmates, "the whole truth must be told: all these men are quite remarkable. These were perhaps the most gifted, the strongest of all our people."[83] Yet when taken as a whole, *Dead House* reveals Dostoevskii's ambivalence towards common convicts; and in a letter to his brother written a week after his release from *katorga* he describes them as more bereft than gifted:

> While still in Tobol´sk I had gotten acquainted with convicts, and there in Omsk I settled down to live with them for four years. They

are a coarse people, irritable and spiteful. Their hatred towards the nobility exceeds all bounds, and therefore they greeted us nobles with hostility and with malicious joy over our woe. They would have eaten us up if they had been allowed to…. 150 enemies couldn't tire of persecuting one, that was a pleasure for them, an amusement, a pastime, and if we could in any way save ourselves from grief, then it was through indifference, moral superiority, which they couldn't help but understand and respect, and through resistance to their will. They always realized that we were higher than they were.

Yet in the same letter he also writes:

Even in prison among brigands, I, in four years, finally distinguished people. Believe it or not, there are profound, strong, marvelous personalities there, and how delightful it was to find gold under a coarse crust. And not one, but two, but several.[84]

Granted that Dostoevskii established genuine friendships with some convicts, the contrast between his and the Decembrists' *katorga* experience is nonetheless stark. Whereas both certainly benefited from their positions as noblemen *vis-à-vis* convicts who originated largely from the peasantry, the tangible comforts afforded the Decembrists were far greater. Spared incarceration alongside the unwashed masses in fetid lice-infested wards, their more benevolent attitude was a result of ignorance as much as *noblesse oblige*. Indeed, ignorance led some to seek contact with rapists and serial murderers they may have even regarded as equals. By contrast, Dostoevskii was tossed like a lamb into the lions' den. Yet his torment was conditioned as much by his own personal failings as by the hatred servants express toward fallen masters. Fellow inmate Szymon Tokarzewski later recalled that the author of *Poor Folk* was aloof and supercilious—incidentally the same accusations Dostoevskii leveled at Tokarzewski and Omsk's other Poles.[85] One despises most in others what one dislikes in oneself; though in all fairness Dostoevskii briefly confesses to these personal foibles in both the aforementioned letter and in *Dead House*.

In addition to their haughty attitudes, the privileges these ennobled prisoners received must have incurred enmity from other prisoners. Like the Decembrists, Dostoevskii did not march into Siberia but rode there in a sleigh. And when he and fellow Petrashevists Sergei F. Durov and Ivan L. Iastrzhembskii arrived in Tobol'sk "the sympathy and lively concern we met with blessed us with almost complete happiness," he wrote his brother. "The exiles of the old days (that is, not they themselves but their wives) looked after us as though we were their own flesh and blood.... [T]hey sent us food and clothing, they consoled us and gave us courage."[86] The wives he was referring to, of course, were those of the Decembrists banished many years earlier. Whereas firsthand accounts are lacking to show what Dostoevskii's criminal inmates really thought about him, evidence does show that Omsk's handful of Poles felt Dostoevskii and Durov enjoyed preferential treatment. General Borislavskii, commander of the Engineer Corps to which Dostoevskii's Penal Company No. 55 belonged, "patronized the Petrashevists," sniffed P. K. Martjanow. Borislavskii supposedly gave them easier jobs and allowed both to clerk in the chancery. I. I. Troitskii, Omsk's senior military physician, was similarly accused of allowing the Petrashevists extended stays in the infirmary—where food and conditions were superior to those in the barracks—despite it being obvious their needs were not, strictly speaking, physiological.[87] Dostoevskii himself discusses these and similar meliorations without considering them from the average convict's point-of-view, but it must be added the Poles also benefited from Troitskii's sympathy and Dostoevskii's clerking job was anyway short-lived.

Dostoevskii's status and notoriety did not always redound to his benefit. Because she was related to Governor-general P. D. Gorchakov, the Decembrist wife Natal´ia Fonvizina promised Dostoevskii during his stay in Tobol´sk that she would intercede on his behalf. Varvara Annenkova similarly promised to write her son-in-law Konstantin I. Ivanov, an officer in Omsk's Engineer Corps. However, Fonvizina later had a falling out with Gorchakov that led to Dostoevskii getting booted out of the chancery; and the gendarme who delivered Annenkova's letter to Ivanov also delivered to Omsk commandant Major Krivtsov an order from the emperor that he was to treat Dostoevskii and Durov "as prisoners in the full sense of the word." Krivstov felt sufficiently emboldened to threaten them with corporal punishment the day they arrived. Dostoevskii's description of Krivtsov as an inhuman beast corresponds to Tokarzewski's, and it has been suggested that his fear of him was even responsible for his epilepsy. Krivtsov truly must have been a monster since he was eventually convicted of maltreating prisoners and drummed out of the military.[88]

Fascinating as *Dead House* is for what it reveals about Dostoevskii, its greater significance lies in what it (alongside a couple of private letters) says about life in a mid-nineteenth century *katorga* prison. Despite

Dostoevskii's near-hallucinatory descriptions of people and situations, as in his two wonderful chapters on a prisoners' visit to the bathhouse and their Christmas theatrical, his factual details withstand scrutiny. That said, Omsk was atypical of *katorga*, since far more penal laborers were assigned to mines or *zavody* than to fortresses. Also, many more penal laborers were in Eastern than in Western Siberia. The year Dostoevskii's imprisonment began only 201 penal laborers, one-quarter of the total exiled that year, were assigned to Western Siberia.[89] Dostoevskii writes that around 150 convicts were at Omsk. His experience was also rendered atypical by assignment to a penal company commanded by the Siberia Corps. Nerchinsk *katorga* was militarized as well, but the prison at Omsk literally formed part of the fortress, and so the regime under which Dostoevskii lived was probably stricter than at a mine or a *zavod*. Nonetheless, *Dead House* portrays many aspects of *katorga* that were common throughout Siberia at that time.

Penal laborers and *brodiagi* were everywhere renowned as master tradesmen. Exiles, most of whom would have been former penal laborers, accounted for over half of Omsk's 176 tradesmen in the early 1840s.[90] Convicts inside the prison also worked as everything from smiths to joiners to cobblers making or repairing items on consignment for guards, soldiers, and local residents during their free time, especially in winter when official work days were shorter. If an officer at Omsk wanted an expensive piece of furniture he would simply contract a convict-joiner and provide him the materials. In such way prisoners earned considerable spending money. Dostoevskii writes that "almost every barrack [*sic*] was transformed into an enormous workshop" by these entrepreneurs.[91] His and the other political prisoners' lack of manual skills probably increased the other inmates' disdain for them.

Those without skills were classified as charworkers (*chernorabochie*) and assigned the simplest tasks during collective assignments. Dostoevskii writes that hauling bricks was practically the first physical labor he had ever done.[92] Crews also cut firewood, made bricks, and constructed and repaired buildings. They sometimes left the prison to work nearby. Once, Dostoevskii's crew dismantled a barge on the Irtysh River. Work slowed down considerably during winter, yet either way "[t]he work itself," he writes, "…did not seem at all the hard, *penal* labour it was supposed to be, and I realized only much later on that its hardness and *penal nature* consisted not so much in its being difficult or unalleviated as in its being *forced*, compulsory, done under the threat of the stick."[93] Even so, he relates how the other prisoners rarely allowed him to help them because of his physical weakness and unfamiliarity with working. Dostoevskii's portrayal of *katorga* as physically undemanding may only characterize his specific time and place. It will be remembered that the Siberian Committee's 1837 report gave shockingly high death rates for *katorga*, and these would have resulted from a combination of living and working conditions. The overabundance of penal laborers at Omsk (and in Western Siberia generally) may have led administrators to impose lower labor quotas and even to tolerate a certain lackadaisicalness, as long as they made a pretense of doing something. Moreover, prison crews would exert enormous collective bursts of energy if their assignment was defined on either a piece-rate or task basis as opposed to an hourly basis. In Dostoevskii's description of the barge's dismantling the crew begins sluggishly with much hemming and hawing until they learn the workday will be over as soon as the job is completed, at which point they work like mad and knock off early.

Despite prisoners' wanting so much to return to their barracks and free time, it was in this rundown building filled to bursting with murderers and other offenders, as well as a fair number who were mentally ill, that *katorga* was at its most oppressive. Omsk was characteristic of most Siberian prisons in that it was falling apart, and if there were any efforts by the local Prison Aid Society to fix it they went unnoticed by Dostoevskii. "Imagine for yourself an old, dilapidated, wooden building which should have been torn down long since and that it could not longer serve," he wrote his brother.

> In the summer the stuffiness is unbearable, in the winter the cold beyond enduring. All the floors have rotted through. The floor is an inch thick with mud, you can slip and fall. The little windows are covered with hoarfrost, so that for the whole day it's almost impossible to read. There's an inch of ice on the windowpanes. There is a drip from the ceiling—it's all full of holes…. If they stoke the stove with six logs there's no warmth (the ice barely melted in the room), but the fumes are unbearable—and that's our whole winter.

The filthy platforms on which prisoners slept beside each other were infested by "[m]ountains of fleas, lice, and cockroaches." Inmates received no bedding except a pillow and had to be content with covering themselves with government sient-issue sheepskin jackets known as *shubki*. "We're like herring in a barrel…," continued Dostoevskii:

> The prisoners do their laundry right there in the barracks and splash water all over the whole little barracks. There's no room to turn

around. It's impossible to go outside to answer the call of nature between sunset and sunrise, because the barracks is locked and a tub is placed in the hall, and therefore the stuffiness is unbearable. All the prisoners stink like pigs and say they can't help doing swinish things because, they say, "a man's a living thing."[94]

Despite noting the existence of "brigand chiefs" Dostoevskii is virtually silent on the hierarchy that organized prison life.[95] The ethnic distinctions that drove convicts apart interested him more. He writes that Caucasians and Muslims tended to stick together, largely because most did not speak Russian. The Poles, whom Dostoevskii says all prisoners hated, were the most aloof, as much for class as for patriotic reasons.

Omsk's prisoners appear to have received sufficient rations, though most had no choice but to eat what they were served, whereas Dostoevskii and other noblemen had money to buy food that vendors sold in the prison or was smuggled in by guards. Nonetheless, he depended for some portion of his diet on prison rations, of which he writes only the bread was "tasty." As for another Russian staple,

The cabbage soup was very unprepossessing. It was cooked in a common cauldron, was slightly thickened with meal and, especially on weekdays, was thin and watery. The enormous quantity of cockroaches it contained horrified me. But the convicts gave this no attention whatsoever.[96]

One aspect of *katorga* that Dostoevskii was never able to resign himself to, judging by his many references to them, was the leg irons all inmates had to wear. "The fetters I wore were not the regulation ones," complains Dostoevskii,

but were designed to be worn outside one's clothes. The regulation prison fetters which were designed to be worn at work consisted not of rings, but of four iron rods, each of almost a finger's thickness, connected by three rings. They had to be worn under one's trousers. To the middle ring a strap was fastened to the belt one wore next to one's shirt.[97]

Because the 8–12-pound bracelets chafed the skin, each convict purchased a pair of leather straps he wrapped around his legs for protection. But with all this in place, walking and especially dressing and undressing remained arts new convicts had to master. The first time he visited the bathhouse Dostoevskii had to be undressed like a child by another convict.

The stresses of prison life naturally affected different individuals in different ways. Some went mad—if indeed they were not insane before they arrived in prison. At Omsk no special care was provided the mentally ill, and so Dostoevskii describes having to endure like everyone else the ravings of those who had lost their minds. Others went insane quietly, withdrawing into catatonia or delusions of grandeur. He recounts a moment when, in the midst of a quiet conversation with a fellow convict he thought completely normal, the man's words suddenly disturbingly revealed he had lost all contact with reality.

As in nearly all prisons throughout history, there existed at Omsk a black market through which inmates could procure what might temporarily relieve them of their burdens. Sex, with either men or women, was a thriving commodity. Penal laborers connived with guards to have local women, who were anyway allowed into the fortress to sell *kalachi* (donut-shaped biscuits) and other items, meet for trysts inside or outside fortress walls. Dostoevskii notes a couple of rare instances when prisoners even sneaked into town for romantic interludes. He also describes in circuitous language Omsk's homosexual prostitutes. "[T]here were perhaps as many as fifteen in our prison," he writes, "it was a strange experience to watch them: only two or three of them had faces that were tolerable to look at."[98] Despite their lack of physical charm these men's services were hotly contested by some inmates. Dostoevskii fondly describes one young man named Sirotkin. After describing his features as feminine and attractive he pointedly adds, "He had no trade, but he received small amounts of money quite frequently." Elsewhere he writes, "Among his companions, Sirotkin was the only good-looking one" and that Sirotkin provided certain "services." When the convicts staged their Christmas play, Sirotkin assumed the female lead role and "looked very sweet dressed up as a young girl. Some of the spectators paid him muttered compliments under their breath."[99] Dostoevskii's loathing for the other prostitutes was not matched by his attitude towards Sirotkin.

Gambling and drinking distracted from the tortures of confinement more frequently than did sex. Prisoners did not necessarily need money to gamble: many staked their clothes and other items to cover bets. Besides various card games there were a host of other games of chance that often assumed epic proportions, lasted all night, and left gamblers exhausted for the coming workday. Gambling was, of course, against prison rules, but the prisoners would hire a "stirrup" (*strëmshchik*) "for five silver kopeks, and his principal responsibility was to watch all night for the guard. For the most part, he froze for six or seven hours in the dark, in the entryway, at 30 degrees below zero, listening to every tap, every sound, every step toward the door."[100]

The procurement of vodka, however, required that a convict steadily save his kopeks. Individuals would squirrel away their money for several months towards the goal of celebrating their name days or some other holiday, during which they would spend every last bit of their savings on a binge that often ended with them being pummeled into silence by the other prisoners so they could sleep. Dostoevskii's descriptions of these episodes are by turns comic, surreal, and ultimately tragic, since these "celebrations" epitomized the frustrations of prison life and next morning left prisoners exactly where they had been before their benders, only now with a hangover and without money or the belongings they had sold to keep drinking. "Prison drinking had its own brand of aristocratism," he wryly notes.[101] Being the most valuable contraband, vodka was never sold openly. Dostoevskii facetiously calls the vodka-seller a *tseloval´nik*, which historically meant both "tavern keeper" and "tax-collector." A confederate from town would hide animal intestines filled with vodka outside the fortress walls where the *tseloval´nik* could find them when he exited with his work crew. When it was time to return to prison he wrapped these vodka sausages around his body beneath his clothes and tried to sneak past the guard. If caught, he might have to surrender some to avoid a flogging but even then usually kept enough to open a *maidan*— a black market commissary. The *tseloval´nik* now faced an internal struggle between wanting to earn money and wanting a drink. He reconciled these desiderata by replacing whatever he drank with water and selling the diluted spirits. Eventually the vodka got so diluted that its alcohol content was almost nil, but so strong was the desire for even this watered-down spirit that convicts paid handsomely "for a little cup, five or six times more than in a tavern."[102]

Thanks to Dostoevskii, Efimov, and a smattering of other sources a reasonable facsimile of what *katorga* was like toward the end of Nicholas I's reign thus emerges. The government provided the bare minimum to maintain this institution, which comprised a dehumanizing netherworld where the maligned and abused slowly gnawed away at themselves like animals caught in a trap. *Katorga*'s malignancy woefully affected all Siberian society, for when penal laborers escaped, as they often did, they visited upon peasants, indigenes, and others revenge for the horrors they had suffered at the hands of the state. Penal laborers found it easy to escape because of their overwhelming numbers, the lack of prison personnel, and the circumstances under which they were held. Between 1823 and 1833 one-quarter of the nearly 3,000 penal laborers assigned to two separate distilleries in Tomsk *guberniia* escaped. Similarly, 259 of the 285 convicts assigned to the Kamenskii distillery fled between 1828 and 1833.[103] Out of the Irkutsk salt works' thousand-man workforce of both exiles and non-exiles, 976 escaped in 1834.[104] Table 7.1 demonstrates that this trend continued at other salt works throughout the decade.

Table 7.1 Annual Escapes from Three Salt Works in Eastern Siberia

	1837	*1838*	*1839*	*1840*
Irkutsk	363	238	248	359
Troitskii	181	164	206	171
Selenginsk	38	74	36	28
Totals	582	476	490	558

Source: Maksimov, "Sibirskaia sol'," 321.

During the period 1838–47, 2,473 penal laborers escaped.[105] Administrators often looked the other way when supernumerary prisoners fled. In 1843 the IGP issued a stern warning to the Nerchinsk Mining Bureau, police, and officials in charge of the Tel´minsk textile mill, salt works, and distilleries, holding each accountable for any penal laborers they allowed to go missing.[106] On 10 February 1859 the Nerchinsk Mining Administration reported that 4,000 of the convicts technically assigned to it were "at large" (*v begakh*).[107] During the period 1856–61, 80 and 75 exiles per annum escaped from Tobol´sk *guberniia*'s Uspensk and Ekaterinsk distilleries, respectively. The 77 penal laborers newly assigned to Uspensk during 1861 hardly made up for the 156 who escaped that same year.[108]

Arrested in Siberia during the period 1838–47 were 9,530 fugitive exile-settlers and prisoners from other categories, as well as 17,316 *brodiagi*.[109] Maksimov calculated that a total of 3,104 convict laborers—that is, not just those sentenced to *katorga*—successfully fled Nerchinsk *zavody* between 1847 and 1859. With the addition of the 508 master craftsmen (*masterovye*) who also escaped during this period these fugitives represented a quarter of the Nerchinsk Mining Administration's labor force.[110]

Hence not every person on the run in Siberia was an escaping convict. Many were soldiers, runaway serfs, or simply others who when detained and unable to produce a passport were declared *brodiagi* and punished accordingly. The MVD reported that 3,323 *brodiagi* were arrested in Siberia and Perm *guberniia* combined in 1844,[111] and reported similar figures throughout the next decade. Perm officials reported arresting 679 fugitives in 1855—a figure that included 79 *brodiagi* (surprisingly evenly distributed between the sexes) and "86 males and 1 female escaping out of Siberia," which means that the majority were soldiers, peasants, or others. Many fugitives were assisted by local residents, 99 of whom were convicted that year as *pristanoderzhateli* (harborers of fugitives).[112] In 1861, 211 fugitives were captured in the same *guberniia*.[113] Six years earlier, Tobol´sk police determined that of the 757 "fugitives and *brodiagi*" arrested in their *guberniia* in 1855, "309 were escaping from exile and 47 were military deserters."[114]

Brodiagi were so plentiful that the Perm administration published a handbook titled *Homilies to Convicts and Those Being Deported to Siberia as Criminals*. Approved by Archimandrite Fomii in his official capacity as Holy Censor, the anonymous author couched his advice in an idiom combining Biblical phraseology with salt-of-the-earth colloquialisms. There is no doubt that the reader (addressed throughout with the formal "You") is guilty of his crime and has committed it because of a lack of faith, and so the first few pages cite scripture to enforce the need for him to repent and surrender to the Lord. But there is also the worldly advice that "confession of the crime before the civil court should be early and full." Those who have sought to conceal their identities by adopting the surname Nepomniashchii (I-Don't-Remember) are taunted with the comment that only those born in a forest would not know their names, before they are implored to "Stop this cunning, good man, this insincerity which so dishonors You!"[115]

Many escapees returned home, of course, but thousands remained in Siberia, especially if they were penal laborers or *brodiagi*, because they had no homes to return to. They often found work in factories or sought refuge in villages. Soldiers punished with assignment to the Siberia Corps sometimes sympathized with and protected fugitives by presenting them to authorities as their civilian friends or assistants. Other fugitives plunged deep into the taiga, surviving with skills sometimes learned from Iakuts or Tungus, though when winter came most pleaded for admittance to the nearest prison, jail, or village to avoid ending up as "snow drops," that is, frozen corpses. If captured, fugitives were usually tattooed, lashed, and exiled (again). During the period 1827–46 a total of 18,328 captured fugitives accounted for 23.5 percent of administrative exiles and 11.5 percent of all exiles combined.[116] With the exile system already in a shambles and escapees roaming the countryside, this vicious cycle did nothing to reduce crime, which, as shown in Chapter 1, was becoming endemic.

In conclusion, *katorga* did not account for an exceedingly large portion of Russia's convicts, and so partly for this reason was not included in the emerging debate about whether or not to abolish exile. Another reason *katorga* eluded scrutiny for so long was that rehabilitation did not figure as strongly in tsarist penology as it did in the emerging penologies of Western Europe and the United States. Like their counterparts, Russians viewed crime as resulting from individuals' moral turpitude; but the tsarist government was less concerned than other governments with trying to instill moral values in convicts. This was because tsarist culture tended to essentialize the criminal as being irrevocably condemned, a view that may in turn have reflected a more general though equally pessimistic one that conceived of all human beings as born sinners. Nevertheless, the state was not about to let these convicts' moral failings stand in the way of efforts to utilize them to achieve its goals. The problem was, these goals were animated by efforts to satisfy both sovereign and governmental forms of power, which were largely antithetical to each other. The primary victims of this antithesis were the tens of thousands sentenced to *katorga*.

Conclusion: Aesthetics, Delusions, Conclusions

Narrative aesthetics call for a story to have a beginning and an end, a plot and a conclusion. History, in the sense of the real-time unfolding of human events, has no such structure—it merely provides the raw material historians fashion into a narrative for the purpose of making it comprehensible and meaningful. The story told in this book forms part of a larger one, which in my previous book *Exile to Siberia, 1590–1822* began with Siberian exile's late sixteenth-century origins and concluded with the promulgation of Speranskii's 1822 Reforms. This larger story will continue with a forthcoming book on the period after 1861. The book at hand, despite lacking an aesthetically gratifying beginning or conclusion, nevertheless does have a plot, by which I have tried to communicate some conclusions that will now be summarized.

My major conclusion is simply that the 1822 Reforms, which Russian historians both before and since 1917 are wont to describe as pivotal in their country's penological development, actually had little practical effect. These historians' tendency to overemphasize the reforms' impact highlights Russian historiography's larger tendency to envisage through a positivistic lens Russia's journey through time. Indeed, late imperial-era scholarship coincided with the heyday of Positivism; and after 1917 Russian historians were for 70 years compelled to conform to the precepts of Marxism, Positivism's single greatest ideological legacy with the possible exception of Liberalism. Despite Communism's collapse, Russian historiography has yet to disengage from Positivism. This is no particular stigma: historians everywhere have a tendency to think inside time-capsules. But it is remarkable the extent to which the thinking of many historians virtually ignores philosophical notions that have been around for many decades. The

1822 Reforms have also been accorded undue significance simply because Russian historians, like most other historians, depend upon the written word in their efforts to reconstruct the past. From the start, this dependence imposes a certain measure of fictiveness upon what are usually demonstrable, and oftentimes laudable, efforts to objectively witness past realities. The reforms doubtlessly remain significant for what they say regarding contemporaneous notions of government, punishment, statecraft, and so on; but their correspondence with the actualities facing exiles and the exile system was practically nugatory.

It will be remembered that Speranskii created six subcategories within the juridical category of "exile to settlement." As of 1862, each of these was not functioning as intended. The so-called incapables category did little more than emblematize exile's continued abusive application. In 1834, two years before he became Western Siberia's governor-general, Petr D. Gorchakov calculated that some 10,000 cripples were residing in Western Siberia alone.[1] Justice minister Dmitrii V. Dashkov acknowledged, though demonstrated little sympathy toward, this problem, and recommended according to a later government report that "[t]he aged, decrepit, maimed, crippled... [be sent] to almshouses; ... and the incapables from the clergy... [be] distributed by the Ministry of Finance to factories to serve as helpers and... for various community needs."[2] Dashkov's call for almshouses repeated what had been legislated in 1822 but continued to be ignored in practice. By 1835, the number of exiles assigned to workshops—institutions that constituted another subcategory and at first sight seem quite progressive—had dwindled to less than 25 per annum. The following year Petersburg closed all Siberia's workshops except that in Irkutsk, which lingered on in disarray until it too closed in 1852. The subcategory of road workers who were tasked with maintaining march-route stations under the Department of Overland Communications seems never to have existed. The subcategory of exiles assigned to the servant guild did exist, though on a small scale and almost wholly within Western Siberia. Its lack of success may be judged by an 1837 letter Gorchakov sent Benkendorf, in which he writes that servant guild exiles had fallen "from being firmly reliable residents to debauchees."[3] Most exiles within this predominantly female contingent were in fact concubines of the military officers they worked for. TobPS assigned several hundred more exiles to this category during the following years, though by the 1850s it still accounted for a very small number. The 1822 provision assigning the most serious offenders among the exile-settlers to factories for one to two years was rarely enforced: between 1823 and 1858 fewer than 4,500 were so assigned, largely because not enough factories were available to employ those in this subcategory.[4] Finally, exile-settlers, when they were assigned to either a state settlement or a *starozhil* village, usually burdened peasants and local administrators to no discernible benefit. They could not or would not become the prosperous state peasants envisaged by Speranskii, whose plans so conspicuously failed to account for these individuals' personal agency, i.e., counter-conduct.

Katorga was the other main category of exile. Because Speranskii had not wanted to lock horns with the MVD, Ministry of Finance, and Ministry of War, each of which maintained a vested interest in *katorga*, his reforms glossed over it. Irrespective of this, *katorga* was by any standards, though particularly those of economic and punitive efficacy, counter-productive as of 1862. The deliberations eventuating in the 1845 *Ulozhenie* presented opportunities to redress *katorga*'s shortcomings but instead produced an even greater reliance on it and thus set the stage for its expansion during the late imperial period. The *Ulozhenie* similarly counterproductively sanctioned the administrative deportation of thousands of persons to Siberia each year, thus completely reversing Speranskii's (and to some extent Alexander I's) previous attempts to end this travesty of justice.

Quite apart from inaugurating positive developments in penology, the 1822 Reforms mark the intensifying struggle between sovereignty and governmentality in Russia between 1823 and 1861. By focusing on the exile system this book has offered a different and more nuanced explanation of early nineteenth-century tsarism than has prevailed, emphasizing not just the importance of the emperor and such institutions as the MVD, GUVS, GUZS, and TobPS, but also the epistemologies of top decision-makers, as well as the decisions and counter-conduct of both individuals (e.g., Lunin and *brodiagi*) and communities (e.g., Siberia's petty official-dom and the *Skoptsy*). Generally speaking, this notion of counter-conduct is especially helpful in better understanding how the state functions and, even more so, how it fails to function. The methodology underpinning this study suggests that the state be seen not as a monolith but as a disorderly collection of processes and negotiations; and it demonstrates how those who benefit from this monolithic myth perpetuate it through political theatrics intended to disguise their own ignorance and helplessness. Because counter-conduct, either within or outside the state apparatus, undermines, ignores, or displaces authoritarian discourse, those who benefit most from the state find it extremely threatening. The struggle between those at the center and those at the extremities of power necessitates that the political script be constantly revised and rewritten, as demonstrated by the *Ulozhenie*, the *Brodiagi* Regulation, and other legislation concerning exile, even if, like the 1822 Reforms, their practical results hardly coincided with what was intended.

It may fairly be said that the tsarist regime controlled subjects to the extent they felt controlled by it, that many believed themselves under its firm control because they were entranced by its theatricality. All the same, the period 1823–61 was dynamic insofar as the public developed a more critical attitude toward tsarism than was possible before. This attitude gained sustenance from witnessing the punishment of those sentenced for deviant behavior, from seeing week after week those bound for Siberia march through your village in chains while you knew from your own experience that many of these wretches had been unjustly condemned. Certainly, this spectacle cowed many, whether or not they sympathized with the plight of the "unfortunates," and conditioned their everyday behavior as officialdom intended it would. But over time the spectacle's impact waned with repetition. More importantly, even if only a small number of spectators may be claimed to have been radicalized by what they saw, they contributed disproportionately to the disenchantment that corroded tsarism's support at the same time that it emboldened its enemies. It is also certainly the case that corporal punishment and exile curbed the behavior of many, if not most, deviants. All the same, many *brodiagi*, *Skoptsy*, and sundry "incorrigibles" perpetuated or even exacerbated their deviancy once they were in Siberia. These individuals' motivations—which were admittedly often homicidal or otherwise antisocial—make no difference to the point being made here, which is that the sum result of their behavior amounted to an antidisciplinary network that, at its broadest, included most Siberian officials. The very attitudes and practices that contributed to tsarism's downfall were cultivated in Siberia by its most repressive activities.

Opposition toward tsarism was largely fueled by the actions of its foremost proponent Nicholas I, who, similar to his civil servant underlings, soon began flailing about in a vain effort to fulfill his self-appointed duties, becoming alternately fixated or detached toward certain issues as his reign careered toward its dénouement. Yet he was probably overwhelmed by his role as head of government from the beginning, as is suggested by his obsession with the military and his tiresome efforts to connect all other matters to it. By all accounts he was a nervous man, like his predecessor Peter I, and for this reason found security in the predictability and regimentation of military life. And, like Peter, he had good reason to be nervous: both shared the fear—which was moreover quite legitimate because it was founded in history—that they would be assassinated. Indeed, had Nicholas not faced a mutiny the very day he laid claim to the throne, might he have adopted a less martial approach toward dealing with social issues and been better disposed to solve the cardinal problems of serfdom and exile?

Narrative aesthetics also call for a trope to be imposed on a given story to better allow readers to appreciate the meaning its author intended for it. Despite some efforts at comedy here and there, this has essentially been a tragedy, one that involves both Nicholas I and the people he ruled. This tragedy operates, of course, at the interpretive level and thus encompasses the historians mentioned above who are wedded to a Positivistic notion of the progressive development of the nation-state. *Exile, Murder and Madness in Siberia, 1823–61* indicates that this notion of progress can lead to tragic consequences for large numbers of people. And yet, as my unapologetic use of the heroic trope for describing Lunin and Lutskii suggests, necessity demands that a notion of individual human betterment be sustained for as long as possible.

Notes

Introduction: Geography, Penality, Power, and Resistance

1 Victor L. Mote, *Siberia: Worlds Apart* (Boulder: Westview Press, 1998), passim; A. P. Gorkin, ed., *Geografiia Rossii* (Moskva: Bol´shaia Rossiiskaia Entsiklopediia, 1998), passim; G. M. Lappo, ed., *Goroda Rossii* (Moskva: Nauchnoe izdatel´stvo, 1994), passim.

2 Quoted in Constantin de Grunwald, *Tsar Nicholas I*, trans. by Brigit Patmore (London: Douglas Saunders with MacGibbon & Kee, 1954), 158.

3 "Perechen´ vedomosti i tabelei, prinadlezhashchikh k otchetu upravliaiush-chago Ministerstvom Vnutrennikh Del, za 1839 god," *ZhMVD* 7 (July 1840): Table III, lit. A.

4 Ivan V. Shcheglov. *Khronologicheskii perechen´ vazhneishikh dannykh iz istorii Sibiri: 1032–1882 gg.* (1883; rpt. Surgut: Severnyi dom, 1993), table, p. 353.

5 "Materialy dlia statistiki Rossii," *ZhMVD* 42 (May 1860): 13.

6 Andrew A. Gentes, *Exile to Siberia, 1590–1822* (New York: Palgrave Macmillan, 2008).

7 "Penality" is a useful term introduced by David Garland that embraces penology, criminal justice, and punishment. David Garland, *Punishment and Modern Society: A Study in Social Theory* (Oxford: Clarendon Press, 1990).

8 *Ssylka v Sibir´: ocherk eia istorii i sovremennago polozheniia* (S.-Peterburg: Tipografiia S.-Peterburgskoi Tiur´my, 1900), appendices, table, pp. 1–2.

9 Emile Durkheim, *The Division of Labor in Society*, trans. by George Simpson (New York: Free Press, 1933), chap. 2; Garland, *Punishment*, 23–39.

10 Michel Foucault, *Discipline & Punish: The Birth of the Prison*, trans. by Alan Sheridan (New York: Vintage, 1977), 209.

11 Quoted in Nicholas V. Riasanovsky, *Nicholas I and Official Nationality in Russia, 1825–1855* (Berkeley: University of California Press, 1961), 193.

12 Frederick W. Kagan, *The Military Reforms of Nicholas I: The Origins of the Modern Russian Army* (New York: St. Martin's Press, 1999).

13 Michel Foucault, *Security, Territory, Population: Lectures at the Collège de France, 1977–1978*, trans. by Graham Burchell (Basingstoke: Palgrave Macmillan, 2007), 66, 67. Two years earlier, during another series of lectures, Foucault asserted that the invention of population resulted in a "massifying" discursive exercise of power "directed not at man-as-body but at man-as-species," and he introduced the term *biopolitics*—the production of knowledges and techniques usually undertaken by, or at least for the benefit of, the state *vis-à-vis* population. Michel Foucault, *Society Must Be Defended*, trans. by David Macey (London: Penguin, 2003), 243.

14 Foucault, *Security*, 248.

15 Ibid., 107–8.

16 Ibid., 108–9.

17 Ibid., 155, 340.

18 Bruce F. Adams, *The Politics of Punishment: Prison Reform in Russia, 1863–1917* (DeKalb: Northern Illinois University Press, 1996), 12–19; Gentes, *Exile*, 114, et passim.

19 Jack Z. Bratich, et al., "Governing the Present," in *Foucault, Cultural Studies, and Governmentality*, ed. by idem (Albany: State University of New York Press, 2003), 5.

20 Mitchell Dean, *Governmentality: Power and Rule in Modern Society* (London: Sage Publications, 1999), 17.

21 See Modris Eksteins, *Rites of Spring: The Great War and the Birth of the Modern Age* (New York: Anchor Books, 1989).

22 Foucault, *Security*, 242–8.

23 Quoted in A. E. Presniakov, *Emperor Nicholas I of Russia: The Apogee of Autocracy, 1825–1855*, ed. and trans. by Judith C. Zacek [including "Nicholas I and the Course of Russian History," by Nicholas V. Riasanovsky] (Gulf Breeze, FL: Academic International Press, 1974), 71.

24 Walter McKenzie Pintner, *Russian Economic Reform under Nicholas I* (Ithaca: Cornell University Press, 1967), 5–6.

25 David F. Lindenfeld, *The Practical Imagination: The German Sciences of State in the Nineteenth Century* (Chicago: University of Chicago Press, 1997), 1. See also Marc Raeff, *The Well-Ordered Police State: Social and Institutional Change through Law in the Germanies and Russia, 1600–1800* (New Haven: Yale University Press, 1983).

26 Foucault, *Security*, 313.

27 Lindenfeld, *Practical*, 18, 20.

28 Dean, *Governmentality*, 95.

29 See Margaret Schabas and Neil De Marchi, "Introduction," in *Oeconomies in the Age of Newton*, ed. by idem [Annual Supplement to Volume 35 of *History of Political Economy*] (Durham: Duke University Press, 2003), 1–13.

30 Colin Gordon, "Governmental Rationality: An Introduction," in *The Foucault Effect: Studies in Governmentality: With Two Lectures by and an Interview with Michel Foucault*, ed. by Graham Burchell, et al. (Chicago: University of Chicago Press, 1991), 12.

31 Elizabeth Fox-Genovese, *The Origins of Physiocracy: Economic Revolution and Social Order in Eighteenth-Century France* (Ithaca: Cornell University Press, 1976), 48, 49. See also Yves Charbit, "The Political Failure of an Economic Theory: Physiocracy," trans. by Arundhati Virmani, *Population (English Edition, 2002–)* 57, no. 6 (2002): 855–83; Jessica Riskin, "The 'Spirit of System' and the Fortunes of Physiocracy," in *Oeconomies*, 42–75.

32 Between 1826 and 1844 the number of factories in Russia grew from only 5,158 to 7,399 and the number of workers in these factories from 206,480 to 469,211. The Crimean War served as an important industrial stimulus: as of 1861 there were 14,148 manufactories (*obrabatyvaiushchie promyshlennosti*) with 522,500 laborers. Nonetheless, these workers represented a miniscule proportion of the empire's total population of nearly 70 million. L. E. Shepelëv, *Apparat vlasti v Rossii: Epokha Aleksandra I i Nikolaia I* (Sankt-Peterburg: Iskusstvo—SPB, 2007), tables, pp. 309, 353; "Materialy dlia statistiki Rossii," *ZhMVD* 42 (May 1860): 13.

33 Between 1823 and 1856 gentry indebtedness soared from 90 million to 398 million silver rubles, yet the state's Loan Bank foreclosed on very few properties and functioned more like a noblemen's welfare agency than an economically rational branch of government. Pintner, *Economic Policy*, Table 3, p. 42.

34   Kagan, *Military*, 10, 15, 97.

35   Pintner, *Economic Policy*, 159.

36   W. Bruce Lincoln, "Count P. D. Kiselev: A Reformer in Imperial Russia," *Australian Journal of Politics & History* 16, no. 2 (1970): 177–86.

37   V. V. Rabtsevich, "Krest´ianskaia obshchina kak organ upravleniia sibirskoi derevnei," in *Krest´ianstvo Sibiri perioda razlozheniia feodalizma i razvitiia kapitalizma (Mezhvuzovskii sbornik nauchnykh trudov)*, ed. by L. I. Postupinskaia (Novosibirsk: Novosibirskii gosudarstvennyi pedagogicheskii institute, 1980), 26–7.

38   M. Iuzefovich, "Neskol´ko slov ob Imperatore Nikolae," *Russkii arkhiv* (1870): 999–1008 [here, p. 1008].

39   Kagan exaggerates Nicholas's reformist proclivities; Orlovsky too readily dismisses them. Cf. Kagan, *Military*, 6*ff*, 238*ff*; Daniel T. Orlovsky, *The Limits of Reform: The Ministry of Internal Affairs in Imperial Russia, 1802–1881* (Cambridge: Harvard University Press, 1981), 27.

40   Presniakov, *Emperor Nicholas I*, 31–2.

41   Quoted in Grunwald, *Tsar Nicholas I*, 158.

42   Orlovsky, *Limits*, 27.

43   W. Bruce Lincoln, *In the Vanguard of Reform: Russia's Enlightened Bureaucrats, 1825–1861* (DeKalb: Northern Illinois University Press, 1982). See also Orlovsky, *Limits*, 121–2, et passim.

44   Foucault, *Security*, 70.

45   John P. LeDonne, *Ruling Russia: Politics and Administration in the Age of Absolutism, 1762–1796* (Princeton: Princeton University Press, 1984).

46   GAIO, f. 435, op. 1, d. 176, ll. 4–8.

47   "Otchet Kazanskago Popechitel'nago tiuremnago komiteta, za 1839 god," *ZhMVD* (January 1840): Table C, p. 328.

48   Gordon, "Governmental Rationality," 4.

49   Peter L. Berger, et al., *The Homeless Mind: Modernization and Consciousness* (Middlesex: Penguin, 1973).

50   Orlovsky, *Limits*, 29.

51   S. Frederick Starr, *Decentralization and Self-Government in Russia, 1830–1870* (Princeton: Princeton University Press, 1972), 28.

52   Marquis de Custine, *Empire of the Czar: A Journey Through Eternal Russia* (1971; rpt. New York: Doubleday, 1989), 488.

53   Berger, *Homeless Mind*, 60 [orig. italics].

54   Apropos this association see Wendy Everett and Peter Wagstaff, "Introduction," in *Cultures of Exile: Images of Displacement*, ed. by idem (New York: Berghahn Books, 2004), x; Edward Said, "Reflections on Exile," *Granta* 13 (1984): 157–72 [here, p. 165].

55   Foucault, *Security*, 177, 193–216.

56   Michel Foucault, *The Use of Pleasure: The History of Sexuality: Volume Two*, trans. by Robert Hurley (London: Penguin, 1985).

57   Michel de Certeau, *The Practice of Everyday Life*, trans. by Steven Rendall (Berkeley: University of California Press, 1984), xv.

58   Ibid., xix [my italics].

59   I. V. Efimov, "Iz zhizni katorzhnykh Ilginskago i Aleksandrovskago, togda kazennykh, vinokurennykh zavodov. 1848–1853 g.," *Russkii arkhiv* 1 (1900): 79–107, 247–72 [here, p. 263].

60 N. P. Matkhanova, *Vysshaia administratsiia Vostochnoi Sibiri v seredine XIX veka: Problemy sotsial´noi stratifikatsii* (Novosibirsk: Sibirskii khronograf, 2002), 37, et passim; George L. Yaney, *The Systematization of Russian Government: Social Evolution in the Domestic Administration of Imperial Russia, 1711–1905* (Urbana: University of Illinois Press, 1973), 218; L. M. Dameshek and A. V. Remnev, eds., *Sibir´ v sostave Rossiiskoi imperii* (Moskva: Novoe literaturnoe obozrenie, 2007), chap. 3; Gentes, *Exile*, passim.

61 William M. Reddy, *The Navigation of Feeling: A Framework for the History of Emotions* (Cambridge: Cambridge University Press, 2001); idem, "The Logic of Action: Indeterminacy, Emotion, and Historical Narrative," *History and Theory* 40, no. 4 (2001): 10–33; Susan Schott, "Emotion and Social Life: A Symbolic Interactionist Analysis," *American Journal of Sociology* 84, no. 6 (1979): 1317–34; Arlie Russell Hochschild, "Emotion Work, Feeling Rules, and Social Structure," *American Journal of Sociology* 85, no. 3 (1979): 551–75.

62 Foucault, *Security*, 357.

63 For an elaboration of this notion see Gentes, *Exile*, 1–6.

64 Jean Bethke Elshtain, *Sovereignty: God, State, and Self* (New York: Basic Books, 2008), 83.

65 I. A. Bartenev, et al., eds., *225 let Akademii khudozhestv SSSR: Katalog vystavki, 1757–1917*, 2nd edn. (Moskva: Izobrazitel´noe iskusstvo, 1985), 404. I saw this medallion on display at the Russian State Historical Museum in Moscow many years ago.

66 Custine, *Empire*, 354–5.

67 Presniakov, *Emperor Nicholas I*, 34.

68 Elise Kimerling Wirtschafter, "Military Justice and Social Relations in the Prereform Army, 1796 to 1855," *Slavic Review* 44, no. 1 (1985): 67–82 [here, p. 82].

69 John L. H. Keep, *Soldiers of the Tsar: Army and Society in Russia, 1462–1874* (Oxford: Clarendon Press, 1985), 307*ff*.

70 See Kagan, *Military*, 9–10. The same was true after 1861. See Andrew A. Gentes, "No Kind of Liberal: Alexander II and the Sakhalin Penal Colony," *Jahrbücher für Geschichte Osteuropas* 54, no. 3 (2006): 321–44; Ana Siljak, *Angel of Vengeance: The "Girl Assassin," the Governor of St. Petersburg, and Russia's Revolutionary World* (New York: St. Martin's Press, 2008).

71 Presniakov, *Emperor Nicholas I*, 31. "...Russia's emperor had not yet come to see the civil service as anything which required special training or talent," writes Lincoln. W. Bruce Lincoln, "The Ministers of Nicholas I: A Brief Inquiry into Their Backgrounds and Service Careers," *Russian Review* 34, no. 3 (1975): 308–23 [here, p. 319].

72 Kagan, *Military*, 146.

Chapter 1 The Surge: Exile and Crime in Siberia

1 Andrew A. Gentes, *Exile to Siberia, 1590–1822* (New York: Palgrave Macmillan, 2008), 201.

2 Lincoln writes that "fifty-five men served Nicholas as ministers from the time he ascended the throne until his death in February 1855." W. Bruce Lincoln, "The Ministers of Nicholas I: A Brief Inquiry into Their Backgrounds and Service Careers," *Russian Review* 34, no. 3 (1975): 308–23 [here, p. 310].

3 Nicholas tormented Speranskii in the aftermath of the Decembrist Uprising but later expressed concern for him in private correspondence. See L. G. Zakharova and S. V. Mironenko, eds., *Perepiska tsesarevicha Aleksandra Nikolaevicha s imperatorom Nikolaem I, 1838–1839* (Moskva: ROSSPEN, 2008), passim. On Speranskii's unpopularity see David Saunders, *Russia in the Age of Reaction and Reform, 1801–1881* (New York: Longman, 1992), 62–3.

4 A. Sergeev, ed., "Gr. A. Kh. Benkendorf o Rossii v 1827–1830 gg. (Ezhegodnye otchety III otdeleniia i korpusa zhandarmov)," *Krasnyi arkhiv* 37 (1929): 138–74 [here, p. 143].

5 Quoted in L. M. Dameshek and A. V. Remnev, eds., *Sibir´ v sostave Rossiiskoi imperii* (Moskva: Novoe literaturnoe obozrenie, 2007), 272–3.

6 Abby M. Schrader, "Unruly Felons and Civilizing Wives: Cultivating Marriage in the Siberian Exile System, 1822–1860," *Slavic Review* 66, no. 2 (2007): 230–56 [here, pp. 236–7].

7 *Uchrezhdenie dlia upravleniia Sibirskikh gubernii* (Sankpeterburg: Pechatano v Senatskoi Tipografii, 1822), passim; Vladimir A. Tomsinov, *Speranskii* (Moskva: Molodaia gvardiia, 2006), 326; Aleksandr A. Vlasenko, "Ugolovnaia ssylka v Zapadnuiu Sibir´ v politike samoderzhaviia XIX veka" (Ph.D. dissertation, Omskii gosudarstvennyi universitet im. F. M. Dostoevskogo, 2008), 53.

8 *Ssylka v Sibir´: ocherk eia istorii i sovremennago polozheniia* (S.-Peterburg: Tipografiia S.-Peterburgskoi Tiur´my, 1900), appendices, table, pp. 1–2.

9 G. Peizen, "Istoricheskii ocherk kolonizatsii Sibiri," *Sovremennik* 9 (1859): 9–46 [here, table, pp. 42–3].

10 S. Maksimov, *Sibir´ i katorga*, 3 vols. (S.-Peterburg: Tipografiia A. Transhelia, 1871) 2: table, p. 320.

11 S. V. Kodan, "Osvoboditel´noe dvizhenie v Rossii i sibirskaia ssylka (1825–1861gg.)," in *Politicheskie ssyl´nye v Sibiri (XVIII-nachalo XX v.)*, ed. by L. M. Goriushkin (Novosibirsk: Nauka, 1983).

12 W. Bruce Lincoln, *Nicholas I: Emperor and Autocrat of All the Russias* (Bloomington: Indiana University Press, 1978), 188, 192–5; idem, "Count P. D. Kiselev: A Reformer in Imperial Russia," *Australian Journal of Politics & History* 16, no. 2 (1970): 177–86.

13 See illustrations in Richard S. Wortman, *Scenarios of Power: Myth and Ceremony in Russian Monarchy: Volume One, From Peter the Great to the Death of Nicholas I* (Princeton: Princeton University Press, 1995), 94–6.

14 Clifford Geertz, *The Interpretation of Cultures: Selected Essays* (New York: Basic Books, 1973), 240–1, 243–4.

15 Alexander Bitis, *Russia and the Eastern Question: Army, Government, and Society, 1815–1833* (New York: Oxford University Press, 2006), 56.

16 Frederick W. Kagan, *The Military Reforms of Nicholas I: The Origins of the Modern Russian Army* (New York: St. Martin's Press, 1999), 8 [orig. italics].

17 Elise Kimerling Wirtschafter, "Military Justice and Social Relations in the Prereform Army, 1796 to 1855," *Slavic Review* 44, no. 1 (1985): 67–82 [here, p. 67].

18 John L. H. Keep, *Soldiers of the Tsar: Army and Society in Russia, 1462–1874* (Oxford: Clarendon Press, 1985), 315.

19 Albert J. Schmidt, "The Restoration of Moscow after 1812," *Slavic Review* 40, no. 1 (1981): 37–48; Andrew Gentes, "The Life, Death and Resurrection of

the Cathedral of Christ the Saviour, Moscow," *History Workshop Journal* 46 (1998): 63–95; Wortman, *Scenarios*, 169–295; Keep, *Soldiers*, 165, 323.

20   Quoted in Wortman, *Scenarios*, 233. General Sergei I. Maevskii similarly wrote of one military colony: "Cleanliness and order were the colony's first concern." Quoted in Michael Jenkins, *Arakcheev: Grand Vizier of the Russian Empire* (New York: Dial Press, 1969), 190.

21   Wortman, *Scenarios*, 297.

22   Quoted in Lincoln, *Nicholas*, 73.

23   John Keep, "Justice for the Troops: A Comparative Study of Nicholas I's Russia and France under Louis-Philippe," *Cahiers du Monde russe et soviétique* 28, no. 1 (1987): 31–54 [here, pp. 33, 35–8, 46]. This counters Kagan's claim that Nicholas valued and even sanctified the law. Kagan, *Military*, 37–8.

24   Keep, *Soldiers*, 224, 262, 298–9; Joseph L. Wieczynski, "The Mutiny of the Semenovsky Regiment in 1820," *Russian Review* 29, no. 2 (1970): 167–80; Sidney Monas, *The Third Section: Police and Society in Russia under Nicholas I* (Cambridge: Harvard University Press, 1961), 45–8; Anatole G. Mazour, *The First Russian Revolution: 1825, the Decembrist Movement: Its Origins, Development, and Significance* (Stanford: University Press, 1937), 58–63; Bitis, *Russia*, 66–7*n*, 85–7.

25   N. M. Iadrintsev, *Sibir´ kak koloniia v geograficheskom, etnograficheskom i dopolnennoe* (S.-Peterburg: Tip. I. M. Sibiriakova, 1892), 246.

26   Evgenii V. Anisimov, *The Reforms of Peter the Great: Progress through Coercion in Russia*, trans. by John T. Alexander (Armonk, NY: M. E. Sharpe, 1993), 229.

27   Adele Lindenmeyr, *Poverty is Not a Vice: Charity, Society, and the State in Imperial Russia* (Princeton: Princeton University Press, 1996), 30–2.

28   For a brief overview of the literature see A. G. Lebedev, "Istoriia borby s nishchenstvom i brodiazhnichestvom v Rossii XIX—nachala XX v. (Opyt ispol´zovaniia penitentsiarnykh uchrezhdenenii)," *Vestnik Moskovskogo universiteta. Seriia 8. Istoriia* 4 (2006): 111–26.

29   Keep, *Soldiers*, 197–9, 335.

30   Bitis, *Russia*, 483–4.

31   Kagan, *Military*, 233.

32   Ibid., 98.

33   Officially titled: "Ob otsylke v Sibir´ na poselenie brodiag i prestupnikov, vmesto otdachi ikh voennuiu sluzhbu i v krepostnyia raboty," *Polnoe sobranie zakonov rossiiskoi imperii. Serie 1*, t. XXXVIII (1830), no. 29329 (23 February 1823).

34   Ibid.

35   Lindenmeyr, *Poverty*, 33–6.

36   RGIA, f. 1281, op. 6, d. 97, l. 14.

37   Vlasenko, "Ugolovnaia ssylka," 148.

38   GARF, f. 1183, op. 1, d. 137, ll.

39   Kagan, *Military*, 89; Bitis, *Russia*, 481; Keep, *Soldiers*, 326–7.

40   Quoted in Bitis, *Russia*, 489.

41   Lincoln, *Nicholas*, 230. See also John S. Curtiss, "The Peasant and the Army," in *The Peasant in Nineteenth-Century Russia*, ed. by Wayne S. Vucinich (Stanford: Stanford University Press, 1968), 110–14; Keep, *Soldiers*, chap. 8, et passim; Elise Kimerling Wirtschafter, "The Lower Ranks in the Peacetime Regimental Economy of the Russian Army, 1796–1855," *Slavonic and East European Review* 64, no. 1 (1986): 40–65.

42   Steven L. Hoch, *Serfdom and Social Control in Russia: Petrovskoe, a Village in Tambov* (Chicago: University of Chicago Press, 1986), 151.
43   E. N. Anuchin, *Izsledovaniia o protsente soslannykh v Sibir´ v period 1827–1846 godov: materialiy dlia ugolovnoi statistiki Rossii* (S.-Peterburg: Tip. Maikova, 1873), table, p. 19.
44   "Ukaz Pravitel´stvuiushchago Senata ot 22 Iiunia 1831 g. o tom, chto zhena chlenovreditelia, otpravliaemago v ssylku s vydacheiu za nego pomeshchiku zachetnoi kvitantsii, dolzhna byt´ priznavaema svobodnoiu ot krepostnoi zvisimosti, a potomu i snabzhaema pasportom na svobodnoe zhitel´stvo," *ZhMVD* 5, no. 5 (1831): 51–3. The Senate had supreme authority over several facets of exile, including the treatment of *brodiagi* and fugitive exiles, provisioning exile-settlers, formation of regional *katorga* administrations, and implementation of the 1822 exile regulations.
45   "Vysochaishe utverzhdennoe v 3 den´ Iiulia 1831 g. mnenie Gosudarstvennago Soveta po voprosu: otsylat´ li v Sibiri s brodiagami maloletnykh detei ikh?," *ZhMVD* 5, no. 6 (1831): 3–5. The military orphanages were created under Emperor Paul. Keep, *Soldiers*, 160.
46   "Otchet Kazanskago Popechitel´nago tiuremnago komiteta, za 1839 god," *ZhMVD* 35, no. 1 (1840): Table C, p. 328; Maksimov, *Sibir´* (1871) 2: table, p. 320; RGIA, f. 1281, op. 6, d. 97, l. 85. See also Andrew A. Gentes, "Towards a Demography of Children in the Tsarist Siberian Exile System," *Sibirica* 5, no. 1 (2006): 1–23.
47   Vlasenko, "Ugolovnaia ssylka," 132 and Appendices.
48   GUVS report dated 28 August 1842, reproduced in L. M. Goriushkin, ed., *Politicheskaia ssylka v Sibiri: Nerchinskaia katorga, Tom 1* (Novosibirsk: Sibirskii khronograf, 1993), doc. no. 45, p. 69 and note.
49   Keep, "Justice": 44.
50   Keep, *Soldiers*, 222.
51   Quoted in Bitis, *Russia*, 490.
52   GAIO, f. 435, op. d. 155, l. 244.
53   Ibid., ll. 334–5.
54   Ibid., l. 308.
55   Kagan, *Military*, 232.
56   Irkutsk constable report, 31 December 1877, GAIO, f. 32, op. 13, d. 95, ll. 5–12.
57   S. V. Maksimov, *Sibir´ i katorga*, 3rd ed. (S.-Peterburg: Izdanie V. I. Gubinskago, 1900), 207.
58   GAIO, f. 435, op. d. 227, l. 11.
59   On the 1831 riot see N. E. Matveev, "Bunt v Staroi-Ruse v 1831 g.," *Russkaia starina* 25 (1879): 389–98; A. F. Ushakov, "Kholernyi bunt v Staroi-Ruse v 1831 g.," *Russkaia starina* 9 (1874): 145–62; [Anon.,] "Bunt v voennykh poseleniiakh v 1831 g.," *Russkaia starina* 25 (1879): 731–8. The potato riots resulted from the state forcing peasants to sow this strange and unfamiliar plant. Walter McKenzie Pintner, *Russian Economic Policy under Nicholas I* (Ithaca: Cornell University Press, 1967), 176–8.
60   Maksimov, *Sibir´* (1900), 207.
61   "Ukaz Pravitel´stvuiushchago Senata, ot 2 Iiunia 1830 goda, o obrashchenii k Prikazy Obshchestvennago Prizreniia brodiag nesposobnykh k sledovaniiu v Sibir´ in a poselenie," *ZhMVD* 3, no. 5 (1830): 34–7.

62 "Ukaz Pravitel´stvuiushchago Senata, ot 12 Iiuna 1830 goda, o merakh predostorozhnosti v soderzhanii liudei, vpadaiushchikh nechaianno v pripadki sumasshestviia," *ZhMVD* 3, no. 5 (1830): 65–8.

63 Lindenmeyr, *Poverty*, 44.

64 "Tsikuliarnoe predpisanie Ministerstva Vnutrennykh Del, Gg. Grazhdanskim Gubernatoram, ot 27 Iiunia 1830 goda, o podvodnoi povinnosti dlia arestantov," *ZhMVD* 4, no. 2 (1831): 3–6.

65 Both quotes in Vlasenko, "Ugolovnaia ssylka," 72, 74–5.

66 Ibid., 71. Vlasenko blames a growing number of exiles for GUZS's reversal. However, numbers fluctuated during this time-span, and 1844 represented only a slight increase over 1839. The decision more likely stemmed from fears that exiles would infect soldiers with either diseases or dangerous ideas.

67 RGIA, f. 1281, op. 6, d. 97, ll. 73–4.

68 I. Ia. Foinitskii, *Uchenie o nakazanii v sviazi s tiur´movedeniem* (S.-Peterburg: Tipografiia Ministerstva putei soobshcheniia [A. Benke], 1889), 290–1. Keep mentions military and civilian "detention companies" being created in 1823 and eventually totaling 55 companies with 13,750 detainees under Nicholas I. These might be the correctional battalions discussed here, though his sources for the date of their origins are problematic. Keep, "Justice": 43 and note; idem, *Soldiers*, 314 and note.

69 RGIA, f. 1281, op. 6, d. 97, ll. 61–3.

70 Anuchin, *Izsledovaniia*, tables, pp. 21, 23.

71 Between 1867 and 1876, 23,383 were exiled to resettlement (*na vodvorenie*), a sentence applied only to *brodiagi*. N. M. Iadrintsev, *Novyia svedeniia o sibirskoi ssylke: Soobshchenniia S.-Peterburgskomu Iuridicheskomu Obshchestv* (appended to Iadrintsev, *Sibir´ kak koloniia: k iubileiu trekhsotletiia. Sovremennoe polozhenie Sibiri. Eia nuzhdy i potrebnosti. Eia proshloe i budushchee* [Sanktpeterburg, 1882]), table, p. 2. See also Andrew A. Gentes, "Vagabondage and Siberia: Disciplinary Modernism in Tsarist Russia," in *Cast Out: Vagrancy and Homelessness in Global and Historical Perspective*, ed. by A. L. Beier and Paul Ocobock (Athens: Ohio University Press, 2008), 184–208.

72 "Ukaz Pravitel´stvuiushchago Senata ot 24 Sentiabria 1830 goda, o vydache zachetnykh rekrutskikh kvitantsii za liudei, postupivshikh v voennuiu sluzhbu za brodiazhestvo i drugie poroki," *ZhMVD* 3, no. 6 (1830): 114–19.

73 Vlasenko, "Ugolovnaia ssylka," 132–3. See also Keep, "Justice": 32; Bitis, *Russia*, 487.

74 Vlasenko claims the statute greatly increased the numbers exiled to Siberia, but this was true only later. Cf. Maksimov, *Sibir´* (1871) 2: table, p. 320.

75 Anuchin, *Izsledovaniia*, tables, pp. 21, 23.

76 As reported in *Ssylka v Sibir´*, table, pp. 26–7.

77 *Statisticheskiia svedeniia o ssyl´nykh v Sibiri, za 1833 i 1834 gody (Izvlechenie iz otcheta o delakh Sibirskago Komiteta)* (Sanktpeterburg: Tip. II Otdeleniia Sobstvennoi E. I. V. Kantseliarii, 1837), appendix to table no. 3, pp. 66–7. Hereafter cited as *Statisticheskiia svedeniia… Sibirskago Komiteta*.

78 Ibid., appendix E, table no. 1, p. 52.

79 Vlasenko, "Ugolovnaia ssylka," 142–3.

80 Richard S. Wortman, *The Development of a Russian Legal Consciousness* (Chicago: University of Chicago Press, 1976), 237.

81   Monas, *Third Section*, 64, 90.
82   Lincoln, *Nicholas*, 103.
83   Samuel Kutscheroff [Kucherov], "Administration of Justice under Nicholas I of Russia," *The American Slavic and East European Review* 7 (1948): 134. See also Wortman, *Russian Legal Consciousness*, 236–42, et passim.
84   N. S. Tagantsev, *Russkoe ugolovnoe pravo: chast´ obshchaia*, 2 vols. (1902; rpt. Tula: Avtograf, 2001) 1: 188*ff*.
85   S. S. Ostroumov, *Prestupnost´ i ee prichiny v dorevoliutsionnoi Rossii* (Moskva: Izdatel´stvo universiteta, 1980), tables 7 and 8, p. 22.
86   Monas, *Third Section*, 70–1. See also pp. 64, 90.
87   Vlasenko, "Ugolovnaia ssylka," 130–1.
88   Anuchin, *Izsledovaniia*, table, p. 22.
89   Richard Pipes, *Russia under the Old Regime* (New York: Charles Scribner's Sons, 1974), 162–3, 211*n*; Marc Raeff, *Imperial Russia, 1682–1825: The Coming of Age in Modern Russia* (New York: Knopf, 1971), 113, 120–1.
90   On *samosud* see Stephen P. Frank, *Crime, Cultural Conflict, and Justice in Rural Russia, 1856–1914* (Berkeley: University of California Press, 1999); idem, "Popular Justice, Community, and Culture among the Russian Peasantry, 1870–1900," in *The World of the Russian Peasant: Post-Emancipation Culture and Society*, ed. by Ben Eklof and Stephen Frank (Boston: Unwin Hyman, 1990), 133–53. Although Frank focuses on the post-emancipation period he notes that *samosud* "remained widespread throughout the nineteenth century...." *Crime*, 134. It should be emphasized that exile was not a primary form of punishment. Within the unofficial ladder of punishments employed by landowners and *obshchestva* exile was the most severe and therefore the rarest. Besides fines and expropriations favored punishments included canings and floggings. See Hoch, *Serfdom*, 163–4; Bruce F. Adams, *The Politics of Punishment: Prison Reform in Russia, 1863–1917* (DeKalb: Northern Illinois University Press, 1996), chap. 1.
91   Anuchin, *Izsledovaniia*, tables, pp. 23, 66–7.
92   *Statisticheskiia svedeniia... Sibirskago Komiteta*, Appendix A, Table No. 1, pp. 49–50.
93   L. E. Shepelëv, *Apparat vlasti v Rossii: Epokha Aleksandra I i Nikolaia I* (Sankt-Peterburg: Iskusstvo—SPB, 2007), 248; Willard Sunderland, *Taming the Wild Field: Colonization and Empire on the Russian Steppes* (Ithaca: Cornell University Press, 2004), 122–3. The government began restricting Roma's itinerancy no later than Peter I's reign. David M. Crowe, *A History of the Gypsies of Eastern Europe and Russia* (New York: St. Martin's Press, 1994), 153*ff*.
94   "Rasporiazheniia: O poriadke soderzhaniia i preprovozhdeniia Tsygan, dlia vodvoreniia ikh v kazennykh seleniiakh," *ZhMVD* 36, no. 4 (April 1840): xxvi–xxxii.
95   Maksimov, *Sibir´* (1900), 207.
96   E.g., leading figures of the Naqshbandiyya, a sufi movement, were exiled from the Caucasus in 1820. Moshe Gammer, *Muslim Resistance to the Tsar: Shamil and the Conquest of Chechnia and Daghestan* (London: Frank Cass, 1994), 39.
97   Robert Lyall, *Travels in Russia, the Krimea, the Caucasus, and Georgia*, 2 vols. (1825; rpt. New York: Arno Press & the New York Times, 1970) I: 459–60.

98 Bitis, *Russia*, 26, 75, 228, et passim; Abby M. Schrader, *Languages of the Lash: Corporal Punishment and Identity in Imperial Russia* (DeKalb: Northern Illinois University Press, 2002), 69–72.

99 See documents in GAIO, f. 435, op. 1, d. 87; d. 94.

100 *Statisticheskiia svedeniia... Sibirskago Komiteta*, Appendix A, Table No. 1, pp. 40–51.

101 Anuchin, *Izsledovaniia*, table, pp. 156–63.

102 "Ukaz Pravitel-stvuiushchago Senata, ot 13 Maia 1830 goda, o neotstuplenii ot obshchikh pravil pri pogrebenii umershikh Magotmetan," *ZhMVD* 3, no. 5 (1830): 17–22.

103 GAIO, f. 24, op. 3, k. 1, d. 10, ll. 17–19, 21.

104 George F. Jewsbury, *The Russian Annexation of Bessarabia: 1774–1828: A Study of Imperial Expansion* (Boulder: East European Quarterly, 1976), 150; Bitis, *Russia*, 441.

105 Anuchin, *Izsledovaniia*, table, pp. 156–63.

106 Anuchin's figures on the religious affiliations of those exiled during the period 1827–46 are practically worthless since they exclude "Catholics exiled from the Kingdom of Poland, Protestants exiled from Finland, and Mohammedans from Siberia and the Caucasus." Ibid., 134.

107 *Statisticheskiia svedeniia... Sibirskago Komiteta*, Appendix A, Table No. 1, p. 40.

108 GAIO, f. 24, op. 3, k. 32, d. 81, ll. 1, 3.

109 A. Sergeev, ed., "Gr. A. Kh, Benkendorf o Rossii v 1827–1830 gg. (Okonchanie)," *Krasnyi arkhiv* 38 (1930): 109–47 [here, p. 144].

110 Ivan Stepanovich Listovskii, "Razskazy iz nedavnei stariny," *Russkii arkhiv* 3 (1878): 507–21 [here, pp. 511–13].

111 GAIO, f. 24, op. 3, k. 36, d. 50, ll. 18–19.

112 RGIA, f. 1281, op. 6, d. 166, l. 17.

113 Ibid., d. 97, l. 48.

114 GAIO, f. 24, op. 3, k. 31, d. 47, ll. 1–2.

115 Ibid., ll. 3, 5, 7, 12.

116 GAIO, f. 24, op. 3, k. 36, d. 69, ll. 1–2.

117 Keep, "Justice": 41.

118 Laura Engelstein, *Castration and the Heavenly Kingdom: A Russian Folktale* (Ithaca: Cornell University Press, 1999), 32.

119 GAIO, f. 24, op. 3, k. 35, d. 12, ll. 1–8.

120 Ibid., k. 36, d. 50, ll. 3–10.

121 GAIO, f. 24, op. 3, k. 35, d. 12, ll. 1–8.

122 Ibid., ll. 14–21.

123 Ibid., ll. 28–31.

124 GAIO, f. 24, op. 3, k. 37, d. 1, ll. 37–44.

125 Ibid., k. 35, d. 12, ll. 1–8.

126 Ibid., ll. 22–70.

127 RGIA, f. 1281, op. 6, d. 97, l. 48.

128 This term is ambiguous insofar as it is impossible to tell if Smorodin castrated himself, someone else, or simply belonged to the *Skoptsy*. Laura Engelstein believes that, strictly speaking, persons were convicted for being *Skoptsy*, not for their roles as castrators. Email to author, 11 May 2009.

129 GAIO, f. 24, op. 3, k. 37, d. 1, ll. 37–44.

130 Ibid., k. 35, d. 5, ll. 2, 9.

131 GAIO, f. 24, op. 3, k. 37, d. 1, ll. 20–3. These figures are approximate: local officials admitted they did not have precise figures. See ibid., ll. 32–3, 34–5.

132 Engelstein, *Castration*, 119.

133 GAIO, f. 24, op. 3, k. 35, d. 12, ll. 2–8, 14–21, 22–70.

134 Ibid., k. 37, d. 1, ll. 1–2.

135 GAIO, f. 24, op. 3, k. 35, d. 12, ll. 28–31.

136 Ibid., ll. 122–201.

137 Bitis, *Russia*, 94–6, et passim.

138 Keep, *Soldiers*, 154. Keep refers to them as "men who had been castrated."

139 "Ukaz Pravitel´stvuiushchago Senata, ot 23 Iiulia 1830 goda, o nevy-davanii zachetnykh rekrutskikh kvitantsii na skoptsov," *ZhMVD* 3, no. 6 (1830): 43–4 [quotation on p. 44].

140 These instructions are referenced in a GUVS memorandum dated 9 October 1837. GAIO, f. 24, op. 3, k. 30, d. 2, ll. 12–14.

141 Ibid., k. 36, d. 50, ll. 3–10.

142 GAIO, f. 24, op. 3, k. 30, d. 2, ll. 57–8.

143 Ibid., ll. 35–6, 37–8, 65, 66–8.

144 Ibid., ll. 101, 102.

145 Ibid., ll. 12–14.

146 GARF, f. 123, op. 1, d. 112, ll. 14–18.

147 Ibid., ll. 10–11.

148 Vlasenko, "Ugolovnaia ssylka," 134; I. V. Shcheglov, *Khronologicheskii perechen´ vazhneishikh dannykh iz istorii Sibiri: 1032–1882 gg.* (1883; rpt. Surgut: Severnyi dom, 1993), 357. Stories of Jewish exiles being involved in smuggling Siberian gold were common. See ibid., 287, 290.

149 Iu. A. Gagemeister, *Statisticheskie obozrenie Sibiri* (SPB, 1856), as reproduced in Kodan, "Osvoboditel´noe," 165; Iu. A. Gagemeister, *Statisticheskoe obozrenie Sibiri*, vol. 2 (SPB, 1854), as reproduced in Shcheglov, *Khronologicheskii perechen´*, table, p. 336; V. M. Kabuzan, *Izmeneniia v razmeshchenii naseleniia Rossii v XVIII–pervoi polovine XIX v. (Po materialam revizii)* (Moskva: Nauka, 1971), appendix 1, table, pp. 55–7; A. S. Nagaev, *Omskoe delo, 1832–1833* (Krasnoiarsk: Krasnoiarskii universitet, 1991), 26; *Ssylka v Sibir´*, table, p. 26; Foinitskii, *Uchenie*, 284–5.

150 Maksimov, *Sibir´* (1871) 2: table, p. 320.

151 I. V. Efimov, "Iz zhizni katorzhnykh Ilginskago i Aleksandrovskago, togda kazennykh, vinokurennykh zavodov. 1848–1853 g.," *Russkii arkhiv* 1 (1900): 79–107, 247–72 [here, p. 95].

152 Cited in Vlasenko, "Ugolovnaia ssylka," 146.

153 Anuchin, *Izsledovaniia*, table, pp. 17–22.

154 *Statisticheskiia svedeniia… Sibirskago Komiteta*, Appendix A, Table No. 1, pp. 42–6.

155 RGIA, f. 1281, op. 6, d. 133, l. 21.

156 According to figures provided that year by the Committee of Ministers, cited in V. A. Volchek, *Osushchestvlenie imperskoi politiki na vostochnykh okrainakh Rossii v deiatel´nosti Vtorogo Sibirskogo komiteta* (Novosibirsk: Sibirskaia nauch-naia kniga, 2006), 94.

157 Vlasenko, "Ugolovnaia ssylka," 146–7.
158 *Statisticheskiia svedeniia… Sibirskago Komiteta*, 30, Table No. V, p. 66, Appendix to Table No. 5, pp. 67–9.
159 "Smes'," *ZhMVD* 8 (1836): table no. 2; "Perechen´ vedomosti i tabelei, prinadlezhashchikh k otchetu upravliaiushchago Ministerstvom Vnutrennykh Del, za 1839 god," *ZhMVD* 7 (July 1840): Table III lit. A.
160 Maksimov, *Sibir´* (1871) 2: table, p. 325.
161 "Perechen´," *ZhMVD* 7 (July 1840): Tables I and III lit. A.
162 "Smes'," *ZhMVD* 8 (1836), table no. 2; "Perechen vedomosti i tabelei, prinadlezhashchikh k otchetu upravliaiushchago Ministerstvom Vnutrennykh Del, za 1839 god," *ZhMVD* 7 (July 1840), Tables I and III lit. A.
163 FBI, "Crime in the United States" http://www.fbi.gov/ucr/cius2006/data/table_16.html, accessed 8 March 2008.
164 "List of Countries by Homicide Rate" http://en.wikipedia.org/wiki/List_of_countries_by_homicide_rate, accessed 8 March 2008.
165 As reported in the following issues of *ZhMVD* 4–12 (April 1842): Table XVIII; 7–8 (1844): Table(s) B; 9–12 (1845): Table(s) B; 29–32 (1850): Table(s) B; 11 (1855): Table(s) B; (May–June 1855): Table B; (July–August 1855): Table B; 14–15 (1855): Table(s) B.
166 V. M. Kabuzan, *Narodonaselenie Rossii v XVIII—pervoi polovine XIX v. (Po materialam revizii)* (Moskva : AN SSSR, 1963), table 17, p. 161.
167 "O prestupleniiakh po vsei Sibiri, v koikh uchastvovali ssyl´nye s 1823 po 1831 god," *ZhMVD* 8 (1833): 224 and table, p. 225.
168 RGIA, f. 1281, op. 6, d. 166, ll. 11–12, 18–19.
169 Ibid., d. 79–1862, l. 128.
170 Ibid., d. 79, ll. 119–21.

Chapter 2 Administering Exile: Malfeasance, Corruption, and Failure

1 N. Evreinov, *Istoriia telesnykh nazanii v Rossii* (New York: Chalidze Publications, 1979), 101.
2 One of the old prisoners Vlas Doroshevich interviewed on Sakhalin remembered his punishment. Vlas Doroshevich, *Russia's Penal Colony in the Far East: A Translation of Vlas Doroshevich's "Sakhalin"*, trans. and intro. by Andrew A. Gentes (New York: Anthem Press, 2009), 375.
3 Evreinov, *Istoriia*, 109–10.
4 Doroshevich, *Russia's Penal Colony*, 450.
5 Quoted in S. Frederick Starr, *Decentralization and Self-Government in Russia, 1830–1870* (Princeton: Princeton University Press, 1972), 45.
6 A. Sergeev, ed., "Gr. A. Kh. Benkendorf o Rossii v 1827–1830 gg. (Ezhegodnye otchety III otdeleniia i korpusa zhandarmov)," *Krasnyi arkhiv* 37 (1929): 138–74 [here, p. 151].
7 L. M. Dameshek and A. V. Remnev, eds., *Sibir´ v sostave Rossiiskoi imperii* (Moskva: Novoe literaturnoe obozrenie, 2007), 100–1.
8 Nicholas B. Breyfogle, *Heretics and Colonizers: Forging Russia's Empire in the South Caucasus* (Ithaca: Cornell University Press, 2005), 36–7, 45.
9 Starr, *Decentralization*, 49.

10   Ibid., 16, 26–7, 29, 48; W. Bruce Lincoln, *Nicholas I: Emperor and Autocrat of All the Russias* (Bloomington: Indiana University Press, 1978), 165. Lincoln writes approvingly that the ratio of civil servants to nobles was 11.8 to 1,000. Ibid., 76.

11   V. A. Volchek, *Osushchestvlenie imperskoi politiki na vostochnykh okrainakh Rossii v deiatel'nosti Vtorogo Sibirskogo komiteta* (Novosibirsk: Sibirskaia nauchnaia kniga, 2006), 158.

12   Aleksandr A. Vlasenko, "Ugolovnaia ssylka v Zapadnuiu Sibir' v politike samoderzhaviia XIX veka" (Ph.D. dissertation, Omskii gosudarstvennyi universitet im. F. M. Dostoevskogo, 2008), Appendices.

13   Dameshek, *Sibir'*, 98–9.

14   Volchek, *Osushchestvlenie*, 67.

15   GAIO, f. 435, op. 1, d. 147, l. 468.

16   Ibid., d. 155, ll. 216–17.

17   GAIO, f. 435, op. 1, d. 168, ll. 24, 27 [same document].

18   Lincoln, *Nicholas*, 167.

19   Ibid., 102.

20   GAIO, f. 435, op. 1, d. 146, l. 360.

21   Ibid., d. 147, ll. 531–5.

22   GAIO, f. 435, op. 1, d. 155, l. 32.

23   Ibid., l. 119.

24   Lincoln, *Nicholas*, 171.

25   Dameshek, *Sibir'*, 103; Volchek, *Osushchestvlenie*, 53.

26   GAIO, f. 435, op. 1, d. 146, l. 407.

27   Abby M. Schrader, "Unruly Felons and Civilizing Wives: Cultivating Marriage in the Siberian Exile System, 1822–1860," *Slavic Review* 66, no. 2 (2007): 230–56 [here, p. 251].

28   Aleksei Bolkovskii, *Ekaterinburgskii tsentral* (Moskva: EKSMO, 2008), 45–62.

29   Frederick W. Kagan, *The Military Reforms of Nicholas I: The Origins of the Modern Russian Army* (New York: St. Martin's Press, 1999), 58–60, et passim.

30   Senator [Aleksei Mikhailovich] Karnilov, *Zamechaniia o Sibiri* (Sanktpeterburg: Pechatno v tipografii Karla Kraila, 1828), 15–16.

31   Whereas "*voisko*" usually means "[Cossack] host," the adjective "*militsionnoe*" suggests an irregular militia.

32   Ibid., 17.

33   Ibid., 17–18 [my italics].

34   Ibid., 18.

35   Ibid., 19.

36   Irkutsk *guberniia* council journal dated 16 March 1829 and redacted in an IGP circular dated 3 May 1829. GAIO, f. 435, op. 1, d. 155, ll. 200–3. Schrader cites a similar document (for which she gives no date) as stating that 60,000 people were exiled "in the five years following Speranskii's reforms...." Schrader, "Unruly Felons": 237.

37   In the document in question this is spelled *Takshintsy* which, given the preceding term, is almost certainly a misspelling of *Tashkintsy* or "people from Tashkent." Thanks to Kit Condill of the Slavic Reference Service at the University of Illinois at Urbana-Champaign for noticing this.

38   Ibid.

39 Walter McKenzie Pintner, *Russian Economic Policy under Nicholas I* (Ithaca: Cornell University Press, 1967), 67–73.

40 GAIO, f. 435, op. 1, d. 155, ll. 200–3.

41 Pintner, *Economic Policy*, 69.

42 Bruce F. Adams, *The Politics of Punishment: Prison Reform in Russia, 1863–1917* (DeKalb: Northern Illinois University Press, 1996), chap. 1.

43 Abby M. Schrader, *Languages of the Lash: Corporal Punishment and Identity in Imperial Russia* (DeKalb: Northern Illinois University Press, 2002), 89–103, quotes on p. 94.

44 I. Ia. Foinitskii, *Uchenie o nakazanii v sviazi s tiur´movedeniem* (S.-Peterburg: Tipografiia Ministerstva putei soobshcheniia [A. Benke], 1889), 287–8. See also Schrader, *Languages*, 90.

45 N. S. Tagantsev, *Russkoe ugolovnoe pravo: chast´ obshchaia*, 2 vols. (1902; rpt. Tula: Avtograf, 2001) 2: 139; Foinitskii, *Uchenie*, 287–8.

46 Foinitskii, *Uchenie*, 287–8; *Ssylka v Sibir´: ocherk eia istorii i sovremennago polozheniia* (S.-Peterburg: Tipografiia S.-Peterburgskoi Tiur´my, 1900), 29–31; Dameshek, *Sibir´*, 97.

47 Foinitskii, *Uchenie*, 284–5.

48 Quoted in *Ssylka v Sibir´*, 33. The source is vague as to the date of this document. Context suggests it was 1835–36.

49 G. Spasskii, "Nechto o Russkikh v Sibiri starozhilakh," *Sibirskii vestnik* 1 (1818): 122–7 [here, pp. 123–5].

50 "O prestupleniiakh po vsei Sibiri, v koikh uchastvovali ssyl´nye s 1823 po 1831 god," *ZhMVD* 8 (1833): 224–33.

51 Foinitskii, *Uchenie*, 288–90; *Ssylka v Sibir´*, 34–5, 37–9. On Walnut Street Prison see Mark Colvin, *Penitentiaries, Reformatories, and Chain Gangs: Social Theory and the History of Punishment in Nineteenth-Century America* (New York: St. Martin's Press, 1997), 54*ff*.

52 Ivan V. Shcheglov, *Khronologicheskii perechen´ vazhneishikh dannykh iz istorii Sibiri: 1032–1882 gg.* (1883; rpt. Surgut: Severnyi dom, 1993), 311–12.

53 Vlasenko, "Ugolovnaia ssylka," 130.

54 Shcheglov, *Khronologicheskii perechen´*, 311–12; Foinitskii, *Uchenie*, 288–90.

55 Vlasenko, "Ugolovnaia ssylka," 139–40.

56 *Statisticheskiia svedeniia o ssyl´nykh v Sibiri, za 1833 i 1834 gody (Izvlechenie iz otcheta o delakh Sibirskago Komiteta)* (Sanktpeterburg: Tip. II Otdeleniia Sobstvennoi E. I. V. Kantseliarii, 1837).

57 The committee's responsibilities were distributed between the State Council and Committee of Ministers. In 1852 Nicholas established a second Siberian Committee, which was disbanded in 1864 and is discussed below. A. P. Okladnikov, et al., eds., *Istoriia Sibiri s drevneishikh vremen do nashikh dnei*, 5 vols. (Leningrad: Izdatel´stvo "Nauka," 1968–9) 2: 476–7; Vlasenko, "Ugolovnaia ssylka," 44.

58 *Statisticheskiia svedeniia... Sibirskago Komiteta*, Appendix to Table No. III, pp. 66–7.

59 Vlasenko, "Ugolovnaia ssylka," 152–3.

60 *Statisticheskiia svedeniia... Sibirskago Komiteta*, Appendix to Table No. III, pp. 66–7.

61 Ibid., Table No. II, p. 57.

62 By way of further comparison, the crude death rate for the United States was 8.25 in 2005. "List of Countries by Death Rate," http://en.wikipedia.org/wiki/List_of_countries_by_death_rate; "Mortality Rate," http://en.wikipedia.org/wiki/Mortality_rate, both accessed 22 August 2006.

63 *Statisticheskiia svedeniia… Sibirskago Komiteta*, Table No. II, pp. 53–7. Note that because there were few infants and children among Western Siberia's exile-settler population, its death rate compares favorably to that given for the United States in the previous footnote.

64 Volchek, *Osushchestvlenie*, 53–4.

65 Vlasenko, "Ugolovnaia ssylka," 144–6.

66 Volchek, *Osushchestvlenie*, 402.

67 Ibid., 55; Vlasenko, "Ugolovnaia ssylka," 169.

68 Vlasenko, "Ugolovnaia ssylka," 169–72.

69 Ibid., 172–5.

70 Quoted in ibid., 181.

71 Volchek, *Osushchestvlenie*, 83–7.

72 Ibid., 103–9.

73 Quoted in ibid., 100.

74 See Mark Bassin, *Imperial Visions: Nationalist Imagination and Geographical Expansion in the Russian Far East, 1840–1865* (New York: Cambridge University Press, 1999); N. A. Troitskaia and A. A. Toropov, eds., *Dal´nii Vostok Rossii v materialakh zakonodatel´stva. 1856–1861 gg.* (Vladivostok: RGIA DV, 2002).

75 Volchek, *Osushchestvlenie*, 284.

76 Vlasenko, "Ugolovnaia ssylka," 82–4 (quote on p. 83).

77 Volchek, *Osushchestvlenie*, 161–3.

78 Quoted in Vlasenko, "Ugolovnaia ssylka," 189.

79 Quoted in ibid., 190–1.

80 S. Maksimov, *Sibir´ i katorga*, 3 vols. (S.-Peterburg: Tipografiia A. Transhelia, 1871) 2: table, p. 320.

81 Quoted in Vlasenko, "Ugolovnaia ssylka," 190–1.

82 Andrew A. Gentes, "Siberian Exile and the 1863 Polish Insurrectionists According to Russian Sources," *Jahrbücher für Geschichte Osteuropas* 51, no. 2 (2003): 197–217.

83 Andrew A. Gentes, "No Kind of Liberal: Alexander II and the Sakhalin Penal Colony," *Jahrbücher für Geschichte Osteuropas* 54, no. 3 (2006): 321–44.

84 David F. Lindenfeld, *The Practical Imagination: The German Sciences of State in the Nineteenth Century* (Chicago: University of Chicago Press, 1997), 40.

85 N. I. Azarova, ed., *Russkie memuary. Nikolai I: Muzh. Otets. Imperator* (Moskva: Slovo, 2000), 462, 463, et passim.

86 Shcheglov, *Khronologicheskii perechen´*, 303.

87 GAIO, f. 435, op. 1, d. 227, l. 11.

Chapter 3   Political Exile and the Martyrdom of the Decembrists

1 A. S. Zuev and N. A. Minenko, *Sekretnye uzniki sibirskikh ostrogov (ocherki istorii politicheskoi ssylki v Sibiri vtoroi chetverti XVIII v.* (Novosibirsk: Nauka, 1992); Andrew A. Gentes, *Exile to Siberia, 1590–1822* (New York: Palgrave Macmillan, 2008), 35, 95*ff*, 117–18.

2 P. S. Squire, *The Third Department: The Establishment and Practices of the Political Police in the Russia of Nicholas I* (Cambridge: Cambridge University Press, 1968), 20, 25–41.

3 Ukase of 28 April 1827 establishing the Corps of Gendarmes. Quoted in ibid., 87.

4 Jonathan W. Daly, *Autocracy under Siege: Security Police and Opposition in Russia, 1866–1905* (DeKalb: Northern Illinois University Press, 1998), 12.

5 W. Bruce Lincoln, *Nicholas I: Emperor and Autocrat of All the Russias* (Bloomington: Indiana University Press, 1978), 265; Ronald Hingley, *The Russian Secret Police: Muscovite, Imperial Russian and Soviet Political Security Operations* (New York: Simon and Schuster, 1970), 41, 44. Both Lincoln and Hingley make the claim about Nadezhdin; Hingley makes the claim about Shevchenko.

6 E. N. Anuchin, *Izsledovaniia o protsente soslannykh v Sibir´ v period 1827–1846 godov: materialy dlia ugolovnoi statistiki Rossii* (S.-Peterburg: Tipografiia Maikova, 1873), table, p. 18.

7 *Statisticheskiia svedeniia o ssyl´nykh v Sibiri, za 1833 i 1834 gody (Izvlechenie iz otcheta o delakh Sibirskago Komiteta)* (Sanktpeterburg: Tip. II Otdeleniia Sobstvennoi E. I. V. Kantseliarii, 1837), 3.

8 John L. H. Keep, *Soldiers of the Tsar: Army and Society in Russia, 1462–1874* (Oxford: Clarendon Press, 1985), 349–50.

9 J. H. Seddon, "The Petrashevtsy: A Reappraisal," *Slavic Review* 43, no. 3 (1984): 434–52; N. Bel´chikov, ed., "Pokazaniia F. M. Dostoevskogo po delu petrashevtsev," *Krasnyi arkhiv* 2 (1931): 130–46; ibid., 3 (1931): 160–78; Joseph Frank, *Dostoevsky: The Years of Ordeal, 1850–1859* (London: Robson Books, 1983), 49, et passim.

10 The exiled Petrashevists were M. V. Butashevich–Petrashevskii, N. P. Grigor´ev, F. M. Dostoevskii, S. F. Durov, F. N. L´vov, N. A. Mombelli, N. A. Speshnev, F.-E. G. Toll´, I.-F. L. Iastrzhembskii. See N. M. Iadrintsev, *Sibir´ kak koloniia v geograficheskom, etnograficheskom i istoricheskom otnoshenii*, ed. by L. M. Goriushkin, et al. (Novosibirsk: Sibirskii khronograf, 2003), 543 [editorial note, which incidentally gives an incorrect year for their convictions]; S. V. Kodan, "Osvoboditel´noe dvizhenie v Rossii i sibirskaia ssylka (1825–1861gg.)," in *Politicheskie ssyl´nye v Sibiri (XVIII–nachalo XX v.)*, ed. by L. M. Goriushkin (Novosibirsk: Nauka, 1983), 152–67 [here, pp. 163–4]; Alan Kimball, "Who Were the Petrashevtsy? A Question Provoked by Some Recent Scholarship," *Mentalities/Mentalités* 5, no. 2 (1988): 1–12.

11 Viach. Polonskii, ed., "M. V. Butashevich-Petrashevskii v Sibiri," *Krasnyi arkhiv* 3 (1925): 184–216 [here, p. 185]. See also V. Prokof´ev, *Petrashevskii* (Moskva: Molodaia Gvardiia, 1962).

12 John J. Stephan, *The Russian Far East: A History* (Stanford: Stanford University Press, 1994), 53.

13 RGIA, f. 1281, op. 6, d. 97, l. 63.

14 M. K. Azodovskii, et al., eds., *Sibirskaia Sovetskaia entsiklopediia. Tom pervyi, A–Zh* (n.p.: Sibirskoe kraevoe izdatel´stvo, 1929), 206–7.

15 GAIO, f. 24, op. 3, k. 39, d. 31, ll. 63–72.

16 S. P. Trubetskoi, "Zapiski 1849–1853 gg.," in *Nikolai I: lichnost´ i epokha. Novye materially*, ed. by A. N. Tsamutali, et al. (SPb.: Izdatel´stvo "Nestor-

Istoriia," 2007), 207–56 [here, p. 229]. Nicholas increased the sentences of some less privileged Decembrists.

17 Aleksei Bolkovskii, *Ekaterinburgskii tsentral* (Moskva: EKSMO, 2008), 37.
18 GAIO, f. 24, op. 3, k. 1, d. 5, ll. 2–3, 4, 21–2, 25–6, 49.
19 Ibid., k. 19, d. 543, ll. 1, 5, 7, 8.
20 GAIO, f. 24, op. 3, k. 2, d. 23, ll. 1, 2–3, 7, 8, 9–10. Use of the term *"uezd"* was a mistake, since the 1822 Reforms replaced it with *"okrug."*
21 Constantin de Grunwald, *Tsar Nicholas I,* trans. by Brigit Patmore (London: Douglas Saunders with MacGibbon & Kee, 1954), 71n2. See also John Gooding, "The Decembrists in the Soviet Union," *Soviet Studies* XL, no. 2 (1988): 196–209; Ludmilla A. Trigos, *The Decembrist Myth in Russian Culture* (New York: Palgrave Macmillan, 2009).
22 Margaret Ziolkowski, "Hagiography and Historiography: The Saintly Prince in the Poetry of the Decembrists," *The Slavic and East European Journal* 30, no. 1 (1986): 29–44.
23 Lewis Bagby, "Aleksandr Bestužev-Marlinskij's 'Roman i Ol´ga': Generation and Degeneration," *The Slavic and East European Journal* 25, no. 4 (1981): 1–15.
24 Abram Tertz [pseudonym of Andrei Siniavskii], *The Trial Begins and On Socialist Realism* (1960; Berkeley: University of California Press, 1982), 200.
25 A. D. Margolis, *Tiur´ma i ssylka v imperatorskoi Rossii: issledovaniia i arkhivnye nakhodki* (Moskva: Lanterna Vita, 1995), 53–76; A. V. Sobolev, "Vel´mozhnaia katorga i ee artel´noe khoziastva," *Voprosy istorii* 2 (2000): 127–35.
26 Cf. Anatole G. Mazour, *The First Russian Revolution: 1825, the Decembrist Movement: Its Origins, Development, and Significance* (Stanford: Stanford University Press, 1937); Marc Raeff, *The Decembrist Movement* (Englewood Cliffs: Prentice-Hall, 1966); Mikhail Zetlin, *The Decembrists,* trans. by George Panin (New York: International University Press, 1958), 283–329; Glynn Barratt, *The Rebel on the Bridge: A Life of the Decembrist Baron Andrey Rozen (1800–84)* (Athens: Ohio University Press, 1975), 97–170; Glynn R. V. Barratt, "A Note on N. A. Bestuzhev and the Academy of Chita," *Canadian Slavonic Papers* 12 (1970): 47–59; Jeanne Haskett, "Decembrist N. A. Bestuzhev in Siberian Exile, 1826–55," *Studies in Romanticism* 4 (1965): 108–205; Glynn R. V. Barratt, ed. and trans., *Voices in Exile: The Decembrist Memoirs* (Montreal: McGill-Queen's University Press, 1974). This latter book consists of excerpts from Decembrists' memoirs interspersed with Barratt's brief commentaries. In their memoirs Decembrists sometimes distorted or even lied about their conspiratorial activities and behavior under interrogation, but tended to be less self-serving about their time in exile. See O. V. Edel´man, "Vospominaniia dekabristov o sledstvii kak istoricheskii istochnik," *Otechestvennaia istoriia* 6 (1995): 34–44.
27 Keep, *Soldiers,* 232, et passim.
28 Kodan, "Osvoboditel´noe dvizhenie," passim; idem, "Nerchinskoe komendantskoe upravlenie i dekabristy," *Voprosy istorii KPSS* 8 (1979): 178–92 [here, pp. 181–2]; P. L. Kazarian, *Olekminskaia politicheskaia ssylka, 1826–1917 gg.,* 2nd ed. (Iakutsk: Sakhapoligrafizdat, 1996), 9, et passim; idem, *Iakutiia v sisteme politicheskoi ssylki Rossii, 1826–1917 gg.* (Iakutsk: GP NIPK Sakhapoligrafizdat, 1998), 6, et passim.

29   As with almost any taxonomy, there are exceptions to this one. A group of officers from the nobility involved in the uprising in the south were not convicted like those in the north by the Supreme Criminal Court, but were instead court-martialed in Kiev for mutiny. Unlike their northern counterparts they marched in chains alongside common criminals and, once in Siberia, engaged in the *katorga* labor the others were exempted from (see below). See Margolis, *Tiur´ma*, 59; S. V. Mironenko, *Dekabristy: Biograficheskii spravochnik* (Moskva: Nauka, 1988), 34, 114, 168–9, 171–2; Rozen, *Voices*, 249.

30   For a list of Decembrists' original sentences see Kodan, "Osvoboditel´noe dvizhenie," 158. The figures for both the number of Decembrists sentenced to exile and those who actually went to Siberia vary according to source. Cf. Iu. P. Pavlov and V. I. Vorob´ev, "Dekabristy v Sibiri (Spravochnye materialy)," in *Sibir´ i dekabristy. Vypusk 5*, ed. by B. S. Meilakh, et al. (Irkutsk: Vostochno-Sibirskoe knizhnoe idatel´stvo, 1988), 238–69; M. V. Konstantinov and R. I. Tsuprik, "Izuchenie dekabristskogo nekropolia v g. Petrovske-Zabaikal´skom," in *Politicheskaia ssylka v Sibiri XIX–nachalo XX v.: Istoriografiia i istochniki*, ed. by L. M. Goriushkin (Novosibirsk: Nauka, 1987), 113; Mazour, *First Russian Revolution*, 212–13.

31   Barratt, *Voices*, 13.

32   Haskett, "Decembrist N. A. Bestuzhev": 188.

33   Vil´gel´m K. Kiukhel´beker, sentenced to 20 years' *katorga*, was instead imprisoned and served in penal battalions in various fortresses until 1835, when he was released for settlement to Siberia. Iosif V. Podzhio (Poggio) and Gavril S. Baten´kov lingered in a variety of prisons for nine and 20 years, respectively, before being released for settlement. A somewhat different case is that of Ivan Iu. Polivanov, who died eight months after being incarcerated in Peter-Paul fortress. Kodan, "Osvoboditel´noe dvizhenie," 158–9; Mironenko, *Dekabristy*, 15–16, 95–6, 145–7.

34   V. A. Fedorov, ed., "'U nas net nikakikh sviazei s vneshnim mirom': Pis´ma dekabrista P. N. Svistunova k bratu Alekseiu. 1831–1832 gg.," *Istoricheskii arkhiv* 1 (1993): 183–93 [here, p. 187].

35   Mazour, *First Russian Revolution*, 171–5, 207; V. A. Fedorov, "Arest dekabristov," *Vestnik Moskovskogo universiteta. Seriia VIII: Istoriia* 5 (1985): 59–71.

36   Iakushkin, *Voices*, 221.

37   Margolis, *Tiur´ma*, table, p. 60.

38   V. A. Fedorov, ed., "Krestnyi put´ dekabristov v Sibir´: Dokumenty ob otpravke osuzhdennykh na katorgu i v ssylku i ob usloviiakh ikh soderzhaniia. 1826–1837 gg.," *Istoricheskii arkhiv* 6 (2000): 46–56 [here, pp. 47–50].

39   Fedorov, "Krestnyi put´": 52.

40   Iakushkin in *Voices*, 215. For other accounts of the journey see ibid., chap. 6. For a full description of the Decembrists' route see Margolis, *Tiur´ma*, 54–7.

41   Quoted in O. S. Tal´skaia, "Pis´ma dekabrista A. F. Briggena v III Otdeleniia," in *Politicheskaia ssylka v Sibiri*, op. cit., 100.

42   This puns on the phrase *poslannye v Sibir´* ("exiled to Siberia"). This translation by Max Eastman is reproduced in John Simpson, ed., *The Oxford Book of Exile* (New York: Oxford University Press, 1995), 179–80.

43   According to an anonymous account written probably by her singing partner of the moment, A. V. Venevitinov. The piece referred to was likely the duet from Mozart's *Don Giovanni*. See [Anon.] "Provody Kniagini Marii Volkonskoi, 1826 g.," *Russkaia starina* 12 (1875): 822–7 [esp. editor's note, p. 824].

44   Sidney Monas, *The Third Section: Police and Society in Russia under Nicholas I* (Cambridge: Harvard University Press, 1961), 75, 78–9; Harriet Murav, "'*Vo Glubine Sibirskikh Rud*': Siberia and the Myth of Exile," in *Between Heaven and Hell: The Myth of Siberia in Russian Culture*, ed. by Galya Diment and Yuri Slezkine (New York: St. Martin's Press, 1993), 96–103.

45   E. E. Iakushkin, "Stikhotvorennie dekabrista," *Krasnyi arkhiv* 10 (1925): 317–19. E. E. Iakushkin was I. D. Iakushkin's grandson.

46   E. E. Iakushkin, "Pesnia dekabristov," *Krasnyi arkhiv* 10 (1925): 319–21; Paul M. Austin, *The Exotic Prisoner in Russian Romanticism* (New York: Peter Lang, 1997).

47   Ziolkowski, "Hagiography and History": 39–40 [her italics].

48   Trans. by Valentine Snow, reproduced in Simpson, *Book of Exile*, 180.

49   Gareth D. Williams, *Banished Voices: Readings in Ovid's Exile Poetry* (Cambridge: Cambridge University Press, 1994), 89.

50   P. V. Il′in, ed., *14 dekabria 1825 goda: Vospominaniia ochevidtsev* (Sankt-Peterburg: Gumanitarnoe Agentstvo "Akademicheskii Proekt," 1999), 724.

51   L. M. Goriushkin, ed., *Politicheskaia ssylka v Sibiri: Nerchinskaia katorga, Tom 1* (Novosibirsk: Sibirskii khronograf, 1993), doc. no. 6.

52   Obolenskii, *Voices*, 230. Barratt gives the Decembrists' labor quota on p. 211.

53   Ibid., 233.

54   Ibid., 224, 230–1.

55   GAIO, f. 24, op. 3, k. 49, d. 278, l. 1.

56   [Anon.] "I. I. Sukhinov (Odin iz Dekabristov)," *Russkii arkhiv* (1870): 907–25; M. Nechkina, "Zagovor v Zerentuiskom rudnike," *Krasnyi arkhiv* 13 (1925): 258–79.

57   Glynn Barratt, *M. S. Lunin: Catholic Decembrist* (The Hague: Mouton, 1976), 80–1.

58   A. S. Nagaev, *"Omskoe Delo" 1832–1833 gg.* (Krasnoiarsk: Krasnoiarskii universitet), 28.

59   A. E. Rozen, *Zapisiki dekabrista*, ed. by G. A. Nevelevyi (Irkutsk: Vostochno-Sibirskoe knizhnoe izdatel′stvo, 1984), 205.

60   These were Shlissel′burg, Keksgol′m, Sveaborg, Svartgol′m, Rochensal′m, and Vyborg. Margolis, *Tiur′ma*, 57; M. N. Gernet, *Istoriia tsarskoi tiur′my*, 3rd ed., 5 vols. (Moskva: Gosudarstvennoe izdatel′stvo iuridicheskoi literatury, 1960–63) 2: 161–72.

61   Rozen, *Zapisiki*, 205.

62   Ibid., 224.

63   Goriushkin, *Nerchinskaia katorga*, doc. no. 3 and editorial note 2, p. 29.

64   See Marc Raeff, *Michael Speransky: Statesman of Imperial Russia, 1772–1822* (The Hague: Martinus Nijhoff, 1957), chap. 10.

65   GAIO, f. 24, op. 3, k. 49, d. 285; Rozen, *Voices*, 246.

66   Fedorov, "Krestnyi put′": 47.

67   Goriushkin, *Nerchinskaia katorga*, doc. no. 3, p. 28.

68 Barratt, *Voices*, 274; O. N. Vilkov, "Trudy dekabristov kak istochnik po istorii gorodov Sibiri (na primere Chity)," in *Politicheskaia ssylka v Sibiri*, op. cit., 90; Gernet, *Istoriia* 2: 177–9, figures 12 and 13, pp. 164, 165.

69 GAIO, f. 24, op. 3, k. 49, d. 292, l. 5; d. 278, l. 6.

70 Orders quoted in Fedorov, "Krestnyi put´": 53.

71 Fedorov, "'U nas net'": 186, 187.

72 Rozen, *Zapisiki*, 221.

73 Dmitrii Zavalishin, *Vospominaniia* (Moskva: Zakharov, 2003), 355–60.

74 Fedorov, "'U nas net'": 185, 191. The possible spying on Leparskii is suggested by Iakushkin in *Voices*, 296. See also Haskett, "Decembrist N. A. Bestuzhev": 190*n*13; Monas, *Third Section*, 79*ff*.

75 M. Iuzefovich, "Neskol´ko slov ob Imperatore Nikolae," *Russkii arkhiv* (1870): 999–1008 [here, pp. 1005–6].

76 Goriushkin, *Nerchinskaia katorga*, doc. no. 5, p. 32.

77 Fedorov, "Krestnyi put´": 54.

78 M. A. Rakhmatullin, "Imperator Nikolai I i sem´i dekabristov," *Otechestvennaia istoriia* 6 (1995): 3–20 [here, pp. 3–4].

79 Anatole G. Mazour, *Women in Exile: Wives of the Decembrists* (Tallahassee: Diplomatic Press, 1975), 7–8, 10; Monas, *Third Section*, 77–8; Kodan, "Osvoboditel´noe dvizhenie," 158–9; Mironenko, *Dekabristy*, passim. On 24 January 1827 the IGP circulated a list of Decembrists' revised sentences. GAIO, f. 435, op. 1, d. 147, l. 80. For a somewhat a dewy-eyed account of the Decembrist wives see Christine Sutherland, *The Princess of Siberia: The Story of Maria Volkonsky and the Decembrist Exiles* (New York: Farrar, Strauss, Giroux, 1984).

80 Rakhmatullin, "Imperator Nikolai": 6, 7.

81 Patrick O'Meara, *The Decembrist Pavel Pestel: Russia's First Republican* (Basingstoke: Palgrave Macmillan, 2003), 65, 103–4.

82 A. N. Murav´ev, *Sochineniia i pis´ma*, ed. by Iu. I. Gerasimova and S. V. Duminyi (Irkutsk: Vostochno-Sibiriskoe knizhnoe izdatel´stvo, 1986), 263.

83 A. V. Podzhio, *Zapiski, pis´ma*, ed. by N. P. Matkhanova (Irkutsk: Vostochno-Sibirskoe knizhnoe izdatel´stvo, 1989), 72.

84 Barratt, "A Note on N. A. Bestuzhev": 50 (see also p. 188*n*11); Haskett, "Decembrist N. A. Bestuzhev": 189.

85 M. A. Bestuzhev, *Voices*, 252; Vilkov, "Trudy dekabristov," 95–7; *Sibir´* (10 May 1887).

86 Goriushkin, *Nerchinskaia katorga*, doc. no. 3.

87 *Voices*, 242.

88 Goriushkin, *Nerchinskaia katorga*, doc. no. 3.

89 Barratt, *Voices*, 242, 274, 294–5; Barratt, "A Note on N. A. Bestuzhev": 55.

90 GAIO, f. 24, op. 3, k. 49, d. 292, l. 42.

91 *Voices*, 260.

92 Ibid., 268.

93 [Anon.] "Vzgliad na Dauriiu i v osobennosti na Nerchinskie gornye zavody," *Sibirskii vestnik* 9 (1823): 107–20 [here, pp. 118–19]; I. I. Komogortsev, "Iz istorii chernoi metallurgii Vostochnoi Sibiri v XVII–XVIII vv.," in *Sibir´ perioda feodalizma. Vypusk 1*, ed. by V. I. Shunkov, et al. (Novosibirsk: Izdatel´stvo Sibirskogo otdeleniia AN SSSR, 1962), 117–20.

94   *Voices*, 287, 289.

95   The three wives were Naryshkina, Fonvizina, and Volkonskaia. During the march Iushnevskii's and Rozen's wives caught up to their husbands by carriage. Iakushkin, *Voices*, 279–80. On 1 August, Chita informed Nerchinsk Zavod that it had 72 state criminals. An unsigned letter drafted at Nerchinsk Zavod, dated 12 August and addressed to the Petrovsk Zavod administration, states: "Upon the transfer of 72 State criminals from Chita Ostrog to Petrovsk zavod, I am ordering [your] office to send me reports about them every month concerning their arrivals and departures." "Arrivals and departures" referred: 1) to the possibility that some Decembrists might still be sent to Petrovsk; and 2) the release of Decembrists to settlements after they completed their labor terms. In other words, both the 1 and 12 August documents indicate that 72 Decembrists were expected to arrive at Petrovsk. On 26 September Petrovsk Zavod reported to Nerchinsk that on the 21st *thirty-six* Decembrists had arrived from Chita; and that two days later *thirty-five* more had arrived—but this totals only seventy-*one*. Monthly reports from Petrovsk continue to list just seventy-*one* Decembrists as late as 30 March 1831. These earlier documents therefore seem to have been mistaken regarding a seventy-second Decembrist. GAIO, f. 24, op. 3, k. 49, d. 292, ll. 49, 50, 51–2, 54, 59.

96   *Voices*, 268–9, 276–82, and notes 8: 1, 12 on pp. 365, 366.

97   Ibid., 279.

98   Ibid., 282.

99   This and other paintings are reproduced in I. S. Zil´bershtein, *Khudozhnik, dekabrist Nikolai Bestuzhev* (Moskva: Izobrazitel´noe iskusstvo, 1988).

100   *Voices*, 277.

101   Basargin in ibid., 276.

102   Barratt, ibid., 274.

103   Ibid., 260, 287–8, 293–5; "Vnutrennii vid odnogo iz dvorov kazemata v Petrovskom zavoda" (1831), a watercolor by N. A. Bestuzhev on display in 1999 at Moscow's State Historical Museum.

104   Fedorov, "'U nas net'": 189.

105   Ibid.: 185, 188.

106   Quoted in L. M. Dameshek and A. V. Remnev, eds., *Sibir´ v sostave Rossiiskoi imperii* (Moskva: Novoe literaturnoe obozrenie, 2007), 292.

107   Konstantinov, "Izuchenie," 114.

108   See GAIO, f. 24, op. 3, k. 49, d. 292; k. 8, d. 150; k. 14, d. 362.

109   Quoted in Russian in Barratt, "A Note on N. A. Bestuzhev": 59. What exactly Cherepanov meant by "120" is unclear, since at the end of 1834 there were only 49 Decembrists left in Petrovsk Zavod. GAIO, f. 24, op. 3, k. 49, d. 292, l. 117. Cherepanov was an interesting figure. A Cossack born in Kiakhta in 1810, he was a writer and journalist who often signed his articles with the *nom de plume* "Siberian Cossack." In 1830–31 he accompanied the Russian mission to Beijing. His expertise in Siberian affairs assured him positions in both the Western and Eastern Siberian administrations. While working for the latter he spent time in Aleksandrovsk Zavod, in Nerchinsk District, where he tried to improve the local administration. While there he became friends with Decembrist D. I. Zavalishin. In 1834 authorities discovered in Cherepanov's possession a letter from Zavalishin. Its contents remain unknown,

but it led to his being charged with "freethinking" and being assigned to a Cossack regiment. When V. I. Rupert became Eastern Siberia governor-general in 1837 he allowed Cherepanov to join the Irkutsk administration. Cherepanov died in Kazan´ in October 1884. V. Modzalevskii, "Cherepanov, Semen Ivanovich," in *Russkii biograficheskii slovar´*, vol. XXII (S.-Peterburg: Tipografiia I. I. Skorokhodova, 1905; rpt. New York: SPE Kraus Reprint Corporation, 1962), 162–4.

110 In addition to the sources above see A. P. Okladnikov, et al., eds., *Istoriia Sibiri s drevneishikh vremen do nashikh dnei*, 5 vols. (Leningrad: Izdatel´stvo "Nauka," 1968–9) 2: 465–74; A. S. Nemzera, *Memuary dekabristov* (Moskva: Pravda, 1988), passim.

111 GAIO, f. 24, op. 3, k. 49, d. 287, ll. 1–2. On Davydova (*née* Potapova) see Mazour, *Women*, 5, 35, 88, 110; Mironenko, *Dekabristy*, 61.

112 *Voices*, 283.

113 Ibid., 289.

114 Ibid., 232.

Chapter 4   Extraordinary Decembrists: Chizhov, Lutskii, and Lunin

1 V. A. Fedorov, ed., "'U nas net nikakikh sviazei s vneshnim mirom': Pis´ma dekabrista P. N. Svistunova k bratu Alekseiu. 1831–1832 gg.," *Istoricheskii arkhiv* 1 (1993): 183–93 [here, pp. 183–4].

2 On the dates of the last Decembrists' departures see ibid. Decembrists began completing their labor terms as early as 1828. Soon after arriving in Siberia a small number petitioned the emperor for clemency and offered in return to serve as regular soldiers in the Caucasus. Nicholas allowed a few to do so. Glynn R. V. Barratt, ed. and trans., *Voices in Exile: The Decembrist Memoirs* (Montreal: McGill-Queen's University Press, 1974), 273, 275, 303. Tal´skaia claims that those Decembrists over 40 years old and with families considered a subsequent offer by Nicholas to serve in the Caucasus a "new punishment." O. S. Tal´skaia, "Pis´ma dekabrista A. F. Briggena v III Otdeleniia," in *Politicheskaia ssylka v Sibiri XIX–nachalo XX v.: Istoriografiia i istochniki*, ed. by L. M. Goriushkin (Novosibirsk: Nauka, 1987), 101. However, A. P. Ermolov, who was in charge of the Caucasus Corps at that time, was publicly known to sympathize with the Decembrists; moreover, his laxness towards all his troops earned him their undying devotion. Bitis writes that "by the beginning of 1827, some 2,700 political dissidents were serving in the Caucasus Corps," and so it would seem Petersburg may have even viewed this as a desirable way to deal with malcontents. Alexander Bitis, *Russia and the Eastern Question: Army, Government, and Society, 1815–1833* (New York: Oxford University Press, 2006), 77.

3 Quoted in O. S. Tal´skaia, "Borba administratsii s vliianiem dekabristov v Zapadnoi Sibiri," in *Ssylka i katorga (XVIII–nachalo XX v.)*, ed. by L. M. Goriushkin (Novosibirsk: Nauka, 1975), 75.

4 Barratt, *Voices*, 303.

5 Zavalishin became a significant figure in GUVS, hashing over policy with Governor-general N. N. Murav´ev. Mark Bassin, "The Russian Geographical

Society, the 'Amur Epoch,' and the Great Siberian Expedition 1855–1863," *Annals of the Association of American Geographers* 73, no. 2 (1983): 240–56. The Bestuzhevs are discussed below.

6 O. S. Tal'skaia, "Ssyl'nye dekabristy na gosudarstvennoi sluzhbe v Sibiri," in *Ssylka i obshchestvenno-politicheskaia zhizn' v Sibiri (XVIII—nachalo XX v.)*, ed. by L. M. Goriushkin (Novosibirsk: Nauka, 1978), 231–51.

7 L. M. Dameshek and A. V. Remnev, eds., *Sibir' v sostave Rossiiskoi imperii* (Moskva: Novoe literaturnoe obozrenie, 2007), 292.

8 *Voices*, 297. There were, of course, a variety of other experiences. See S. V. Mironenko, *Dekabristy: Biograficheskii spravochnik* (Moskva: Nauka, 1988).

9 A. I. Dmitriev-Mamonov, *Dekabristy v Zapadnoi Sibiri* (S.-Peterburg: Tip. Montvida. Ug. Konnoi, 1905), 127–8.

10 Tal'skaia, "Borba," 72–93. Gorchakov was an insufferable bastard who insisted on using the informal "you" with subordinates. Briggen called him "the pasha of Omsk." See Anatolii Remnev, "'Tigr, zakolotyi gusinym perom.' Kazus zapadnosibirskogo general-gubernatora kniazia P. D. Gorchakova," *Acta Slavica Iaponica* 27 (2009): 55–75.

11 GAIO, f. 28, op. 1, d. 4, l. 9; d. 3, l. 3; Dmitrii Zavalishin, *Vospominaniia* (Moskva: Zakharov, 2003), 368–9, 451–2.

12 Dmitriev-Mamonov, *Dekabristy*, 39–41, 65–9; I. V. Shcheglov. *Khronologicheskii perechen' vazhneishikh dannykh iz istorii Sibiri: 1032–1882 gg.* (1883; rpt. Surgut: Severnyi dom, 1993), table, 281–2.

13 P. L. Kazarian, *Iakutiia v sisteme politicheskoi ssylki Rossii, 1826–1917 gg.* (Iakutsk: GP NIPK Sakhapoligrafizdat, 1998), 279; Mironenko, *Dekabristy*, 155–6.

14 Quoted in A. M. Larin, *Gosudarstvennye prestupleniia: Rossiia. XIX vek* (Tula: Aftograf, 2000), 116.

15 GAIO, f. 24, op. 3, k. 5, d. 105, ll. 2–4 (copy).

16 P. L. Kazarian, *Olekminskaia politicheskaia ssylka, 1826–1917 gg.*, 2nd ed. (Iakutsk: GP NIPK Sakhapoligrafizdat, 1996), 16, 28.

17 GAIO, f. 24, op. 3, k. 5, d. 105, ll. 2–4 (copy).

18 Ibid., ll. 5, 6–7.

19 A. Sergeev, ed., "Gr. A. Kh. Benkendorf o Rossii v 1831–1832 gg.," *Krasnyi arkhiv* 46 (1931): 132–59 [here, p. 157].

20 GAIO, f. 24, op. 3, k. 5, d. 105, ll. 9, 10, 13; Kazarian, *Iakutiia*, 279.

21 Mironenko, *Dekabristy*, 196.

22 GAIO, f. 24, op. 3, k. 7, d. 129, ll. 1, 6–7, 11–12, 13; Mironenko, *Dekabristy*, 196.

23 GAIO, f. 24, op. 3, k. 8, d. 167, l. 1.

24 Fedorov, "'U nas net'": 184.

25 P. V. Il'in, ed., "'Gosudar! Ispoveduiu tebe iako boiashchiisia boga': Prosheniia rodstvennikov dekabristov o pomilovanii arestovannykh. 1826 g.," *Istoricheskii arkhiv* 1 (2001): 156–77 [here, p. 157].

26 GAIO, f. 24, op. 3, k. 7, d. 129, ll. 11–12.

27 Dameshek, *Sibir'*, 292.

28 Quoted in Tal'skaia, "Borba," 86.

29 GAIO, f. 24, op. 3, k. 8, d. 167, ll. 21, 35.

30 Lorer's case is especially instructive. After completing his term at Petrovsk Zavod in 1832, he was initially sent to a log cabin in a Lake Baikal outpost

named Mertvyi Kultuk (Russo-Tatar for "Dead End") but soon allowed to join other Decembrists in Kurgan, Tobol´sk *guberniia*. Barratt, *Voices*, 304–14; Mironenko, *Dekabristy*, 104.

31 A. D. Margolis, *Tiur´ma i ssylka v imperatorskoi Rossii: issledovaniia i arkhivnye nakhodki* (Moskva: Lanterna Vita, 1995), 45–52, 62–3, 67–8. Noblemen lost their exemption to corporal punishment when, as part of their sentences, they were stripped of their class rights and consigned to a "civil death." On mortality rates in the Caucasus see Thomas M. Barrett, "Lines of Uncertainty: The Frontiers of the Northern Caucasus," in *Imperial Russia: New Histories for the Empire*, ed. by Jane Burbank and David L. Ransel (Bloomington: Indiana University Press, 1998), 152; John L. H. Keep, *Soldiers of the Tsar: Army and Society in Russia, 1462–1874* (Oxford: Clarendon Press, 1985), 340, 343. Over 100 *"chernigovtsy"* appear to have been exiled to settlement in Siberia. Shcheglov, *Khronologicheskii perechen´*, 287; Anatole G. Mazour, *The First Russian Revolution: 1825, the Decembrist Movement: Its Origins, Development, and Significance* (Stanford: Stanford University Press, 1937), 221.

32 Bruce F. Adams, *The Politics of Punishment: Prison Reform in Russia, 1863–1917* (DeKalb: Northern Illinois University Press, 1996), 20. See also Margolis, *Tiur´ma*, 67; Keep, *Soldiers*, 167–8; Abby M. Schrader, *Languages of the Lash: Corporal Punishment and Identity in Imperial Russia* (DeKalb: Northern Illinois University Press, 2002), passim. For a rather sanitized dramatization of the gauntlet see Stanley Kubrick's film *Barry Lyndon* (1975).

33 John Keep, "Justice for the Troops: A Comparative Study of Nicholas I's Russia and France under Louis-Philippe," *Cahiers du Monde russe et soviétique* 28, no. 1 (1987): 31–54 [here, p. 41].

34 Margolis, *Tiur´ma*, 63–4.

35 Ibid., 70–6.

36 Barratt writes: "Of the thirty-one persons sentenced to death by decapitation (as 'second degree victims') by the Special Supreme Court that pronounced its verdicts on 9 July 1826, none deserved his fate more than N. A. Bestuzhev." Glynn R. V. Barratt, "A Note on N. A. Bestuzhev and the Academy of Chita," *Canadian Slavonic Papers* 12 (1970): 47–59 [here, p. 48].

37 Mironenko, *Dekabristy*, 107.

38 Similar to his brothers, A. A. Bestuzhev was originally sentenced to 20 years *katorga*, subsequently reduced to exile to settlement. He left Petersburg on 6 November 1827 and arrived in Iakutsk on 31 December 1827, where he remained until July 1829. During his stay he obtained permission to re-enlist as a private and left to serve in the Caucasus. He arrived in Tbilisi in August 1829 and died in combat in 1836. Ibid., 20.

39 GAIO, f. 24, op. 3, k. 4, d. 69, ll. 1–3, 7–8. See also Mironenko, *Dekabristy*, 107; Margolis, *Tiur´ma*, 70–1.

40 Margolis, *Tiur´ma*, 73.

41 GAIO, f. 24, op. 3, k. 4, d. 69, ll. 5, 7–8.

42 Nicholas's orders are described in Margolis, *Tiur´ma*, 73. GUVS's Police Department transmitted Benkendorf's communication to Lavinskii on 11 November 1829. GAIO, f. 24, op. 3, k. 4, d. 69, ll. 38–39. There is some uncertainty as to whether Lutskii received 100 or 90 blows. Cf. Margolis and GAIO, f. 24, op. 3, k. 11, d. 258, ll. 2–5.

43   GAIO, f. 24, op. 3, k. 4, d. 69, ll. 77, 80–1. Lutskii's physical description appears in ibid., k. 11, d. 258, ll. 6–7. The exact date of his departure for Novozerentuisk is uncertain, though the dates Margolis and Mironenko give for his punishment appear incorrect. Cf. Margolis, *Tiur´ma*, 73; Mironenko, *Dekabristy*, 107.

44   GAIO, f. 24, op. 3, k. 11, d. 258, ll. 2–5; Mironenko, *Dekabristy*, 107; Margolis, *Tiur´ma*, 75.

45   GAIO, f. 24, op. 3, k. 5, d. 82, ll. 1–2*ff*. See also the comment in a communication dated 27 September 1835 from EOGU to GUVS: "...Lutskii has already been captured three times in Achinsk *okrug* [Eniseisk *guberniia*], these escapes occurring in 1829, 1830, and 1831...." Ibid., k. 11, d. 258, l. 1.

46   GAIO, f. 24, op. 3, k. 5, d. 82, ll. 25–6.

47   Ibid., k. 11, d. 258, ll. 1, 6–7, 12.

48   Ibid., ll. 28, 30, 61. The Kuenskie works were in Stretensk *volost´*, Nerchinsk *okrug*. See [Anon.,] "Vzgliad na Dauriiu i v osobennosti na Nerchinskie gornye zavody," *Sibirskii vestnik* 5 (1823): 49–58 [here, pp. 56–7].

49   S. V. Kodan, "Amnistiia dekabristam (1856 g.)," *Voprosy istorii*, 4 (1982): 178–82.

50   Margolis, *Tiur´ma*, 76; Mironenko, *Dekabristy*, 107. These authors say nothing about the fate of Lutskii's family.

51   GAIO, f. 435, op. 1, d. 133; d. 147, l. 468; d. 146, l. 114.

52   Zavalishin, *Vospominaniia*, 264.

53   Quoted in Barratt, *M. S. Lunin*, 82–3.

54   All following quotations of Lunin's letters are from M. S. Lunin, *Pis´ma iz Sibiri*, ed. by I. A. Zhelvakova and N. Ia. Eidel´man (Moskva: Nauka, 1987). They can be referenced by date.

55   Barratt, *M. S. Lunin*, 88–9.

56   V. A. Fedorov, ed., "Krestnyi put´ dekabristov v Sibir´: Dokumenty ob otpravke osuzhdennykh na katorgu i v ssylku i ob usloviiakh ikh soderzhaniia. 1826–1837 gg.," *Istoricheskii arkhiv* 6 (2000): 46–56 [here, pp. 54–5].

57   Quoted in Barratt, *M. S. Lunin*, 87. I have replaced "supreme" with "sovereign's."

58   Lunin originally wrote "duty" (*obiazannost´*) but crossed it out.

59   Quoted in Barratt, *M. S. Lunin*, 114–15 [orig. italics].

60   Ibid., 116.

61   Ibid.

62   Quotations below are from M. S. Lunin, *Pis´ma iz Sibiri*, op. cit.

63   Ann Radcliffe (1764–1823), English writer who pioneered the Gothic novel.

64   This translation is based on the Russian translation.

Chapter 5   Paranoia and Conspiracy: Polish Exiles and the Omsk Affair

1   Adam Zoltowski, *Border of Europe: A Study of the Polish Eastern Provinces* (London: Hollis & Carter, 1950), 42.

2   P. Iudin, "Ssyl´nye 1812 goda v Orenburgskom krae: K istoriia Otechestvennoi voiny," *Russkii arkhiv* 3 (1896): 5–33 [here, p. 25].

3   S. V. Maksimov, *Sibir´ i katorga*, 3rd ed. (S.-Peterburg: Izdanie V. I. Gubinskago, 1900), 339. See also A. S. Nagaev, *Omskoe delo, 1832–1833* (Krasnoiarsk: Krasnoiarskii universitet, 1991), 96.

4   See Piotr S. Wandycz, *The Lands of Partitioned Poland, 1795–1918* (Seattle: University of Washington Press, 1974), 3–4, 17–18, 74; Norman Davies, *God's Playground: A History of Poland in Two Volumes: Volume 1, The Origins to 1795* (New York: Columbia University Press, 1982), 162; Pieter M. Judson and Marsha L. Rozenblit, eds., *Constructing Nationalities in East Central Europe* (New York: Berghahn Books, 2005).

5   On the war see R. F. Leslie, *Polish Politics and the Revolution of November 1830* (London: University of London, Athlone Press, 1956); Tadeusz Stachowski, "The Polish-Russian War of 1831," *History Today* [Great Britain] (29 May 1979): 310–17; ibid. (6 June 1979): 386–93; Wandycz, *Lands*, 112. On Russia's manpower shortage see Frederick W. Kagan, *The Military Reforms of Nicholas I: The Origins of the Modern Russian Army* (New York: St. Martin's Press, 1999), 212–13 et passim.

6   "Tsirkuliarnoe predpisanie Upravliaiushchago Minsiterstvom Vnutrennikh Del Grazhdanskim Gubernatoram ot 13 Marta 1831 goda, O Vysochaishem povelenii, kasatel´no propuska iz Tsarstva Pol´skago liudei vo vnutrenniia nashi gubernii," *ZhMVD* 4, no. 2 (1831): 84–6.

7   Because this chapter quotes liberally from Russian sources I use the Russian version of this word.

8   Davies, *God's Playground*, 201–55; Wandycz, *Lands*, 4–6. Wandycz contends that "many Jews adopted a pro-Polish stand during the November Insurrection" (p. 91) but offers no evidence. He casts further doubt on this claim by adding only that "individual Jews fought in the army...." (p. 111).

9   Nagaev, *Omskoe delo*, 4, 30–1, 160; I. A. Khrenov, *Ocherki revoliutsionnykh sviazei narodov Rossii i Pol´shi. 1815–1917 gg.* (Moskva: Nauka, 1976), 123. Khrenov writes that nearly 15,000 Poles were assigned to the Caucasus between 1835 and 1846.

10 Leslie, *Polish Politics*, 217.

11 Wandycz, *Lands*, 125.

12 Ibid., 126.

13 Cf. Jerzy Skowronek, "The Direction of Political Change in the Era of National Insurrection, 1795–1864," in *A Republic of Nobles: Studies in Polish History to 1864*, ed. and trans. by J. K. Fedorowicz, et al. (New York: Cambridge University Press, 1982), 273.

14 M. D. Filin, "Pol´skie revoliutsionery v zabaikal´skoi politicheskoi ssylke v 30–40-e gg. XIX v. (po materialam Gosudarstvennogo arkhiva Chitinskoi oblasti)," in *Politicheskie ssyl´nye v Sibiri (XVIII–nachalo XX v.)*, ed. by L. M. Goriushkin (Novosibirsk: Nauka, 1983), 171 [my italics].

15 S. V. Kodan, "Sibirskaia ssylka uchastnikov oppozitsionnykh vystuplenii i dvizhenii v Tsarstve Pol´skom 1830–1840-x gg. (Politiko-iuridicheskii srez)," p. [8], www.lib.pomorsu.ru/exile/Polska_ssylka/Kodan.doc (accessed 15 January 2009).

16 Norman Davies, *Heart of Europe: A Short History of Poland* (New York: Oxford University Press, 1986), 167.

17 M. S. Lunin, *Pis´ma iz Sibiri*, ed. by I. A. Zhelvakova and I. Ia. Eidel´man (Moskva: Nauka, 1987), 20, 390.

18 Kodan, "Sibirskaia ssylka," p. [2].

19 F. F. Bolonev, A. A. Liutsidarskaia, and A. I. Shinkovoi, *Ssyl´nye poliaki v Sibiri: XVII, XIX vv.* (Novosibirsk: Knizhita, 2007), 61–2, 153–6.

20 A. I. Shinkovoi, "Dokumenty Gosudarstvennogo arkhiva Irkutskoi oblasti o ssyl'nykh poliakakh v Vostochnoi Sibiri," in ibid., 55.

21 GAIO, f. 24, op. 3, k. 5, d. 93, ll. 5–7.

22 [Anon.,] "Svedeniia o Eniseiskoi Gubernii (Iz zapisok Statskago-Sovetnika Pestova)," *ZhMVD* 5, no. 4 (1831): 75–113 [here, p. 108; orig. italics].

23 "Tsirkuliarnoe predpisanie Upravliaiushchago Ministerstvom Vnutrennikh Del Gg. Grazhdanskim Gubernatoram ot 19 Avgusta 1831 g. o platezh Prikazam deneg za pogrebenie umershikh v bol'nitsakh onykh arestantov," *ZhMVD* 5, no. 5 (1831): 59.

24 Beata Gruszczynska and Elzbieta Kaczynska, "Poles in the Russian Penal System and Siberia as a Penal Colony (1815–1914): A Quantitative Examination," *Historical Social Research* 15, no. 4 (1990): 95–120 [here, p. 100].

25 Lunin, *Pis'ma*, 21.

26 Gruszczynska, "Poles": Table 1, p. 112. This corresponds to the large number exiled to Siberia that year for "crimes against the government," according to the Siberian Committee. See Chapter 3.

27 Ibid.: Table 4, p. 115.

28 M. Zaseleiskii, "Statistika Tsarstva Pol'skago," *ZhMVD* 4–12 (1842): Tables 15 and 17.

29 Ibid.: Table 15.

30 GAIO, f. 24, op. 3, k. 14, d. 352, ll. 5–7, et passim.

31 Maksimov, *Sibir'* (1900), 341*n*. The 1832 Organic Statute abolished Poland's status as a kingdom.

32 Ibid. These figures are corroborated in E. N. Anuchin, *Izsledovaniia o protsente soslannykh v Sibir' v period 1827–1846 godov: materialy dlia ugolovnoi statistiki Rossii* (S.-Peterburg: Tipografiia Maikova, 1873), tables, pp. 156–7.

33 L. M. Goriushkin, ed., *Politicheskaia ssylka v Sibiri: Nerchinskaia katorga, Tom 1* (Novosibirsk: Sibirskii khronograf, 1993), doc. no. 45, pp. 78, 81.

34 GAIO, f. 24, op. 3, k. 33, d. 147, ll. 1–3, 55–108, 122–48.

35 Reproduced in Bolonev, *Ssyl'nye*, 61. Once again, "*uezd*" is mistakenly used in place of "*okrug*."

36 Wandycz, *Lands*, 119.

37 Roster entry reproduced in Bolonev, *Ssyl'nye*, 86.

38 GAIO, f. 24, op. 3, k. 31, d. 32, ll. 34–85.

39 Quoted in B. S. Shostakovich, *Istoriia Poliakov v Sibiri (XVII—XIX vv.)* (Irkutsk: Irkut. un-t, 1995), 62.

40 GAIO, f. 24, op. 3, k. 31, d. 32, ll. 145–84.

41 Ibid., k. 33, d. 147, ll. 55–108, 122–48.

42 Kodan, "Sibirskaia ssylka," p. [2].

43 Ibid., pp. [2–3].

44 Shostakovich, *Istoriia*, 55–6.

45 Quoted in ibid., 56.

46 Maksimov, *Sibir'* (1900), 342.

47 Ibid., 342.

48 Ibid., 342–3.

49 Lunin, *Pis'ma*, 21.

50 Letters dated 29 June, 29 October, and 6 November 1835, reproduced in Goriushkin, *Nerchinskaia katorga*, docs. nos. 17, 21, 22.

51 Ibid., doc. nos. 25, 55; Maksimov, *Sibir´* (1900), 353–5; Kodan, "Sibirskaia ssylka," p. [6].

52 Goriushkin, *Nerchinskaia katorga*, doc. no. 45.

53 GAIO, f. 24, op. 3, k. 14, d. 362, l. 47.

54 Maksimov, *Sibir´* (1900), 343–4.

55 I. V. Efimov, "Iz zhizni katorzhnykh Ilginskago i Aleksandrovskago, togda kazennykh, vinokurennykh zavodov. 1848–1853 g.," *Russkii arkhiv* 1 (1900): 79–107, 247–72 [here, p. 261].

56 Simon Tokarzewski, "In Siberian Prisons, 1846–1857," trans. by the staff, *Sarmatian Review* 25, no. 2 (2005), http://www.ruf.rice.edu/~sarmatia/405/254tokar.html (accessed 14 April 2009). This is a translation of pp. 137–73 and 230–1 from Szymon Tokarzewski, *Siedem lat katorgi. 1846–1857*, 2nd ed. (Warsaw: Gebethner and Wolff, 1918).

57 Letter dated 2 August 1835 reproduced in Goriushkin, *Nerchinskaia katorga*, doc. no. 18, p. 42.

58 GAIO, f. 24, op. 3, k. 30, d. 1, passim.

59 Letter reproduced in Goriushkin, *Nerchinskaia katorga*, doc. no. 46.

60 Kodan, "Sibirskaia ssylka," pp. [7, 9, 10].

61 Shostakovich, *Istoriia*, 57–8.

62 Lunin, *Pis´ma*, 20.

63 Shostakovich, *Istoriia*, 68–70.

64 Reproduced in ibid., 66–7.

65 Ibid., 38–47.

66 See R. Darrell Meadows, "Engineering Exile: Social Networks and the French Atlantic Community, 1789–1809," *French Historical Studies* 23, no. 1 (2000): 67–102; Andrew Dawson and Mark Johnson, "Migration, Exile and Landscapes of the Imagination," in *Contested Landscapes: Movement, Exile and Place*, ed. by Barbara Bender and Margot Winer (New York: Berg, 2001); Julia Kristeva, "A New Type of Intellectual: The Dissident," in *The Kristeva Reader*, ed. by Toril Moi (New York: Columbia University Press, 1986); Mahnaz Afkhami, *Women in Exile* (Charlottesville: University Press of Virginia, 1994); Hamid Naficy, *The Making of Exile Cultures: Iranian Television in Los Angeles* (Minneapolis: University of Minnesota Press, 1993).

67 Quoted in L. M. Dameshek and A. V. Remnev, eds., *Sibir´ v sostave Rossiiskoi imperii* (Moskva: Novoe literaturnoe obozrenie, 2007), 294.

68 M. M. Gromyko, "Novyi dokument o dekabristskoi i pol´skoi ssylke v Zapadnoi Sibiri," in *Ssylka i obshchestvenno-politicheskaia zhizn´ v Sibiri (XVIII—nachalo XX v.)*, ed. by L. M. Goriushkin (Novosibirsk: Nauka, 1978); A. P. Okladnikov, et al., eds., *Istoriia Sibiri s drevneishikh vremen do nashikh dnei*, 5 vols. (Leningrad: Izdatel´stvo "Nauka," 1968–9) 2; 475; Nagaev, *Omskoe delo*, 135*ff*.

69 Internal Nerchinsk Mining Bureau report dated 2 March 1843 in Goriushkin, *Nerchinskaia katorga*, doc. no. 47.

70 GAIO, f. 24, op. 3, k. 31, d. 32, ll. 2–3, 27, 34–85, 108–9; ibid., k. 33, d. 147, ll. 55–108, 122–48.

71 GAIO, f. 24, op. 3, k. 39, d. 31, ll. 63–72.

72 Ibid., ll. 160–78.

73 Ibid., ll. 90–151.

74   Amnesty cited in a letter dated 9 June 1840 from MVD to GUVS. Goriushkin, *Nerchinskaia katorga*, doc. no. 37.

75   Amnesty cited in letter dated 21 February 1851 from the Irkutsk Exile Bureau to the Nerchinsk Mining Bureau. Ibid., doc. no. 60.

76   Maksimov, *Sibir´* (1900), 346.

77   Nagaev, *Omskoe delo*, 4, 30–1, 160. Kagan gives a figure of 21,172 men in the Siberia Corps as of 1834. Kagan, *Military*, 224. The figure for Krasnoiarsk is in [Anon.,] "Svedenie o Eniseiskoi Gubernii (Iz zapisok Statskago-Sovetnika Pestova)," *ZhMVD* 5, no. 4 (1831): 75–113 [here, p. 84*n*].

78   I. V. Shcheglov, *Khronologicheskii perechen´ vazhneishikh dannykh iz istorii Sibiri: 1032–1882 gg.* (1883; rpt. Surgut: Severnyi dom, 1993), 271 and table, pp. 281–2. These data contradict Nagaev's claim that the population of 12,000 when the Poles arrived consisted almost entirely of soldiers, administrators, and their families. Cf. Nagaev, *Omskoe delo*, 29–31.

79   Prof. Virginia Martin, email to the author, 3 February 2000; Joseph L. Wieczynski, *The Modern Encyclopedia of Russian and Soviet History*, vol. 51 (supplement) (Gulf Breeze, FL: Academic International Press, 1989), 44; Shcheglov, *Khronologicheskii perechen´*, 313.

80   P. Kallinikov and I. Korneeva, eds., *Russkii biograficheskii slovar´: V 20 t.* (Moskva: TERRA-Knizhnyi klub, 1998) 3: 243.

81   The government began publishing newspapers in Siberia's four *guberniia* cities in 1857. Shcheglov, *Khronologicheskii perechen´*, 348.

82   D. D. Akhsharumov, "Kholera v Malorossii v 1830–1831 gg.," *Russkaia starina* 47 (1885): 209–22 [here, p. 210].

83   [Anon.,] "Kratkoe nastavlenie k raspoznanie priznakov kholery, pre-dokhraneiiu ot onoi, i k pervonachal´nomu eia lecheniiu," *ZhMVD* 4 (1831): 149–82.

84   [Anon.,] "Tsirkuliarnoe predpisanie Upravliaiushchago Ministerstvom Vnutrennikh Del, Gg. Grazhdanskim Gubernatorom, ot 8 Ianvaria 1831 g., o priostanovlennykh v nekotorykh Guberniiakh ssyl´nykh arestantov," *ZhMVD* 4 (1831): 11–12.

85   Akhsharumov, "Kholera": 222.

86   W. Bruce Lincoln, *Nicholas I: Emperor and Autocrat of All the Russias* (Bloomington: Indiana University Press, 1978), 142.

87   Vasilii Ostroglazov, "Kholera v Moskve v 1830 godu," *Russkii arkhiv* 3 (1893): 93–106; [Anon.] "Kholera v Moskve (1830): Iz pisem Kristina k grafine S. A. Bobrinskoi," *Russkii arkhiv* 3 (1884): 136–51.

88   N. E. Matveev, "Bunt v Staroi-Ruse v 1831 g.," *Russkaia starina* 25 (1879): 389–98; A. F. Ushakov, "Kholernyi bunt v Staroi-Ruse v 1831 g.," *Russkaia starina* 9 (1874): 145–62; [Anon.,] "Bunt v voennykh poseleniiakh v 1831 g.," *Russkaia starina* 25 (1879): 731–8; John L. H. Keep, *Soldiers of the Tsar: Army and Society in Russia, 1462–1874* (Oxford: Clarendon Press, 1985), 301–2.

89   Orenburg governor quoted in a letter from Tseidler to GUVS dated 12 November 1831. GAIO, f. 24, op. 3, k. 4, d. 96, ll. 1–2. Tseidler apparently learned of the Cheliabinsk episode from Tobol´sk officials.

90   Ibid., l. 3.

91   Ibid., ll. 7–8, 9–10. Osipov's letter to Kovalev is dated 24 October 1831.

92   Ibid., l. 11.

93 GAIO, f. 24, op. 3, k. 8, d. 169, ll. 11–12. The specific origin and date of this document are not clear, but it was written by a Siberian official sometime during 1834.

94 As spelled in documents.

95 Ibid., passim.

96 For the following account I will use the Russian spelling of names since I repeatedly quote Russian sources.

97 Quoted in Nagaev, *Omskoe delo*, 32–3. (Nagaev writes that Grudzinskii did not arrive in Siberia until September 1832, i.e., two months *after* his letter was received by Bronevskii. It is unclear if this is a mistake in his chronology or if it means that Grudzinskii sent his letter prior to or during his march into exile.) The following is drawn from Nagaev's book, which is based largely on archival documents. For a discussion of these and other sources see A. S. Nagaev, "Istochniki i literatura po istorii 'omskogo dela,' 1832–1833 gg.," in *Politicheskaia ssylka v Sibiri XIX–nachalo XX v. Istoriografiia i istochniki*, ed. by L. M. Goriushkin (Novosibirsk: Nauka, 1987), 130–7. The Omsk Affair is also recounted in Maksimov, *Sibir´* (1900), 350*ff*; Okladnikov, *Istoriia* 2: 474–5.

98 Nagaev, *Omskoe delo*, 33–4.

99 Ibid., 34.

100 Ibid., 35–6.

101 Quoted in ibid., 36–7.

102 Ibid., 38–9.

103 Information concerning all three comes from a report issued 19 October 1836 in Petersburg on the commission's findings, and from the editor's notes. Goriushkin, *Nerchinskaia katorga*, doc. no. 26. Nagaev describes Serotsinskii as a former priest. Cf. Nagaev, *Omskoe delo*, 39.

104 Nagaev, *Omskoe delo*, 122–3; Okladnikov, *Istoriia* 2: 475–6.

105 Shostakovich, *Istoriia*, 37.

106 G. K. Repinskii, "Narodnye tolki o Tsesareviche Konstantine Pavloviche 1836 g.," *Russkaia starina* 23 (1878): 135–42.

107 Lincoln, *Nicholas*, 139–40; Joseph L. Wieczynski, *The Modern Encyclopedia of Russian and Soviet History*, vol. 17 (Gulf Breeze, FL: Academic International Press, 1980), 163–70; Wandycz, *Lands*, 77–8, 88–90; Mariia Kucherskaia, "Konstantin Pavlovich–'pol´skii korol´'," and Ol´ga Kashtanova, "Balkanskie vneshnepoliticheskie proekty kontsa XVIII–pervoi chetverti XIX v. i velikii kniaz´ Konstantin Pavlovich," *Dva veka, zhurnal rossiiskoi istorii XVIII–XIX stoletii* 1–2 [c. 2001] [internet journal, site now defunct, articles in my possession].

108 Quoted in Filin, "Pol´skie revoliutsionery," 168–9. Filin refers to Koz´linskii as Koz´minskii. However, in the government document cited below, his name appears as I have spelled it above. As above, Russian versions of these names will be used.

109 Ibid., 170. Filin mistakenly identifies Irkutsk's governor as a "P. Kirillov." Tseidler governed Irkutsk from 1821 to 1835.

110 Quoted in ibid., 170–1. It is quite possible that the difference in the spelling of Kolychevskii's name between the two sources from which Filin quotes is due to a publishing error, since Filin makes no mention of the difference.

111 Goriushkin, *Nerchinskaia katorga*, doc. no. 13; Filin, "Pol′skie revoliut-sionery," 171.
112 I. S. Shunshintsev, "Delo o poliakakh v Orenburge 1833 goda (Po arkhivnym dannym)," *Russkii arkhiv* 2 (1902): 661–6.
113 Nagaev, *Omskoe delo*, 122–23; Okladnikov, *Istoriia* 2: 475.
114 GAIO, f. 24, op. 3, k. 8, d. 151, ll. 2–3.
115 Ibid., l. 1.
116 The date of Morozov's removal is uncertain. A letter from EOGU to GUVS dated 14 April 1834 states that Morozov was recalled on 9 February, but this date conflicts with other documents citing Morozov's presence in Eniseisk following the 4 March assault. Ibid., ll. 1, 2–3, 6–7.
117 Frantsov's statements and actions are related in EOGU's 14 April report to GUVS. Ibid., ll. 6–7.
118 Okladnikov, *Istoriia* 2: 475–6.
119 See Franklin A. Walker, "Poland in the Decembrists' Strategy of Revolution," *Polish Review* 15 (1970): 43–4.
120 Nagaev, *Omskoe delo*, 39, 54, 80–81, 84, 96, et passim.
121 Ibid., 98, 102, et passim.
122 Ibid., 80, 148–9.
123 Nagaev, "Istochniki i literatura," 130–1; Nagaev, *Omskoe delo*, 135. Details for the 17 sentenced to *katorga* are in the investigatory commission's October 1836 report. Goriushkin, *Nerchinskaia katorga*, doc. no. 26.
124 John Keep, "Justice for the Troops: A Comparative Study of Nicholas I's Russia and France under Louis-Philippe," *Cahiers du Monde russe et sovié-tique* 28, no. 1 (1987): 31–54 [here, p. 45].
125 Nagaev, "Istochniki i literatura," 130–37. Maksimov's version can also be found in the third edition of his work. Maksimov, *Sibir′* (1900), 340*ff*.
126 Okladnikov, *Istoriia* 2: 476.
127 A. V. Remnev, *Rossiia dal′nego vostoka. Imperskaia geografiia vlasti XIX–nachala XX vekov* (Omsk: Izd-vo Omsk. gos. un-ta, 2004), 132.

Chapter 6   Exile to Settlement

1 Laura Engelstein, *Castration and the Heavenly Kingdom: A Russian Folktale* (Ithaca: Cornell University Press, 1999), 119.
2 [Anon.,] "Svedenie o Eniseiskoi Gubernii (Iz zapisok Statskago-Sovetnika Pestova)," *ZhMVD* 5, no. 4 (1831): 75–113 [here, pp. 104–8].
3 GAIO, f. 24, op. 3, k. 35, d. 12, ll. 2–8, 22–70; k. 37, d. 1, ll. 20–3.
4 Ibid., ll. 22–70.
5 GAIO, f. 24, op. 3, k. 30, d. 2, ll. 69–70, 71.
6 Ibid., k. 36, d. 78, ll. 1, 3.
7 GAIO, f. 24, op. 3, k. 36, d. 69, ll. 4–5.
8 S. Maksimov, *Sibir′ i katorga*, 3 vols. (S.-Peterburg: Tipografiia A. Transhelia, 1871) 2: table, p. 323. Maksimov's total of 200,280 includes persons exiled to residence (*na zhit′e*), but they would have totaled only a few thousand at most.
9 One historian estimates "less than 70% of [male] exiles participated in reproducing the population and were in fact doomed to extinction."

L. M. Dameshek and A. V. Remnev, eds., *Sibir´ v sostave Rossiiskoi imperii* (Moskva: Novoe literaturnoe obozrenie, 2007), 282–3.

10 Cf. Nicholas B. Breyfogle, et al., "Russian Colonizations: An Introduction," in *Peopling the Russian Periphery: Borderland Colonization in Eurasian History*, ed. by idem (New York: Routledge, 2007), 7–8.

11 Aleksandr A. Vlasenko, "Ugolovnaia ssylka v Zapadnuiu Sibir´ v politike samoderzhaviia XIX veka" (Ph.D. dissertation, Omskii gosudarstvennyi universitet im. F. M. Dostoevskogo, 2008), 45–6.

12 Walter McKenzie Pintner, *Russian Economic Policy under Nicholas I* (Ithaca: Cornell University Press, 1967), 164; Willard Sunderland, *Taming the Wild Field: Colonization and Empire on the Russian Steppes* (Ithaca: Cornell University Press, 2004), 139.

13 Vlasenko, "Ugolovnaia ssylka," 61–2.

14 [Anon.,] "Pis´ma iz Sibiri. XIX. Barnaul, 21 Maia [1810]," *Aziatskii vestnik* (July–December 1825): 48.

15 Vlasenko, "Ugolovnaia ssylka," 41, 134.

16 Breyfogle, *Peopling*; Donald W. Treadgold, *The Great Siberian Migration: Government and Peasant Resettlement from Emancipation to the First World War* (Princeton: Princeton University Press, 1957); Willard Sunderland, "Peasants on the Move: State Peasant Resettlement in Imperial Russia, 1805–1830s," *Russian Review* 52, no. 4 (1993): 472–85.

17 Quoted in Pintner, *Economic Policy*, 158.

18 Vlasenko, "Ugolovnaia ssylka," 154–5, 156, 158, 161–2.

19 *Statisticheskiia svedeniia o ssyl´nykh v Sibiri, za 1833 i 1834 gody (Izvlechenie iz otcheta o delakh Sibirskago Komiteta)* (Sanktpeterburg: Tip. II Otdeleniia Sobstvennoi E. I. V. Kantseliarii, 1837), 18, 21.

20 Quoted in Vlasenko, "Ugolovnaia ssylka," 61.

21 [Anon.,] "Zapiski o Sibiri. (Prolozhenie.) Kratkoe opisanie Zabaikal'skago kraia," *ZhMVD* 3 (1830): 165–82 [here, pp. 167–8].

22 [Anon.,] "Zapiski o Sibiri. (Okonchanie)," *ZhMVD* 4 (1830): 149–58 [here, p. 150].

23 Quoted in Vlasenko, "Ugolovnaia ssylka," 62–3. Murav´ev worked for the administration in 1832–33, until a conflict with Governor-general I. A. Vel´iaminov resulted in his being transferred out of Siberia. It is not clear if this conflict concerned corruption. V. Fedorchenko, *Imperatorskii Dom. Vydaiushchiesia sanovniki: Entsiklopediia biografiia*, 2 vols. (Krasnoiarsk: BONUS, 2001) 2: 81.

24 GAIO, f. 24, op. 3, k. 5, d. 93, l. 1.

25 *Ssylka v Sibir´: ocherk eia istorii i sovremennago polozheniia* (S.-Peterburg: Tipografiia S.-Peterburgskoi Tiur´my, 1900), 115–16.

26 Vlasenko, "Ugolovnaia ssylka," 128–9, 138.

27 Ibid., 135–6, Appendices.

28 RGIA, f. 1281, op. 6, d. 97, ll. 14–15.

29 Vlasenko, "Ugolovnaia ssylka," 134.

30 "Smes´," *ZhMVD* 8 (1836): table no. 2; "Perechen´ vedomosti i tabelei, prinadlezhashchikh k otchetu upravliaiushchago Ministerstvom Vnutrennykh Del, za 1839 god," *ZhMVD* 7 (1840): Tables I, III lit. A; "Smes´," *ZhMVD* 32 (1850): Table B. Tobol´sk's male population was just over 200,000 in 1839.

31 RGIA, f. 1281, op. 6, d. 133, l. 21.

32 Dameshek, *Sibir'*, 279.

33 Vlasenko, "Ugolovnaia ssylka," 60, 77, 135–6, 142–3, Appendices.

34 Andrew A. Gentes, *Exile to Siberia, 1590–1822* (New York: Palgrave Macmillan, 2008), passim.

35 Sunderland, *Taming*, 114–15.

36 Pintner, *Economic Policy*, 69.

37 A. P. Okladnikov, et al., eds., *Istoriia Sibiri s drevneishikh vremen do nashikh dnei*, 5 vols. (Leningrad: Izdatel'stvo "Nauka," 1968–9) 2: 191–2.

38 A. Bitis and Janet Hartley, "The Russian Military Colonies in 1826," *Slavonic and East European Review* 78, no. 2 (2000): 321–30 [here, pp. 321, 324–5].

39 John L. H. Keep, *Soldiers of the Tsar: Army and Society in Russia, 1462–1874* (Oxford: Clarendon Press, 1985), 305–06. See also Richard E. Pipes, "The Russian Military Colonies, 1810–1831," *Journal of Modern History* 22, no. 3 (1950): 205–19.

40 Sunderland, *Taming*, 116.

41 Schafer suggests using this term alongside *raison d'état*. Sylvia Schafer, "When the Child is the Father of the Man: Work, Sexual Difference and the Guardian-State in Third Republic France," *History and Theory* 31, no. 4 (1992): 98–115 [here, p. 102].

42 Maksimov, *Sibir'* (1871) 2: table, p. 319. Due to the Crimean War's impact the number of convicts exiled to *katorga* rose precipitously in 1855.

43 In 1840 Western Siberia governor-general P. D. Gorchakov floated a plan to establish state settlements in his region, but after conferring with his Eastern Siberia counterpart and calculating that such an operation would cost over five million silver rubles he cancelled it. Vlasenko, "Ugolovnaia ssylka," 58–61.

44 With the exception of one *volost'* each in Biisk and Kuznetsk *okruga*. Ibid., 121–7, 133–5.

45 *Statisticheskiia svedeniia… Sibirskago Komiteta*, 19–20; *Ssylka v Sibir'*, 19–20nn1, 3. The settlements were located and named as follows: Kansk *okrug*: Lovatsk, Elizavetinsk, Lavinsk, Cheremkhovsk, Taraisk, Malovsk, Prirechinsk, Niko-laevsk, Nagornoe, Anginsk, Aleksandrovsk, Borodinsk, Verkhnerybinsk, and Kansko-Perevozinsk; Minusinsk *okrug*: Vostochnoe, Sagaisk, Tigritsk, Dubensk, Ermakovsk, and Sabinsk; Achinsk *okrug*: Pokrovsk and Malouluisk. The Cher-emkhovsk and Kansko-Perevozinsk settlements may have been established earlier in 1819.

46 Quoted in Dameshek, *Sibir'*, 281.

47 *Ssylka v Sibir'*, 20–1; G. Peizen, "Istoricheskii ocherk kolonizatsii Sibiri," *Sovremennik* 9 (1859): 9–46 [here, pp. 40–1]. There is disagreement as to how long the settlements took to be built. Cf. [Anon.,] "Novyia knigi [review of I. Pestov, *Zapiski ob Eniseiskoi gubernii Vostochnoi Sibiri 1831 goda* (1833)]," *ZhMVD* 10 (1833): 240; G. S. Fel'dstein, *Ssylka: eia genezisa, znacheniia, istorii i sovremennogo sostoianiia* (Moskva: T-vo skoropechatni A. A. Levenson, 1893), 160–1; I. Ia. Foinitskii, *Uchenie o nakazanii v sviazi s tiur'movedeniem* (S.-Peter-burg: Tipografiia Ministerstva putei soobshcheniia [A. Benke], 1889), 286–7.

48 *Statisticheskiia svedeniia… Sibirskago Komiteta*, 18–19, 21.

49 *Ssylka v Sibir'*, 20.

50 Nagaev identifies three—Stepanovsk, Elizavetinsk, and Lavinsk. A. S. Nagaev, *Omskoe delo, 1832–1833* (Krasnoiarsk: Krasnoiarskii universitet, 1991), 123. I have found no other reference to a Stepanovsk.

51 *Ssylka v Sibir´*, 21–2.
52 *Statisticheskiia svedeniia… Sibirskago Komiteta*, 19*n*.
53 A. Sergeev, ed., "Gr. A. Kh, Benkendorf o Rossii v 1827–1830 gg. (Okonchanie)," *Krasnyi arkhiv* 38 (1930): 109–47 [here, p. 123].
54 *Statisticheskiia svedeniia… Sibirskago Komiteta*, 20.
55 Ibid., 20–1.
56 Maksimov, *Sibir´* (1871) 2: table, p. 323.
57 Andrew A. Gentes, "'Licentious Girls' and Frontier Domesticators: Women and Siberian Exile from the Late 16th to the Early 19th Century," *Sibirica* 3, no. 1 (2003): 3–20.
58 Abby M. Schrader, "Unruly Felons and Civilizing Wives: Cultivating Marriage in the Siberian Exile System, 1822–1860," *Slavic Review* 66, no. 2 (2007): 230–56 [here, p. 256].
59 Maksimov, *Sibir´* (1871) 2: table, p. 320.
60 Vlasenko, "Ugolovnaia ssylka," 70–1.
61 Fel´dstein, *Ssylka*, 169–70. See also I. V. Shcheglov, *Khronologicheskii perechen´ vazhneishikh dannykh iz istorii Sibiri: 1032–1882 gg.* (1883; rpt. Surgut: Severnyi dom, 1993), 279; Foinitskii, *Uchenie*, 286–7.
62 Basil Dmytryshyn, et al., eds., *Russia's Conquest of Siberia, 1558–1700: A Documentary Record*, Vol. 1 (Portland: Oregon Historical Society Press, 1985), doc. nos. 71 and 112.
63 Marc Raeff, *Siberia and the Reforms of 1822* (Seattle: University of Washington Press, 1956), 13–14, 62; Lev Dameshek, "'Ustav ob upravlenii inorodtsev' Speranskogo," *Zemlia irkutskaia* 8 (1997): 17–19; James Forsyth, *A History of the Peoples of Siberia: Russia's North Asian Colony, 1581–1990* (Cambridge: Cambridge University Press, 1994), 67–9; John J. Stephan, *The Russian Far East: A History* (Stanford: Stanford University Press, 1994), 23–4. On the history of Russian slavery and its relationship to serfdom see Richard Hellie, *Slavery in Russia, 1450–1725* (Chicago: University of Chicago Press, 1982); Evgenii V. Anisimov, *The Reforms of Peter the Great: Progress through Coercion in Russia*, trans. by John T. Alexander (Armonk, NY: M. E. Sharpe, 1993), 197–202.
64 S. V. Maksimov, *Sibir´ i katorga*, 3rd ed. (S.-Peterburg: Izdanie V. I. Gubinskago, 1900), 105. See also Raeff, *Siberia*, 62–3; Fel´dstein, *Ssylka*, 169–70; *Ssylka v Sibir´*, 23; Shcheglov, *Khronologicheskii perechen´*, 303; Foinitskii, *Uchenie*, 286–7.
65 Vlasenko, "Ugolovnaia ssylka," 131, 138–9.
66 *Statisticheskiia svedeniia… Sibirskago Komiteta*, appendix A for table no. 1, pp. 50–1.
67 Ibid., table no. 2, p. 57.
68 GAIO, f. 435, op. 1, d. 155, l. 244.
69 Ibid., d. 217, l. 15. As of 1825 only 169 houses made of stone existed in Siberia. Shcheglov, *Khronologicheskii perechen´*, table, pp. 281–2.
70 V. I. Semevskii, *Rabochie na sibirskikh zolotykh promyslakh: istoricheskoe izsledovanie*, 2 vols. (S.-Peterburg: Tipografiia M. Stasiulevicha, 1898) 1: 544, tables, pp. 557–63.
71 Ibid., xxxi.
72 Peizen, "Istoricheskii ocherk": 40–1; Semevskii, *Rabochie* 1: 13–14, tables, pp. 540–3; Maksimov, *Sibir´* (1871) 2: table, p. 323.
73 Semevskii, *Rabochie* 1: xxxii–xxxiii, xxxvi–xxxvii, lvii,13–14.

74 Ibid., lx–lxi, lxvi.

75 Ibid., 27–31. P. D. Gorchakov, appointed governor-general in 1836, probably issued this order.

76 Ibid., 37, 40. Grebeshchikov's title was *unter-shikhtmeister*, a position within the mining hierarchy equivalent to the twelfth *chin* in the Table of Ranks. L. V. Belovinskii, *Rossiiskii istoriko-bytovoi slovar´* (Moskva: RIO Rossiiskii Arkhiv, 1999), 510; Iu. A. Fedosiuk, *Chto neponiatno u klassikov, ili Entsiklopediia russkogo byta XIX veka*, 2nd ed. (Moskva: Nauka, 1999), 93, 121.

77 Semevskii, *Rabochie* 1: 31–6, 40–6, 48–9.

78 Vlasenko, "Ugolovnaia ssylka," 57–8.

79 *Ssylka v Sibir´*, 25.

80 Andrew A. Gentes, "The Institution of Russia's Sakhalin Policy, from 1868 to 1875," *Journal of Asian History* 36, no. 1 (2002): 1–31; idem, "No Kind of Liberal: Alexander II and the Sakhalin Penal Colony," *Jahrbücher für Geschichte Osteuropas* 54, no. 3 (2006): 321–44.

81 Figures for 1823 and 1851 in Shcheglov, *Khronologicheskii perechen´*, table, p. 337; figure for 1843 in N. Cherniakovskii, "Statisticheskoe opisanie Ishimskago Okruga Tobol´skoi Gubernii," *ZhMVD* 2 (1843): 3–48, 200–55 [here, pp. 22, 252].

82 This term had previously designated an administrative exile, but Cherniakovskii uses it idiosyncratically as a diminutive of *poselenets*, which officially meant "exile-settler."

83 Cherniakovskii, "Statisticheskoe opisanie": 24, 244, 247–9, 252.

84 Maksimov, *Sibir´* (1900), 103.

Chapter 7 *Katorga* and the 1845 *Ulozhenie*

1 S. Maksimov, *Sibir´ i katorga*, 3 vols. (S.-Peterburg: Tipografiia A. Transhelia, 1871) 2: tables, pp. 319, 320. The precise number of penal laborers cannot be determined due to the fact that figures for the years 1852–53 include convicts exiled to settlement.

2 [Anon.,] "Predstoiashchee preobrazovanie katorga," *Tiuremnyi vestnik* 6–7 (1910): 897–922 [here, p. 898].

3 *Statisticheskiia svedeniia o ssyl´nykh v Sibiri, za 1833 i 1834 gody (Izvlechenie iz otcheta o delakh Sibirskago Komiteta)* (Sanktpeterburg: Tip. II Otdeleniia Sobstvennoi E. I. V. Kantseliarii, 1837), 17.

4 Aleksandr A. Vlasenko, "Ugolovnaia ssylka v Zapadnuiu Sibir´ v politike samoderzhaviia XIX veka" (Ph.D. dissertation, Omskii gosudarstvennyi universitet im. F. M. Dostoevskogo, 2008), 160.

5 Maksimov, *Sibir´* (1871) 2: table, p. 319.

6 GAIO, f. 435, op. 1, d. 155, ll. 334–5.

7 *Ssylka v Sibir´: ocherk eia istorii i sovremennago polozheniia* (S.-Peterburg: Tipografiia S.-Peterburgskoi Tiur´my, 1900), 18, 28–9.

8 *Ssylka v Sibir´*, 18, 25, table, pp. 26–7; Maksimov, *Sibir´* (1871), table, p. 319.

9 Vlasenko, "Ugolovnaia ssylka," Appendices.

10 Maksimov, *Sibir´* (1871), table, p. 319.

11 "Perechen´ vedomosti i tabelei, prinadlezhashchikh k otchetu upravliaiushchago Ministerstvom Vnutrennykh Del, za 1839 god," *ZhMVD* 7 (July 1840): Table III, lit. A.

12 As figures for both 1825 and 1858 show. I. V. Shcheglov, *Khronologicheskii perechen´ vazhneishikh dannykh iz istorii Sibiri: 1032–1882 gg.* (1883; rpt. Surgut: Severnyi dom, 1993), tables, pp. 281–2, 353.

13 Maksimov, *Sibir´* (1871) 2: table, p. 319.

14 GAIO, f. 435, op. 1, d. 227, l. 11; d. 263, l. 100.

15 [Anon.,] "Vzgliad na Dauriiu i v osobennosti na Nerchinskie gornye zavody," *Sibirskii vestnik* 3 (1823): 27–48 [here, pp. 35–6, 41].

16 L. M. Goriushkin, ed., *Politicheskaia ssylka v Sibiri. Nerchinskaia katorga, Tom 1* (Novosibirsk: Sibirskii khronograf, 1993), doc. no. 74, p. 139. Many more were "at large" and are discussed below.

17 I. V. Efimov, "Iz zhizni katorzhnykh Ilginskago i Aleksandrovskago, togda kazennykh, vinokurennykh zavodov. 1848–1853 g.," *Russkii arkhiv* 1 (1900): 79–107, 247–72 [here, p. 259].

18 N. V. Sushkov, "O Sibirskikh solianykh promyslakh," *Sibirskii vestnik* 14 (1821): 255–74, 315–26 [here, p. 273]; S. V. Maksimov, *Sibir´ i katorga*, 3rd ed. (S.-Peterburg: Izdanie V. I. Gubinskago, 1900), 477, 478–9. Similar figures for this period provided in idem, "Sibirskaia sol´," in *Zhivopisnaia Rossiia. Otechestvo nashe v ego zemel´nom, istoricheskom, plemennom, ekonomicheskom i bytovom znachenii*, ed. by P. P Semenov (S.-Peterburg: Izdanie Tovarishchestva M. O. Vol´f, 1895), 321.

19 Efimov, "Iz zhizni katorzhnykh": 259.

20 Ibid.: 259–61.

21 GAIO, f. 435, op. 1, d. 193 [there are no numbers written on this *delo's* pages].

22 [Anon.,] "Vzgliad na Dauriiu i v osobennosti na Nerchinskie gornye zavody," *Sibirskii vestnik* 9 (1823): 107–20 [here, p. 107].

23 N. V. Sushkov, "O Sibirskikh solianykh promyslakh (okonchanie)," *Sibirskii vestnik*, 15 (1821): 91–9; G. Golenishchev, "Statistika: O sostoianii Kamchatskoi oblasti v 1830 i 1831 godakh," *ZhMVD*, 10 (1833): 1–29 [here, pp. 2–3, and table].

24 John Dundas Cochrane, *A Pedestrian Journey through Russia and Siberian Tartary to the Frontiers of China, the Frozen Sea and Kamchatka*, ed. and intro. by Mervyn Horder (1823; rpt. London: Folio Society, 1983), 180–2.

25 E.... ....v, "Ocherki, razskazy i vospominaniia: Ssyl´no-katorzhnye v Okhotskom solevarennom zavode," *Russkaia starina* 22 (1878): 301–16.

26 An affectionate diminutive of *katorzhnye* (penal laborers).

27 Ibid.: 306.

28 V. M. Doroshevich, *Sakhalin (Katorga)*, 2 vols. (Moskva: I. D. Sytin, 1903) 1: 270–1. This passage may be found in English in Vlas Doroshevich, *Russia's Penal Colony in the Far East: A Translation of Vlas Doroshevich's "Sakhalin"*, trans. and intro. by Andrew A. Gentes (New York: Anthem Press, 2009), 184–5.

29 Efimov, "Iz zhizni katorzhnykh": 250–3.

30 V. I. Semevskii, *Rabochie na sibirskikh zolotykh promyslakh: istoricheskoe izsledovanie*, 2 vols. (S.-Peterburg: Tipografiia M. Stasiulevicha, 1898) 1: 314–24.

31 In Russian: *Kak v nedavnikh to godakh/ Na Kariiskikh promyslakh/ Tsarstvoval Ivan!/ Ne Ivan Vasil´ich Groznyi/ Inzhener-ot byl on gornyi/ Razgil´deev sam!* Ibid.: 24. See also N. P. Matkhanova, ed., *Graf N. N. Murav´ev-Amurskii v*

vospominaniiakh sovremennikov (Novosibirsk: Sibirskii khronograf, 1998), 320*n*14.

32 [Anon.,] "Izvlechenie iz otcheta po Upravleniiu Irkutskoiu Gubernieiu, za 1839 god. (Okanchanie)," *ZhMVD* (October 1840): 25–7.

33 [Anon.,] "Kratkii otchet o polozhenii i deistviiakh Obshchestva popechitel′nago o tiur′makh, za 1840 god," *ZhMVD* 41 (1841): 314, 321–2.

34 GAIO, f. 435, op. 1, d. 125, ll. 1–2.

35 Bruce F. Adams, *The Politics of Punishment: Prison Reform in Russia, 1863–1917* (DeKalb: Northern Illinois University Press, 1996), 40–45; [Anon.,] *Materialy k izsledovaniiu istorii russkikh tiurem v sviazi s istoriei uchrezhdeniia Obshchestva Popechitel′nago o tiur′makh* (Chernigov: Tipografiia Gubernskago Zemstva, 1912), 66–97.

36 Adele Lindenmeyr, *Poverty is Not a Vice: Charity, Society, and the State in Imperial Russia* (Princeton: Princeton University Press, 1996), 39.

37 *Materialy k izsledovaniiu istorii russkikh tiurem*, 72, 80.

38 Ibid., 85.

39 Ibid., 89–90, 97, 103–4.

40 Ibid., 108. See also S. K. Gogel′, *Voprosy ugolovnago prava, protsessa i tiur′movedeniia* (S.-Peterburg: Obshchestvennaia pol′za, 1906), 612.

41 GARF, f. 123, op. 1, d. 97, ll. 1–3, 4, 6–7, 9, 10, 18–19.

42 Vlasenko, "Ugolovnaia ssylka," 56.

43 GARF, f. 123, op. 1, d. 20, passim.

44 Ibid., d. 125, passim; ibid., d. 112, passim.

45 RGIA, f. 1281, op. 6, d. 166, ll. 19–20.

46 GUVS Council journal of 31 January 1853. GARF, f. 123, op. 1, d. 97, ll. 20–4.

47 Ibid., ll. 9, 10.

48 Ibid., ll. 18–19.

49 Ibid., l. 27.

50 Adams, *Politics*, 45.

51 GARF, f. 123, op. 1, d. 97, ll. 37–40, 42.

52 N. S. Tagantsev, *Russkoe ugolovnoe pravo: chast′ obshchaia*, 2 vols. (1902; rpt. Tula: Avtograf, 2001) 1: 189, 676*n*392; V. D. Spasovich, *Uchebnik ugolovnago prava* (Sanktpeterburg: Tip. I. Ogrizko, 1863), 323. See also Abby M. Schrader, *Languages of the Lash: Corporal Punishment and Identity in Imperial Russia* (DeKalb: Northern Illinois University Press, 2002), 13, 19–20.

53 [Anon.,] *Tiuremnoe preobrazovanie, I. Ispravitel′nyi dom, zakliuchenie v kreposti i tiur′ma* ([S.-Peterburg]: Tipo-lit. S.-Peterburgskoi tiur′my, 1905), 4–5; I. Ia. Foinitskii, *Uchenie o nakazanii v sviazi s tiur′movedeniem* (S.-Peterburg: Tipografiia Ministerstva putei soobshcheniia [A. Benke], 1889), 295*n*2; Adams, *Politics*, 10, 39.

54 Spasovich, *Uchebnik*, 325; I. Gol′denberg, *Reforma telesnykh nakazanii. Velikia reformy shestidesiatykh v ikh proshlom i nastoiashchem* (S.-Peterburg: M. I. Semenov [1913]), 21.

55 N. Evreinov, *Istoriia telesnykh nazanii v Rossii* (New York: Chalidze Publications, 1979), 110.

56 Abby M. Schrader, "Containing the Spectacle of Punishment: The Russian Autocracy and the Abolition of the Knout, 1817–1845," *Slavic Review* 56, no. 4 (1997): 613–44; Adams, *Politics*, chap. 1.

57 Stephen P. Frank, "Emancipation and the Birch: The Perpetuation of Corporal Punishment in Rural Russia, 1861–1907," *Jahrbücher für Geschichte Osteuropas* 45, no. 3 (1997): 401–16.

58 Adams writes that during the post-Reform era "Russia... gradually made its prisons cleaner, roomier, healthier places." Adams, *Politics*, 9. See also Jonathan W. Daly, "Criminal Punishment and Europeanization in Late Imperial Russia," *Jahrbücher für Geschichte Osteuropas* 47 (2000): 341–62.

59 Efimov, "Iz zhizni katorzhnykh": 264.

60 New York Public Library, Rare Books and Manuscripts Division, George Kennan Papers, Box 3, Doc. 22–4102, pp. 3–7.

61 Tagantsev, *Russkoe ugolovnoe pravo* 2: 139.

62 Ibid.: tables, pp. 246–8.

63 *Ministerstvo vnutrennykh del, 1802–1902: Istoricheskii ocherk*, 3 vols. (S.-Peterburg: Tip. MVD, 1902) 1: 66.

64 Tagantsev, *Russkoe ugolovnoe pravo* 1: 142, 665n294.

65 Spasovich, *Uchebnik*, 326.

66 G. S. Fel´dstein, *Ssylka: eia genezisa, znacheniia, istorii i sovremennogo sostoianiia* (Moskva: T-vo skoropechatni A. A. Levenson, 1893), 145–6.

67 "Vysochaishe utverzhdennyia dopolnitel´nyia postavleniia o raspredelenii i upotreblenii o suzhdennykh v katorzhnyia raboty," *Polnoe sobranie zakonov rossiiskoi imperii. Serie 2*, t. XX (1846), no. 19284 (15 August 1845). I have also made use of a separately bound booklet found in Moscow's Lenin Library: *Dopolnitel´nyia postanovleniia o raspredelenii i upotreblenii osuzhdennykh v katorzhnyia raboty. Polozhenie o ispravitel´nykh arestantskikh rotakh grazhdanskago vedomstva. Dopolnitel´nyia pravila k ustavu o soderzhashchikhsia pod strazheiu* ([n.p.: n.p.], 1845).

68 Foinitskii, *Uchenie*, 291–2.

69 Article 49, no. 19284.

70 "Vysochaishe utverzhdennoe polozhenie ispravitel´nykh arestantskikh rotakh grazhdanskago vedomstva," *Polnoe sobranie zakonov rossiiskoi imperii. Serie 2*, t. XX (1846), no. 19285 (15 August 1845).

71 Articles 82–4, 90, no. 19285.

72 *Ssylka v Sibir´*, 55n.

73 Article 5, no. 19285

74 Foinitskii, *Uchenie*, 295n1.

75 Quoted in David Magarshack, *Dostoevsky* (London: Secker & Warburg, 1962), 168.

76 Letter to Mikhail, 30 January–22 February 1854, Omsk. David Lowe and Ronald Meyer, eds. and trans., *Fyodor Dostoevsky: Complete Letters, Volume One: 1832–1859* (Ann Arbor: Ardis, 1988), 188.

77 N. Bel´chikov, ed., "Pis´mo F. M. Dostoevskogo iz kreposti," *Krasnyi arkhiv* 2 (1922): 234–9.

78 Fyodor Dostoyevsky, *The House of the Dead*, trans. by David McDuff (New York: Penguin, 1985), 140. On Dostoevskii's comments over the years about his prison experience see Jacques Catteau, "F. M. Dostoevskij et la Sibérie," in *Sibérie II: Questions sibériennes*, ed. by Boris Chichlo (Paris: Insitut d'études slaves, 1999).

79 Dostoyevsky, *House*, 242.

260 *Notes*

80 For an interesting speculation on Russian society's *masochistic* drives
    see Daniel Rancour-Laferriere, *The Slave Soul of Russia: Moral Masochism
    and the Cult of Suffering* (New York: New York University Press, 1995).

81 For an account of Dostoevskii's activities immediately after release see
    Ronald Hingley, *Dostoyevsky: His Life and Work* (New York: Charles
    Scribner's Sons, 1978), chaps. 4 and 5. According to D´iakov, Dostoevskii
    completed writing *Dead House* by the time he was released from the
    military in March 1859. Fragments of the work first appeared in the
    journal *Russkii mir* in 1860–61; the full text was serialized in *Vremia*
    (published by Mikhail Dostoevskii) in 1861–62. In 1862 the work
    appeared as a separate volume. V. A. D´iakov, "Katorzhnye gody
    F.M. Dostoevskogo (Po novym istochnikam)," in *Politicheskaia ssylka v Sibiri
    XIX–nachalo XX v.: Istoriografiia i istochniki*, ed. by L. M. Goriushkin,
    (Novosibirsk: Nauka, 1987), 197.

82 *Dead House* is not easily classifiable as a memoir, *roman à clef*, or anything
    else. Dostoevskii fictionalized some events and incorporated other convicts'
    experiences, sometimes from outside Omsk. See Robert Louis Jackson,
    "The Narrator in Dostoevsky's *Notes from the House of the Dead*," in *Studies in
    Russian and Polish Literature, in Honor of Waclaw Lednicki*, ed. by Zbigniew
    Folejewski (The Hague: Mouton, 1962); Lewis Bagby, "Dostoevsky's *Notes
    From A Dead House*: The Poetics of the Introductory Paragraph," *Modern
    Language Review* 81 (1986): 139–52. Because it so influenced Solzhenitsyn's
    Gulag Archipelago, one is tempted to use Solzhenitsyn's subtitle "A Literary
    Investigation" to describe Dostoevskii's book. On *Dead House* as an historical
    document see M. M. Gromyko, "'Zapiski iz mertvogo doma' F. M. Dostoevs-
    kogo kak istochnik po istorii sibirskoi katorgi 50–x godov XIX v.," in *Ssylka i
    katorga v Sibiri (XVIII–nachalo XX v.)*, ed. by L. M. Goriushkin, et al. (Novo-
    sibirsk: Nauka Sibirskoe otdelenie, 1975); Leonard A. Polakiewicz, "The Rus-
    sian Prison System as Seen through the Eyes of Chekhov and Dostoevsky,"
    The Soviet and Post-Soviet Review 28, nos. 1–2 (2001 [2002]): 157–86; Joseph
    Frank, *Dostoevsky: The Years of Ordeal, 1850–1859* (London: Robson Books,
    1983), 89.

83 Dostoyevsky, *House*, 355.

84 Letter to Mikhail, 30 January–22 February 1854, *Complete Letters*, op. cit.,
    186–7, 190. Hingley and Magarshack each comment on Dostoevskii's
    bitterness towards those he would later praise. Hingley, *Dostoyevsky*, 76,
    81; Magarshack, *Dostoyevsky*, 179*ff*. The painting "Christmas in Omsk
    Prison," which portrays Dostoevskii horror-stricken at the carousing
    convicts surrounding him and being comforted by a fellow prisoner, cap-
    tures the essence of his worst experiences there. Reproduced in Hingley,
    Dostoyevsky, 77.

85 Tokarzewski's remarks are cited in Hingley, *Dostoyevsky*, 81. For brief
    biographies of Omsk's Poles see D´iakov, "Katorzhnye," 200*ff*.

86 Quoted in Frank, *Dostoevsky*, 71.

87 D´iakov, "Katorzhnye," 199.

88 M. M. Gromyko, "F. M. Dostoevskii i sem´ia dekabrista I. A. Annen-
    kova," in *Politicheskie ssyl´nye v Sibiri (XVIII—nachalo XX v.)*, ed. by
    L. M. Goriushkin (Novosibirsk: Nauka, 1983), 102–2; Frank, *Dostoevsky*,
    71, 73–5, 78–9, 81, 84–5.

89 Maksimov, *Sibir´* (1871) 2: table, p. 319.

90 Vlasenko, "Ugolovnaia ssylka," Appendices.

91 However, he contradicts himself somewhat, writing for instance a few pages later that "perhaps only a third of the convicts had work of their own...." Dostoyevsky, *House*, 38, 44, 84, 86.

92 Dostoevskii and the Poles were all *chernorabochie*—another reason General Borislavskii and others tried to help them. D´iakov, "Katorzhnye," 200.

93 Dostoyevsky, *House*, 43 [orig. italics].

94 Letter to Mikhail, 30 January–22 February 1854, *Collected Letters*, 187.

95 Unfortunately, I have found no sources on this topic for the period ending in 1861. Concerning the social organization of prison life after this date see Andrew A. Gentes, "'Beat the Devil!': Prison Society and Anarchy in Tsarist Siberia," *Ab Imperio* 2 (2009): 201–24.

96 Dostoyevsky, *House*, 45.

97 Ibid.

98 Ibid., 72.

99 Ibid., 69, 72, 135–6, 200–1.

100 F. M. Dostoevskii, *Polnoe sobranie sochinenii v tridtsati tomakh*, 30 vols. (Leningrad: Nauka, 1972) 4: 49.

101 Dostoyevsky, *House*, 64.

102 Dostoevskii, *Polnoe sobranie sochinenii* 4: 37.

103 *Ssylka v Sibir´*, 29n.

104 Maksimov, "Sibirskaia sol´," 321.

105 Maksimov, *Sibir´* (1871) 2: table, p. 325.

106 GAIO, f. 435, op. 1, d. 227, l. 11.

107 Goriushkin, *Politicheskaia ssylka v Sibiri*, doc. no. 74, p. 139.

108 Vlasenko, "Ugolovnaia ssylka," Appendices.

109 Maksimov, *Sibir´* (1871) 2: table, p. 325.

110 Maksimov, *Sibir´* (1900), 474–5; Maksimov, *Sibir´* (1871) 1: 102*n*, 182.

111 "Smes´," *ZhMVD* 8–10 (1844–45): Table(s) B. This source contains no data for Tobol´sk *guberniia* for November–December, and so the number arrested would have been even higher.

112 RGIA, f. 1281, op. 6, d. 79, ll. 21–2.

113 Ibid., d. 79–1862, l. 26.

114 Ibid., d. 166, l. 18.

115 [Anon.,] *Poucheniia k podsudimym i k peresylaemym v Sibir´ prestupnikam* (Perm´: V gubernskoi tipografii, 1859), 23, 38–9.

116 E. N. Anuchin, *Izsledovaniia o protsente soslannykh v Sibir´ v period 1827–1846 godov: materialiy dlia ugolovnoi statistiki Rossii* (S.-Peterburg: Tip. Maikova, 1873), table, p. 23.

Conclusion: Aesthetics, Delusions, Conclusions

1 I. Ia. Foinitskii, *Uchenie o nakazanii v sviazi s tiur´movedeniem* (S.-Peterburg: Tipografiia Ministerstva putei soobshcheniia [A. Benke], 1889), 287.

2 *Ssylka v Sibir´: ocherk eia istorii i sovremennago polozheniia* (S.-Peterburg: Tipografiia S.-Peterburgskoi Tiur´my, 1900), 34–5.
3 Quoted in ibid., 18*n*1.
4 S. Maksimov, *Sibir´ i katorga*, 3 vols. (S.-Peterburg: Tipografiia A. Transhelia, 1871) 2: table, p. 321.

Bibliography

Archival Sources

Abbreviations: f.=*fond* (collection); op.=*opis´* (listing); k.=*karton* (carton); d.=*delo* (sheaf); l.=*list* (sheet)

GAIO—Irkutsk District State Archive (*Gosudarstvennyi arkhiv Irkutstkoi oblasti*), Irkutsk, Russia:

Fond 24: Main Administration of Eastern Siberia (*Glavnoe upravlenie Vostochnoi Sibiri*) 1822–1887

Fond 32: Irkutsk Provincial Administration (*Irkutskoe gubernskoe upravlenie*) 1834–1917

Fond 137: Ust´-Kutsk Salt Works (*Ust´-Kutskii solevarennyi zavod*) 1840–1912

Fond 435: Kirensk City Government (*Kirenskaia gorodskaia uprava*) 1784–1867

GARF—Russian Federation State Archive (*Gosudarstvennyi arkhiv Rossiiskoi Federatsii*), Moscow, Russia:

Fond 123: Prison Aid Society of the Ministry of Justice (*Obshchestvo popegatel´nykh o tiur´makh Ministerstva iustitsii*) 1819–1917

Fond 1183: Tobol´sk Exile Office (*Tobol´skii prikaz o ssyl´nykh*) 1822–1890

RGIA—Russian State Historical Archive (*Rossiiskii Gosudarstvennyi Istoricheskii Arkhiv*), St Petersburg, Russia:

Fond 1281: Council of the Ministry of Internal Affairs (*Sovet Ministerstva Vnutrennikh Del*) 1804– [sic]

Legal Documents

Dopolnitel´nyia postanovleniia o raspredelenii i upotreblenii osuzhdennykh v katorzhnyia raboty. Polozhenie o ispravitel´nykh arestantskikh rotakh grazhdanskago vedomstva. Dopolnitel´nyia pravila k ustavu o soderzhashchikhsia pod strazheiu. [n.l.: n.p.], 1845.

Polnoe sobranie zakonov rossiiskoi imperii. Serie 1, t. XXXVIII. [S.-Peterburg] V Tip. II otd-niia sobstvennoi Ego Imp. Velichestva Kantseliarii, 1830.

Polnoe sobranie zakonov rossiiskoi imperii. Serie 2, t. XX. [S.-Peterburg] V Tip. II otd-niia sobstvennoi Ego Imp. Velichestva Kantseliarii, 1846.

Uchrezhdenie dlia upravleniia Sibirskikh gubernii. Sankpeterburg: Pechatano v Senatskoi Tipografii, 1822.

Published Documents Collections

Baten´kov, G. S. *Sochineneiia i pis´ma. Tom 1. Pis´ma (1813–1856).* Irkutsk: Vostochno-Sibirskoe knizhnoe izdatel´stvo, 1989.

Bel´chikov, N. (Ed.) "Pis´mo F. M. Dostoevskogo iz kreposti." *Krasnyi arkhiv* 2 (1922): 234–9.

Bel´chikov, N. (Ed.) "Pokazaniia F. M. Dostoevskogo po delu petrashevtsev." *Krasnyi arkhiv* 2 (1931): 130–46; 3 (1931): 160–78.

Dmytryshyn, Basil, et al. (Eds.) *Russia's Conquest of Siberia, 1558–1700: A Documentary Record*. Vol. 1. Portland: Oregon Historical Society Press, 1985.

Fedorov, V. A. (Ed.) "Krestnyi put´ dekabristov v Sibir´: Dokumenty ob otpravke osuzhdennykh na katorgu i v ssylku i ob usloviiakh ikh soderzhaniia. 1826–1837 gg." *Istoricheskii arkhiv* 6 (2000): 46–56.

Fedorov, V. A. (Ed.) "'U nas net nikakikh sviazei s vneshnim mirom': Pis´ma dekabrista P. N. Svistunova k bratu Alekseiu. 1831–1832 gg." *Istoricheskii arkhiv* 1 (1993): 183–93.

Gorbachevskii, I. I. *Zapiski. Pis´ma*. Moskva: Izdatel´stvo Akademii nauk SSSR, 1963.

Goriushkin, L. M. (Ed.) *Politicheskaia ssylka v Sibiri: Nerchinskaia katorga, Tom 1*. Novosibirsk: Sibirskii khronograf, 1993.

Iakushkin, E. E. "Pesnia dekabristov." *Krasnyi arkhiv* 10 (1925): 319–21.

Iakushkin, E. E. "Stikhotvorennie dekabrista." *Krasnyi arkhiv* 10 (1925): 317–19.

Il´in, P. V. (Ed.) "'Gosudar! Ispoveduiu tebe iako boiashchiisia boga': Prosheniia rodstvennikov dekabristov o pomilovanii arestovannykh. 1826 g." *Istoricheskii arkhiv* 1 (2001): 156–77.

Lowe, David, and Ronald Meyer. (Eds. and trans.) *Fyodor Dostoevsky: Complete Letters, Volume One: 1832–1859*. Ann Arbor: Ardis, 1988.

Lunin, M. S. *Pis´ma iz Sibiri*. Ed. by I. A. Zhelvakova and N. Ia. Eidel´man. Moskva: Nauka, 1987.

Murav´ev, A. N. *Sochineniia i pis´ma*. Ed. by Iu. I. Gerasimova and S. V. Duminyi. Irkutsk: Vostochno-Sibiriskoe knizhnoe izdatel´stvo, 1986.

Podzhio, A. V. *Zapiski, pis´ma*. Ed. by N. P. Matkhanova. Irkutsk: Vostochno-Sibirskoe knizhnoe izdatel´stvo, 1989.

Polonskii, Viach. (Ed.) "M. V. Butashevich-Petrashevskii v Sibiri." *Krasnyi arkhiv* 3 (1925): 184–216.

Sergeev, A. (Ed.) "Gr. A. Kh. Benkendorf o Rossii v 1827–1830 gg. (Okonchanie)." *Krasnyi arkhiv* 38 (1930): 109–47.

Sergeev, A. (Ed.) "Gr. A. Kh. Benkendorf o Rossii v 1827–1830 gg. (Ezhegodnye otchety III otdeleniia i korpusa zhandarmov)." *Krasnyi arkhiv* 37 (1929): 138–74.

Sergeev, A. (Ed.) "Gr. A. Kh. Benkendorf o Rossii v 1831–1832 gg." *Krasnyi arkhiv* 46 (1931): 132–59.

Tsamutali, A. N., et al. (Eds.) *Nikolai I: lichnost´ i epokha. Novye materialy*. SPb.: Izdatel´stvo "Nestor-Istoriia," 2007.

Zakharova, L. G., and S. V. Mironenko. (Eds.) *Perepiska tsesarevicha Aleksandra Nikolaevicha s imperatorom Nikolaem I, 1838–1839*. Moskva: ROSSPEN, 2008.

Memoirs and Autobiographies

Azarova, N. I. (Ed.) *Russkie memuary. Nikolai I: Muzh. Otets. Imperator*. Moskva: Slovo, 2000.

Barratt, Glynn R. V. (Ed. and trans.) *Voices in Exile: The Decembrist Memoirs*. Montreal: McGill-Queen's University Press, 1974.

Cochrane, John Dundas. *A Pedestrian Journey through Russia and Siberian Tartary to the Frontiers of China, the Frozen Sea and Kamchatka*. Ed. and intro. by Mervyn Horder. 1823; rpt. London: Folio Society, 1983.

Custine, Marquis de. *Empire of the Czar: A Journey through Eternal Russia*. New York: Doubleday, 1989.

De Choiseul-Gouffier, Madame la Comtesse. *Historical Memoirs of the Emperor Alexander I and the Court of Russia*. Trans. by Mary Berenice Patterson. Chicago: A.C. McClurg and Co., 1900.

Dostoevskii, F. M. *Polnoe sobranie sochinenii v tridtsati tomakh*. Vol. 4. Leningrad: Nauka, 1972.

Dostoyevsky, Fyodor. *The House of the Dead*. Trans. by David McDuff. New York: Penguin, 1985.

Henderson, Thulia S. (Ed.) *Memorials of John Venning, Esq., with Numerous Notices from His Manuscripts Relative to the Imperial Family of Russia*. 1862; rpt. Cambridge, England: Oriental Research Partners, 1975.

Howard, John. *The State of the Prisons*. New York: E. P. Dutton & Co., 1929.

Il´in, P. V. (Ed.) *14 dekabria 1825 goda: Vospominaniia ochevidtsev*. Sankt-Peterburg: Gumanitarnoe Agentstvo "Akademicheskii Proekt," 1999.

Kennan, George. *Siberia and the Exile System*. 2 vols. New York: The Century Co., 1891.

Lansdell, Henry. *Through Siberia*. 3rd ed. Boston: Houghton Mifflin, 1882.

Lyall, Robert. *Travels in Russia, the Krimea, the Caucasus, and Georgia*. 2 vols. 1825; rpt. New York: Arno Press & the New York Times, 1970.

Matkhanova, N. P. (Ed.) *Graf N. N. Murav´ev-Amurskii v vospominaniiakh sovremennikov*. Novosibirsk: Sibirskii khronograf, 1998.

Rozen, A. E. *Zapisiki dekabrista*. Ed. by G. A. Nevelevyi. Irkutsk: Vostochno-Sibirskoe knizhnoe izdatel´stvo, 1984.

Spottiswoode, William. *A Tarantasse Journey through Eastern Russia in the Autumn of 1856*. 1857; rpt. New York: Arno Press & the New York Times, 1970.

Tokarzewski, Simon. "In Siberian Prisons, 1846–1857." Trans. by the staff. *Sarmatian Review* 25, no. 2 (2005). http://www.ruf.rice.edu/~sarmatia/405/254tokar.html (accessed 14 April 2009).

Wilson, William Rae. *Travels in Russia*. 2 vols. 1828; rpt. New York: Arno Press and the New York Times, 1970.

Zavalishin, Dmitrii. *Vospominaniia*. Moskva: Zakharov, 2003.

Imperial Era Publications

[Anon.] *Materialy k izsledovaniiu istorii russkikh tiurem v sviazi s istoriei uchrezhdeniia Obshchestva Popechitel´nago o tiur´makh*. Chernigov: Tipografiia Gubernskago Zemstva, 1912.

[Anon.] *Ministerstvo vnutrennykh del, 1802–1902: Istoricheskii ocherk*. 3 vols. S.-Peterbug: Tip. MVD, 1902.

[Anon.] *Poucheniia k podsudimym i k peresylaemym v Sibir´ prestupnikam*. Perm´: V gubernskoi tipografii, 1859.

[Anon.] *Ssylka v Sibir´: ocherk eia istorii i sovremennago polozheniia*. S.-Peterburg: Tipografiia S.-Peterburgskoi Tiur´my, 1900.

[Anon.] *Tiuremnoe preobrazovanie, I. Ispravitel´nyi dom, zakliuchenie v kreposti i tiur´ma*. [S.-Peterburg]: Tipo-lit. S.-Peterburgskoi tiur´my, 1905.

Anuchin, E. N. *Izsledovaniia o protsente soslannykh v Sibir´ v period 1827–1846 godov: materialy dlia ugolovnoi statistiki Rossii*. S.-Peterburg: Tipografiia Maikova, 1873.

266 *Bibliography*

Anuchin, E. N. *Materialy dlia ugolovnoi statistiki Rossii. Izsledovaniia o protsente ssylaemykh v Sibir'*. Tobol'sk: V Tipografii Tobol'skago Gubernskago Pravleniia, 1866.

Bogoliubskii, I. *Istoriko-statisticheskii ocherk proizvoditel'nosti Nerchinskago Gornago Okruga s 1703 po 1871 god*. S.-Peterburg: V Tip. V. Demakova, 1872.

[Butin, M.] *Nikolaevskii chugunno-plavil'nyi, zhelezodelatel'nyi i mekhanicheskii zavod, prinadlezhashchii torgovomu domu Nerchinskikh 1-i gil'dii kuptsov Brat'ev Butinykh, nakhodiashchiisia v Irkutskoi gubernii*. S.-Peterburg: Tipografiia O. Unfug, 1892.

Dal', V. I. *Tolkovyi slovar' zhivogo velikorusskogo iazyka*. 4 vols. 1882; rpt. Moskva: Russkii iazyk, 1999.

Dmitriev-Mamonov, A. I. *Dekabristy v Zapadnoi Sibiri*. S.-Peterburg: Tip. Montvida. Ug. Konnoi, 1905.

Doroshevich, V. M. *Sakhalin (Katorga)*. 2 vols. Moskva: I. D. Sytin, 1903.

Doroshevich, Vlas. *Russia's Penal Colony in the Far East: A Translation of Vlas Doroshevich's "Sakhalin"*. Trans. and intro. by Andrew A. Gentes. New York: Anthem Press, 2009.

Fel'dstein, G. S. *Ssylka: eia genezisa, znacheniia, istorii i sovremennogo sostoianiia*. Moskva: T-vo skoropechatni A. A. Levenson, 1893.

Foinitskii, I. Ia. *Uchenie o nakazanii v sviazi s tiur'movedeniem*. S.-Peterburg: Tipografiia Ministerstva putei soobshcheniia (A. Benke), 1889.

Gogel', S. K. *Voprosy ugolovnago prava, protsessa i tiur'movedeniia*. S.-Peterburg: Obshchestvennaia pol'za, 1906.

Gol'denberg, I. *Reforma telesnykh nakazanii. Velikia reformy shestidesiatykh v ikh proshlom i nastoiashchem*. S.-Peterburg: M. I. Semenov [1913].

Iadrintsev, N. M. *Russkaia obshchina v tiur'me i ssylke*. S.-Peterburg: Tipografiia A. Morigerovskago, 1872.

Iadrintsev, N. M. *Sibir' kak koloniia v geograficheskom, etnograficheskom i istoricheskom otnoshenii*. Ed. by L. M. Goriushkin, et al. Novosibirsk: Sibirskii khronograf, 2003.

Iadrintsev, N. M. *Sibir' kak koloniia v geograficheskom, etnograficheskom i dopolnennoe*. S.-Peterburg: Izdanie I.M. Sibiriakova, 1892.

Iadrintsev, N. M. *Sibir' kak koloniia: k iubileiu trekhsotletiia. Sovremennoe polozhenie Sibiri. Eia nuzhdy i potrebnosti. Eia proshloe i budushchee* [bound with *Novyia svedeniia o sibirskoi ssylke: Soobshchenniia S.-Peterburgskomu Iuridicheskomu Obshchestv*]. Sanktpeterburg: Tipografiia M.M. Stasiulevicha, 1882.

Karnilov, Senator [Aleksei Mikhailovich]. *Zamechaniia o Sibiri*. Sanktpeterburg: Pechatno v tipografii Karla Kraila, 1828.

Maksimov, S. *Ssyl'nye i tiur'my. Tom 1. Neschastnye*. Sanktpeterburg: V tipografii Morskago ministerstva, 1862.

Maksimov, S. *Sibir' i katorga*. 3 vols. S.-Peterburg: Tipografiia A. Transhelia, 1871.

Maksimov, S. "Sibirskaia sol'." *Zhivopisnaia Rossiia. Otechestvo nashe v ego zemel'nom, istoricheskom, plemennom, ekonomicheskom i bytovom znachenii*. Ed. by P. P. Semenov. S.-Peterburg: Izdanie Tovarishchestva M. O. Vol'f, 1895.

Maksimov, S. V. *Sibir' i katorga*. 3rd ed. S.-Peterburg: Izdanie V. I. Gubinskago, 1900.

Nikitin, V. N. *Tiur'ma i ssylka: Istoricheskoe, zakonodatel'noe, administrativnoe i bytovoe polozhenie zakliuchennykh, peresyl'nykh, ikh detei i osvobozhnennykh iz pod strazhi, so vremeni vozniknoveniia russkoi tiur'my, do nashikh dnei, 1560–1880 g*. S.-Peterburg: Tipografiia G. Shparvart, 1880.

Russkii biograficheskii slovar´. S.-Peterburg: Tipografiia I. I. Skorokhodova, 1905; rpt. New York: SPE Kraus Reprint Corporation, 1962.

Sapozhnikov, V. V., and N. A. Gavrilov. "Zemli Kabineta Ego Velichestva." *Aziatskaia Rossiia: Tom pervyi: Liudi i poriadki za Uralom*. S. Peterburg: Izdanie Pereselencheskago upravleniia glavnago upravleniia zemleustroistva i zemledeliia, 1914.

Semevskii, V. I. *Rabochie na sibirskikh zolotykh promyslakh: istoricheskoe izsledovanie*. 2 vols. S.-Peterburg: Tipografiia M. Stasiulevicha, 1898.

Shcheglov, I. V. *Khronologicheskii perechen´ vazhneishikh dannykh iz istorii Sibiri: 1032–1882 gg.* 1883; rpt. Surgut: Severnyi dom, 1993.

Slovtsov, Petr Andreevich. *Progulki vokrug Tobol'ska v 1830 g.* M.: Tipografiia Semena Selivanovskogo, 1834.

Spasovich, V. D. *Uchebnik ugolovnago prava*. Sanktpeterburg: Tip. I. Ogrizko, 1863.

Statisticheskiia svedeniia o ssyl´nykh v Sibiri, za 1833 i 1834 gody (Izvlechenie iz otcheta o delakh Sibirskago Komiteta). Sanktpeterburg: Tip. II Otdeleniia Sobstvennoi E. I. V. Kantseliarii, 1837.

Tagantsev, N. S. *Russkoe ugolovnoe pravo: chast´ obshchaia*. 2 vols. 1902; rpt. Tula: Avtograf, 2001.

Imperial Era Periodicals

Aziatskii vestnik
Russkaia starina
Russkii arkhiv
Sibir´
Sibirskii vestnik
Sovremennik
Tiuremnyi vestnik
Zhurnal Ministerstva vnutrennikh del

Secondary Works

Adams, Bruce F. *The Politics of Punishment: Prison Reform in Russia, 1863–1917*. DeKalb: Northern Illinois University Press, 1996.

Adler, Jeffrey S. "Vagging the Demons and Scoundrels: Vagrancy and the Growth of St. Louis, 1830–1861." *Journal of Urban History* 13, no. 1 (1986): 3–30.

Adorno, Theodor W. *History and Freedom: Lectures, 1964–1965*. Ed. by Rolf Tiedemann. Trans. by Rodney Livingstone. Malden, MA: Polity Press, 2006.

Afkhami, Mahnaz. *Women in Exile*. Charlottesville: University Press of Virginia, 1994.

Albrow, Martin. *Bureaucracy*. London: Pall Mall Press, 1970.

Alexander, John T. *Bubonic Plague in Early Modern Russia: Public Health and Urban Disaster*. New York: Oxford University Press, 2002.

Anderson, Benedict R. O'G. *Imagined Communities: Reflections on the Origin and Spread of Nationalisms*. New York: Verso, 1991.

Anisimov, Evgenii V. *The Reforms of Peter the Great: Progress through Coercion in Russia*. Trans. by John T. Alexander. Armonk, NY: M. E. Sharpe, 1993.

Anisimov, Evgenii. *Dyba i knut: politicheskii sysk i russkoe obshchestvo v XVIII veke*. Moskva: Novoe Literaturnoe Obozrenie, 1999.

[Anon.] *Administrativno-territorial'noe delenie Primorskogo kraia, 1856–1980 gg.* Vladivostok: DVNTs AN SSSR, 1984.

Armstrong, John A. "Old-Regime Governors: Bureaucratic and Patrimonial Attributes." *Comparative Studies in Society and History* 14, no. 1 (1972): 2–29.

Austin, Paul M. *The Exotic Prisoner in Russian Romanticism*. New York: Peter Lang, 1997.

Azodovskii, M. K., et al. (Eds.) *Sibirskaia Sovetskaia entsiklopediia. Tom pervyi, A–Zh.* N.p.: Sibirskoe kraevoe izdatel'stvo, 1929.

Bagby, Lewis. "Aleksandr Bestužev-Marlinskij's 'Roman i Ol'ga': Generation and Degeneration." *The Slavic and East European Journal* 25, no. 4 (1981): 1–15.

Bagby, Lewis. "Dostoevsky's *Notes From A Dead House:* The Poetics of the Introductory Paragraph." *Modern Language Review* 81 (1986): 139–52.

Barratt, Glynn R. "A Note on N.A. Bestuzhev and the Academy of Chita." *Canadian Slavonic Papers* 12 (1970): 47–59.

Barratt, Glynn. *M. S. Lunin: Catholic Decembrist*. The Hague: Mouton, 1976.

Barratt, Glynn. *The Rebel on the Bridge: A Life of the Decembrist Baron Andrey Rozen (1800–84)*. Athens: Ohio University Press, 1975.

Barry, Kathleen. *The Prostitution of Sexuality*. New York: NYU Press, 1995.

Bassin, Mark. "Inventing Siberia: Visions of the Russian East in the Early Nineteenth Century." *American Historical Review* 96, no. 3 (1991): 763–94.

Bassin, Mark. "The Russian Geographical Society, the 'Amur Epoch,' and the Great Siberan Expedition 1855–1863." *Annals of the Association of American Geographers* 73, no. 2 (1983): 240–56.

Bassin, Mark. *Imperial Visions: Nationalist Imagination and Geographical Expansion in the Russian Far East, 1840–1865*. Cambridge: Cambridge University Press, 1999.

Bazarzhapov, V. B., et al. (Eds.) *Poliaki v Buriatii*. Ulan-Ude: VSGTU, 1996.

Beier, A. L. *Masterless Men: The Vagrancy Problem in England, 1560–1640*. New York: Routledge, 1985.

Belovinskii, L. V. *Rossiiskii istoriko-bytovoi slovar'*. Moskva: RIO "Rossiiskii Arkhiv," 1999.

Bender, Barbara. (Ed.) *Landscape: Politics and Perspectives*. Oxford: Berg, 1993.

Bender, Barbara, and Margot Winer. (Eds.) *Contested Landscapes: Movement, Exile and Place*. New York: Berg, 2001.

Berger, Peter L., et al. *The Homeless Mind: Modernization and Consciousness*. Middlesex: Penguin, 1973.

Bitis, Alexander. *Russia and the Eastern Question: Army, Government, and Society, 1815–1833*. New York: Oxford University Press, 2006.

Bitis, A., and Janet Hartley. "The Russian Military Colonies in 1826." *Slavonic and East European Review* 78, no. 2 (2000): 321–30.

Blondel, Jean, and Nick Manning. "Do Ministers Do What They Say? Ministerial Unreliability, Collegial and Hierarchical Governments." *Political Studies* 50 (2002): 455–76.

Blum, Jerome. *Lord and Peasant in Russia: From the Ninth to the Nineteenth Century*. Princeton: Princeton University Press, 1961.

Bobrick, Benson. *East of the Sun: The Epic Conquest and Tragic History of Siberia*. New York: Poseiden Press, 1992.

Bogdanov, L. P. "Voennye poseleniia." *Voprosy istorii* 2 (1980): 178–83.

Bolkovskii, Aleksei. *Ekaterinburgskii tsentral*. Moskva: EKSMO, 2008.

Bolonev, F. F., A. A. Liutsidarskaia, and A. I. Shinkovoi. *Ssyl´nye poliaki v Sibiri: XVII, XIX vv*. Novosibirsk: Knizhita, 2007.

Borodaev, V. B., et al. (Eds.) *Guliaevskie chteniia. Vyp. 1: Materialy pervoi, vtoroi i tret´ei istoriko-arkhivnykh konferentsii*. Barnaul: Upravlenie arkhivnogo dela administratsii Altaiskogo kraia and Laboratoriia istoricheskogo kraevedeniia Barnaul´skogo gosudarstvennogo pedagogicheskogo universiteta, 1998.

Braginskii, M. A. *Nerchinskaia katorga: Sbornik nerchinskogo zemliachestva*. Moskva: Politkatorzhan, 1933.

Bratich, Jack Z., et al. (Eds.) *Foucault, Cultural Studies, and Governmentality*. Albany: State University of New York Press, 2003.

Breyfogle, Nicholas B. *Heretics and Colonizers: Forging Russia's Empire in the South Caucasus*. Ithaca: Cornell University Press, 2005.

Breyfogle, Nicholas B., et al. (Eds.) *Peopling the Russian Periphery: Borderland Colonization in Eurasian History*. New York: Routledge, 2007.

Bubis, Nadezhda. "Irkutskii tiuremnyi zamok." *Zemlia irkutskaia* 10 (1998): 51–6.

Burbank, Jane, and David L. Ransel. (Eds.) *Imperial Russia: New Histories for the Empire*. Bloomington: Indiana University Press, 1998.

Burchell, Graham, et al. (Eds.) *The Foucault Effect: Studies in Governmentality: With Two Lectures by and An Interview with Michel Foucault*. Chicago: University of Chicago Press, 1991.

Canning, Kathleen. "The Body as Method? Reflections on the Place of the Body in Gender History." *Gender & History* 11, no. 3 (1999): 499–513.

Certeau, Michel de. *The Practice of Everyday Life*. Trans. by Steven Rendall. Berkeley: University of California Press, 1984.

Charbit, Yves. "The Political Failure of an Economic Theory: Physiocracy." Trans. by Arundhati Virmani. *Population (English Edition, 2002–)* 57, no. 6 (2002): 855–83.

Chibiriaev, S. A. *Velikii russkii reformator: Zhizn´, deiatel´nost´, politicheskie vzgliady M. M. Speranskogo*. Moskva: Nauka, 1989.

Chichlo, Boris. (Ed.) *Sibérie II: Questions sibériennes*. Paris: Insitut d'études slaves, 1999.

Colvin, Mark. *Penitentiaries, Reformatories, and Chain Gangs: Social Theory and the History of Punishment in Nineteenth-Century America*. New York: St. Martin's Press, 1997.

Cosgrove, Denis E. *Social Formation and Symbolic Landscape*. London: Croom Helm, 1984.

Cosgrove, Denis, and Stephen Daniels. (Eds.) *The Iconography of Landscape: Essays on the Symbolic Representation, Design and Use of Past Environments*. New York: Cambridge University Press, 1988.

Crowe, David M. *A History of the Gypsies of Eastern Europe and Russia*. New York: St. Martin's Press, 1994.

Dameshek, L. M., and A. V. Remnev. (Eds.) *Sibir´ v sostave Rossiiskoi imperii*. Moskva: Novoe literaturnoe obozrenie, 2007.

D´iakov, V. A. *Osvoboditel´noe dvizhenie v Rossii, 1825–1861gg*. Moskva: Mysl´, 1979.

D´iakov, V. A., et al. (Eds.) *Russko-pol´skie revoliutsionnye sviazi 60-kh godov i vosstanie 1863 goda: Sbornik statei i materialov*. Moskva: AN SSSR, 1962.

Daly, Jonathan W. "Criminal Punishment and Europeanization in Late Imperial Russia." *Jahrbücher für Geschichte Osteuropas* 47 (2000): 341–62.

Daly, Jonathan W. *Autocracy under Siege: Security Police and Opposition in Russia, 1866–1905*. DeKalb: Northern Illinois University Press, 1998.

Dameshek, Lev "'Ustav ob upravlenii inorodtsev' Speranskogo." *Zemlia irkutskaia* 8 (1997): 17–19.

Davies, Norman. *God's Playground: A History of Poland in Two Volumes: Volume 1, The Origins to 1795*. New York: Columbia University Press, 1982.

Davies, Norman. *Heart of Europe: A Short History of Poland*. New York: Oxford University Press, 1986.

Davies, Sue. "Working Their Way to Respectability: Women, Vagrancy and Reform in Late Nineteenth Century Melbourne." *Lilith* 6 (1989): 50–63.

Dean, Mitchell. *Governmentality: Power and Rule in Modern Society*. London: Sage Publications, 1999.

Dikovskaia-Iakimova, A., and V. Pleskov. (Eds.) *Kara i drugie tiur´my nerchinskoi katorgi: Sbornik vospominanii, dokumentov i materialov*. Moskva: Izd-vo Politkatorzhan, 1927.

Diment, Galya, and Yuri Slezkine. (Eds.) *Between Heaven and Hell: The Myth of Siberia in Russian Culture*. New York: St. Martin's Press, 1993.

Dorrian, Mark, and Gillian Rose. (Eds.) *Deterritorialisations... Revisioning Landscapes and Politics*. New York: Black Dog Pub. Ltd., 2003.

Durkheim, Emile. *The Division of Labor in Society*. Trans. by George Simpson. New York: Free Press, 1933.

Dvorianov, V. N. *V Sibirskoi dal´nei storone... (ocherki istorii politicheskoi katorgi i ssylki. 60-e gody XVIII v.—1917 g.)*. Minsk: Nauka i tekhnika, 1985.

Edel´man, O. V. "Vospominaniia dekabristov o sledstvii kak istoricheskii istochnik." *Otechestvennaia istoriia* 6 (1995): 34–44.

Eisenstadt, S. N. (Ed.) *Max Weber on Charisma and Institution Building*. Chicago: University of Chicago Press, 1968.

Ekirch, A. Roger. *Bound for America: The Transportation of British Convicts to the Colonies 1718–1775*. Oxford: Clarendon Press, 1987.

Eklof, Ben, and Stephen Frank. (Eds.) *The World of the Russian Peasant: Post-Emancipation Culture and Society*. Boston: Unwin Hyman, 1990.

Eklof, Ben, et al. (Eds.) *Russia's Great Reforms, 1855–1881*. Bloomington: Indiana University Press, 1994.

Eksteins, Modris. *Rites of Spring: The Great War and the Birth of the Modern Age*. New York: Anchor Books, 1989.

Elshtain, Jean Bethke. *Sovereignty: God, State, and Self*. New York: Basic Books, 2008.

Engelstein, Laura. *Castration and the Heavenly Kingdom: A Russian Folktale*. Ithaca: Cornell University Press, 1999.

Engelstein, Laura. *The Keys to Happiness: Sex and the Search for Modernity in Fin-de-Siècle Russia*. Ithaca: Cornell University Press, 1992.

Entsiklopedicheskii slovar´ Brokgauz i Efron biografii. Moskva: Bol´shaia Rossiiskaia Entsiklopediia, 1993.

Eroshkin, N. P. *Ocherki istorii gosudarstvennykh uchrezhdenii dorevoliutsionnoi Rossii*. Moskva: Gosudarstvennoe Uchebno-Pedagogicheskoe Izdatel´stvo Ministerstva Prosveshcheniia RSFSR, 1960.

Everett, Wendy, and Peter Wagstaff. (Eds.) *Cultures of Exile: Images of Displacement*. New York: Berghahn Books, 2004.

Evreinov, N. *Istoriia telesnykh nakazanii v Rossii*. New York: Chalidze Publications, 1979.

Farnsworth, Beatrice, and Lynne Viola. (Eds.) *Russian Peasant Women*. New York: Oxford University Press, 1992.

Fedorchenko, V. *Imperatorskii Dom. Vydaiushchiesia sanovniki: Entsiklopediia biografiia*. 2 vols. Krasnoiarsk: BONUS, 2001.

Fedorov, V. A. "Arest dekabristov." *Vestnik Moskovskogo universiteta. Seriia VIII: Istoriia* 5 (1985): 59–71.

Fedosiuk, Iu. A. *Chto neponiatno u klassikov, ili Entsiklopediia russkogo byta XIX veka*. 2nd ed. Moskva: Nauka, 1999.

Fey, Ingrid E., and Karen Racine. (Eds.) *Strange Pilgrimages: Exile, Travel, and National Identity in Latin America, 1800–1990s*. Wilmington, DE: Scholarly Resources, 2000.

Finzsch, Norbert, and Robert Jütte. *Institutions of Confinement: Hospitals, Asylums, and Prisons in Western Europe and North America, 1500–1950*. Cambridge: Cambridge University Press, 1996.

Flowers, R. Barri. *The Prostitution of Women and Girls*. Jefferson, NC: McFarland & Co., 1998.

Flynn, James T. "Uvarov and the 'Western Provinces': A Study of Russia's Polish Problem." *The Slavonic and East European Review* 64, no. 2 (April 1986): 212–36.

Forsyth, James. *A History of the Peoples of Siberia: Russia's North Asian Colony, 1581–1990*. Cambridge: Cambridge University Press, 1994.

Foucault, Michel. *Abnormal: Lectures at the Collège de France, 1974–1975*. Trans. by Graham Burchell. New York: Picador, 2003.

Foucault, Michel. *Discipline & Punish: The Birth of the Prison*. Trans. by Alan Sheridan. New York: Vintage, 1977.

Foucault, Michel. *Power/Knowledge: Selected Interviews & Other Writings, 1972–1977*. Ed. by Colin Gordon. New York: Pantheon, 1980.

Foucault, Michel. *Security, Territory, Population: Lectures at the Collège de France, 1977–1978*. Trans. by Graham Burchell. Basingstoke: Palgrave Macmillan, 2007.

Foucault, Michel. *Society Must Be Defended*. Trans. by David Macey. London: Penguin, 2003.

Foucault, Michel. *The History of Sexuality: An Introduction. Volume 1*. New York: Vintage, 1990.

Foucault, Michel. *The Use of Pleasure: The History of Sexuality: Volume Two*. Trans. by Robert Hurley. London: Penguin, 1985.

Fox-Genovese, Elizabeth. *The Origins of Physiocracy: Economic Revolution and Social Order in Eighteenth-Century France*. Ithaca: Cornell University Press, 1976.

Frank, Joseph. *Dostoevsky: The Years of Ordeal, 1850–1859*. London: Robson Books, 1983.

Frank, Stephen P. "Emancipation and the Birch: The Perpetuation of Corporal Punishment in Rural Russia, 1861–1907." *Jahrbücher für Geschichte Osteuropas* 45, no. 3 (1997): 401–16.

Frank, Stephen P. "Narratives within Numbers: Women, Crime and Judicial Statistics in Imperial Russia, 1834–1913." *Russian Review* 55, no. 4 (1996): 541–66.

Frank, Stephen P. *Crime, Cultural Conflict, and Justice in Rural Russia, 1856–1914*. Berkeley: University of California Press, 1999.

Freeze, Gregory L. "The Soslovie (Estate) Paradigm and Russian Social History." *The American Historical Review* 91, no. 1 (February 1986): 11–36.

Gaiduk, Sergei Leonidovich. *Tiuremnaia politika i tiuremnoe zakonodatel´stvo pore-formennoi Rossii.* Ph.D. Dissertation. Moskva: Moskovskii gosudarstvennyi universitet im. M. V. Lomonosova, 1987.

Gammer, Moshe. *Muslim Resistance to the Tsar: Shamil and Conquest of Chechnia and Daghestan.* London: Frank Cass, 1994.

Garland, David. *Punishment and Modern Society: A Study in Social Theory.* Oxford: Clarendon Press, 1990.

Geertz, Clifford. *The Interpretation of Cultures: Selected Essays.* New York: Basic Books, 1973.

Gentes, Andrew A. "The Life, Death and Resurrection of the Cathedral of Christ the Saviour, Moscow." *History Workshop Journal* 46 (1998): 63–95.

Gentes, Andrew A. "'Licentious Girls' and Frontier Domesticators: Women and Siberian Exile from the Late 16th to the Early 19th Century." *Sibirica* 3, no. 1 (2003): 3–20.

Gentes, Andrew A. "Siberian Exile and the 1863 Polish Insurrectionists According to Russian Sources." *Jahrbücher für Geschichte Osteuropas* 51, no. 2 (2003): 197–217.

Gentes, Andrew A. "*Katorga*: Penal Labor and Tsarist Siberia." *The Siberian Saga: A History of Russia's Wild East.* Ed. by Eva-Maria Stolberg. Frankfurt am Main: Peter Lang, 2005.

Gentes, Andrew A. "No Kind of Liberal: Alexander II and the Sakhalin Penal Colony." *Jahrbücher für Geschichte Osteuropas* 54, no. 3 (2006): 321–44.

Gentes, Andrew A. "Towards a Demography of Children in the Tsarist Siberian Exile System." *Sibirica* 5, no. 1 (2006): 1–23.

Gentes, Andrew A. "Other Decembrists: The Chizhov Case and Lutskii Affair as Signifiers of the Decembrists in Siberia." *Slavonica* 13, no. 2 (2007): 134–49.

Gentes, Andrew A. *Exile to Siberia, 1590–1822.* New York: Palgrave Macmillan, 2008.

Gentes, Andrew A. "Vagabondage and Siberia: Disciplinary Modernism in Tsarist Russia." *Cast Out: Vagrancy and Homelessness in Global and Historical Perspective.* Ed. by A. L. Beier and Paul Ocobock. Athens: Ohio University Press, 2008.

Gentes, Andrew A. "'Beat the Devil!': Prison Society and Anarchy in Tsarist Siberia." *Ab Imperio* 2 (2009): 201–24.

Gernet, M. N. *Istoriia tsarskoi tiur´my.* 5 vols. 3rd ed. Moskva: Gosudarstvennoe izdatel´stvo iuridicheskoi literatury, 1960–63.

Gleason, Abbott. *Young Russia: The Genesis of Russian Radicalism in the 1860s.* New York: Viking, 1980.

Gooding, John. "The Decembrists in the Soviet Union." *Soviet Studies* XL, no. 2 (1988): 196–209.

Goriushkin, L. M. (Ed.) *Politicheskaia ssylka v Sibiri XIX-nachalo XX v.: Istoriografiia i istochniki.* Novosibirsk: Nauka, 1987.

Goriushkin, L. M. (Ed.) *Politicheskie ssyl´nye v Sibiri (XVIII—nachalo XX v.).* Novosibirsk: Nauka, 1983.

Goriushkin, L. M. (Ed.) *Ssyl´nye dekabristy v Sibiri.* Novosibirsk: Nauka, 1985.

Goriushkin, L. M. (Ed.) *Ssylka i obshchestvenno-politicheskaia zhizn´ v Sibiri (XVIII—nachalo XX v.).* Novosibirsk: Nauka, 1978.

Goriushkin, L. M., et al. (Eds.) *Ssylka i katorga v Sibiri (XVIII—nachalo XX v.).* Novosibirsk: "Nauka" Sibirskoe otdelenie, 1975.

Gorkin, A. P. (Ed.) *Geografiia Rossii*. Moskva: Bol´shaia Rossiiskaia Entsiklopediia, 1998.

Gruszczynska, Beata, and Elzbieta Kaczynska. "Poles in the Russian Penal System and Siberia as a Penal Colony (1815–1914): A Quantitative Examination." *Historical Social Research* 15, no. 4 (1990): 95–120.

Grunwald, Constantin de. *Tsar Nicholas I*. Trans. by Brigit Patmore. London: Douglas Saunders with MacGibbon & Kee, 1954.

Haskett, Jeanne. "Decembrist N.A. Bestuzhev in Siberian Exile, 1826–55." *Studies in Romanticism* 4, no. 4 (1965).

Hellie, Richard. *Slavery in Russia, 1450–1725*. Chicago: University of Chicago Press, 1982.

Hingley, Ronald. *Dostoyevsky: His Life and Work*. New York: Charles Scribner's Sons, 1978.

Hingley, Ronald. *The Russian Secret Police: Muscovite, Imperial Russian and Soviet Political Security Operations*. New York: Simon and Schuster, 1970.

Hoch, Steven L. "Famine, Disease, and Mortality Patterns in the Parish of Borshevka, Russia, 1830–1912." *Population Studies* 52, no. 3 (1998): 357–68.

Hoch, Steven L. *Serfdom and Social Control in Russia: Petrovskoe, a Village in Tambov*. Chicago: University of Chicago Press, 1986.

Hochschild, Arlie Russell. "Emotion Work, Feeling Rules, and Social Structure." *American Journal of Sociology* 85, no. 3 (1979): 551–75.

Hollingsworth, Barry. "John Venning and Prison Reform in Russia, 1819–1830." *Slavonic and East European Review* 48, no. 113 (1970): 537–56.

Hood, Christopher C. *The Limits of Administration*. London: John Wiley & Sons, 1976.

Hufton, Olwen. "Begging, Vagrancy, Vagabondage and the Law: An Aspect of the Problem of Poverty in Eighteenth-century France." *European Studies Review* 2, no. 2 (1972): 97–123.

Ianson, Ia. D. "Pered Oktiabrem." *Irkutskaia ssylka: Sbornik irkutskogo zemliachestva*. Ed. by V. V. Bustrem. Moskva: Politkatorzhan, 1934.

Jackson, Robert Louis. "The Narrator in Dostoevsky's *Notes from the House of the Dead*." *Studies in Russian and Polish Literature, in Honor of Waclaw Lednicki*. Ed. by Zbigniew Folejewski. The Hague: Mouton, 1962.

Jenkins, Michael. *Arakcheev: Grand Vizier of the Russian Empire*. New York: Dial Press, 1969.

Jewsbury, George F. *The Russian Annexation of Bessarabia: 1774–1828: A Study of Imperial Expansion*. Boulder: East European Quarterly, 1976.

Judson, Pieter M., and Marsha L. Rozenblit. (Eds.) *Constructing Nationalities in East Central Europe*. New York: Berghahn Books, 2005.

Kabuzan, V. M. *Izmeneniia v razmeshchenii naseleniia Rossii v XVIII-pervoi polovine XIX v. (Po materialam revizii)*. Moskva: Izdatel´stvo "Nauka," 1971.

Kabuzan, V. M. *Narodonaselenie Rossii v XVIII-pervoi polovine XIX v.* Moskva: AN SSSR, 1963.

Kagan, Frederick W. *The Military Reforms of Nicholas I: The Origins of the Modern Russian Army*. New York: St. Martin's Press, 1999.

Kallinikov, P., and I. Korneeva. (Eds.) *Russkii biograficheskii slovar´: V 20 t.* Moskva: TERRA-Knizhnyi klub, 1998.

Kandaurova, T. N., and B. B. Davydov. "Voennye poseleniia v otsenke." *Vestnik Moskovskogo Universiteta. Seriia VIII: Istoriia* 2 (1992): 44–55.

Karpenko, Z. G. *Gornaia i metallurgicheskaia promyshlennost´ Zapadnoi Sibiri v 1700–1860 godakh.* Novosibirsk: Izdatel´stvo Sibirskogo otdeleniia AN SSSR, 1963.

Kashtanova, Ol´ga. "Balkanskie vneshnepoliticheskie proekty kontsa XVIII—pervoi chetverti XIX v. i velikii kniaz´ Konstantin Pavlovich." *Dva veka, zhurnal rossiiskoi istorii XVIII–XIX stoletii* 1–2 [c. 2001] [internet journal, site now defunct, article in author's possession].

Kazarian, P. L. *Iakutiia v sisteme politicheskoi ssylki Rossii, 1826–1917 gg.* Iakutsk: GP NIPK Sakhapoligrafizdat, 1998.

Kazarian, P. L. *Istoriia Verkhoianska.* Iakutsk: GP NIPK Sakhapoligrafizdat, 1998.

Kazarian, P. L. *Olekminskaia politicheskaia ssylka, 1826–1917 gg.* 2nd ed. Iakutsk: Sakhapoligrafizdat, 1996.

Keep, John L. H. *Soldiers of the Tsar: Army and Society in Russia, 1462–1874.* Oxford: Clarendon Press, 1985.

Keep, John. "Justice for the Troops: A Comparative Study of Nicholas I's Russia and France under Louis-Philippe." *Cahiers du Monde russe et soviétique* 28, no. 1 (1987): 31–54.

Khrenov, I. A. *Ocherki revoliutsionnykh sviazei narodov Rossii i Pol´shi. 1815–1917 gg.* Moskva: Nauka, 1976.

Kimball, Alan. "Who Were the Petrashevtsy? A Question Provoked by Some Recent Scholarship." *Mentalities/Mentalités* 2 (1988): 1–12.

Kingston-Mann, Esther, and Timothy Mixter. (Eds.) *Peasant Economy, Culture, and Politics of European Russia, 1800–1921.* Princeton: Princeton University Press, 1991.

Kirchheimer, Otto. *Political Justice: The Use of Legal Procedure for Political Ends.* 1961; Westport, CT: Greenwood Press, 1980.

Kodan, S. V. "Amnistiia dekabristam (1856 g.)." *Voprosy istorii,* 4 (1982): 178–82.

Kodan, S. V. "Nerchinskoe komendantskoe upravlenie i dekabristy." *Voprosy istorii KPSS* 8 (1979): 178–92.

Kodan, S. V. "Sibirskaia ssylka uchastnikov oppozitsionnykh vystuplenii i dvizhenii v Tsarstve Pol´skom 1830–1840-x gg. (Politiko-iuridicheskii srez)." www.lib.pomorsu.ru/exile/Polska_ssylka/Kodan.doc (accessed 15 January 2009).

Kodan, S. V. *Sibirskaia ssylka dekabristov: istoriko-iuridicheskoe issledovanie.* Irkutsk: Izd-vo Irkut. un-ta, 1983.

Kodan, S. V. *Upravlenie politicheskoi ssylkoi v Sibir´: 1826–1856 gg.* Irkutsk: Irkutskii gos. universitet im. A. A. Zhdanova, 1980.

Komogortsev, I. I. "Iz istorii chernoi metallurgii Vostochnoi Sibiri v XVII–XVIII vv." *Sibir´ perioda feodalizma. Vypusk 1.* Ed. by V. I. Shunkov, et al. Novosibirsk: Izdatel´stvo Sibirskogo otdeleniia AN SSSR, 1962.

Kristeva, Julia. "A New Type of Intellectual: The Dissident." *The Kristeva Reader.* Ed. by Toril Moi. New York: Columbia University Press, 1986.

[Kucherov] Kutscheroff, Samuel. "Administration of Justice under Nicholas I of Russia." *The American Slavic and East European Review* 7 (1948).

Kucherov, Samuel. *Courts, Lawyers and Trials under the Last Three Tsars.* 1953; rpt. Westport, CT: Greenwood Press, 1974.

Kucherskaia, Mariia. "Konstantin Pavlovich—'pol´skii korol´.'" *Dva veka, zhurnal rossiiskoi istorii XVIII–XIX stoletii* 1–2 [c. 2001] [internet journal, site defunct, article in author's possession].

Lacey, Nicola. *State Punishment: Political Principles and Community Values.* London: Routledge, 1988.

Lappo, G. M. (Ed.) *Goroda Rossii*. Moscow: Nauchnoe izdatel´stvo, 1994.

Larin, A. M. *Gosudarstvennye prestupleniia: Rossiia. XIX vek*. Tula: Aftograf, 2000.

Lebedev, A. G. "Istoriia borby s nishchenstvom i brodiazhnichestvom v Rossii XIX—nachala XX v. (Opyt ispol´zovaniia penitentsiarnykh uchrezhdenenii)." *Vestnik Moskovskogo universiteta. Seriia 8. Istoriia* 4 (2006): 111–26.

LeDonne, John P. *Ruling Russia: Politics and Administration in the Age of Absolutism, 1762–1796*. Princeton: Princeton University Press, 1984.

Leslie, R. F. *Polish Politics and the Revolution of November 1830*. London: University of London, Athlone Press, 1956.

Lincoln, W. Bruce. "Count P. D. Kiselev: A Reformer in Imperial Russia." *Australian Journal of Politics & History* 16, no. 2 (1970): 177–86.

Lincoln, W. Bruce. "The Ministers of Nicholas I: A Brief Inquiry into Their Backgrounds and Service Careers." *Russian Review* 34, no. 3 (1975): 308–23.

Lincoln, W. Bruce. *Nicholas I: Emperor and Autocrat of All the Russias*. Bloomington: Indiana University Press, 1978.

Lincoln, W. Bruce. *In the Vanguard of Reform: Russia's Enlightened Bureaucrats, 1825–1861*. DeKalb: Northern Illinois University Press, 1982.

Lincoln, W. Bruce. *The Conquest of a Continent: Siberia and the Russians*. New York: Random House, 1994.

Lindenfeld, David F. *The Practical Imagination: The German Sciences of State in the Nineteenth Century*. Chicago: University of Chicago Press, 1997.

Lindenmeyr, Adele. *Poverty is Not a Vice: Charity, Society, and the State in Imperial Russia*. Princeton: Princeton University Press, 1996.

Lyashchenko, Peter I. *History of the National Economy of Russia to the 1917 Revolution*. Trans. by L. M. Herman. New York: Macmillan, 1949.

Magarshack, David. *Dostoevsky*. London: Secker & Warburg, 1962.

Mailick, Sidney, and Edward H. Van Ness. (Eds.) *Concepts and Issues in Administrative Behavior*. Englewood Cliffs, NJ: Prentice-Hall, 1962.

March, G. Patrick. *Eastern Destiny: Russia in Asia and the North Pacific*. Westport, CT: Praeger, 1996.

Margolis, A. D. *Tiur´ma i ssylka v imperatorskoi Rossii: issledovaniia i arkhivnye nakhodki*. Moskva: Lanterna, 1995.

Marks, Steven G. *Road to Power: The Trans-Siberian Railroad and the Colonization of Asian Russia, 1850–1917*. Ithaca: Cornell University Press, 1991.

Matkhanova, N. P. *Vysshaia administratsiia Vostochnoi Sibiri v seredine XIX veka: Problemy sotsial´noi stratifikatsii*. Novosibirsk: Sibirskii khronograf, 2002.

Mazour, Anatole G. *The First Russian Revolution: 1825, the Decembrist Movement: Its Origins, Development, and Significance*. Stanford: Stanford University Press, 1937.

Mazour, Anatole G. *Women in Exile: Wives of the Decembrists*. Tallahassee: Diplomatic Press, 1975.

McClintock, Anne. *Imperial Leather: Race, Gender and Sexuality in the Colonial Contest*. London: Routledge, 1995.

McConnell, Allen. *Tsar Alexander I: Paternalistic Reformer*. New York: Thomas Y. Crowell Co., 1970.

Meadows, R. Darrell. "Engineering Exile: Social Networks and the French Atlantic Community, 1789–1809." *French Historical Studies* 23, no. 1 (2000): 67–102.

Meilakh, B. S., et al. (Eds.) *Sibir´ i dekabristy. Vypusk 5*. Irkutsk: Vostochno-Sibirskoe knizhnoe idatel´stvo, 1988.

Merton, Robert K., et al. (Eds.) *Reader in Bureaucracy*. Glencoe, IL: Free Press, 1952.

Minenko, N. A. "Obshchinnyi skhod v Zapadnoi Sibiri XVIII-pervoi poloviny XIX v." *Obshchestvennyi byt i kul´tura russkogo naseleniia Sibiri (XVIII-nachalo XX v.)*. Ed. by L. M. Rusakova. Novosibirsk: Nauka, 1983.

Mironenko, S. V. *Dekabristy: Biograficheskii spravochnik*. Moskva: Nauka, 1988.

Mirzoev, V. G. *Istoriografiia Sibiri (Domarksistskii period)*. Moskva: Izdatel´stvo "Mysl´," 1970.

Mitchell, W. J. T. (Ed.) *Landscape and Power*. 2nd ed. Chicago: University of Chicago Press, 2002.

Monas, Sidney. *The Third Section: Police and Society in Russia under Nicholas I*. Cambridge: Harvard University Press, 1961.

Morris, Norval, and David L. Rothman. (Eds.) *The Oxford History of the Prison: The Practice of Punishment in Western Society*. New York: Oxford University Press, 1998.

Mote, Victor L. *Siberia: Worlds Apart*. Boulder: Westview Press, 1998.

Murphy, Jeffrie G. *Punishment and Rehabiliation*. 3rd ed. Belmont, CA: Wadsworth, 1995.

Naficy, Hamid. *The Making of Exile Cultures: Iranian Television in Los Angeles*. Minneapolis: University of Minnesota Press, 1993.

Nagaev, A. S. *Omskoe delo, 1832–1833*. Krasnoiarsk: Krasnoiarskii universitet, 1991.

Nechkina, M. "Zagovor v Zerentuiskom rudnike." *Krasnyi arkhiv* 13 (1925): 258–79.

Nechkina, M. V. *Dvizhenie dekabristov*. 2 vols. Moskva: Izd-vo Akademii Nauk SSSR, 1955.

Nechkina, M. V. *Griboedov i dekabristy*. 2nd ed. Moskva: Izdatel´stvo Akademii nauk SSSR, 1951.

Nemzera, A. S. *Memuary dekabristov*. Moskva: Pravda, 1988.

O'Meara, Patrick. *The Decembrist Pavel Pestel: Russia's First Republican*. Basingstoke: Palgrave Macmillan, 2003.

Okladnikov, A. P., et al. (Eds.) *Istoriia Sibiri s drevneishikh vremen do nashikh dnei*. 5 vols. Leningrad: Izdatel´stvo Nauka, 1968–69.

Orlovsky, Daniel T. "Recent Studies on the Russian Bureaucracy." *Russian Review* 35, no. 4 (1976): 448–67.

Orlovsky, Daniel T. *The Limits of Reform: The Ministry of Internal Affairs in Imperial Russia, 1802–1881*. Cambridge: Harvard University Press, 1981.

Ostroumov, S. S. *Prestupnost´ i ee prichiny v dorevoliutsionnoi Rossii*. Moskva: Izdatel´stvo universiteta, 1980.

Oxley, Deborah. *Convict Maids: The Forced Migration of Women to Australia*. Cambridge: Cambridge University Press, 1996.

Page, Edward C. *Political Authority and Bureaucratic Power*. Brighton, Eng.: Wheatsheaf Books Ltd., 1985.

Palmer, Alan. *Alexander I: Tsar of War and Peace*. New York: Harper and Row, 1974.

Parker, Andrew, et al. (Eds.) *Nationalisms & Sexualities*. London: Routledge, 1992.

Phillips, Kim M., and Barry Reay. (Eds.) *Sexualities in History: A Reader*. London: Routledge, 2002.

Phoenix, Joanna. "Prostitute Identities: Men, Money and Violence." *British Journal of Criminology* 40, no. 1 (2000).

Pintner, Walter McKenzie. *Russian Economic Reform under Nicholas I*. Ithaca: Cornell University Press, 1967.

Pintner, Walter McKenzie, and Don Karl Rowney. (Eds.) *Russian Officialdom: The Bureaucratization of Russian Society from the Seventeenth to the Twentieth Century*. London: Macmillan, 1980.

Pipes, Richard E. "The Russian Military Colonies, 1810–1831." *Journal of Modern History* 22, no. 3 (1950): 205–19.

Pipes, Richard. *Russia under the Old Regime*. New York: Charles Scribner's Sons, 1974.

Polakiewicz, Leonard A. "The Russian Prison System as Seen through the Eyes of Chekhov and Dostoevsky." *The Soviet and Post-Soviet Review* 28, nos. 1–2 (2001 [2002]): 157–86.

Pratt, John. "The Return of the Wheelbarrow Men; or, The Arrival of Postmodern Penality?" *British Journal of Criminology* 40, no. 1 (2000): 127–45.

Presniakov, A. E. *Emperor Nicholas I of Russia: The Apogee of Autocracy, 1825–1855*. Ed. and trans. by Judith C. Zacek. With "Nicholas I and the Course of Russian History." By Nicholas V. Riasanovsky. Gulf Breeze, FL: Academic International Press, 1974.

Prikhod´ko, Mikhail. "Sozdanie ministerskoi sistemy upravleniia v Rossii pervoi treti XIX veka." *Dva veka, zhurnal rossiiskoi istorii XVIII-XIX stoletii* 4 (2001) [Internet journal. Site now defunct, article in author's possession].

Prokof´ev, V. *Petrashevskii*. Moskva: Molodaia Gvardiia, 1962.

Protopopov, K. I. "Eniseiskaia politicheskaia ssylka ot dekabristov do 1917 goda." *Eniseiskaia ssylka: Sbornik eniseiskogo zemliachestva*. Ed. by V. N. Sokolov. Moskva: Politkatorzhan, 1934.

Rabtsevich, V. V. "Krest´ianskaia obshchina kak organ upravleniia sibirskoi derevnei." *Krest´ianstvo Sibiri perioda razlozheniia feodalizma i razvitiia kapitalizma (Mezhvuzovskii sbornik nauchnykh trudov)*. Ed. by L. I. Postupinskaia. Novosibirsk: Novosibirskii gosudarstvennyi pedagogicheskii institute, 1980.

Raeff, Marc. *Imperial Russia, 1682–1825: The Coming of Age in Modern Russia*. New York: Knopf, 1971.

Raeff, Marc. *Michael Speransky: Statesman of Imperial Russia, 1772–1822*. The Hague: Martinus Nijhoff, 1957.

Raeff, Marc. *Siberia and the Reforms of 1822*. Seattle: University of Washington Press, 1956.

Raeff, Marc. *The Decembrist Movement*. Englewood Cliffs: Prentice-Hall, 1966.

Raeff, Marc. *The Well-Ordered Police State: Social and Institutional Change through Law in the Germanies and Russia, 1600–1800*. New Haven: Yale University Press, 1983.

Rakhmatullin, M. A. "Imperator Nikolai I i sem´i dekabristov." *Otechestvennaia istoriia* 6 (1995): 3–20.

Rancour-Laferriere, Daniel. *The Slave Soul of Russia: Moral Masochism and the Cult of Suffering*. New York: New York University Press, 1995.

Reddy, William M. "The Logic of Action: Indeterminacy, Emotion, and Historical Narrative." *History and Theory* 40, no. 4 (2001): 10–33.

Reddy, William M. *The Navigation of Feeling: A Framework for the History of Emotions*. Cambridge: Cambridge University Press, 2001.

Remnev, A. V. *Rossiia dal´nego vostoka. Imperskaia geografiia vlasti XIX—nachala XX vekov*. Omsk: Izd-vo Omsk. gos. un-ta, 2004.

Remnev, Anatolii. "'Tigr, zakolotyi gusinym perom.' Kazus zapadnosibirskogo general-gubernatora kniazia P. D. Gochakova." *Acta Slavica Iaponica* 27 (2009): 55–75.

Riasanovsky, Nicholas V. *Nicholas I and Official Nationality in Russia, 1825–1855.* Berkeley: University of California Press, 1961.

Roberts, M. J. D. "Public and Private in Early Nineteenth-Century London: The Vagrant Act of 1822 and Its Enforcement." *Social History* 13, no. 3 (1988): 273–94.

Robinson, Marc. (Ed.) *Altogether Elsewhere: Writers on Exile.* Boston: Faber and Faber, 1994.

Rose, Lionel. *"Rogues and Vagabonds": Vagrant Underworld in Britain, 1815–1985.* New York: Routledge, 1988.

Ross, Jeffrey Ian, and Stephen C. Richards. (Eds.) *Convict Criminology.* Belmont, CA: Wadsworth, 2003.

Rothman, David J. *The Discovery of the Asylum: Social Order and Disorder in the New Republic.* Boston: Little, Brown, 1971.

Rowney, Karl. "Structure, Class, and Career: The Problem of Bureaucracy and Society in Russia, 1801–1917." *Social Science History* 6, no. 1 (1982): 87–110.

Rusche, Georg, and Otto Kirchheimer. *Punishment and Social Structure.* 1939; rpt. New Brunswick: Transaction, 2003.

Safronov, F. G. *Russkie krest´iane v Iakutii (XVII-nachalo XX vv.).* Iakutsk: Iakutskoe knizhnoe izdatel´stvo, 1961.

Said, Edward. "Reflections on Exile." *Granta* 13 (1984): 157–72.

Saunders, David. *Russia in the Age of Reaction and Reform, 1801–1881.* New York: Longman, 1992.

Schabas, Margaret, and Neil De Marchi. (Eds.) *Oeconomies in the Age of Newton.* [Annual Supplement to Volume 35 of *History of Political Economy*.] Durham: Duke University Press, 2003.

Schafer, Sylvia. "When the Child is the Father of the Man: Work, Sexual Difference and the Guardian-State in Third Republic France." *History and Theory* 31, no. 4 (1992): 98–115.

Schmidt, Albert J. "The Restoration of Moscow after 1812." *Slavic Review* 40, no. 1 (1981): 37–48.

Schott, Susan. "Emotion and Social Life: A Symbolic Interactionist Analysis." *American Journal of Sociology* 84, no. 6 (1979): 1317–34.

Schrader, Abby M. "Containing the Spectacle of Punishment: The Russian Autocracy and the Abolition of the Knout, 1817–1845." *Slavic Review* 56, no. 4 (winter 1997): 613–44.

Schrader, Abby M. "Unruly Felons and Civilizing Wives: Cultivating Marriage in the Siberian Exile System, 1822–1860." *Slavic Review* 66, no. 2 (2007): 230–56.

Schrader, Abby M. *Languages of the Lash: Corporal Punishment and Identity in Imperial Russia.* DeKalb: Northern Illinois University Press, 2002.

Seddon, J. H. "The Petrashevtsy: A Reappraisal." *Slavic Review* 43, no. 3 (1984): 434–52.

Selishchev, A. M. *Zabaikal´skie staroobriadtsy. Semeiskie.* Irkutsk: Irkutskii universitet, 1920.

Sellin, J. Thorsten. *Slavery and the Penal System.* New York: Elsevier, 1976.

Sergeev, M. D., et al. (Eds.) *Dekabristy i Sibir´.* Moskva: Izobrazitel´noe iskusstvo, 1988.

Shepelёv, L. E. *Apparat vlasti v Rossii: Epokha Aleksandra I i Nikolaia I.* Sankt-Peterburg: Iskusstvo—SPB, 2007.

Shobodoev, E., et al. "Ot gubernii—k oblasti: sobytiia i liudi." *Zemlia irkutskaia* 8 (1997).

Shostakovich, B. S. *Istoriia Poliakov v Sibiri (XVII—XIX vv.).* Irkutsk: Irkut. un-t, 1995.

Simpson, John. (Ed.) *The Oxford Book of Exile.* New York: Oxford University Press, 1995.

Skowronek, Jerzy. "The Direction of Political Change in the Era of National Insurrection, 1795–1864." *A Republic of Nobles: Studies in Polish History to 1864.* Ed. and trans. by J. K. Fedorowicz, et al. New York: Cambridge University Press, 1982.

Slezkine, Yuri. *Arctic Mirrors: Russia and the Small Peoples of the North.* Ithaca: Cornell University Press, 1994.

Sobolev, A. V. "Vel´mozhnaia katorga i ee artel´noe khoziastva." *Voprosy istorii* 2 (2000): 127–35.

Stachowski, Tadeusz. "The Polish-Russian War of 1831." *History Today* [Great Britain] (29 May 1979): 310–17; (6 June 1979): 386–93.

Starr, S. Frederick. *Decentralization and Self-Government in Russia, 1830–1870.* Princeton: Princeton University Press, 1972.

Stephan, John J. *The Russian Far East: A History.* Stanford: Stanford University Press, 1994.

Strauss, E. *The Ruling Servants: Bureaucracy in Russia, France—and Britain?* London: George Allen & Unwin Ltd., 1961.

Squire, P. S. *The Third Department: The Establishment and Practices of the Political Police in the Russia of Nicholas I.* Cambridge: Cambridge University Press, 1968.

Sunderland, Willard. "Peasants on the Move: State Peasant Resettlement in Imperial Russia, 1805–1830s." *Russian Review* 52, no. 4 (1993): 472–85.

Sunderland, Willard. *Taming the Wild Field: Colonization and Empire on the Russian Steppes.* Ithaca: Cornell University Press, 2004.

Sutherland, Christine. *The Princess of Siberia: The Story of Maria Volkonsky and the Decembrist Exiles.* New York: Farrar, Strauss, Giroux, 1984.

Tertz, Abram. [Pseud. of Andrei Siniavskii.] *The Trial Begins and On Socialist Realism.* 1960; rpt. Berkeley: University of California Press, 1982.

Tomsinov, Vladimir A. *Speranskii.* Moskva: Molodaia gvardiia, 2006.

Treadgold, Donald W. *The Great Siberian Migration: Government and Peasant Resettlement from Emancipation to the First World War.* Princeton: Princeton University Press, 1957.

Trigos, Ludmilla A. *The Decembrist Myth in Russian Culture.* New York: Palgrave Macmillan, 2009.

Troitskaia, N. A., and A. A. Toropov. (Eds.) *Dal´nii Vostok Rossii: Iz istorii sistemy upravleniia. Dokumenty i materialy.* Vladivostok: RGIA DV, 1999.

Van Gunsteren, Herman R. *The Quest for Control: A Critique of the Rational-Central-Rule Approach in Public Affairs.* London: John Wiley & Sons, 1976.

Vlasenko, Aleksandr A. "Ugolovnaia ssylka v Zapadnuiu Sibir´ v politike samoderzhaviia XIX veka." Ph.D. dissertation. Omskii gosudarstvennyi universitet im. F. M. Dostoevskogo, 2008.

Volchek, V. A. *Osushchestvlenie imperskoi politiki na vostochnykh okrainakh Rossii v deiatel´nosti Vtorogo Sibirskogo komiteta.* Novosibirsk: Sibirskaia nauchnaia kniga, 2006.

Vucinich, Wayne S. (Ed.) *The Peasant in Nineteenth-Century Russia*. Stanford: Stanford University Press, 1968.

Waley-Cohen, Joanna. *Exile in Mid-Qing China: Banishment to Xinjiang, 1758–1820*. New Haven: Yale University Press, 1991.

Walker, Franklin A. "Poland in the Decembrists' Strategy of Revolution." *Polish Review* 15 (1970): 43–54.

Wandycz, Piotr S. *The Lands of Partitioned Poland, 1795–1918*. Seattle: University of Washington Press, 1974.

Weber, Max. *Economy and Society: An Outline of Interpretive Sociology*. 3 vols. New York: Bedminster Press, 1968.

Weber, Max. *The Theory of Social and Economic Organization*. Ed. by Talcott Parsons. New York: Macmillan, 1964.

White, Hayden. "The Question of Narrative in Contemporary Historical Theory." *History and Theory* 23, no. 1 (1984): 1–33.

Wieczynski, Joseph L. (Ed.) *The Modern Encyclopedia of Russian and Soviet History*. Gulf Breeze, FL: Academic International Press, 1978.

Williams, Gareth D. *Banished Voices: Readings in Ovid's Exile Poetry*. Cambridge: Cambridge University Press, 1994.

Wirtschafter, Elise Kimerling. "Military Justice and Social Relations in the Prereform Army, 1796 to 1855." *Slavic Review* 44, no. 1 (1985): 67–82.

Wirtschafter, Elise Kimerling. "The Lower Ranks in the Peacetime Regimental Economy of the Russian Army, 1796–1855." *Slavonic and East European Review* 64, no. 1 (1986): 40–65.

Wood, Alan. "Administrative Exile and the Criminals' Commune in Siberia." *Land Commune and Peasant Community in Russia: Communal Forms in Imperial and Early Soviet Society*. Ed. by Roger Bartlett. New York: St. Martin's Press, 1990.

Wood, Alan. "Crime and Punishment in the House of the Dead." *Civil Rights in Imperial Russia*. Ed. by Olga Crisp and Linda Edmondson. Oxford: Clarendon Press, 1989.

Wood, Alan. "Sex and Violence in Siberia: Aspects of the Tsarist Exile System." *Siberia: Two Historical Perspectives*. London: The Great Britain-USSR Association and The School of Slavonic and East European Studies, 1984.

Wood, Alan. "The Use and Abuse of Administrative Exile to Siberia." *Irish Slavonic Studies* 6 (1985): 65–81.

Wortman, Richard S. *Scenarios of Power: Myth and Ceremony in Russian Monarchy: Volume One, From Peter the Great to the Death of Nicholas I*. Princeton: Princeton University Press, 1995.

Wortman, Richard S. *The Development of a Russian Legal Consciousness*. Chicago: University of Chicago Press, 1976.

Yaney, George L. "Law Society and the Domestic Regime in Russia, In Historical Perspective." *The American Political Science Review* 59, no. 2 (1965): 379–90.

Yaney, George L. *The Systematization of Russian Government: Social Evolution in the Domestic Administration of Imperial Russia, 1711–1905*. Urbana: University of Illinois Press, 1973.

Zacek, Judith C. "A Case Study in Russian Philanthropy: The Prison Reform Movement in the Reign of Alexander I." *Canadian Slavic Studies/Revue canadienne d'études slaves* 1, no. 2 (1967): 196–211.

Zacek, Judith Cohen. "The Lancastrian School Movement in Russia." *Slavonic and East European Review* 45, no. 105 (1967): 343–67.

Zen´kovskii, Sergei. *Russkoe staroobriadchestvo: Dukhovnye dvizheniia semnadtsatogo veka*. Moskva: Tserkov, 1995.

Zetlin, Mikhail. *The Decembrists*. Trans. by George Panin. New York: International University Press, 1958.

Zil´bershtein, I. S. *Khudozhnik dekabrist Nikolai Bestuzhev*. 3rd ed. Moskva: Izobrazitel´noe iskusstvo, 1988.

Ziolkowski, Margaret. "Hagiography and Historiography: The Saintly Prince in the Poetry of the Decembrists." *The Slavic and East European Journal* 30, no. 1 (1986): 29–44.

Zoltowski, Adam. *Border of Europe: A Study of the Polish Eastern Provinces*. London: Hollis & Carter, 1950.

Zuev, A. S., and N. A. Minenko. *Sekretnye uzniki sibirskikh ostrogov (ocherki istorii politicheskoi ssylki v Sibiri vtoroi chetverti XVIII v*. Novosibirsk: Nauka, 1992.

Index